THE VISUAL
DICTIONARY OF
S<u>E</u>X

onveyed
red with
l under-
ff refuse
'erage
tem of,
ter]

sown. See sew.

sĕx, n. Being male or female, males or females collectively, (*without distinction of age or s.;* *the fair, gentle, softer, weaker, s.,* women ; *the sterner s.,* men ; *the* *s., women).* [L *sexus*]

sĕxagēnăr′ian, see QUAD-RAGENARIAN ; **Sĕxagĕs′ĭma,** QUADRAGESIMA.

THE VISUAL DICTIONARY OF SEX

PAN BOOKS

in association with Macmillan London

First published 1978 by
Macmillan London Ltd
This edition published 1979 by
Pan Books Ltd, Cavaye Place,
London SW10 9PG
in association with Macmillan
London Ltd

9 8 7 6 5 4 3 2

© Trewin Copplestone
Publishing Ltd 1978

ISBN 0 330 25890 7

Created, designed and produced
by Trewin Copplestone
Publishing Ltd
Printed in Hong Kong

CONTENTS

In the entries appearing in the sections listed on this page, there are definitions or explanations of other associated words, printed in SMALL CAPITALS. Other words, which are printed in italics *with an asterisk** are to be checked in the Index, which will refer the reader to the relevant page for further information.

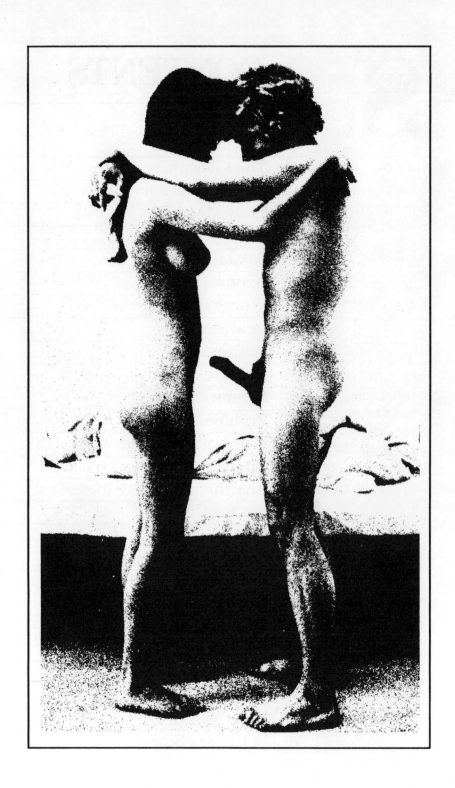

SEX-WORDS ARE DYNAMITE. AND LIKE certain explosives, many of them are unstable and must be handled carefully. Bringing them all together in a dictionary which aims to explain their meanings coolly and precisely could be a dangerous job. For one thing, they are an awkward mixture of scientific terms and intimate slang. Many of them come from the medical vocabulary and refer to bodily things in a clinical way like setting a fracture or treating TB. Others, sounding just as scientific, have been compounded in the misty regions of psychology and psychoanalysis; these often required a considerable effort on the part of an untrained person to try and understand to what they refer. The new procedures of sex therapy have brought in another jargon that needs translating into plain English. Then there are all the "naughty" words, whose origins can be traced in English speech and literature, from the Middle Ages to the newest West Coast in-talk.

In spite of enlightenment and permissiveness, sexual ignorance, often leading to sexual unhappiness, still exists, and this ignorance actually thrives on the way that sex-words are frequently used. For it is as a smoke-screen rather than out of frankness that some of us—if we are honest with ourselves—talk about sex. Many psychoanalytical terms are in circulation, without their meanings being fully taken in by the people who use them. And how many times do we avoid showing ourselves up by not asking what something *really* means?

Then there are the sex swear-words—that extraordinary switch of value when the desirable object's name serves to express extreme contempt. 'That stupid *cunt,* that *prick!'* we say, spitting out the words as if they were literally dirty. But do we feel that way about the things named? Saying them sometimes gives a kind of excitement, and for some people, 'talking dirty' to a sexual partner can be arousing. Even more confusing is the meaningless repetition of a four-letter word in ordinary speech. This is a sort of ritual, meant to proclaim a don't-care machismo and insubordination. A person's most frequent adjective may be 'fucking', but it bears no relation to his sex-life.

The biggest inhibition of all is when someone's own personal sexual security is far from being what he or she would wish others to think. One then frequently hears sex-words being brashly used to give the idea that all's well. A sense of shame or inadequacy in sex is very different to reveal openly and we take refuge in using sexy language.

Sexual equality of men and women does not mean sexual sameness, and the presentation of factual information about the nature of arousal and orgasm must take into account the differences of feeling and expectation in men and women if the book is to be as valid for one as for the other. The experience of the women's liberation movement means that in any discussion of women's roles in society different perspectives must be considered. The acknowledgement of female sexual needs has seen to that. This undertstanding of what a women feels about herself, about what she needs from her sexual partner, is now very different from that generally accepted prior to Masters' and Johnson's research. Following on from there, the humane practical work of other leading sex therapists and physicians of various disciplines has given us a new picture of female sexuality.

This in turn opens up the whole question of gender. Traditional assumptions about what boys and girls are like and what people should do with their lives if they are not happy in their normal sexual roles, have been challenged constructively by research into gender identity. The difficulties of people who for various reasons do not fit into conventional male or female patterns can now often be helped by medical treatment. Those who choose relationships with their own sex now do so more openly than ever before. The discussion of all topics in this book reflects recent advances in medical and educational thinking, as much on gender as on homosexual relationships of all kinds.

The easing up of sexual constraints founded on ignorance and prejudice, and the greater personal freedom to choose and to change in sexual relationships, also give rise to their own new problems. Instead of feeling the old shame of sex, people are often scared that their sexual performance is lower than is expected of them. The myth of 'super-sex' finds no support in the facts presented in this book.

Illustrations relating to sex are no less varied than sex-words, from immortal art to porno magazines, from goddesses to gynecology. Some are lyrical dream-images, some are outrageous fantasies or erotic titillation. Some are just plain funny.

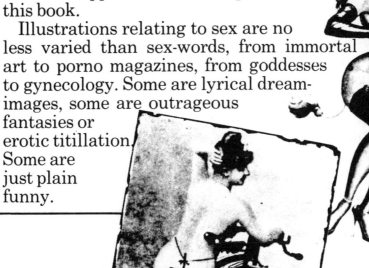

But whether funny or physical, shocking or arousing, each one throws light on a facet of sexual behaviour.

In trying to create the right book, we faced many difficulties. For we are dealing with a basic, overwhelming, but puzzling human experience. Sex is still surrounded by taboos, yet it is constantly being thrust at our eyes and ears. 'Sexploitation' describes the way sex is made to sell a product, however remote the connection. 'Permissiveness' describes the new public attitude of non-interference in people's sex lives. All this can be cold and unhelpful. Warmth and sympathy are more liberating than commercialized full-frontalism, and warmth and sympathy are a major contribution by the authors and experts who worked on this dictionary.

The contents are grouped in a number of main sections which are listed on page 5. Some of them provide information on hard-edged subjects to do with our bodies and ways of making love. Others suggest approaches to an understanding of each other, and of other people's sex problems. This organisation of the contents allows the dictionary to be used in two ways. The definitions of words by themselves are found by looking them up in the Index, where a page reference is given. On the other hand, the reader can enlarge on some area of sexual knowledge by turning to any of the main headings, where all the words used in connection with it are grouped together and explained. This is a direct and open book about things that were once hushed up, and have lately been over-exposed. A book that thinks that love needs sex, and *vice versa* —and that neither can flourish without a good measure of humour.

1

THE LIBERATORS

Profiles of the major pioneers in understanding human sex life.

Sexual Liberation

This compendium deals primarily with the words of the language of sex and their synonyms and derivations, but to exclude the history of certain aspects of sexual information would fall short of a true understanding. Unless it is possible to relate sexual attitudes to the circumstances of the past as well as of the present, much will remain unclear. The fact that the ancient Egyptians had different sex taboos to modern mankind is interesting but has little direct relevance for us, but when we look at the writing of the pioneer thinkers of ancient Greece, they make a connection with the sexual activity of modern people. 20th-century sexual ideas and practices can be seen not as examples of decadence, but as evidence of a sexual renaissance, perhaps over-long delayed.

The Greeks looked upon all sexual activity in the same way as they did eating and drinking, believing that sexual enjoyments were among the greatest happinesses of mankind. The common paraphilias that we choose to call sexual perversions today, were defined by the Greeks as being parallel to love. We owe the idea of sexual indecency to the Romans, who called all diseases of the sexual organs, *morbus indecens*. Later, the medieval mind, especially that of the church, was obsessed with sex to an almost hysterical degree. Fresh fuel was added to a vast cauldron of sexual repression.

The main foundation of modern sexual repressiveness was laid in the mid-19th century. Queen Victoria was on the throne of Britain and Victorianism was the name for the public morality of the modern world, so far as sex was concerned. It is difficult to be sure how far private sexual behaviour was influenced by Victorian attitudes, but clearly much present-day sexual worry, fear and exploitation was present at that time. Writers on sexology saw the whole of life as a

Havelock Ellis   Masters   Schrenck-Notzing   Magnus Hirschfeld   Kinsey   Wilhelm Reich   Pavlov

struggle against sexual temptation. It was not until the end of the century that sexual researchers, who were also men of science (for example Krafft-Ebing, Havelock Ellis and Freud), began to feel able to look at sexual activity logically rather than in a purely judgemental way. Freud's theories, although misunderstood and abhorred at the outset, eventually did much to put sex on the map as a proper scientific discipline.

These liberators, who stunned society at the turn of the century with the publication of 'carnal' knowledge, turned an impatient ear to the reactions of an outraged public. They were persistent explorers and theorizers, and

opened the way for valuable clinical experiment and practical therapy by their successors. Their enlightened studies of the mind revealed associations that startled even themselves. At first, Freud resisted his discovery of the sexuality of children, but went on courageously to chart the unconscious human mind. Women had been warned off masturbation and had made love in the 'missionary' position for so long that it was not surprising that at first, female subjects were ignorant of orgasm. Homosexuality was first identified as separate from transvestism by Hirschfeld as late as 1910. The work of Havelock Ellis was banned in England soon after trials of Oscar Wilde.

Now perhaps, the climate, both in Europe and America, is right for a better knowledge of sex to be promulgated. This gives new hope for scientific observation, and for working at systems of sexual medicine in a healthy rather than in a pathological social background. Although not necessarily Freudian in the psychoanalytical sense, sexologists today can pursue their studies, research and practice in an atmosphere of truth rather than of folklore and prejudice, thanks to the liberating life's work of these great pioneers.

ohnson   Krafft-Ebing   Margaret Sanger   Sacher-Masoch   de Sade   Marie Stopes   Freud

De Sade

Some 70 years after Sade's death, his name was used by the Viennese sexologist Krafft-Ebing to coin a new term to describe a particular sexual impulse. This is found in the person for whom inflicting pain and degradation on a human 'sex object' is a satisfying sexual experience—it is 'sadism'.

In fact, Sade has several claims to be remembered as a sexual liberator. He wrote in exhaustive detail about the sexual tastes for which he is notorious; he catalogued every unusual sexual activity he could think of, and—perhaps most important—he wrote without apology, furiously defending his right (and by implication, everyone's) to his own instincts.

Donatien-Alphonse-François, Marquis de Sade, was born to a wealthy, aristocratic family in Paris in 1740. He was not raised by his parents but had a somewhat subservient childhood in the household of a yet wealthier and more aristocratic uncle. Between the ages of 14 and 23 he served in the cavalry, fighting in the Seven Years' War.

Only a short time after his arranged marriage to a wealthy girl of the middle class, the first scandal broke. Some prostitutes complained that he had forced them into sexual abuses which were no part of the bargain, and Sade spent a few weeks in prison. His notoriety increased when a whore reported that Sade (now 26) had, after whipping her, wounded her with a pen-knife and filled the wounds with hot wax. Later still, Sade was accused of trying to poison some prostitutes by feeding them the supposed aphodisiac Spanish Fly, a highly dangerous irritant.

He and an accomplice-servant had to escape to Sardinia, being condemned to death at Aix in their absence. Returning to France in 1776, Sade had one last long fling before the law closed in on him. It seems that the innocent if uninteresting bourgeoise he had married was now wholly corrupted by him. Together, they now organized a series of 'orgies' involving numerous children of both sexes. Sade's mother-in-law finally brought about his arrest in Paris in 1777. The extraordinary period of licence he had known ended in a twelve-year spell in prison. His wife retreated to a nunnery for the rest of her life. After five years of boredom, frustration, rage, and intrigues, Sade began writing in earnest to occupy himself. His first work of note, *Dialogue Between a Priest and a Dying Man* (1782) made clear his atheism, another grave defiance of society and its conventions. Sade was transferred to the Bastille. There he wrote *The 120 Days of Sodom* (1785) on a carefully concealed roll of paper, 39 feet long. A few days before the Revolution broke out in Paris, this provocative aristocrat shouted through the bars to passersby: 'They are massacring the prisoners; you must come and free them!' Sade was promptly removed to the lunatic asylum at Charenton, thus missing by only a few days the storming of the Bastille.

Released in April 1790, Sade emerged into freedom in the years of the Revolution. He continued his literary productivity with the novels *Justine* (1791) and *Juliette* (1792). During Napoleon's rule he continued to write but again got into trouble. He was arrested in 1801 and sent back to Charenton. He died there in 1814.

Sacher-Masoch

As with the Marquis de Sade, it was Sacher-Masoch's obsessional 'one-track-mind', seen in his most famous literary efforts, that gave Krafft-Ebing the idea of using the second half of his name to coin the term 'masochism'. Masochism is thus the logical converse of sadism, and although the two men from whom these words derive make a strange pair, the sadist and the masochist are ideal sexual partners.

Leopold von Sacher-Masoch was born in 1836 at Lemberg (Lvov) in Galicia, then part of the Austro-Hungarian Empire. The origin of his sexual desire for pain and humiliation is not entirely clear, although there may be a clue in his father being the chief of police. According to the memoirs of his second wife, his fetish for furs and his love of punishment had roots in a childhood passion for his Aunt Zenobia. Hidden among the furs in her wardrobe he watched her and her lover making love and this gave him a profoundly exciting sexual response. His adult sexual life seems to have consisted of a series of liaisons with women who were willing to re-enact this and other private dramas by keeping him in bondage (he was their 'slave'), humiliating him (he always insisted they take another lover so that he could surreptitiously observe them making love); and physically abusing him (corporal punishment, especially whipping, was crucial to his sexual arousal).

Though his books mainly seem to be celebrations of his own fantasies about cruel women dressed in furs and brandishing scourges, Sacher-Masoch had some literary talent. His success as a journalist and writer allowed him to abandon a career in law and at one time he had quite a following, especially in France. In the year 1886, his most famous and most autobiographical novel, *Venus in Furs,* was published and his fame was at its height. He was given a grand reception in Paris by *Le Figaro* and the *Revue des Deux Mondes,* and was made a chevalier of the Legion of Honour.

Sacher-Masoch had a direct and vivid style but prudishly (or prudently) he avoided all physical detail in his novels, and he also supplied a moral at the end. Severin, the central character in *Venus in Furs,* explains the moral of his tale of bondage thus: '... woman, as nature has created her and as man is at present educating her, is his enemy. She can only be his slave or his despot, but *never his companion.* This she can become only when she has the same rights as he, and is his equal in education and work.'

Although his novels, like Sade's tend

to be obsessively preoccupied with his particular sexual preferences, Sacher-Masoch did not (as Sade did) invite social and legal retribution. He did not fancy the real-life punishments of ostracism and prison, any more than Sade relished the real-life orgies of the guillotine. (Modern defenders of *sado-masochism** have claimed not only that its chief element is play, but also that playing at hurting and being hurt is a way of channelling emotions which can otherwise lead to real-life tyranny.)

Krafft-Ebing published the first edition of his *Psychopathia Sexualis* in 1886, Sacher-Masoch's year of greatest success. In this book, he first defined 'sadism' and 'masochism' as two poles of the same phenomenon, often existing in the same person. This would not have been news to Sade, and did not escape the notice of Sacher-Masoch himself – at the climax of *Venus in Furs*, Severin switches from a masochist attitude towards women to a sadistic one.

Like Sade, Sacher-Masoch ended his life in a lunatic asylum (whether he was mad or just unusual is arguable). He was committed in 1895 and is believed to have died shortly after.

Freud

Freud's discovery of the great influence of sexuality on the development of personality revolutionized the study of the mind. All subsequent developments in psychiatry and psychiatric treatment are in some way based on it. His courageous insistence on his discovery at a time when Western society was horrified by it, and the undeniable authority with which he established his findings, encouraged others working in related fields, and opened up our culture to an honest assessment of the interrelatedness of sexuality to all aspects of human development.

Freud was born in 1856 in Freiberg (Pribor), Moravia (now Czechoslovakia), but after the failure of his father's textile business, his family moved to Vienna when he was four. Freud chose medicine for a career partly at his father's insistence and partly in the hope that it would satisfy his already keenly developed curiosity about human nature. In the early part of his career, Freud became a sound research student. He received intellectual stimulus from many sources. He qualified and began working in neurology, the diseases of the brain and spinal cord. Only gradually did his energy and ambitions focus on the medical condition of hysteria. (It was a common belief from the time of Hippocrates that hysteria was confined to women and although Freud knew this to be untrue, the vast majority of patients with hysterical symptoms were female.) Hypnosis was the newly-established technique for getting through to a patient with such 'hysterical' symptoms as paralysis of a perfectly healthy arm.

However, Freud found he was inept as a hypnotist and, realizing that the effects of hypnotism stemmed from suggestion, he was led to develop the 'talking technique' as a substitute. The famous couch had been there for hypnosis; he continued to get his patients to lie on it because it helped them to relax, and he sat behind them largely because he was a shy man and could not bear to be stared at all day. By 1896, he had abandoned hypnosis, having stumbled upon the use of free association, and was using the term psychoanalysis to describe his 'talking' method.

In this procedure, patients relax comfortably, pick out something of emotional significance in their lives (the 'opening emotional elements') and then let their thoughts flow unimpeded in whatever direction they spontaneously carry them. Freud noticed that patients often found their starting material in *dreams** they remembered, and he began to develop a first 'model' of how the mind works. At this time, he began to develop his hypothesis that the mind has three parts – or rather, three states which exist together. It was not for another 30 years (in 1923) that he fully set out his well-known triad of Id, Ego and Superego. Freud proposed that the ID is unconscious and instinctual, without moral judgment; that the SUPEREGO is partly conscious and represents the rules instilled by one's parents and society (the voice of guilt); and the EGO is the conscious go-between which is able to relate and adapt to the outside world. As Freud's clinical experience

built up, consistent patterns began to emerge: all his cases of hysteria had sexual causes. Each woman had apparently been seduced, molested or frightened as a child by some perverse adult. Just as Freud was beginning to accept one revolutionary idea – that women could and did have sexual feelings – he received a terrible shock. He discovered that many of his patients had been lying to him.

Instead of abandoning his work or suppressing his discovery, he re-examined his theory to see if he could explain *why* the women had all reported traumatic sexual experiences from childhood. In 1886, he had married his great love, Martha Bernays, after a long and frustrating engagement, and he now had several children in whom he took an intense interest. He began to look to them for clues about all these invented childhood seductions. At the same time, he turned for answers to the one patient whom he knew could be consistently coerced into telling the truth – himself. In the next three years he analyzed himself. Recalling his own early sexual excitement when he accidentally saw his mother dressing, and observing his own children, he was confirmed in his belief that most of the early seductions 'remembered' by his patients were not lies but fantasies – events not feared but desired. He came to the startling realization that children, too, were sexual beings.

There was prudery, even puritanism, in Freud's many-faceted character and he resisted the idea of childhood sexuality. Once he had accepted the idea, he would not let censure by his colleagues or the horror of society stop him in his work.

Freud now proposed that everything we did which was not in aid of self-preservation was in pursuit of pleasure, and that all pleasure-seeking activity was, in a wide sense, erotic. He came to call this sexual energy the LIBIDO and he argued that if sexual energy was prevented from finding a direct outlet (as society and civilization mostly demanded) it must find some alternative means of expression. With luck the alternative channel would be some kind of creative activity (he called it SUBLIMATION). Sexual energy with no other outlet would express itself in disturbance of the mind or the body or both.

All Freud's work developed from this. In 1899, he finished *The Interpretation of Dreams*. In this book, he examined the mechanisms by which dreams enable the unconscious to cope with facts or events of our lives which our conscious minds are too frightened or simply too preoccupied to face. He explained his principle of wish-fulfilment, showed the enormous effect the life of the infant had on conditioning the human adult and described the OEDIPUS COMPLEX, relying as he often did on his classical and literary education for models.

Freud's influence began to spread. He was made a professor in 1902, two years after publishing *The Interpretation of Dreams*. He had by now founded the Wednesday Circle which became the Vienna Psychoanalytical Society (with Alfred Adler among the first participants). Carl-Gustav Jung joined Freud's circle by 1907. The first break in Freud's circle came in 1911 and was with Adler (1870–1937). For Adler, not sexuality but will-to-power came to be viewed as the primary driving force of the personality. He introduced the concept of the Inferiority and Superiority Complexes to explain emotional unbalance.

Jung (1875–1961), in his turn, dissented from Freud's emphasis on the centrality of sex in the development of the mind. He took the view that libido did not merely encourage the search for pleasure, but was an energy of mind that encourages the appetite for food, drink and feelings. He came to concentrate on the neuroses of people in middle age in whom the sexual and aggressive drives (particularly if they had been successful) were less important than the search for meaning.

From early in the 1920s, Freud suffered from cancer of the jaw and underwent frequent and painful operations for the rest of his life. In 1938, after Hitler's occupation of Austria, Freud, as a Jew though a non-practicing one, was persuaded to escape to London with his daughter, Anna (herself a noted child psychiatrist who refined his work on defence mechanisms). Freud continued working on his theories until his death in 1939.

Havelock Ellis

A man of wide interests and a prolific writer, Henry Havelock Ellis is chiefly remembered for the seven volumes of his *Studies in the Psychology of Sex* (published between 1896 and 1928) – the first of which gained him immediate notoriety, being banned as an obscene publication. He was born in Croydon, England in 1859, and his strict family instilled in him many of the sexual

myths and inhibitions of the Victorian era, making a torment of his youth. He went to Australia to be a teacher at 16.

He returned to England aged 19 to study medicine at St. Thomas' Hospital in London. Like Freud, he had little interest in being a practising physician; he wanted the respectability of a medical degree to prove his scientific credentials when he began to write. He remarked in later years that 'in my own medical training, the psychological aspects of sex had no existence whatsoever'. Only the physical processes of sex – in the study of women's diseases, for example – were considered by his medical teachers.

In 1890 he published *The Criminal* and *The New Spirit*, the first of his efforts to introduce criminology and sexology as sciences.

He married Edith Lees in 1891 when he was 32, and his personal experiences and those of his wife seem to have led to his writing *Man and Woman* (1894), a book in which he made an early attempt to present a balanced view of homosexuality and bisexuality. When *Sexual Inversion,* volume I of his *Studies,* was published in 1897, only two years after the trials of Oscar Wilde, it led to the prolonged court case which prevented the publication and acceptance of Ellis' work in England for some time, although his books were highly successful in some circles in America.

As he said, his was the first book in English 'to set forth the earliest results reached by Freud'. The *Studies* described the physical aspects of sexual function alongside less appreciated elements like the significance of touch, smell, sight and hearing in sexual *courtship** and mating. He considered eroticism applied to the self, not only in masturbation but also in the nature of erotic dreams, and wrote about these in a most enlightened fashion for a

medical man at that time. Havelock Ellis also broke new ground in sexual discussion by considering sexual deviations in practice, and their likely origins. He wrote about sadism and masochism, for example, as well as explaining *fetishism** and *exhibitionism**.

He campaigned all his life for early sex education for children, for birth control, for an end to the concept of illegitimacy, for experimental unions of couples without marriage, for changes in divorce laws and for the repeal of criminal laws against homosexual acts between consenting adults. His investigations into every sexual idiosyncracy were powered by a moral fervour, as if he could infect his readers with open-mindedness. Terms that have become part of everyone's language, and were even adopted by Freud, such as 'auto-eroticism' and *narcissism**, were coined by him. He believed that love is an art, and that feminine 'frigidity' may arise from a failure in the art of love by the male partner.

Ellis lived out his beliefs in his private life. He and Edith decided not to have children and agreed to end sexual contact with each other, while accepting each other's extramarital relationships – Edith's were all with women. In his sixties, after she died, Ellis formed the first totally satisfying sexual union of his life: he fell in love with Françoise Delisle, 30 years younger than he, and they lived together for the remaining 20 years of his life without getting married.

By the time of his death in 1939, Ellis was widely admired for his work, his learning, his compassion and his calm scepticism.

Krafft-Ebing

Richard von Krafft-Ebing was famous in his own day, and is still noted now, for his contributions to the study of sexual aberrations, chiefly in his book *Psychopathia Sexualis*, the most massively comprehensive collection of case studies of psychotic sexual data that had ever been published.

Perhaps because his work as a forensic psychiatrist meant that most of his case-histories were taken from criminals, Krafft-Ebing was firmly at the non-permissive end of the spectrum of opinion, and he condemned most, though not quite all, forms of sexual activity. His place in the still developing history of sexual liberation is due not to these emotive attitudes but to his scientist's approach to his work, which established the factual study of sexual aberration as a respectable pursuit. *Psychopathia Sexualis* provided Freud with data which he used in his *Three Contributions to the Theory of Sex* (1905).

It was Krafft-Ebing who derived some of the descriptive terms from names in sexual literature. For example, he coined the term 'sadism', after the Marquis de Sade, to describe sexual pleasure derived from inflicting pain on others. He also coined the term 'masochism', after the stories by Sacher-Masoch in which self-affliction brings a form of sexual relief. Born in 1840, Richard, Freiherr (Baron) von Krafft-Ebing was chairman at the important Psychiatry and Neurology Convention in 1896 when Freud first presented his views on the cause of hysteria. Later, he was one of the specialists who is said to have recommended Freud for a Professorship in Vienna. Krafft-Ebing distinguished himself in research into the then ill-understood diseases of the brain and nervous system. The illness known as general paralysis of the insane (GPI) still puzzled the specialists in nervous diseases. It presented a mixture of brain changes (claims of grandeur yet loss of memory) and physical changes (weakness and loss of power in the limbs). Krafft-Ebing carried out the research experiments which confirmed that GPI is caused by the syphilis organism in the nervous system.

Krafft-Ebing intended his *Psychopathia Sexualis* (first published in German in 1886) to be read by doctors only. He did his best to ensure this by using Latin wherever he had to describe the details of sexual activities in his cases. The book nevertheless became immensely popular. Improving and expanding the book were major occupations for the rest of his life and his final reworking of it was for the twelfth edition. He died in 1902. *Psychopathia Sexualis* makes quaint reading today.

Magnus Hirschfeld

Magnus Hirschfeld, whose dates (1868–1935) fall within Freud's life-span, was one of the few genuinely sympathetic German psychiatrists to specialize in homosexuality. A brilliant and energetic man, he founded the first scientific journal of sexual pathology in 1899. This annual publication was to be a forum for important discussions on the subject of sex, and in it he gave a strongly favourable review of Freud's crucial and controversial *Three Essays on the Sexual Theory* (1905). Hirschfeld coined a number of terms for sexual practices. For example, he used the work 'ipsation' when an individual actively masturbates and is sexually gratified without having any associated psychic fantasies. He also used 'automonosexualism' to describe men who are so narcissistic that only their own bodies give them sexual satisfaction. He was the first person to make a proper distinction between homosexuality and transvestism (1910) and he and others in his journal campaigned for the reform of laws which penalized homosexuals.

Schrenck-Notzing

Albert, Freiherr von Schrenck-Notzing (1826–1929) was one of the psychiatric pioneers working at the same time as Freud and helping to create the climate in which Freud's major discoveries became acceptable. A striking feature of his work were his attempts to 'cure' homosexuality (for which the standard medical term was the revealingly enough, 'contrary sexual instinct') with the help of suggestion under hypnosis and visits to brothels. He was not the first person to offer homosexuals this kind of refuge from social persecution, and his book on modifying sexual orientation (1892) in part foreshadowed Pavlov's achievements on conditioned reflexes.

Pavlov

The work of the Russian experimental psychologist Ivan Petrovich Pavlov (1849–1936) on the processes of digestion had brought him a Nobel prize in 1904. In the course of this work, using animals for his experiments, he found that once dogs were trained to expect dinner at the sound of a bell, they would salivate when he rang the bell, no matter whether dinner turned up or not. These observations (published from 1910 onwards) established that some kinds of behaviour (salivation) were the result of reflex reactions to a familiar stimulus (dinner) and that such responses could be manipulated by bringing in stimuli that were associated with the familiar one (bells). Pavlov called these responses CONDITIONED REFLEXES and argued that they play a significant part in determining human as well as animal behaviour.

One application of Pavlov's work has been in attempts to 'recondition' sexual tastes through aversion therapy. His findings have been applied in a more practical and successful way in varying kinds of sex therapy, notably by Masters and Johnson, in overcoming reactions in problems like premature ejaculation, impotence and frigidity.

Margaret Sanger

Margaret Sanger was the founder of the American birth control movement. Her writings and speeches publicized the need for birth control – she coined the term – and opened up a way of discussing this formerly taboo subject. Unlike her English counterpart, *Marie Stopes**, who at first thought of fulfillment within conventional and rather well-to-do marriages, Margaret Sanger's lifelong campaign for birth control grew out of direct experience of the needs of poor families and single mothers.

Born Margaret Higgins in Corning, New York, in 1883, she was herself one of 11 children. She married architect William Sanger in 1900. (She later divorced him and in 1922 remarried, but like Marie Stopes she kept the name of her first husband for professional reasons.) After the birth of her second child, she went to work as an obstetrical nurse on the lower East Side of Manhattan. Here she witnessed results of uncontrolled bith rates – high infant and maternal mortality, and appalling psychological pressures. After a young woman had died in her arms from the effects of a self-induced abortion, Margaret Sanger determined to emancipate women from unwanted pregnancy. She founded her magazine *The Woman Rebel* (later called *Birth Control Review*) in 1914 and began publicizing contraception through that and through her pamphlet *Family Limitation*. Liable to charges of obscenity under the 1873 Comstock Act, she was constantly harrassed by the law (and by Comstock himself while he lived) and spent 30 days in jail after opening the first US birth control clinic in 1916.

In the long run, the publicity which her harrassment gave her won her support. She founded the American Birth Control League in 1921, by which time she had help from many prominent people, among them her friend *Havelock Ellis.** She organized the first World Population Conference in Geneva in 1927 and was elected first president of the International Planned Parenthood Federation (1953). In 1936, the Comstock Act was reinterpreted to permit physicians to prescribe contraceptives. Her view of birth control had expanded a great deal and she came, like Marie Stopes, to work for birth control in overpopulated countries. She died in 1966 in Tucson, Arizona.

Marie Stopes

Born in 1880 in Edinburgh, Marie Carmichael Stopes, who proclaimed every women's right to freedom from unwanted pregnancy, was the first English women liberator in the field of sexuality, dominated so far by men. She had the advantage of a scientific education, which allowed her a practical and theoretical basis for her statements and activities. She lectured at University College, London, on palaeobotany, the study of extinct or fossil plants, particularly in coal seams. Her success as a scientist at that time showed the capacity and right of every woman to have careers in spite of male hostility.

Her first marriage was emotionally and sexually unhappy for her, and by the time it was annulled in 1916 she had become concerned for the personal and sexual satisfaction of women in marriage. With the encouragement of her second husband, Vernon Roe, she wrote *Married Love* (1918) and its immense success led her to bring out *Wise Parenthood*, which was specifically about contraception, in the same year. She believed that successful birth con-

trol, especially if women had control themselves, would enable women to enjoy wanted children as well as their marriage relationship with more personal fulfilment and satisfaction. She continued to publicize her ideas with growing success, despite protest and public opposition, especially from Catholic groups. She opened the first British birth control clinic in north London in 1921, and founded the Society for Constructive Birth Control (precursor of the Family Planning Association) in 1922 to spread information, especially among poor and ill-educated women. The occlusive diaphragm which prevents sperm passing into the neck of the uterus was named the 'Stopes cap'.

She continued to work, lecture and write for the birth control movement until her death in 1958.

Wilhelm Reich

Reich is the most paradoxical of the sexual liberators: anti-authoritarian authoritarian, outcast, puritan, crank, prophet – and in all the history of sexology, perhaps the most single-minded believer in the centrality of sex to human lives.

He was born in 1897 in Galicia into a cultured and well-to-do farming family. At 14, his childhood ended abruptly with his mother's suicide, an event to which he may have contributed by telling his father of her affair with the family tutor. His father developed tuberculosis and died three years later. Reich was trained in physics applied to living matter, but the First World War intervened. At 19 he joined the Austrian army and at 21, the war over, he turned up in Vienna in search of a career and promptly settled on psychiatric medicine.

Over the next ten years he seems to have been in the mainstream of the Viennese psychoanalytic group: but around 1927 his path began to diverge from theirs. In that year, Reich was refused an analysis by Freud, and it has been suggested that this refusal was the long-term cause of Reich's extreme heterodoxy. An active Marxist over the next five years, Reich tried hard to establish a political context for his work. He suggested, for example, that the death instinct – described by Freud as the opposite of the pleasure principle and sex drive – may in fact derive from the pattern of the capitalist system. In 1930, having moved to Berlin, he found-

ed the suggestively titled German Association for Proletarian Sexual Politics, which sought widespread legal reform on sexual matters.

In trying to cross Marx with Freud, Reich was of course trying to bridge the gulf between vastly different attitudes to human change and development: Marx's work was focussed on change from without and Freud's on change from within. In any case, Reich was not orthodox enough for either side. He was expelled in 1933 from the Communist Party and in 1934 from the Psychoanalytic Association. For the rest of his life, Reich was on his own.

It is interesting to note that while most of Freud's dissenting colleagues (Adler and Jung, for instance) thought that he emphasized sex to the exclusion of other factors in human psychology, Reich thought he failed to give sex anything like its due. As far as Reich was concerned, sex was the potential cure for almost all the ills of civilization.

The catch was that not any old form of sex would do: it had to be 'real' sex as defined by Reich himself. 'Real' sex turned out to be a complex and rather restrictive activity, confined to heterosexual couples whose orgasms were not only reached in the course of intercourse alone, but conformed to a variety of requirements (including timing and degrees of excitement) which were measurable on a graph. Reich stated these theories in his much-revised *Function of the Orgasm* (originally published in 1927).

In 1939, Reich had to flee Europe in the face of Nazi antagonism. In New York, he once again showed an interest in his original scientific arena of biophysics. However, the stimulus of a new environment and a receptive new audience encouraged him to reveal a 'new discovery'. Early on in Reich's solitary journey as a research psychoanalyst, he had put forward the notion that 'orgone energy' – a concept roughly equivalent to that of the life force – was at large in the universe in vast quantities and could be tapped by artificial means. To this end he developed various forms of body-therapy, culminating in the famous Orgone Box which he marketed, claiming that it would infuse with orgone energy anyone who stepped inside it. Among those who did so were members of the US Food and Drug Administration, and finding it empty of measurable life-force or anything else they proclaimed it to be a fraud. Reich continued to distribute his box and in 1956 he was given a two-year prison sentence for contempt of court and violation of the Food, Drug and Cosmetic Act. He died in prison in 1957, under psychiatric care.

Kinsey

Alfred Charles Kinsey pioneered a type of research which was badly needed to test the theories of Freud and his immediate successors. He collected and analyzed statistical information about the sexual behaviour of thousands of ordinary men and women. As a direct result of his work, people's knowledge of their own sexual behaviour has grown spectacularly, and a tradition was established that led to the Masters and Johnson studies and the setting up of sex therapy clinics.

Born in New Jersey in 1894, his upbringing was strict and as a young child he suffered from rheumatic fever and rickets. He grew up with a fervent interest in the outdoors and with wholly conventional attitudes towards sex. (When a college friend confessed to him his agony over masturbation, Kinsey persuaded the friend to join him in prayer for strength to stop.) He began his career as a zoologist after studying at Bowdoin College and getting a science doctorate at Harvard in 1920. He worked for 17 years at Indiana University on the entomology of the gall wasp. He collected, measured and classified between two and four million examples and became recognized as the world's leading authority on the insect.

During his years as a zoologist Kinsey married. There were four children; it was by all accounts a happy marriage and Kinsey was satisfied with his career. But the work of his life changed when his university decided to introduce a course in marriage in 1937, and Kinsey was put in charge of it. He was distressed to find that there were no statistical studies of sexual behaviour and response to validate or support many theories and beliefs then held, and which he was expected to teach. He had to teach facts for his course and, since they did not exist in a scientifically valid form, he decided to collect them himself. Applying his zoological data methods, he began interviewing willing subjects in small numbers and slowly shaped his interviewing techniques and questions. As he proceeded, he found his students and the men and women he was interviewing asking him urgent questions. Would premarital intercourse spoil their chances of happy marriage? Would masturbation drive them insane or affect their children? Should they overcome their homosexual desires and if so how? Kinsey packed up his gall-wasp collection and donated it to the American Museum of National History, and spent the rest of his life collecting the information that might answer these questions.

In 1942, Indiana supported Kinsey's establishment of the Institute for Sexual Research at the University. He had acquired Clyde E. Martin as an assistant in 1939; Wardell B. Pomeroy joined him in 1943 and Dr. Paul Gebbard (who was to continue in charge of the Institute after Kinsey's death) in 1946. Pomeroy, Martin and other assistants helped analyze and write up the data which appeared as the first report of the institute in 1948: *Sexual Behavior in the Human Male*. This technical study became a best-seller, as did its successor, *Sexual Behavior in the Human Female* (1953).

The reports startled many people and undermined many myths. Based on the case histories of over 5000 white males and over 5000 white females, he reported, for instance, that 96% of men masturbated, as did 85% of all women. Only 4% of American males were exclusively homosexual but 37% had had at least one homosexual experience to the point of orgasm. Among women 28% had some lesbian experience by the age of 45. And all this in an age when the official version of 'normal' sexual behaviour was defined within narrow, puritanical limits, the holdovers of 19th-century ideas. Kinsey's report on the multiple female orgasm caused consternation and even disbelief to a degree that nothing else in his reports did. Doctors Edmund Bergler and William S. Kroger wrote a book entitled *Kinsey's Myth of Female Sexuality* and dismissed the reports of multiple orgasm as 'fantastic tales which the female volunteers told Kinsey', a strange echo of the common medical belief in the 19th century that only 'perverted' women had any sexual feelings at all. The report (which was also based on detailed gynecological examinations of 879 women) further noted that the interior of the vagina was an area of little or no sensitivity in virtually all women and that only the clitoris and labia minor played important roles in stimulation and orgasm, facts later confirmed by Masters and Johnson's direct observation. The report even included the suggestion (a courageous one in 1953) that women might learn to enjoy orgasm and increase enjoyment in sex if they practised by masturbating. Studies were also made of the erotic behaviour of infants and the Kinsey team reported that one 11-month old baby had 14 orgasms in 38 minutes.

Responsible criticism of the reports focussed on possible irregularities in Kinsey's sampling. Nevertheless, later studies of all sorts have tended to confirm the findings and figures of the reports. Kinsey himself was concerned that with the best will in the world respondents could not answer some kinds of question from experience. The 1948 report stated: 'Erotic arousal is a material phenomenon which involves an extended series of physical, physiologic, and psychologic changes. Many of these could be subjected to precise instrumental measurement if objectivity among scientists and public respect for scientific research allowed such laboratory investigation'.

At about the time Kinsey died in 1956, however, Dr. Masters and his assistant Mrs Johnson were embarking on their work at Washington University at St Louis, Missouri.

Masters & Johnson

The laboratory work of Dr. William H. Masters and Virginia E. Johnson built upon Kinsey's work and was helped by the change in public opinion which the 'Kinsey reports' provoked. In their turn, they have greatly increased our knowledge of what happens in the body during sexual experiences.

Masters was born in comfortable circumstances in Cleveland, Ohio, in 1915. In 1943, when he was a qualified doctor with a successful student career behind him, he decided to research into the human physiology of sex. Realizing he would have to wait until he was considered mature by others, until he had established a reputation as a researcher in some less controversial subject, and until he could do his studies under respectable auspices, he became a gynecologist. He published many papers, establishing himself particularly in the field of hormone replacement therapy for post-menopausal women. In 1954 he embarked upon the research that was to carry out work envisaged by Kinsey:

the backing up of subjective case histories with objective observation. He worked at the School of Medicine in Washington University, St Louis, until private financing enabled him to establish the Reproductive Biology Research Foundation in 1964.

Dr Masters began his work with prostitutes of both sexes, but realized almost immediately that they were untypical of the 'average' American citizen in whom he was primarily interested. Setting out to find 'respectable' volunteers, Masters decided to hire a woman to help interview and screen them. He found Mrs. Johnson. She was born in 1925 in the Missouri Ozarks, where she was brought up with a rare lack of sexual ignorance and hypocrisy. While studying music, she had become interested in sociology and psychology. Married, with two children, she had separated from her husband and was looking for a job just when Masters advertised for an assistant. Theirs was to be one of the great 20th-century research partnerships, and nearly twenty years later they married.

Of 1273 men and women who volunteered, 694 were accepted after screening and became participants in laboratory observations of sexual activity over the next 11 years. There were 276 married couples plus 106 single women and 36 single men. The age range was enormous: 21 to 89 for men, 18 to 78 for women. Interestingly, of 7500 attempts on the part of women to reach orgasm – with or without a partner – there were only 118 failures. For men the failure rate was six times higher.

The report of their work, *Human Sexual Response* (1966), not only confirmed objectively some of the controversial findings of the Kinsey reports, it exploded three more myths. It proved that a man's sexual performance is in no way related to the size of his penis. It proved that there is no such thing as a vaginal orgasm however the orgasm is triggered (thus finally unburdening women of one of Freud's most unpleasant legacies – his insistence that not only were vaginal and clitoral orgasms distinct but that the vaginal orgasm alone was 'mature' and 'real'). It proved, too, that women do not necessarily experience satisfaction or need rest after an orgasm, as men do, but are capable of multiple orgasms.

By 1959, Masters and Johnson had begun to apply their observations to people's problems. In 'sex therapy' clinics for couples they concentrated on treating impotence and frigidity, beginning with an examination of the sexual history of both partners and their interrelationship. They gathered information about sexual dysfunction as they went along, and in the first ten years of their clinic, with follow-ups lasting five years, Masters and Johnson reported success rates of 97.8% in overcoming premature ejaculation; of 80.7% with female frigidity; of 73.8% in cases of male impotence which had started after some sexual experience; and of 59.4% in male impotence cases that went back to earliest experiences. Many of the techniques that Dr. Masters learned from the male and female prostitutes he had used as early subjects have found direct application in therapy of sexual inadequacy. The report of this work, *Human Sexual Inadequacy* (1970), has become a standard work for sex therapists and has led to the adoption of new treatments for sexual distress and dysfunction.

2

A SEXUAL GALLERY

Roles and attitudes that people adopt for their sexual personalities.

Roles & Attitudes

Shakespeare said 'All the world's a stage', and people probably act their lives out more than they realize. The scripts are handed down from parents and grandparents with a certain number of rules about who can play which parts. In particular, there seems to be one group of ROLES which are for men only, and another group which are for women only. If we tresspass and steal each other's roles, we will not be called 'manly' or 'feminine'—terms of praise for those who perform the roles of their own sex successfully—but 'mannish' or 'effeminite', derogatory words which suggest that there is something wrong with these roles when the wrong people play them.

Among the most time-honoured sex roles are those of the woman who acts helpless and the man who acts as if he has someone helpless to look after. The woman's role might include waiting for the man to open doors and light her cigarettes, claiming to be incapable of performing simple sums of arithmetic and expecting to be paid for. Her clothes and shoes support her in her role—they are not meant to be practical for walking or getting wet in. Clearly, in her behaviour, her 'costume', her expectations and attitudes, she is saying 'I am incapable'. And the man who walks beside her in practical clothes, opens doors for her, lights her cigarettes, displays his knowledge of simple arithmetic and pays for her evening's food and entertainment is saying the same thing—'that's right, you're helpless (but you don't have to worry about it because I'm here)'.

Not all sex roles are so obvious. For example, there is the familiar character of the Nagging Wife, whose lines go something like this: 'don't forget to call the garage, did you feed the dog, I wish you wouldn't smoke so much, that stair carpet is loose again, your tie needs straightening'. She is probably partnered by the equally familiar character of the Long-Suffering Husband, whose message tends to be non-verbal: in response to her monologue he tightens his lips ('I could say plenty but I'm too noble'), squares his shoulders ('listening to you is really a burden') and sighs deeply ('I suffer more than you can understand').

It would be unfair to suggest that sex roles are always only games or relics of behaviour from an earlier age. There is no doubt that a number of different functions need to be fulfilled in any family: money must be earned; shopping, cooking and cleaning must be done; children must be looked after. The *roles* of wage-earner, housekeeper and child-minder must be filled, somehow, by the adults of the family. The rules about who does what have scarcely begun to relax, and they undoubtedly affect our behaviour because they represent an unequal division of power: earning the money (and having the once-necessary extra muscle) meant

that men had very much more power than women, and by and large they still do.

All kinds of subsidiary roles and attitudes spring up where power is concerned: in particular the powerful seek to justify their position by attributing it to the characteristics of both themselves and the group which they dominate. We like to think that we behave according to higher laws than the laws of the jungle, and if those who are physically strongest dominate there must be 'good' and 'moral' reasons for it—and not just the obvious reason that they are in a position to clobber anyone who challenges them.

This is probably the chief reason why women in the past were often given rather unnatural character types. According to some, women were innately pure, good, gentle, simple, etc., and therefore needed protecting. The women who tried to live up to this good-little-girl type of role almost inevitably became prudes and hypocrites, apparently lacking in sexual feeling, common sense or the capacity for making decisions. Another (and quite contradictory) line of argument said that women were innately impure, dangerous, seductive, scheming, complex, etc. If you broke the rules of current sexual morality and happened to be female, you found yourself cast as the scarlet woman—with all the attendant characterization of someone ruthless, predatory, 'unwifely' and 'unmotherly'. (Who ever heard of a scarlet man?—men who broke the same moral laws had different parts to play.)

However, women were by no means the only ones to find themselves limited to playing certain roles. Faced with a problem which affects both him and his wife equally, as for instance a neighbour playing rock until 4 am., a man can not, according to his script, say 'what are you going to do?' (that's her line). His line is something like 'leave this to me' and—whether he feels like it or not—he's stuck with the role of boss.

Probably most sex roles are variants on this basic duo of boss and bossed, dominant and subordinate. Heterosexuals have been given great—and sometimes painful—insight into their sexual behaviour by the imitations which are enacted by some homosexuals. Possibly, however, homosexuals will provide the others with new models as well as with mirror-images. When bisexuals develop a relationship with someone of their own sex they may discover their behaviour seems incongruous—is, in fact, play-acting in the wrong place.

There is no reason why we should be totally free of role-playing in life, but there seems to be no virtue in being trapped in roles which merely limit us to one stereotyped kind of behaviour—possibly one which may not even be natural to our individual personalities. Shakespeare also said that each man in his time plays many parts. Perhaps now is the time for both men and women to expand their repertoire.

Chris Jones

Dreams

Freud's brilliant ideas helped to chart the seemingly incomprehensible morass of our dream life. He thought that what a dreamer remembers is merely a façade that hides a dream's true meaning. He named the memory 'manifest content' and the true meaning 'latent content'. The 'residue' or events of the previous day, Freud believed, are sometimes used in dreams to express deepseated wishes and perhaps to offer solutions to problems. Certain processes occur which distort dreams' real meaning. For instance, in the phenomenon of 'condensation', parts of a dream's true meaning are abridged and appear in the memory. Thus one person from real life may represent several people or ideas in dreams. 'Displacement' is another dream distortion in which emotions attached to one thing or event are linked to something else which seems to be irrelevant or unconnected. In the process of 'symbolism', certain symbols or events signify particular things in all dreams.

Jung found that many symbols occurring in dreams resembled drawings found in caves and elsewhere by ancient primitive people. He believed that just as we have vestigial primitive organs in our bodies (for example, the appendix, which is used in the bodies of rabbits and other herbivores to digest cellulose), so we have similar structures in our minds. He went on to describe a 'collective subconscious' common to all human beings: being so similar in form and chemistry to our primitive ancestors, it may be that we share much of our dream life with them.

Freud called dreams the 'royal road to the unconscious' and spent much time with his patients analysing their dreams, but modern ideas about the relevance of dreams have not completely supported his views about their importance—especially in regard to hidden or subconscious conflicts which result in sexual problems or anxiety.

In the 1960s, scientists discovered that there are two sorts of sleep which alternate during the night and which have different electrical brain patterns associated with them. In one type, the eyes move about rapidly from side to side, giving it the name Rapid Eye Movement (REM) sleep. This occurs every ninety minutes or so throughout the night and is associated with bursts of brain activity, with dreaming and male erections during dreams.

Promiscuity

This is a label for people who have sex relations on a casual basis with different partners over a short period of time. Promiscuity doesn't usually describe people who form longer term relationships with more than one person, although sometimes it includes them as well. Most people seek out things in life that give them pleasure, and there is no doubt that sex is pleasurable. Anyone who lives solely for pleasure—which includes being promiscuous—is called a HEDONIST, from the Greek word for pleasure. LIBERTINE or VOLUPTUARY are the old-fashioned terms (mostly describing promiscuous men) for those who take delight in 'pleasures of the flesh'. Labels for sexual activity with multiple partners have historically been uncomplimentary, although a DON JUAN or a CASANOVA is usually thought of with some envy as being successful sexually and romantically with women.

Throughout the ages more men then women have had the opportunity, riches, power or freedom to indulge in promiscuity. But it is interesting that certain women, when obtaining power or social position, behaved with as much sexual energy as men in the same position. Messalina, wife of the Roman Emperor Claudius, is one good example —she is famous for her droves of lovers. NYMPHOMANIA traditionally described such exceptionally promiscuous female behaviour, a sort of frenetic quest for endless sexual gratification. The word has generally gone out of favour, since it is known that all women are capable of multiple orgasms, not just nymphomaniacs. The word is not even very popular anymore in describing women who have a deep psychological or physical need for frequent orgasm. In recent decades some couples in a quest to make their sexual lives more exciting have engaged in *partner swapping** (swinging), preferring this to more casual promiscuity or adultery.

There are both positive and negative sides to promiscuity. On the one hand, it enables a man or woman to become familiar with the physical and the emotional side of sexual relationships. People often make better lovers and have happier sex lives if they learn something practical about technique. In some cases, previous promiscuous behaviour may avert a couple's discovering after the honeymoon that they have made a mistake simply because they were blinded by sexual attraction prior to marriage. On the negative side, people who behave promiscuously may have difficulties in forming stable loving relationships and in some ways may be immature. Promiscuous behaviour spreads diseases which are sexually transmitted, and it is recognised that such diseases are on the increase world-wide (*health**). Also, it is now a medically accepted fact that a girl who engages in sexual intercourse from a young age with multiple partners is much more likely to develop certain cancers of the cervix or the womb in maturity than a girl who has not been promiscuous.

Modesty

Modesty is an adjective usually applied to girls or women which indicates that one's manner and conduct is retiring or bashful or scrupulously chaste. At various periods in history and in many different cultures, a different mode of behaviour and plain, unpretentious dress were considered the necessary attributes of femininity. Human ideas about what constitutes modesty are very arbitrary. A woman strictly brought up in the Islamic faith and used to wearing a veil might modestly cover her face rather than her genitals if surprised by an outsider while in the nude. The conditioning of a Western woman would lead her to cover her breasts and her genitals.

Prude

A person who is extremely circumspect in the use of words and behaviour regarding sexual matters is a prude. A prude's behaviour disguises any real human sexuality or feelings and emotions about sex. The term is often applied to a woman of affected modesty or one who pretends extreme propriety, but it can also describe a man. A prudent woman might be one who is careful, for example, to use some means of contraceptive to prevent an unwanted pregnancy, but a *prudish* woman might pretend to such modesty that she would deny any knowledge of contraception.

Prudish behaviour often goes hand in hand with hypocrisy, a pretence of virtue or goodness, or with an obsessive but unadmitted interest in sex. Examples of prudishness can be found in most cultures and in many different historical times, and the zeal with which prudes have meted out punishment to the 'wicked and sinful' seems to support the Marquis de Sade's aphorism that puritanism is an ally of the devil.

The Victorian era in England was famous both for its prudery and its hypocrisy. William Acton, a prominent Victorian physician, was an almost perfect example of his age—he wrote at great length in a serious medical fashion on sexual diseases and related problems, even describing prostitution at great length from a sociological and statistical point of view. On the other hand, he actually wrote 'a modest woman seldom desires any sexual gratification for herself' and he also catalogued the supposed horrific diseases that would afflict a masturbator.

Perhaps the best example of current prudish attitudes in Western society is public *sex education** on sexually-transmitted diseases. Such diseases are now known to constitute a world-wide epidemic and yet so-called public morality dictates that the topic be handled with discretion and even clinics in hospitals specializing in such disease often have a substitute name such as 'L-clinic' rather than a direct name such as 'sex disease clinic'. Examples of prudery in the use of words connected with sex are so rampant as to be hilarious. 'Intimacy' for intercourse or 'private parts' for genitals are just two examples. This is direct sexual INHIBITION, the restraint of straight-forward expression of a natural activity.

Peter Till.

Dominance

In many relationships and marriages a struggle for power or dominance goes on. Men and women with maturity problems or sexual difficulties are often unable to compromise or give in to a partner because they find such a loss of power or control too emotionally threatening or humiliating.

Dominance in sexual relations can take many forms ranging from acting out *sado-masochistic** fantasies to a woman who demands to be wined and dined before making love, or a man who insists that his partner always lies on her back during intercourse.

Women who demand ideal sexual performance from men—and show their contempt for anything less—are some-times called BALL BREAKERS or ball busters. These terms also describe women who do not conform to a stereo-typed male idea of sexual femininity.

On the other hand, some men are excited by a woman acting out a domin-ant role as a school teacher or gov-erness (usually dressed up in intimate or fantasy clothing) and who chastises (*flagellation**) or otherwise humiliates them (*erotic bondage**). Such activi-ties may be engaged in by a man with a prostitute or a call girl, while with his unsuspecting wife he engages in a more usual form of love-making. Married and other couples engage in dominance games too as an adjunct or stimulant to love making.

MACHISMO is a current word which comes from the Spanish *macho*, mean-ing male. It implies a need to express an arrogant style of virility, probably be-cause many Mediterranean or Latin-American males feel they must live up to a popular image of dominant, flam-boyant masculinity. Machismo in sex tends to imply *sexism** or exploitation of females. However, some women en-joy being sexually dominated, and find dominance games, such as being tied up before making love or being mildly chastised, stimulating and exciting.

Not every person who seeks or enjoys a relationship in which one partner is strongly dominant will be aware of psychological motives which may un-derline their attitude. Provided natural unequal partners are emotionally com-plementary to each other the dominance of one over the other is unlikely to cause unhappiness, unless at some time the submissive one discovers that he or she is no longer willing to be emotionally exploited.

Submission

A submissive person characteristically acts with meekness and a willing obedience to the wishes and demands of a person or persons in authority. As with *dominance**, submission forms a part of the sexual climate of many relationships and marriages. Submissive behaviour, especially where a compulsive element is present, is thought to be caused by a person's upbringing and may reflect a deprivation trauma suffered in childhood.

Between sexual partners, submissive behaviour may take many forms. On the one hand, a woman may always play a 'feminine' role by never taking the first steps in any sexual activity and by acting a completely passive role even while intercourse takes place. At the other extreme, the desire of some men and women to be humiliated by their partners, to grovel and beg forgiveness for 'misbehaviour' borders on pathology or mental disease. Some men love women who reject and humiliate them; the more skilled a woman becomes at such rejection the more devoted her partner becomes.

Throughout history, sexual *sadism** and dominance-submission patterns of behaviour were often linked to the use of slaves as objects rather than as people with dignity. The Roman Empire provides a good example of extreme patterns of sexual submission. As Rome conquered territories throughout Europe, North Africa and Asia, thousands of slaves were sent back to the capital to provide public entertainment in the arenas of a violent and often sexual nature. Slaves were used by wealthy citizens of Rome to provide sexual entertainment at orgies. The submission of slaves to any sort of sexual indignity or activity was not unique to Rome; the notion of people as *sex objects** has flourished throughout the pages of history.

Today, a sub-culture exists devoted to *erotic bondage** and discipline which involves interest in and the practice of submission-dominance behaviour. Magazines giving contact names of people with such interests are published, and they describe boots, spurs, spike heels, chains, whips and other equipment of a sexually sadistic nature. Such magazines usually contain stories about women who administer 'strict discipline' with illustrations depicting them in erotic 'B & D' gear, looking suitably cruel and authoritative.

Tomi Ungerer

Sex Object

Any person or thing to which sexual emotions and activity are directed is quite literally a sex object. Any material thing from a pornographic magazine to a human being which stimulates sexual excitement and arousal can be a sex object, but the phrase 'sex object' is currently used as a derogatory term, implying sexual exploitation of women in fact or fantasy by men. It implies a *sexist** attitude in which women are considered as child bearers and sexual stimulants, apart from their human qualities. When slaves were used to satisfy the sexual proclivities of their owners with no regard for their own feelings or dignity, they represented *par excellence* the use of other human beings as sex objects. Throughout history, animals have also been used for human sexual purposes. Even today such practices occur, but are usually resorted to by the sexually inadequate or the mentally disturbed.

'Girlie' magazines with erotic pictures of all different sizes and shapes of women are sex objects themselves as they provide visual stimulation of a sexual nature. The women depicted are, of course, sex objects in that they provide emotional sexual stimulation and in some cases physical arousal in readers. There are magazines on the market in which men are photographed as sex objects, offering stimulation for women as well as for homosexual men.

It is a fact of life that the human female between the ages of puberty and menopause is sexually stimulating to the human male. Objections by women to being sex objects can arise from feelings of degradation and inequality. Many women complain that their husbands only want them 'for one thing' and as a result they become unresponsive sexually. Often husbands are surprised both by this attitude and their wives' lack of response, and much of the work of sex counselling and marriage guidance is to reconcile these differences. In some respects, the different sexual arousal patterns of men and women contribute to female resentment about being sex objects. Men can be as sensitive as women about being treated as sex objects rather than worthy human beings with individual personalities.

Sexism

'Sexism' describes attitudes and emotions concerning the sexual roles enacted by men and women, both historically and in day-to-day encounters. It has come to mean the placing of men and of women into traditional 'feminine' and 'masculine' roles without regard for their individual preferences or abilities.

Sexual liberation for both men and women has begun to challenge these deeply-rooted attitudes to the roles of male and female. The traditional male role of bread-winner and aggressor complemented by a female role of passive acquiescence and support is part of the psyche of most Western adults. Emancipation and improved independence for women seem to threaten men who may feel they are losing their 'self-image', their identities. Increasing female liberation in many areas of day-to-day life is seen as threatening 'traditional' male roles.

Sexual liberation, while it is welcomed by men as giving them much more opportunity for sexual expression with a greater variety of women, is also detested because it makes women less 'feminine'. Many men seem to be shocked to be on the receiving end of female instigated sexual attention or sexual aggression, especially as women become more direct. A double standard of behaviour is part of the doctrine of sexism.

Biologically, the male's function is to chase and impregnate, and if this were not so the human race would die out. In the male sex role, the penetration and thrusting actions of coitus have an aggressive element. At the height of passion, a male shows a directed energy which climaxes in ejaculation. Despite this physical aggressive energy, emotional aggression towards women is part of sexism. In its extreme form, it has been called male chauvinism—a bellicose masculinity which fervently believes that all females are *sex objects** and should play their traditional role.

Sexist attitudes are exceptionally widespread and wide-ranging: male factory workers have gone on strike when their pay was the same as females; men murder their wives in a fit of sexual jealousy and are treated with sympathy by the courts (homicide is not the charge, manslaughter usually is). Sexual attacks upon women are a common occurrence, and sexist attitudes underly most of them.

Narcissism

(From Narkissos, a boy in Greek mythology who fell so in love with his own reflection in a pool that he starved to death looking at it.) The term is used in psychoanalysis to describe a phase in childhood development, often at about the age of three, when a child's love-object is its own person (*sexual development**). Certain adults with sexual difficulties persist neurotically in the self-love stage. An example is a lover who cannot respond sexually without actually seeing his or her partner getting pleasure during love-making. Some *pedophiles** are narcissistic and will kiss their mirror-images on occasions.

Femme Fatale

The French term 'Femme Fatale' describes the traditional image of a woman with a fascination over men, who are likely to throw away everything for her. The type of the smouldering VAMP, behaving as if she is irresistible to men, is a familiar character. (There is usually one at every party.) Some, in fact, *are* irresistible—perhaps because they exude an obvious sexuality (or at least availability) and are single-minded in their pursuit of sexual mates. More often, the role is adopted by certain women whose own insecurity leads them into an intensively competitive attitude to other women. The idea that men are drawn to them, like moths to a candle, also nourishes an immature attitude to sexual relationships.

Tease

There are degrees of teasing. The low-cut dress or tight trousers represent a 'first degree'—it is not directed at anybody in particular and signals a general sexual availability. The 'second-degree' tease is shown by smiles and winks—direct personal interaction involving no physical contact. Physical contact is expressed in the 'third degree' tease when touching and kissing are common, yet still with no commitment to ultimate sexual gratification.

Teasing is a normal part of the development of a sexual relationship. It is useful when one of the partners is unsure of himself or the partner. It is a try-on, testing period, when the partners say to each other, this-is-what-I-might-be-if-you-are-what-I-think-you-are. In adolescence it is quite common, but it is part of adult courtship, too. When a relationship never progresses beyond the tease phase, it may be a sign of an immature personality.

A tease is usually thought of as female. The roots of this probably lie in our male-dominated traditions of seduction. It is the man who instigates action. He asks for the first date, moves for the first kiss and makes the proposal of marriage. The female is still not expected to make passes at the male, so she can only inaugurate action by indirect action, by flirting with or teasing the male. She hopes that he will take up her suggestion, and develop it into sexual activity.

There are some people who enjoy flirting not because they are really inviting further sexual play but because they enjoy the power it gives them over a willing partner who can be kept dangling. In a restricted social group, like a small town or a youth club, a girl who works her way through several partners without actually having intercourse will become known as a '*prick-tease*' or '*cock-tease*'. More elegantly, a girl who will allow everything short of penetration is known by the old-fashioned French term DEMI-VIERGE ('half virgin').

Courtly Love

Minstrels in the early Middle Ages composed and performed songs on the theme of courtly love at the courts of rulers and the nobility. Courtly love denotes a special attitude of (conveniently) hopeless passion and non-sexual devotion. Songs of unrequited love were addressed to a usually married lady, often of higher social rank than the 'lover', who called her his mistress. To her he offered his dedicated service, in exchange for some mere token like a handkerchief or even a single glance. Chastity on both sides was taken for granted, and real sexual success was the last thing the minstrel pined for.

Most poems of courtly love extol the mistress's virtue and graciousness in elaborate but formalized terms—followed by complaints about her scorn for the suitor. A somewhat masochistic attitude can be detected in this adoration of a proud, idealized woman.

The phenomenon of courtly love originated in Provence in the period just before the first Crusade. The poet-lovers were known there as *troubadours*. They were song writers, performers and courtiers rolled into one, and mostly members of the nobility. From France courtly love spread to Spain, Italy and Germany setting a new tone of romance in personal relations among the aristocracy.

Two influences may have helped to foster the early formula for courtly love. One came from the Greeks and Romans, who did not view romantic love as necessary in marriage. Love was regarded as a disease that unsettled people and could bring matrimonial disaster. The other influence came from the early Christian Church fathers, who often shuddered over the sexuality of women. In the second century AD., Tertullian described women as 'temples built over sewers', and the temptations of St. Jerome and St. Anthony traditionally took the form of erotic fantasies. Together, both influences tended to separate marriage and sex from romantic love, which might be cultivated as a physically sexless but ecstatically spiritual relationship.

The courtly love attitude—ecstatic in words, inhibited in action—degenerated in time into the sentimentality ridiculed by Cervantes in *Don Quixote*. Many women's magazines, pulp fiction and teenage love or romance comics still portray love and sex in the same unrealistic but romantic fashion.

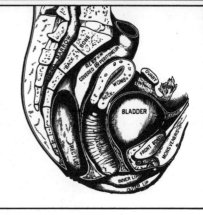

3

BODY MAPS

The location and action of the genital organs in both sexes.

Woman

Areola

Literally the Latin for 'a little space', areola is, in sexual terms, the coloured area around the *nipple*.* Often the earliest sign of the breasts starting to develop is an enlargement of the areola —the so-called areola 'budding'. Once this has happened, the whole breast starts to fill out. The areola changes again during early pregnancy, becoming darker and larger.

Breast

One of the major areas of femaleness, the breast is a mass of fatty tissue that contains glandular structures, the function of which is to produce milk. Breasts vary greatly in size and shape and are often unequal, but size is no measure of a woman's fertility or 'sexiness', nor is there any indication that it has anything to do with breast function. Breasts develop before a girl starts to menstruate and at the change of life, they may shrink a little. Breasts tend to become tense and sometimes painful just prior to a period, and firmer during sexual excitement. Lumps or bumps in the breast should always be examined and diagnosed urgently by a doctor.

Cervix

Cervix means 'a neck' in Latin, and in the gynecological sense it is the neck of the womb. It is a barrel-shaped organ about 1-1½ in (2.5-3.5 cm) in length. Half of it projects into the vagina and feels like the tip of the nose. It has a tiny canal passing through it and thus the vagina communicates with the womb. The cervix is often covered with mucus. Cells scraped from its surface show changes if examined under the microscope in various conditions. This is the basis of the cervical smear test for early cancer. The cervix is capable of expanding enormously prior to child-birth.

Clitoris

Generally accepted as having the same origin in the embryo as the male penis, the clitoris lies on the front of the pubic bone, almost hidden by the labia majora. Consisting of erectile tissue, and richly supplied with nerves, it is one of the most sensitive parts of the vulva. The whole clitoris is about ¾ in (20 cm) in length. Most of the body of the clitoris can only be felt if squeezed against the pubic bone. Its tip (glans) is visible under its hood (prepuce). The part that the clitoris plays in sexual intercourse

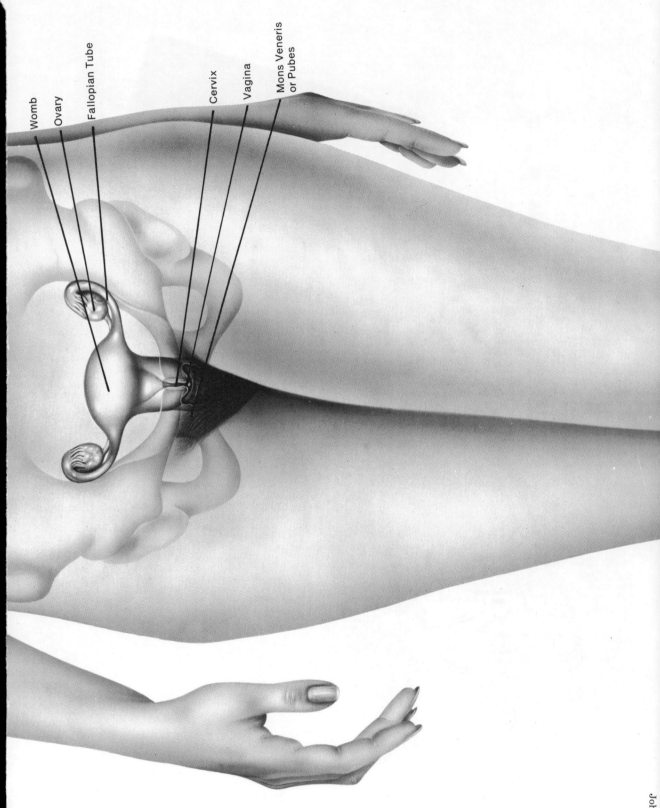

Womb

Ovary

Fallopian Tube

Cervix

Vagina

Mons Veneris
or Pubes

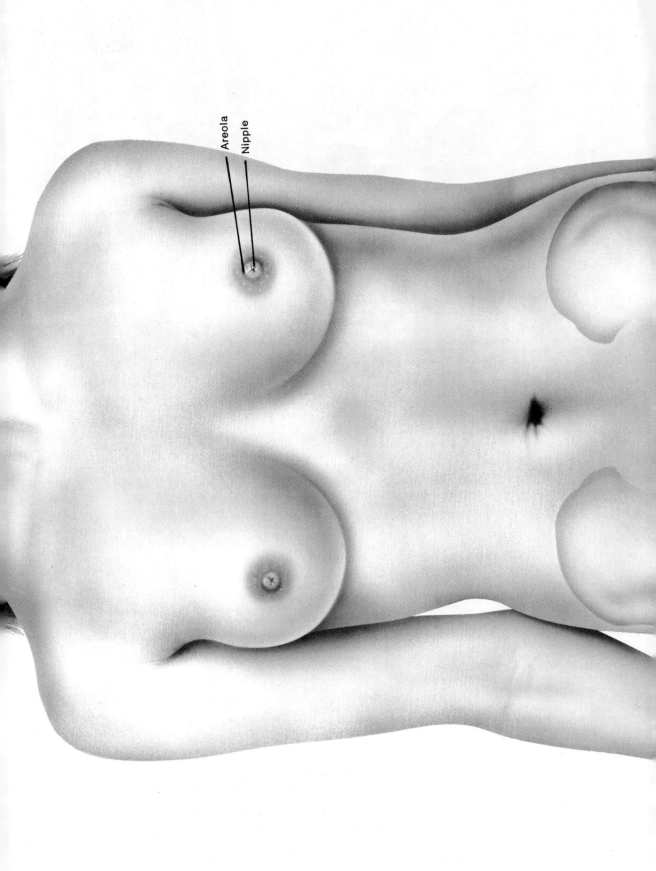

Areola

Nipple

is not fully understood, but it seems to be more involved in female excitement techniques than actual coitus.

Egg (Ovum)

The female reproductive cell of any animal or plant. Eggs vary immensely in size, but basically they are all very similar structures. The *ovum* (Latin for 'egg') is expelled from the ovary, having undergone a reduction in the number of its chromosomes from 46 to 23. (The superfluous chromosome material stays inside the cell, apparently functionless.) Unless fertilized in the Fallopian tube by the male sperm cell, the egg dies within a few days.

Fallopian Tubes

These paired structures extend from the ovaries to the womb, one on either side. Each is about 4 in (10 cm) in length, communicating with the womb at one end and the inside of the abdomen (peritoneal cavity) at the other (*Fallopian tube**). The fact that there is a free way between the vagina, *via* the cervical canal, the womb and the Fallopian tube, right into the inside of the cavity explains how occasionally peritonitis can occur after douching or infection of the vagina.

Fourchette

French for 'little fork'. This is the rearmost part of the vaginal opening (*introitus*), formed by the two labia minora fusing at this point. It only gets a special name to describe a skin area that frequently gets torn during childbirth and sometimes (together with the hymen) during the first act of intercourse.

Hymen

An incomplete membrane partially closing the entrance to the vagina. Usually, there is only one hole in the hymen through which the menstrual fluid (menses) can escape, but sometimes there are several holes present, in which case the hymen gains several fanciful adjectives like 'crescentic' 'annular', 'septate' and so on. When the hymen is ruptured or torn, it usually bleeds a little. As so many things can tear a hymen, its presence has no necessary relationship to virginity. Childbirth fragments the hymen into tiny skin tags called *carunculae*. (The original Greek word *humen* means a 'film' or 'membrane', and by extension it acquired a lot of meanings connected with the marriage rites.)

Woman

Labia Majora

The 'larger lips' or skin around the vaginal opening, with underlying deposits of fat in them. Anatomically, they are the female counterpart of the scrotum. In the front, they run up to join together at the mons veneris. At the back they join to become the perineum. Their outer parts are covered with hair, their inner surface is smooth and moistened by the secretions of various glands and the vaginal secretion. Except when the labia minora push between them, they remain close together and close off the entrance to the vagina. Sweat glands on the labia majora secrete a sexual scent (odours*).

Labia Minora

The 'smaller lips' which lie within the labia majora. They are soft, and vary considerably in size from woman to woman, and thus may project or remain hidden by the larger lips to the vagina's mouth. In the front, the minor lips join together and give the clitoris its prepuce (foreskin) or hood. At the back they fuse to form the fourchette*. The specialized skin of the labia minora is full of blood vessels and this allows them to become erect or 'pout' during sexual excitement.

Mons Veneris

'Mount of Venus' is the name given to the hair-bearing pubic skin of the woman, which covers the upper part of the pubic bone where its two halves join (the pubic symphysis) and the lower part of the abdominal muscles. There is a fatty pad beneath the mons veneris.

Nipple

This cone-shaped elevation in the centre of the areola* is larger and more extensive in women than in men. In both sexes it can be seen to be erectile either in sexual excitement or in the cold. It is an erogenous zone as well as a structure designed by nature for baby feeding. Milk flows from the nipple and its areola in the nursing mother, and it may also do so if she is sexually excited during the postnatal period.

Os

The Latin word for 'mouth' is os (genitive oris) and in the gynecological and sexual sense, it refers to the mouths of the cervix, which has one os at each end. The mouth in the vagina (external os) is joined to another in the womb (in-

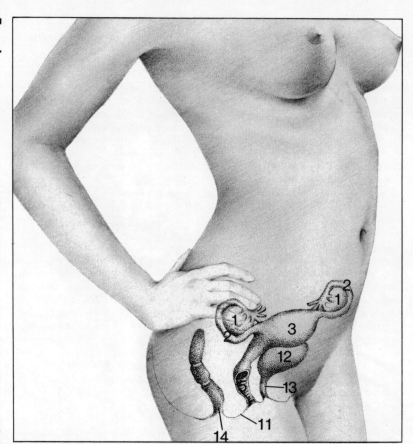

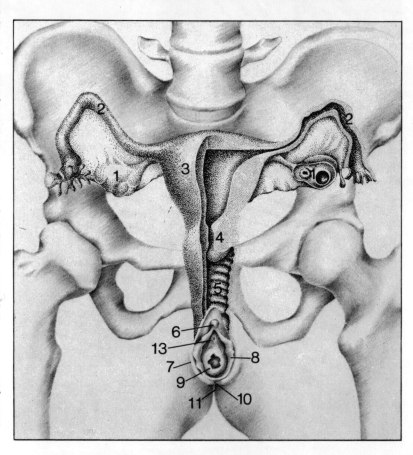

ternal os) by the cervical canal. In anatomy, the Latin *os* (genitive *ossis*), which means 'bone', is also used, and can be confused with the word above.

Ovary

The female sex gland, lying one on either side of the womb. The paired ovaries, 1⅜ in (3.5 cm) in length and ¾ in (2 cm) thick, weigh about .14-.28 oz (4-8 g) each, the right one tending to be bigger than the left. They are corrugated on the surface and pale in colour. When viewed through the laparascope, small lumps can be seen on them in a fertile woman. These are the developing ovarian *follicles,* which contain the ripening egg cells. The inner part of the ovary is mainly composed of blood vessels, but the outer part stores about half a million potential egg cells, about five hundred of which are destined to mature during a woman's life-time. At the age of 16 or 17, the first follicle ripens and then explodes, throwing out an egg cell *(ovum)*. It continues to do this once a month, roughly, until she is about 45 or 50 *(menopause*)*. Where an gg cell has recently escaped, the surface colour turns yellowish.

Perineum

The less hairy skin area which lies between the vaginal opening and the anus. Its length is about ¾-2 in (2-5 cm). The perineum is of concern to the obstetrician, as it is an area prone to damage during childbirth.

Pubes

Two meanings exist. It is either the pubic hair or the area covered by it. It can also refer to the underlying pubic bone, the *os pubis.*

Rectum

(Latin for 'straight'.) In anatomy, it is in fact the straight last part of the large intestine before the anal canal leads to the anus. The rectum is often free of bowel contents. As it is about 5 inches (13 cm) in length, it can learly accom-

1 Ovary
2 Fallopian Tube
3 Womb (Uterus)
4 Cervix
5 Vagina
6 Clitoris
7 Labia Majora
8 Labia Minora
9 Hymen
10 Fourchette
11 Perineum
12 Bladder
13 Urethra
14 Rectum

modate an erect penis or a vibrator, but in doing so it probably exceeds its natural function.

Urethra

The tube through which the urine passes on its way from the bladder to the outside. In the female, it ends in the vestibule or 'forecourt'. The sides of this forecourt are the labia minora. The front is occupied by the clitoris and the back is the hymen or its remnants.

Womb (Uterus)

A thick-walled, muscular, hollow organ rather like a pear in shape, the pointed end of which is the cervix. It is about 3¼-3½ in (8-9 cm) in length, 2½ in (6 cm) across in its widest part and about ¾ in (4 cm) thick in the thickest part. In other words, it is like a pear that somebody has gently trodden on. The walls of the womb are about ½-¾ in (1-2 cm) thick and the length of the internal cavity is about 3-3¼ in (7.5-8 cm), measured from the external os. The womb has a body and a *cervix**. The *Fallopian tubes** are inserted into it on each side. The womb is held in place by several ligaments, the most important of which run out from the cervix and upper vagina like the spokes from the hub of a wheel to the rim of the surrounding pelvic structures.

Vagina

Its Latin name, meaning 'sheath' or 'scabbard', describes the vagina's role, ensheathing the penis during intercourse. Internally, it is made of modified skin which covers an elastic fibomuscular structure. It runs backwards from its opening at an angle of 60-70° from the horizontal plane. It is not straight even then, but is bent backwards further about half way down its length. Because the cervix 'points' into it at the top, its forward wall is about 3¼ in (8 cm) in length and its pear wall is about 4 in (10 cm) in length. Measurements are really pointless because, like the stomach and the womb, the organ is vastly distentable. The vagina undergoes active changes during coitus *(Orgasmic Response**)*.

Vulva

A composite term for the external genitals of the female, including the mons veneris, the clitoris, the vestibule, the urethral opening, the labia, the hymen or its remnants, the fourchette and perhaps for completeness the perineum, although this is not a truly sexual area.

Man

Adam's Apple

The popular name for the prominent part of the male larynx (voice box). At puberty and under the influence of male hormones, the larynx grows, the vocal cords become longer and thus change their natural vibration characteristics, and the voice changes or breaks. If male hormones are given to women, similar changes occur, but without the appearance of an Adam's apple.

Appendix Testes

A small oval body about the size of a rice grain that lies on top of the testes. It is the remnant of a structure related to the kidney during the growth of the fetus.

Corpora Cavernosa

Latin for 'bodies of caverns'. The main structure of the *penis** is formed of a *corpus spongiosum** and two corpora cavernosa, the latter making up most of the shaft. They divide at the base and are attached to the pubic bone. The 'caverns' of the penis fill with blood during sexual excitement (the process called ENGORGEMENT) and produce an erection.

Corpus Spongiosum

The third body of erectile tissue in the *penis**, through which the *urethra** passes. Even when the penis is erect, the corpus spongiosum remains fairly soft and spongy, which allows sperm to pass along the urethra as the man ejaculates.

Epididymis

A small structure composed mainly of a mass of small, convoluted tubes that collect up the semen from the *testes** and eventually take it down to the *vas deferens**. The epididymis gets its name from two Greek words meaning 'on top of the twins', referring to where it sits, on and behind each of the twinned testicles. It is described as having a head, a body and a tail. Just behind the head of the epidiymis lies the *appendix testes**.

Glans

This is the tip of the *penis**. It is an expansion of the *corpus spongiosum**. The base of the glans projects out from the main body of the penis and this projecting margin is called the *corona**.

Man

1 Testis
2 Epididymis
3 Vas Deferens or Spermatic Duct
4 Os Pubis
5 Seminal Vesicle
6 Prostate
7 Prostatic Utricle
8 Urethra
9 Meatus
10 Corpora Cavernosa
11 Corpus Spongiosum
12 Glans
13 Prepuce
14 Bladder
15 Perineum
16 Rectum

(left) *Adam and Eve by Albrecht Dürer,*

The areas of *secondary sexual characteristics** of male and female bodies are shown as follows:

hair on head and face

body hair (heavier growth on men)

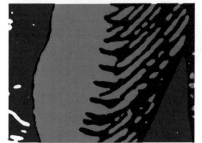

skeletal and muscular differences

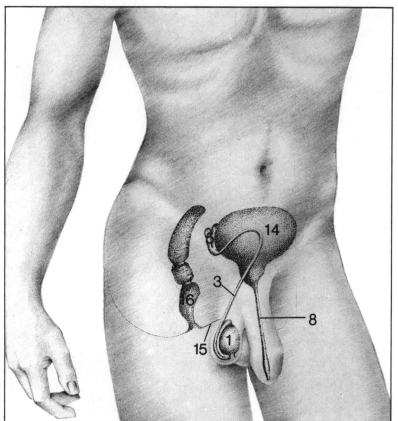

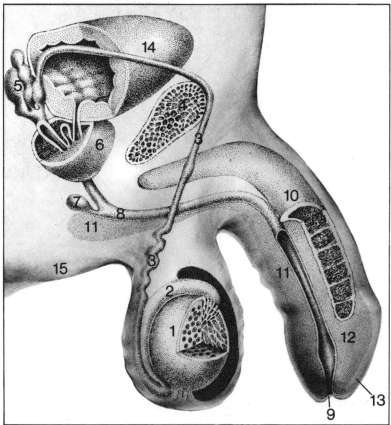

Man

Penis

This is the male organ of coitus. It is made up of the three 'bodies' or corpora, and is covered with skin. It is a very variable organ as far as size is concerned and ranges in length from $2\frac{7}{8}$–$4\frac{1}{2}$in (7.25–11.5cm) in the flaccid state to $4\frac{3}{8}$–$8\frac{1}{4}$in (12-21cm) when erect. The circumference ranges from 3–$4\frac{1}{2}$in (7.5–10.5cm) flaccid to $3\frac{3}{8}$–$4\frac{3}{4}$in (8.5–12cm erect). A new concept of penis size is the comparative volume index, an indication of the *mass* or filling capacity of the penis. This varies in the erect state from 5.7–28.8in^3 (94–423 cm^3) in different men.

Perineum

The less hairy skin area which lies between the back of the scrotum and the anus. A central ridge, called the median raphe, is plainly evident.

Prepuce (Foreskin)

In the uncircumcised male, the skin of the penis projects over the *glans** and is reflected back upon itself to run into and be joined to the neck of the penis. The skin in this area is thin, and continuous with the urethral opening. When the penis is flaccid, the *foreskin** has to be pulled back to show the glans, but once the penis is erect, the glans is usually pretty fully exposed (*circumcision**).

Prostate

This gland appears to be a sexual organ, since in animals which have seasonal sexuality, the prostate enlarges during a mating season and then shrinks until the next. In the adult human male, it is about $1\frac{5}{8}$in (4cm) across at its base and is the size of a chestnut. The prostate is composed of muscular and glandular tissue. Its secretions pass down about 20 small ducts which lead to the section of the *urethra** that pierces the prostate gland, but their purpose is not yet fully understood.

Scrotal Bag

The scrotum is a sack-like structure containing the testicles. It is made of skin, muscle and various planes of connective tissue. The skin of the *penis** blends into the skin of the scrotum in front. The pouch of the scrotum is divided into right and left portions, the left one hanging down lower than the right. This dividing ridge is continued forward along the base of the penis and backwards through the perineum towards the anus. The scrotal skin is

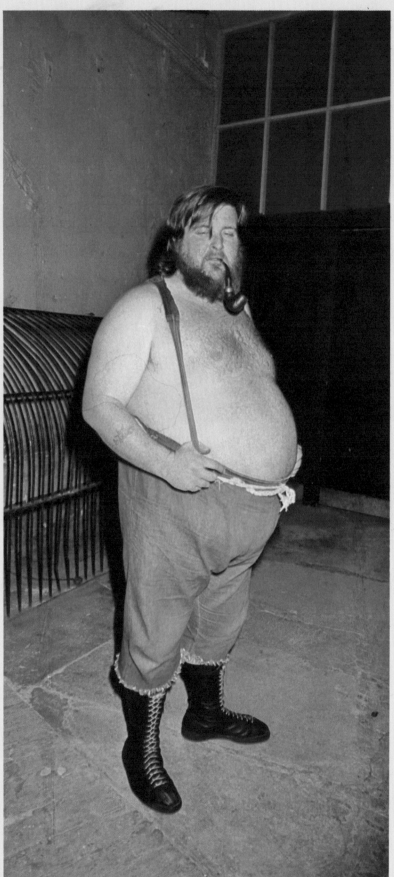

Sphincter

Greek for 'binder'. A term applied to muscles that run around a body orifice or internal structure. For example, the anus has a powerful sphincter muscle, and so do the bladder and stomach.

Testes

(Testis or testicle in the singular.) The semen-secreting glands of the male. The testes are fairly uniform in size 1⅝–2in (4–5cm) in length, 1in (2.5cm) in breadth and 1¼in (3cm) in width, and lie in the scrotum, surrounded by various tough coverings. Inside them are about 250 glandular lobes. Tiny tubes collect the spermatozoa and eventually they enter the *epididymus** where a maturing process usually occurs. At the tail of the epididymus, the *vas deferens** is formed which, together with a burden of blood vessels and nerves, is ensheathed into the spermatic cord. This can be felt in the groin in the male.

Urethra

The tube through which the urine passes on its way from the bladder to the outside. In the male, it ends at the top of the *penis** and is, in all 8–10in (20.5–25.5cm) long.

Vas Deferens (Spermatic Duct)

Latin for 'the vessel that carries away,' which is exactly what the vas does. One on each side of the body carries sperm from the *epididymis** up through the groin in the spermatic cord. Then it separates from the spermatic cord and eventually enters the pubic cavity, to run between the base of the bladder and the upper end of the seminal vesicle. As it continues its downward path, it meets its fellow from the other side and eventually joins the duct of the seminal vesicle as it runs into the *prostate** gland. This now becomes called the EJACULATORY DUCT, which travels on to the prostatic urethra, near to where the prostatic ducts enter it. This meeting place of the three components of the semen, the sperm, the secretions of the *seminal vesicles** and those of the prostate gland, is called the PROSTATIC UTRICLE. A utricle is a bag, and this is a little bag-like cul-de-sac off the main part of the prostatic urethra. Interestingly, this structure corresponds to the vagina in the female. During ejaculation, semen is ejected from the utricle and the prostatic urethra and up into the *penis**.

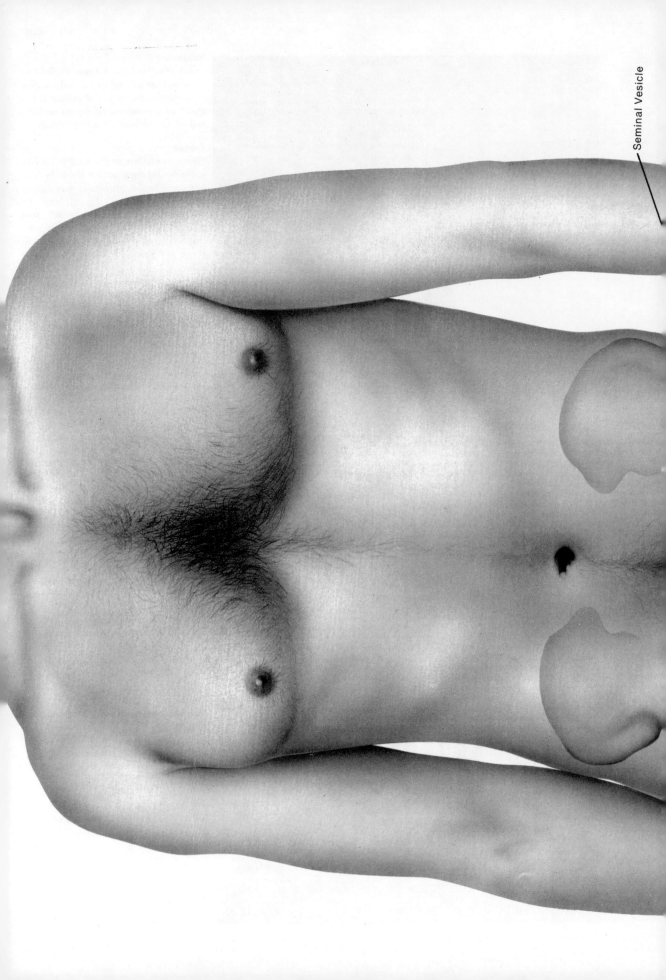

Seminal Vesicle

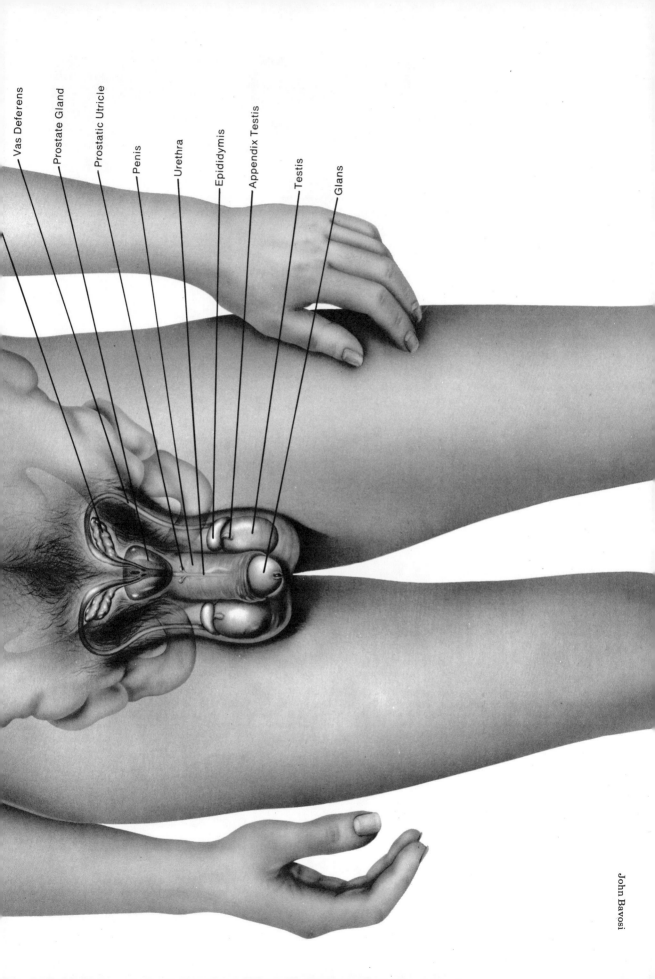

Vas Deferens

Prostate Gland

Prostatic Utricle

Penis

Urethra

Epididymis

Appendix Testis

Testis

Glans

John Bavosi

corrugated and can be seen to move, noticeably in cold weather and during coitus.

Semen

A mixture of spermatozoa from the *testes** and secretions from the *prostate** gland, the *seminal vesicles** and possibly from other rudimentary glands as well. At orgasm in the male, semen is shot out of the *penis** under pressure (*ejaculation**). Usually, after two days continence .07–.21 fl oz (2–6ml) of semen are ejaculated. More frequent ejaculation diminishes the volume of semen each time.

Seminal Vesicles

These provide the bulk of fluid in the semen. There are two of them, placed on each side between the base of the bladder and the rectum. Each one is about 2in (5cm) in length and consists of a tube coiled upon itself like a spring, from which bulge several little chambers or diverticula. The lower end of this curiously shaped tube becomes narrow and joins the *vas deferens**. Together they form the ejaculatory ducts which conduct the semen into the prostatic urethra and thence, as ejaculation occurs, onwards up the *penis**.

Smegma

Greek for 'soap'. Smegma is a mixture of dead skin cells and skin grease and does look a bit like soap as it hides under the foreskin. It can, however, also be found under the prepuce of the clitoris and in the upper (front) parts of the labia minora. The presence of smegma denotes a poor standard of personal hygiene, and it can be a contributory factor in transmitting disease.

Sperm

Greek for 'seed'. It is an abbreviation of *spermatozoon* (single) or *spermatozoa* (plural), which denotes the male germ cell capable of penetrating the ovum. Each sperm cell has an oval shaped head, a centre portion and a long tail. They mature in the tubules of the *testes** and once ejaculated they live only a few hours in the female reproductive tract. Many sperm cells seem to cluster around an egg cell before one pierces the exterior by means of enzyme action and penetrates it. Once inside, the sperm combines with the egg and a change occurs, hardening the barrier around the cell to prevent further penetration by other sperms.

Leonard McCombe/Life © Time Inc. 1977

4

GENDER

The influences that determine a person's place in the spectrum of sex.

Intersex

Between the type of the completely male and of the completely female person there is a variety of possible physical or psychological anomalies which occur from time to time. This range of possibilities is known as INTERSEX. Influences which may place a human being in an intersex category can be visualized as pinballs striking the obstacles on a pin-ball board, before dropping eventually into a particular slot, as illustrated on this page.

A. FEMALE: physical and psychological identity is completely female; fertile, with full female gonads; XX chromosomes.

B. BISEXUAL FEMALE: physically completely female; sexually attracted to members of both sexes; fertile; XX chromosomes.

C. FEMALE HOMOSEXUAL: physical identity is female; sexually attracted only to another female; fertile; XX chromosomes.

D. BUTCH FEMALE HOMOSEXUAL: physical identity is female; full female genitals; psychological identity is male; sexually attracted only to another female; fertile; XX chromosomes.

E. TRANSSEXUAL FEMALE: physically completely female, with female gonads; possibly has an enlarged clitoris, with envy of male role; psychological identity is male or neutral; fertile; XX chromosomes.

F. TESTICULAR FEMINIZATION SYNDROME: has outward sexual characteristics of a female (breasts, normal clitoris) but with internal testes and male chromosomes; psychological identity is female; infertile; XY chromosomes.

Female
1 Upbringing & conditioning
2 Male envy role
3 Masculine imprinting
4 Hostile father
5 Absent father

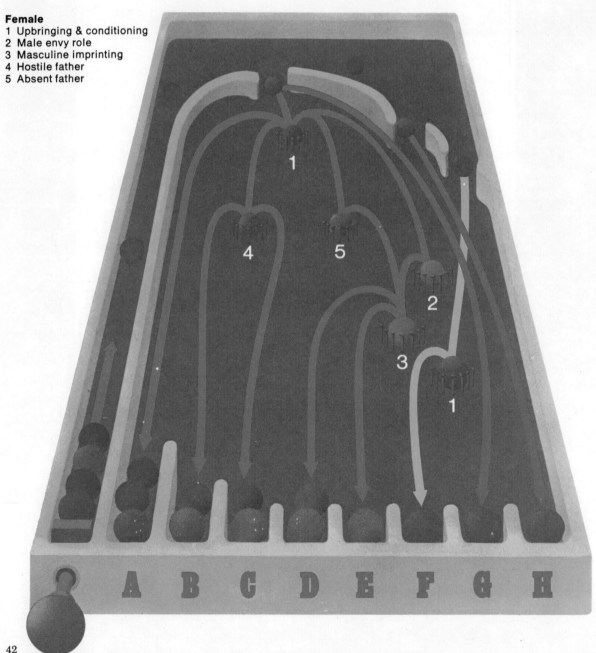

G. GYNANDROUS FEMALE: physically female with all female sex organs, but very masculine in appearance (facial hair, broad frame); male secondary sexual characteristics; most likely fertile; XX chromosomes.

H. TURNER'S SYNDROME: outward appearance and psychological identity more or less female, but with internal testes; Y-typical congenital malformation (shortness of stature, webbing of neck); infertile; XO chromosomes.

I. KLINEFELTER'S SYNDROME: outward appearance male; penis and gonads small, and tendency to obesity; infertile; XXY chromosomes.

J. GYNANDROUS MALE: has fully male sex organs, but is deficient in male hormones; feminine appearance (lack of facial hair, broad hips); most likely fertile; XY chromosomes.

K. TRANSSEXUAL MALE: physically male, with male gonads and small penis; has envy of female role; psychological identity is female or neutral; probably fertile; XY chromosomes.

L. TRANSVESTITE MALE: physically completely male, but enjoys adopting a female role by wearing women's clothes; fertile; XY chromosomes.

M. FEMININE MALE HOMOSEXUAL: physical identity is male; male gonads and genitals; psychological identity is female; attracted only to another male; fertile; XY chromosomes.

N. BUTCH MALE HOMOSEXUAL: physical and psychological identity is male; sexually attracted only to another male; fertile; XY chromosomes.

O. BISEXUAL MALE: physically completely male; sexually attracted to members of both sexes; fertile; XY chromosomes.

P. MALE: physical and psychological identity is male; male gonads and genitals; fertile; XY chromosomes.

Male
1 Upbringing & conditioning
2 Female role envy
3 Feminine imprinting
4 Hostile father
5 Feminine clothes envy
6 Possessive mother
7 Weak father and/or
  hostile mother

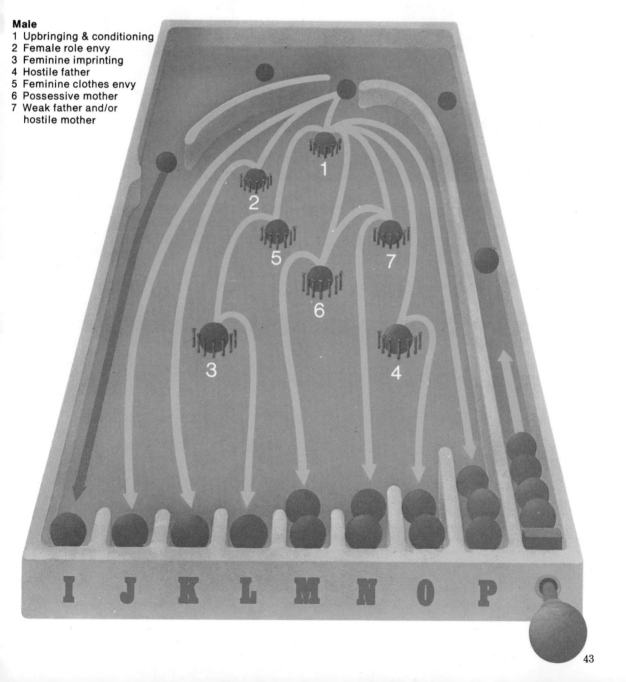

Transsexual: Male to Female

Transvestite

(opposite page) *Transsexual: Female to Male*

Gender Identity

The term 'gender', as in gender role or gender identity, was borrowed from ordinary grammar and introduced into sexological writing in the 1950s. This was done to try and bypass some of the confusion due to the multiple meanings of the term 'sex' itself, especially when dealing with hermaphroditism. The sex of the sex organs is not inevitably the same as a person's sexuality of sex role in the erotic sense, and one's 'masculine' or 'feminine' erotic sex role is not inevitably identical with the overall social behaviour in which one is arbitrarily placed because of one's physical sex organs.

Gender *identity* is a sameness, a unity and a persistence of one's individuality which can be male, female or ambivalent (i.e., both at once). Gender *role* is everything a person says or does to indicate to others, or to oneself, the degree to which one is male, female or ambivalent. It includes (but is not limited to) a person's sexual arousal and response. Gender role is the public expression of one's gender identity.

It is possible for a newborn baby to have the sex chromosomes and internal reproductive organs of a female, but the external genitals of a male, except that there are no testes. If reared as a male, this baby will 'grow' a boy's gender identity/role, despite the fact that the chromosomes and gonads are really female. Near puberty, this boy might find himself developing breasts and menstruating through his penis. His conception of himself as a male would then be totally incompatible with the pubertal feminization that was actually happening to him. But a boy in this case does not usually consider 'reassigning' himself as a female. He will probably choose to undergo surgery to remove the newly developed breasts and female sex organs. It is wrong to say that this person is a female. He has the chromosomal and gonadal sex of a female, yet the gender identity/role of a male. Put like this, we make distinctions between the sex of his sex organs, his sexual role in using them, and his overall role in society as a male.

In the foregoing example, the person described was an illustration of what is known as hermaphroditism or intersexuality. A HERMAPHRODITE is a person for whom at least one variable or feature of sex is incongruous with the others. The boy is considered hermaphroditic because of the fully formed penis, which is incongruous with the external genitals expected for females. It is not possible for a hermaphrodite to have both a fully functional penis and fully functional vagina simultaneously.

ANDROGYNY is a word used to refer to sexual ambiguity of body build. In a new and fashionable usage, it means sharing gender roles (especially vocational roles) regardless of procreational functioning—in the fashion world, it means the same as unisex. Androgyny may or may not include erotic BISEXUALITY (or ambisexuality) which traditionally means the ability to switch to being either male or female and back again. More popularly, it refers to the experience of being attracted to and performing erotically with a partner of either sex. The bisexual ratio may be 50 : 50, 1 : 99, or somewhere in between. The term EPICENE means either sharing the traits of both sexes, or being incompletely of either sex. Often it is used to suggest effeminacy in a male.

In a colloquial and limited usage, SEX CHANGE refers to genital surgery, the so-called sex-change operation of transsexuals. In the strict and literal sense, it is not possible to change a person's sex, whereas it is possible to 'reannounce' or 'reassign' it and sexologists prefer the more precise term, 'sex reassignment'.

It is only common sense to use the appearance of the genitals as the criterion of sex determination, because in a majority of individuals the shape of the genitals (morphologic sex) agrees with their chromosomal, gonadal and hormonal sex, and, as it subsequently develops, with their gender identity/role.

If there are defects of the sex organs at birth (such as the hermaphroditism referred to above, and agenesis or nonformation of the penis) the morphology of the genitals cannot be used as the criterion of sex as declared on a birth certificate. Some medical practitioners turn, therefore, to the criterion of chromosomal or gonadal sex. Neither by itself alone is adequate, however, for neither permits an exact prediction of what the hormonal sex will become at puberty, or the adequacy of the genitals (even allowing for surgical repair) for copulation in adulthood. The best thing to do in all such cases is therefore to assign the baby to that sex in which it is going to be possible later on for the adult (after being treated by hormones and surgery) to have intercourse as a man or woman.

One's gender identity/role is not, any more than one's native language, completely there at birth. In the postnatal phase of one's life, it almost invariably follows and agrees with the sex of assignment and rearing. Judiciously sex-assigning a baby born with a defect of the sex organs can be very satisfactory indeed to his/her ultimate development. As an adult, the person can live in good health and with a sense of psychosexual well-being.

A TRANSSEXUAL is a person who appears without question a male or a female when the genitals are examined, and is in a majority of instances reproductively fertile, but who experiences a gender identity that is in opposition to his or her bodily sex, and who has an obsessive need for sex reassignment. It is impossible for an ordinary person to be propelled into the condition of transsexualism, as it has nothing to do with free will or voluntary choice. The process of sex reassignment that can be undergone by a transsexual includes hormonal, surgical, social and legal steps. The person may ultimately achieve the social status and the cosmetic appearance of a member of the sex of reassignment, minus of course fertility.

Male-to-female transsexuals take estrogenic hormones which induce all or some of the following: breast growth, softening of the skin, decreased muscle strength, increase and redistribution of subcutaneous body fat, and lessened body hair growth. Breast and hip size can be augmented by surgically implanting silicone inserts. Hair on the face, arms and legs may be permanently removed by electrolysis. Although neither voice pitch nor the size of the Adam's apple is affected by estrogen, most male-to-female transsexuals manage to speak habitually with a more feminine pitch, without relapsing to a deeper one. Some even have their vocal cords surgically shortened to raise the voice, and the Adam's apple reduced in size by surgery.

Female genitals are achieved surgically by removing the testes and using the scrotal skin to form the labia majora. The inside of the penis is removed and its skin used as the lining of a surgically created vagina. Skin from the inner thigh may be used to help augment the penile skin. The outcome of this genital surgery is variable, but in most cases it looks and works satisfactorily and the person enjoys erotic sensitivity.

Female to male transsexuals take androgen, the male hormone, which induces in varying degrees the following

changes: increased muscle strength, increased body hair growth, cessation of menstruation, redistribution and reduction of body fat, permanent lowering of vocal pitch, increased libido, and enlargement of the clitoris. The breasts are surgically removed, as are the internal female reproductive organs (hysterectomy).

It is not yet possible for plastic surgery to create a normal looking, functioning penis. However, some female-to-male transsexuals do undergo partially masculinizing surgery, which results in a tube of skin (possibly reinforced with muscle tissue), which hangs down in the male position, resembling a penis. One surgical technique permits the insertion of various implants into the tube for sufficient firmness to permit insertion into the vagina of the partner in copulation. The clitoris is left intact, so that the female-to-male transsexual easily attains orgasm. The urethra remains in the female position. Surgical attempts to construct a phallus complete with urethra have not been satisfactory. Many female-to-male transsexuals prefer to skip these complicated procedures of genital reconstruction, and use a dildo instead.

Partners of reassigned transsexuals may themselves be bisexual, but not necessarily so. The partner responds to the reassigned person's resulting behaviour and appearance, not to the sex of the body as it was born.

In every day usage, MASCULINE and FEMININE are adjectives derived from the terms 'male' and 'female' respectively. In the recent literature on transsexualism, however, some writers have related the terms 'male' and 'female' to biological sex and the terms 'masculine' or 'feminine' to social or psychological sex (which they erroneously define as synonymous with gender). This splitting up of 'sex' and 'gender' seems to perpetuate the age-old division of body and mind. Sex is as much in the brain as in the pelvis. The two are intimately connected and, whether in human relations or in scientific studies, they should not be separated.

Renee in California, Richard in New York

Tennis doctor's dilemma

Dr Renee Richards has entered for the Dewar Cup tennis tournament in London next week. The chances of her playing are remote. First, she is on the list of "alternates" for the qualifying competition. Beyond that is an even bigger obstacle, the imposition by the Women's Tennis Association of a chromosome test for all players. Dr Richards, who was once Dr Richard Raskind, has said she will refuse to take such a test, for reasons made clear in the following article by GLADYS HELDMAN, reproduced from the October issue of the American magazine "World Tennis".

On July 11, 1976, Renee Richards, MD, of Newport Beach, California, won the La Jolla women's singles championship, defeating Robin Harris in the final, 6—1, 6—1. Within a week, Dr Richards was receiving some 20 phone calls a day from newspapers, television and radio stations, and magazines. To each inquiry, she replied: "No comment."

Dr Renee Richards of California was formerly Dr Richard Raskind of New York, a successful ophthalmologist and a well-known and popular eastern tennis star. As Dr Raskind, he had reached the final of the National Junior veterans' clay courts in 1972. As Renee Richards, she had won the La Jolla women's singles and had applied for entry in the United States open women's championship.

I had known her years before as Richard Raskind. As a matter of fact, I had seen Richard defeat my husband in the 1961 United States National Indoors, 8—6, 2—6, 9—7.

Although I now thought of her as a woman, I stuttered when Dr Richards's receptionist asked who was calling. I identified myself and added, "He knows me . . . she knows me". The personal pronoun problem remained, although that evening it seemed natural to say to my husband, "She remembers when you played him in the National Indoors".

When Renee got on the phone, I heard a very friendly and warm voice. I asked her if she wanted to talk first or if she would prefer direct questions. Renee said to ask away, which I promptly did.

When did you first decide you wanted to be a woman?

It was something I had always been waiting for. I had been living my life as a lie, and I overcompensated in athletics. Ultimately, I had the surgery in August, 1975, but I had been preparing physically with hormones for five years.

Weren't you married?

Yes, I married Barbara in 1969. She knew about my problems, but we were both hopeful that marriage would turn me around. It was a futile attempt. The divorce was friendly. We are still very close, and I try to see her and my child regularly.

I understand you entered the La Jolla tournament as Renee Clark. Are you married now?

No. That was a pseudonym to maintain anonymity. However, I should have known that anyone would recognize my wind-up and left-handed forehand. Originally, when I moved to Newport Beach in February, I had planned to take up the game right-handed. I joined John Wayne Tennis Club, but forgot my old resolutions and played as a lefty. The members were extremely nice and very encouraging. None of them were aware of my past.

Why did you move to California?

I wanted a life of anonymity. I had been a professor at Cornell Medical School, where I had a very large practice, and my friends and family were located in the East. However, I felt I couldn't live the life of a normal woman if people knew my background.

What made you decide to play La-Jolla?

For the first five months I refused to enter tournaments. Finally, through the pressure of my new friends and my old competitive urge, I decided to play.

Did you send in your entry for the National Clay Courts?

No. I wrote for an entry blank, but they never sent one. However, I did apply to enter the United States Open at Forest Hills as an amateur. I wrote a personal note to the referee, Mike Blanchard. I said he undoubtedly had heard about what had happened and that I had no wish to create any difficulties, but I am now a woman under the law. My driver's licence, my passport, and my doctor can attest to this. I also told Mike I couldn't play men's tournaments any more. In my last sentence I wrote that I recalled him from junior days.

Did you apply to join the Women's Tennis Association?

I sent in my application mainly because of Forest Hills. I didn't know the workings of the new system, and I thought I had to be a member in order to compete. All I wanted was the chance to play the top women in the world. The WTA replied that I would be eligible to play in their fall circuit.

Do you want to play the Virginia Slims tournaments?

No. I am an ophthalmologist first and a tennis player second. I love competition, but I am not about to tour on Virginia Slims as a pro. Your husband and I are probably the last of the true amateur players.

If the US Open asks you to take a chromosome test, would you qualify as a woman?

Legally and medically I am a woman, but I might fail the lab tests for chromosomes. I have never had a chromosome test. However, millions of women have chromosome abnormalities. I know the Olympics use the chromosome test for screening, but there is a physical test that follows. Even if I drew a negative on the chromosome test, I would pass the pelvic and blood tests. One must base diagnosis of sex on the total clinical picture. In medicine, a laboratory test is a small part of a total diagnosis, and you go by a physical examination for the definitive answer. A chromosome test tells whether a person has a male chromatin pattern, a female pattern, or an unusual abnormal pattern. It doesn't say whether someone is a man or a woman.

In your opinion, why did the Olympics institute a chromosome test?

The object was to uncover female impersonators from countries trying to disguise a male athlete so that he could compete in a womens' event. It wasn't designed to uncover people with abnormal chromosome patterns who were legitimate males or females.

Do you feel you would have an unfair advantage over women in a tennis tournament?

I think I have an advantage over many women because I am a good athlete and I am tall, but that's the same advantage Betty Stove has in tennis and Carol Mann in golf. Both of them are bigger and stronger than I. That's a physical advantage unrelated to sex because all three of us have the same degree of estrogen and the same lack of testosterone circulating in our blood. The advantage we have in being tall is neutralized by the agility and speed of smaller players, such as Billie Jean King and Evonne Goolagong.

Has your muscle configuration changed?

Definitely. My muscles are no longer the bulky, well-defined, testosteron-laden muscle mass. The biceps and triceps in my arms are no longer that of a man. I would have looked silly a few years ago in a sleeveless top; I don't any more. The subcutaneous fat has been redistributed to the areas where women have it and men don't.

Taking into account the normal decline in tennis ability you would have experienced with age, are you playing as well today as Dick Raskind would have played?

I think I am playing very well because I am playing every day and my timing is as good as ever, but I have to admit that when I say that to friends who knew Dick a few years ago, they reply, "Renee, you forget what a good player Dick was". It's frustrating to play against my present coach, Attilio Rosetti, a former Argentine Davis Cup player, and to be beaten, 6—0, 6—0, whenever he feels like it. I know damn well he could never have done that to Dick. I practise with Betty Ann Stewart, and we play close matches; she couldn't have done that well against Dick. The biggest differences are in the power of my serve and in my ability to produce sudden bursts of speed on the court.

What if another man who didn't have a high sex urge but had a strong tennis drive did what you did just so that he could play the Virginia Slims circuit?

That's a very sticky issue. One would have to individualize, as in my case. The physical suffering, the pain, and the anguish of the change are so great that not even a deranged man would willingly undergo it for such a reason.

Did you think your entry would be accepted by the United States Open?

Some of my New York friends said Forest Hills would never accept the entry. My California friends said that they couldn't refuse me. New York sees me as Dick, but California only knows me as Renee. I was hopeful that Forest Hills would let me play. . . Maybe they were worrying about any nut who comes along. More likely, they were considering that my appearance would tarnish the event. I don't want that to happen any more than they do.

Do you think you would win the United States Open?

I am not absolutely sure. I am not undefeated as a woman. I have played in two mixed doubles where I lost to another woman. In one of them I teamed with Scott Carnahan, who played No 1 for the University of California at Irvine. We were beaten by Gail Hansen Glascow and Dennis Prout, 6—4, in the third. I also played in another local mixed doubles, and there I was beaten by Diane Desfor.

What has happened to you since you played La Jolla?

I have been swamped with calls from the members of the press, but I haven't talked to anyone. I didn't want a stranger intruding in my private life. You are the only one I would talk to.

Richard Raskind (extreme left) at Yale, Renee Richards (extreme right) at La Jolla.

Tomi Ungerer

5

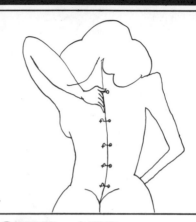

SEXUAL DISPLAY

Dress (and undressing) as self-expression, since before the fig-leaf.

Fashion

David English

Swinging Hellenes let it all hang out. Walking to work, they slung a see-through business coat over their shoulders, covering *everything* down to the navel. For important activities, like leaning on a pole or picking up a crate of houmous, they eased off such constricting gear in favour of an Attic tan. Hence the expression "Red Figure Wear". (Later in the holiday season, as all classical scholars know, they were into "Black Figure Wear".)

After the good Lord had smitten Adam and Eve with embarrassment about their external sex organs, they immediately proceeded to invent sexually arousing fashion. Adam wore his fig leaf on a low-slung hipster line, to show off his good bottom, while Eve shattered Eden with the first topless bikini. Gratitude? Schmattertude!

Reach-me-down furs were the best a cave-man's girl-friend could hope for. (Licences being filled out in those days on chipped rocks in triplicate, most couples found marriage a drag, and kept their liaisons dangereuses.) All the rage were sensible things that kept the wet out and the grease in. The trend may be back with us any day now.

But only once was it ever high mode for men to – shall we say – take a public stand, put their meat on the table, show the hard with the smooth. For all of a hundred years, the stylish gallant walked to Church, visited his mother-in-law and dined out wearing ten inches of padded taffeta poking out of his flies.

It is a common misconception that if a man sports a plume in his hat, frilly silk knickers, sparkles on his pumps and coloured suitings that cross the spectrum, he must be some kind of fag in drag. Take a look at the Three Musketeers, then! How's that for all-male mustachioed braggadoccio in full fairy fig? In those days, men rode, swore, whored and crossed swords in costumes that make Liberace look like the guy next door.

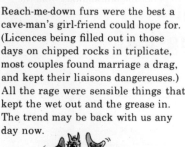

The Ages of Faith (sometimes spelt "Fath") were a costumier's paradise. Pell-mell went the fashion changes from Lindisfarne to the Holy Land. The Robber Baron look (steel knitteds and warm rust for the inner seams) was hardly in before Minstrel Pants (such *savers* with their non-match legs) were all the rage. But for macho appeal who can beat slim-line Crusaders? (Well, Saracens could, but then we always *loved* baggy pants.)

If fashion trends for women show one thing more than any other through the whole of history (until right *now*, of course) it is that dress designers have just never been satisfied with the actual female shape as it really is. From the "pregnant wife" look (immortalized by Flemish artists like van der Weyden) onwards, women have been clothed as walking caricatures of some line or other. Above all, of hip lines and buttock lines. Padding and paniers gave an impression of monstrous fat thighs, bustles added bulges to existing bottoms, and crinolines enveloped the whole below-waist zone in a quivering dome under which the secrets of a lady's true physique were entombed.

People began to show through their clothes after the First World War in history had cracked the complacency of society. Hair was bobbed, short and workmanlike. Boobs that had been sculptured bulges became lifelike little tits. The word sex was discovered to mean more than the difference between pink and blue. Men and women worked hard to unleash the fiery tigers of virility and voluptuousness that they felt were caged within their decently clothed selves. Often, all they got were hangovers and creditors, but life had never been like this before.

Fashion

Hollywood invented the sweater girl in time to give the Second World War its peace aims: cokes, smokes and pokes for all, regardless of age, colour or physical condition. The flavour of that era of uplift bras and pencil-skirts is still nostalgically preserved for us by the artists who cater for the dreams of fladge and bondage fans—in picture or those dominant whiplash ladies who seem to have walked straight out of the 1940s.

The Adam are back in town. Pulsating with the primal wails of orgasm and birth, the group finger their erectile guitars with a rhythmic grasp that recalls the earlier Wank to which some of them used to belong. Slipping their dark glasses down from time to time, to reveal the hollow sockets of optics long ago blinded by heavy agents of their one-time manager Chronos, with whom they are currently litigating for the return of their deep-frozen eyeballs from a vault in Nevada. The Adam have that mastery of the catatonic mode that single out the fantabulous from the merely frenzied. This is where fashion ends, not with a style but an explosion.

Leather Scene

In certain circles, such as the leather fraternity, the meaning of the terms S/M or S & M has altered from the original 'Sado-Mascochism' to SLAVE/ MASTER, in keeping with *erotic bondage** and *flagellation** patterns of behaviour. Costume plays a major part in the leather scene and homosexual dress codes are at their most sophisticated here. Leather and Levi's are mandatory whatever the sexual role, but the Master usually prefers black leather from top to toe, while the Slave may

wear ripped, worn Levi's (in private, and in some bars, the Slave's jeans may be almost disintegrating).

The Master will wear a leather motorbike jacket embellished with studs and removable functional chains. A sleeveless denim overjacket, decorated with the insignia of the wearer's bike or leather club, is often worn on top. Pants are either black leather, worn Levi's or black leather chaps worn in public over Levi's, but in private with a variety of other leather jockstrap-type devices. Bike or engineer boots are the normal footwear. When not riding his bike (preferably a large

BMW), the full kit is topped off with a black military-style leather cap, decorated with chains and/or a club insignia.

A tee-shirt or leather shirt may be worn under the jacket, but if the weather permits, skin is preferred. Underwear is not worn except for jockstraps or devices such as leather pouches, some of which separate the testicles from the penis, or hold the penis in some kind of restraint. A cockring may be worn instead. A 'masterharness' is sometimes worn beneath the jacket; this is a series of straps in black leather designed in a variety of configurations across the torso, but usually with a cock-ring through which

the flaccid penis is fitted, and a series of buckles on the chest. The nipples are left free so that clamps may be applied. Studded belts and wristbands are the nearest thing to jewellery. The wristband is worn on the left for the Master, who also has the belt buckled to the left. Handcuffs are sometimes suspended from the left rear. Slaves may be dressed similarly but usually they will wear a bike jacket with Levi's. A Slave harness may also be worn under the clothing. This usually has more restraint attachments fitted to it and its lower straps are designed to leave the anus free.

Fashion

The prime purpose of wearing clothes has always been to protect the human body from the discomforts of the environment. The second reason is to show off the body with a view to attracting a mate. Throughout the animal kingdom there are examples of sexual display in which some physical feature of an animal is exaggerated, perhaps in shape or colour, to attract the attention of a potential mate. Not surprisingly, men and women have adapted this natural phenomenon into the idea of using clothing as a means of attracting a mate. At different times and in different places, people have worn a number of different styles of clothing to maintain an everchanging and renewed level of excitement. This is the fundamental reason for the very existence of what is regarded as fashion in dress . . . or undress.

There are several means of using fashion to enhance sexual appeal. First, there is novelty. A man or woman who has the courage and fashion sense to be different draws attention at once. In the Regency period when men wore elaborate and brightly coloured brocades and silks, Beau Brummel stood out by wearing plain black and white. Fashion followed him. Today, a man who wears casual clothing to a formal occasion may attract opprobrium, but he certainly stands out from the crowd. Novelties which have become fashionable because of their sexual attractiveness are such things as bikinis, mini skirts, see-through clothes, ankle bracelets, long boots, earrings and pendants for men and crotch-hugging trousers. There is nothing new about these fashion gimmicks, but their rediscovery has been a novelty to Western society.

Fashion also uses concealment to suggest sex appeal. There is an aspect of human imagination that is stimulated by the sheer visual absence of the things it would like to see. So a totally naked body is usually less provocative than a partly-clad one. The technique of exposing large areas of the body while completely hiding a part with primary sex appeal can be very effective. A long skirt slashed to the hips, which casually displays the outside of the thigh but keeps the inside hidden, can be tantalizing. So is swathing the body virtually from the neck to the feet with garments that makes its shape almost indistinguishable. In the 1920s, for example, the high fashion for women was to look as if they had no breasts at all.

Sex appeal can be suggested by exaggeration, a technique of selecting some particular part of the body for attention and using everything fashion can invent to focus attraction on it. Beauty spots stuck on the face near an attractive dimple or the lips or near a nipple were popular at times. The decolleté neckline has gone in and out of fashion; at times there has been competition as to how low women's gowns could be cut to display the breasts without revealing the nipples. Necklines eventually dropped to below the nipples. The topless craze of recent years is a close parallel. In order to expose the breasts, women wear nothing at all above the waist. For a while this caught on in higher society circles and among the daring, but the fashion has remained only in some bars and other places of entertainment where dancers and waitresses are paid to go topless. In medieval times, the exaggerated and decorated codpiece drew attention to the male genital area. In Africa and Asia some tribes have worn penis sheaths of wood or leather to attract female eyes to the decorated organ. Today, skin-tight levis or jeans are a similar exaggerated male fashion.

The buttocks exert a powerful sexual attraction, and they too have been subjected to fashionable exaggeration. The bustle worn at the end of the last century was a supported truss of material poised over the area. This drew the onlooker's eyes because it moved provocatively from side to side when a woman was walking, thus exaggerating not only the shape but the movement of the buttocks. A bustle worn with a wasp waist, a form of brutal corset that pulled the waist into perhaps a mere 16in, displayed a sharp contrast between narrowness and opulent bulges and attracted the men of the times. The waist nipper or elasticated wide belt, the basque or longline bra and corset combination and other forms of laced-in foundation garments have been fashionable at many different times and even in recent decades.

A fourth technique of using fashion in aid of sex appeal is deliberate exposure. To be effective, the exposure is usually of parts previously hidden by fashion—this was the case when thighs and panties were exposed by mini skirts. Striptease or sexily undressing as a form of quasi-dancing entertainment depends upon provocative exposure. A strip-tease performer usually begins the act fully clothed and slowly reveals parts of the body in time to music (*Sex Shows**).

Finally, there are the accessories of fashion which are a form of enhancing sexual display. Any additional decoration to clothing or to the body such as jewellery, scarfs, hats, gloves, ties, belts, garters and so on can be both fashionable and attractive. Wigs, male and female, and changes in natural hair styles with the addition of curls, colouring and so forth are powerful sexual stimulants. Even hair pieces for the pubic region have had a limited appeal—in 17th century England pubic wigs were called MERKINS and later known as BOWSERS. In 16th century France, it was considered elegant in high society for a woman to pomade her pubic hair to encourage its growth and then to decorate the pubic hair with coloured silk bows or ribbons. Recently there has been a brief fashion for shaving pubic hair into various shapes—heart-shaped pubic hair was a cheerful and popularly appealing joke in the late 1960s.

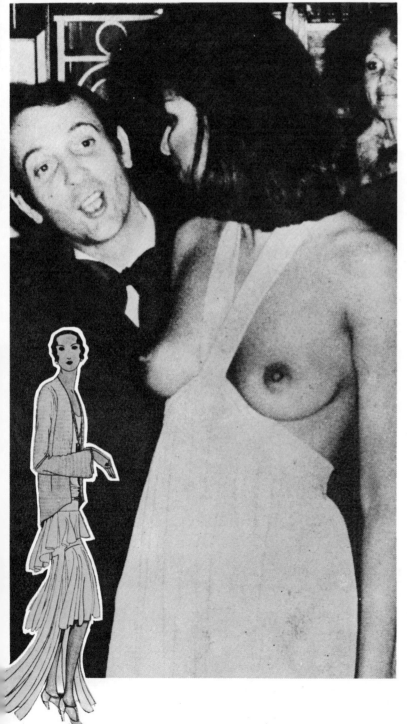

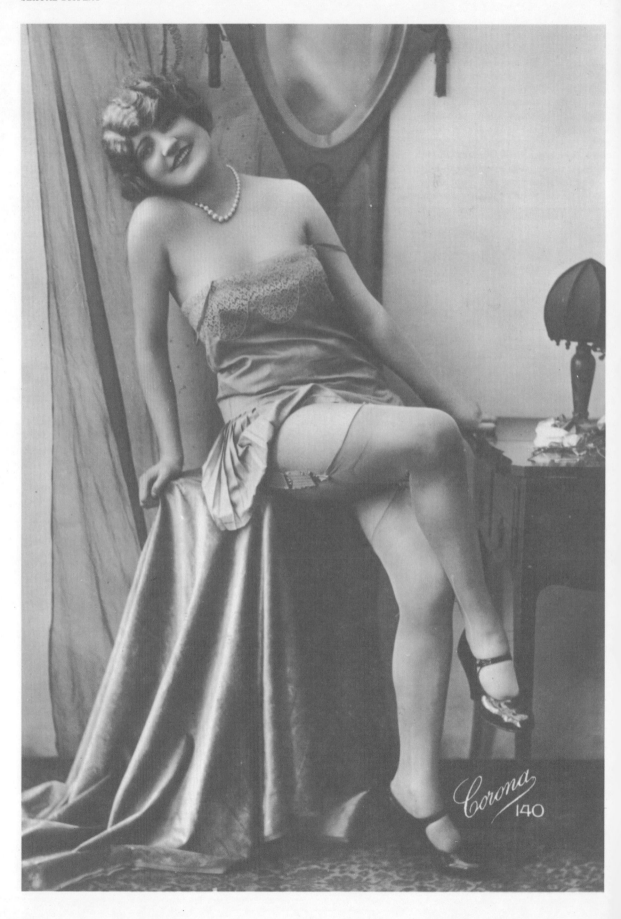

Naturism

This is the name of a movement that originated at the beginning of the century in Germany and gained popularity elsewhere during the 1930s. Naturists enjoy sporting and other social activities without wearing clothes, usually in organized, members-only clubs and groups.

NUDISM was the original name for this cult, but as the word had unwelcome sexual associations and the so-called nudists proclaimed themselves less interested in sex than in the healthy and beneficial effects of sun, light and air on the naked body, naturism was generally adopted by the 1960s. Naturist groups are often called sun clubs or open air clubs.

In the 1960s and 1970s, topless and even nude sunbathing became more widespread, especially in the Mediterranean areas and on the Pacific Coast. Attire on other beaches throughout the world became briefer and nudity generally occasioned less public censure. So although the novelty of naturist groups has worn off, there is still a small proportion of dedicated followers. The groups have often been subjected to vigorous campaigns by self-appointed moralists who disapprove of exposure of the naked human body, and therefore there has been careful selection and strict rules of acceptance for members of naturist groups in order to avoid allegations of sexual activities or *voyeurism**. Naturism encourages families to participate in their group or club activities.

Some people at naturist gatherings retain a measure of shyness and keep their genitals covered. During sporting activities, men sometimes wear a tiny athletic support for comfort and protective restraint. Its French name is *le minimum*.

Undoubtedly the naked human body is sexually attractive and also a source of aesthetic inspiration to poets, sculptors and artists. However idealized nude portraits and sculptures are, it is not possible to deny that the inspiration and attraction of even great works of art is basically sexual, when the nude human figure is displayed. Similarly, the naturist way of life has undoubted advantages and benefits (sun, light and heat *are* health giving), but that the movement has a strong sexual undercurrent is undeniable, although this constitutes no grounds for objection.

Cosmetic Deformities

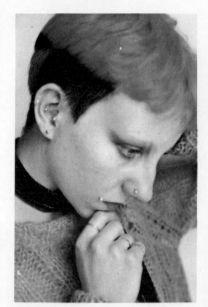

While the use of decorative adornments and provocative clothing is a normal and accepted method of enhancing sexual attraction in Western society, actually adapting the body physically is less well known. There is evidence, however, that some so-called cosmetic deformities or deliberate bodily modifications for the purposes of increasing sexuality and sexual appeal are becoming more widespread. Cosmetic deformities can be major physical changes such as PLASTIC SURGERY to change the shape of breasts, buttocks, legs, faces and so on to minor deformities such as piercing the ears. These two types of deformity specially imposed on the body are perhaps the best known in 20th century society.

One well-known although not so widely practiced technique of cosmetic deformation is TATTOOING. In the West there are masculine associations with male symbols tattooed over arm muscles, the back and the chest (anchors, snakes, daggers and so forth). Some tattooing is flagrantly sexual—coloring the penis itself in grotesque patterns or designs. A sense of protection and domination is achieved when some women are tattooed, often in intimate places, with a man's name.

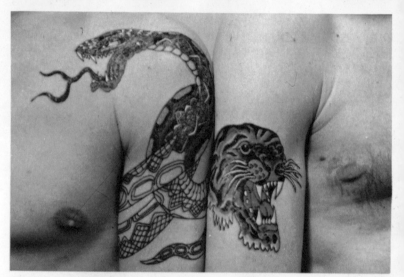

Some primitive tribes cover their bodies with large-scale geometric patterns. This tattooing is often accompanied by purposeful SCARIFICATION. Faces, arms and chests are often blemished in traditional patterns. In Western society, there are sado-masochistic associations with the deliberate scarring of buttocks, breasts or other areas, and such sights are inflammatory to the passions of some deviants. There are other kinds of scarring which have sexual overtones, usually because of their association with either images of masculinity or femininity. A sword slash scar across one cheek was a mark of manliness among Prussian noblemen who were trained in the martial arts and duelling.

The extreme and unexpected nudity of normally hair-covered portions of the body may, to some extent, explain the phenomena of DEPILATION, or the removal of body hair. Many women remove hair under the armpits, on the legs and even on the arms. The PUDENDA (the entire genital, groin and anal areas) are sometimes shaved. Sanskrit manuscripts show Indian women with shaved pudenda.

Body Piercing

Rods or discs of wood or metal inserted into the lips, and bone or metal inserted through the nasal septum, are well-known examples of ornamental piercing in men and women of Asian, African, North and South American and Oceanic cultures. Many Hindu women wear nose rings of precious metals or gemstones in the nostrils. Pierced ears for pendants are a popular personal decoration in Western society and may unconsciously symbolize the possibility of other concealed ornaments of a more sexual kind.

Rings and studs piercing almost any part of the skin—including the nipples of both sexes, the labia, the hood of the clitoris, the male foreskin, scrotum

and perineum, even the head of the penis itself— are erotically exciting to some people. Psychologically, a Sado-Masochistic motivation surely lies behind such practices, but little research has been done in this area. Perhaps only half of the people who begin to have piercings done enjoy *dominance** or *bondage** encounters as well. For many, the physical feeling of the insertions is sufficiently satisfying on its own. Among the *apadravyas* or penis-enhancers described in the *Kama Sutra,* there is specific mention of perforating the male organ 'as for earrings', and inserting various hard objects to improve the pleasure of intercourse.

The operation is a quick one, and must be carried out under 100 per cent hygienic conditions, with a local freezing agent to numb the pain. Once healed, the piercing does not need to have a ring kept in it permanently. In penile piercing, urine has no harmful effect on the healing process. For some, the operation itself can be exciting, and sometimes, a person will remove the sleeper before healing and have it done all over again. Body hair on areas of piercing is in some cases removed by electrolysis.

Some men claim that their nipples gave them no sexual pleasure before they were pierced. A ring through the glans itself is claimed to increase sensitivity during intercourse, and is known as the PRINCE ALBERT or dressing ring. This type, according to tradition, was used in Victorian times to secure the penis in the right or left trouser leg. A DYDO is a stud through the rim of the glans, usually inserted in groups. It consists of a gold, silver or stainless steel rod with a screw-on ball at each end. A GUICHE is a ring piercing the *perineum** and is said to have been inspired by South Pacific customs. Light pressure on the guiche is claimed to increase arousal, and gently tugging on it at the climax to prolong orgasm.

The secret knowledge that one is sexually adorned with rings and studs can itself give satisfaction. Generally, the ornamentation starts in a small way, but grows more extravagant with time as the wearer discovers its compelling nature and learns new possibilities from ellow-piercers or from seeing photographs. The craving for more and more holes is often combined with an interest in tattooing. Very few clubs exist for pierced people of either sex, but groups tend to form spontaneously.

INFIBULATION is a form of body piercing that is found among a few primitive communities, and is usually intended to restrict sexual intercourse. The edges of the foreskin or of the labia are pierced and kept permanently clipped together. Female infibulation in such cases seems to combine the idea of a wife as property with a puritanical view of the enjoyment of sex. Among Western body-piercers, another kind of infibulation is practised, in which partners put a padlock through the foreskin or the labia, and keep the keys with each other's consent, thus allowing for a variety of dominance situations.

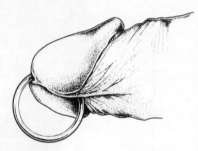

A 'Prince Albert'

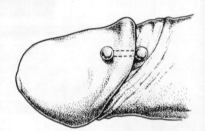

A dydo

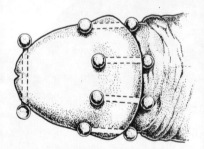

Dydoes with (left) an ampallang

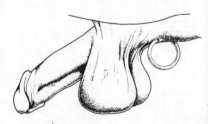

A guiche

6

AROUSAL

The how, when and why of being turned on.

Turned on

Sexual arousal is the process by which the male and female bodies become capable of uniting in the act of sexual intercourse. In modern slang, the state of sexual arousal is often described as being 'turned on'. This involves complex changes throughout the body. The most obvious change in the turned on male is erection of the penis which enables it to be inserted into the vagina of the female partner. To facilitate this, glands at the entrance of the vagina and the lining of the vagina itself produce a lubricating fluid (*lubrication**) as the female becomes turned on. The external female genital organs swell and the clitoris becomes erect with its tip (the glans clitoris) exposed between the folds of the labia.

Either sex can be turned on without direct physical contact. Sexual arousal frequently results from erotic mental images or fantasies. The sight of an erotic situation involving the opposite sex often turns people on. Some people can be sexually aroused by hearing a particular melody or by the smell of a particular odour. It is obviously impossible for every episode of sexual arousal to be concluded in sexual intercourse. When someone is turned on and intercourse is inappropiate at the time, sexual tension may be relieved by *masturbation**, either solitarily or mutually with one's sexual partner. If the tension is neglected altogether, the effects of being turned on will normally subside.

During love making the sight of the loved one and the knowledge that sexual advances may be reciprocated usually provides a stimulus towards sexual arousal. Between this and the release from sexual tension which occurs at orgasm, intensification of sexual arousal is brought about by the mutual stimulation of all the senses and body areas (*body maps**). Sexual contact between partners which produces mutual stimulation before the penis is actually inserted into the vagina is known as FOREPLAY.

Who should make the initiatives or the first moves? At many different times in history, it has been considered improper for a female to initiate foreplay. In fact it was often considered improper for her to reciprocate at all in sexual activity. Now that women are accepted as sexual beings in their own right with sexual desires and feelings, it is acceptable for either partner to make the first move to initiate foreplay

thereby turning the other partner on.

SEDUCTION plays an important role in both male and female sexual behaviour. It is normally a continuous process from initial non-sexual contact through a phase of platonic friendship to eventual sexual consummation. Throughout this process there are almost predetermined moves, each one calculated to arouse sexual interest and desire in the partner. Whether the male or female makes the first move, foreplay involves increasing degrees of physical and emotional contact between the partners, progressing from holding hands to genital stimulation. During foreplay verbal communication with the whispering of endearments and communication with the eyes form important erotic stimuli.

Foreplay is conventionally divided into two phases. NECKING refers to love play during which all areas of the body above the waist are stimulated. This, of course, includes *kissing**. And there is PETTING which refers to any love play that is beyond the limits of necking but which falls short of sexual intercourse. In normal love making there is a gradual transition between the two phases, though the length of time spent necking compared to petting varies from couple to couple and from time to time for the same couple.

As a couple become more turned on during the early stages of necking, the extent of the physical contact between them becomes greater and more intimate. At first, contact will be confined to those areas of the body that are readily exposed while dressed—the hands, face, neck, ears and legs particularly. The hands will wander over the partner's clothed body. The breasts will be caressed by the male, while the female partner's hands may find and stroke the bulge in the trousers produced by the erect penis.

After a time, exploratory excursions of the hands pass under the clothing. The couple may undress completely if the situation is suitable, or they may undo sufficient garments to allow more intimate HEAVY PETTING, or stimulation of the genital areas. When a person in a potentially sexual situation allows their partner to touch those areas of the body that are normally out of bounds it implies that the person will allow further and more intense love play, though it does not always mean the person wishes sexual intercourse.

TOUCHING is sexually arousing for each partner. The fingers are extremely sensitive parts of the body. Those areas of the body that give most sexual

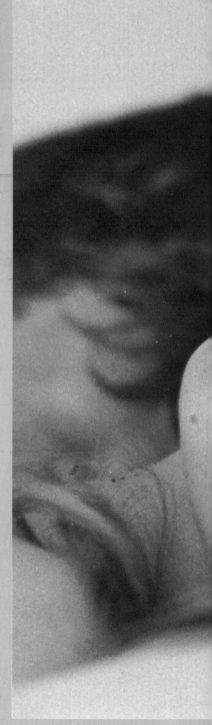

pleasure and stimulation when touched are called *erogenous zones**. They vary slightly from person to person. The form of touch which provides maximum stimulation varies widely—some people find that a very light stroking touch is highly erotic whereas others are left cold by this and desire a heavier approach. Frequently, as a person becomes more turned on, a heavier and more forceful touch is desired, though this is not always the case.

Touching normally stimulates the nerve endings in the skin. Many people find that they are more intensely stimulated by vigorous handling of the body involving rubbing and kneading the deeper tissues beneath the skin, such as the muscles. This type of activity is known as MASSAGE. It can be used in nonsexual situations to stimulate the muscles and joints after illness or injury, or to relax tension, but it can also have highly erotic connotations and may be incorporated into sexual foreplay. Many people find that they can intensify the sensations of touching if they gently massage a body lotion into their lover's body.

During foreplay, touching extends from the secondary erogenous zones to the genital areas. A woman usually rubs the penis along its shaft with a pump-like action and fondles the scrotum containing the testes. The male rhythmically rubs the external female sexual organs. Many women find direct rubbing of the exposed part of the clitoris uncomfortable and even painful, especially if the area is not lubricated, and prefer to be stimulated further up its shaft. During genital stimulation the male may insert one or two fingers into the vagina and move them in and out simulating the movement of the penis in the vagina during intercourse. This often stimulates the vaginal walls to produce more lubricating fluid. Few women find stimulation pleasurable if there is vaginal dryness. Genital stimulation in both sexes may also be produced during foreplay by the mouth and tongue (*oral sex**). The male sucks, licks or kisses the vulva area and may insert his tongue into the entrance of the vagina. The female licks and sucks her lover's penis.

Although the main biological purpose of foreplay is sexual arousal (turning each partner on in readiness for sexual intercourse), foreplay may be extremely pleasurable even when it is not possible or desirable to go any further. Heavy petting may continue until each partner has achieved orgasm and relief from sexual tension.

Aphrodisiac

The term aphrodisiac describes anything that is capable of increasing sexual desire or performance. The word itself is derived from Aphrodite, the goddess of love in Greek mythology. Usually aphrodisiac refers to drugs or love potions containing stimulating herbal concoctions, but erotic films and books, for example, are also regarded as aphrodisiacs.

Throughout the ages there has been a continuous search for an ideal, safe aphrodisiac—a preparation that has specific and reliable stimulating effects on sexual desire and activity without any other effects on the body. The ideal has not yet been discovered, but there are numerous preparations derived from plants and animals that have been reputed to have aphrodisiac properties. The ideal aphrodisiac may well be discovered in the coming years as medical scientists find out more about the intricate chemical changes that occur in the parts of the brain where sexual desire is initiated.

At the time of writing, orthodox medical opinion is sceptical about the actual properties of the so-called aphrodisiac preparations that are currently available without prescription from herbalists, health food and sex aid shops. Many of these preparations or their constituents have been used as aphrodisiacs for centuries and in all four corners of the earth. No doubt they will continue to be used until science somes up with something better.

While the search for drugs to stimulate sexual desire and performance goes on, research effort is also being devoted to finding drugs that will suppress sexual desire. Such drugs, collectively called ANAPHRODISIACS, are required to control excessive sexual desire, particularly when it leads to antisocial behaviour and conflict with the law. In some countries men who have been committed to prison on account of sexual offences are sometimes paroled on the agreement that they will take, or have administered by injection, drugs that will suppress their sex drive (see also *drugs and sex**).

Sarsaparilla

The natives of South America regarded concoctions made from various parts of the sarsaparilla plant as valuable aphrodisiacs. It is used as a general tonic and has been shown to contain hormones.

Asafetida

This is a resin with a very pungent odour derived from an Asian plant. A tonic made from asafetida has been used as an aphrodisiac in the East and there is some evidence that it does have stimulant properties.

Ginseng

Ginseng which has been used for thousands of years by the Chinese has become popular in the West in recent years and is readily available in many forms. Its root is shaped like that of the mandrake, and the plant is grown in large quantities in the Appalachian mountain region in the U.S. Ginseng is considered to be an effective general tonic for both physical and emotional debility, and is claimed by many to enhance sexual desire and performance.

Hops

Tea made from hops has long been used as a general tonic and remedy for headache and gastric disorders. Pillows filled with hops are claimed to induce sleep. Hops have been shown to contain very small quantities of female sex hormone so there may be some basis for the Gypsy belief that hops beneficially affect female sexual functioning.

Liquorice

Liquorice has many medicinal properties. Liquorice water, which can be made by mixing a teaspoonful of powdered liquorice in a glass of soda water, is well established in France as an aphrodisiac for women. The powdered root is a constituent of several commercially available preparations. Liquorice has been found to contain chemicals similar in structure to the sex hormones.

Fennel

From ancient times fennel has been considered to have aphrodisiac properties. Fennel tea is prepared from the dried leaves or by simmering the crushed seeds in water. Crushed seeds of fennel are included in commercially available aphrodisiac preparations.

Pollen

Pollen as a source of energy and vitality has been known since antiquity. It has a reputation for maintaining male sex drive and sexual performance and has been used in the treatment of prostate disorders in males and menopausal problems in females. Pollen can be purchased in various forms from health food shops. Scientific analysis of pollen has revealed that it contains very small amounts of testosterone and other hormones affecting sexual functions, so there may be a basis for its medicinal reputation.

Hydrocotyle Asiatica

This is a plant that grows in the tropical jungles of the East. It is regarded as a superb rejuvenator and has been found to contain chemicals that can have stimulating effects on the sex glands.

Yohimbine

This is a chemical derived from the bark of the yohimbine tree which grows in Africa. It probably exerts its aphrodisiac action by increasing the blood flow to the genital organs, thereby giving the sensation of sexual arousal and aiding the changes that occur when a person is *turned on**. Yohimbine is incorporated in a preparation that many doctors prescribe for patients with loss of sexual desire and ability.

Mandrake Root

The root obtained from the mandragora plant was considered to have aphrodisiac properties. The root bears a likeness to the human body. In Medieval times the roots were employed as an *amulet** tied around the waist in the belief that mandrake root would prevent or cure impotence.

Vitamin E

This vitamin has received much publicity in recent years, although its exact role in human sexual activity is not known. There is a general agreement that this vitamin is essential for normal sexual behaviour and fertility. The chemical name of the vitamin is *alpha tocopherol* and there is evidence that it may prevent the arteries from becoming furred up. It is taken by a very large number of people routinely in the hope that it will help maintain youth and vitality. There is no evidence that it is an aphrodisiac in humans.

Foods

Throughout the ages various foods have been considered to have aphrodisiac properties. Beef, eggs, particularly egg yolks, onions and oysters, just to mention a few, have all been eaten in large quantities in the quest for a sexual stimulant. 'Prairie oysters' mentioned in Victorian literature are bull's testicles which were regarded as possessing aphrodisiac properties. They do contain male sex hormone and therefore could possibly work, but they would have to be eaten raw and it is likely that the hormones would be destroyed in the stomach during digestion.

Spanish Fly

Of all reputed aphrodisiacs, Spanish fly is perhaps the most commonly thought of, but it is *lethal*. The 'flies', in fact, are small, shiny blister beetles, native to France and Spain, called *Lytta vesicatoria*. They are killed, dried and pulverized and a chemical, *cantharidin,* is extracted. When swallowed, it passes through the kidneys and into the bladder from where it is passed with the urine. Cantharidin is a powerful irritant to the body; it specifically irritates the bladder which stimulates the sexual organs causing very high degrees of sexual arousal. In fact, the penis can

become so erect that it fails to return to a flaccid state—this continuous erection is called *priapism** and often requires surgical treatment. Spanish fly should never be used by humans as death from convulsions can result. The dosage which causes sexual arousal also kills.

Rhinoceros Horn

Powdered rhinoceros horn was widely favoured by the Chinese as an aphrodisiac. It may be that the Chinese thought along the lines of 'like breeds like', and hoped that by taking powdered horn their penises would become perpetually hard.

Testosterone

This is the most important male sex hormone produced in the human body. In males and females sexual desire is dependent upon this hormone; in the male, testosterone is essential for sexual functioning. It is often prescribed to increase sexual desire and performance, if a patient is lacking in production of the hormone. It may be given to women to stimulate sexual desire, but only for short periods as it causes women to develop masculine features such as a deep voice and beard. Testosterone is only obtainable on prescription.

Erogenous Zones

Erogenous zones are particular areas of the body which become very sensitive during sexual arousal. Stimulation of these areas by touching or kissing produces increased sexual excitement and may lead to orgasm under certain circumstances. During sexual *foreplay** when wandering hands explore a partner's body, an increase in sexual response follows the touching of erogenous zones.

The first zones normally to be discovered in early stages of love play are the lips, the back and sides of the neck and the ears in both sexes and the base of the spine in men. These areas are known as SECONDARY EROGENOUS ZONES not being directly connected with the sex organs. The inner surfaces of the thighs are very sensitive to stimulation and stroking them can produce marked sexual arousal. Breasts are another secondary erogenous zone; caressing them gives pleasure to the male partner as well as the female. The nipples of both men and women are very sensitive to stimulation by either the hand or mouth and respond by stiffening into firm points. The sensitivity of secondary erogenous zones varies much from one person to another. Some people are highly stimulated by a lover running fingers lightly up and down the spine or back, others are turned on by their partners stroking the lower part of their abdomens.

More intense foreplay leads to the recognition of the PRIMARY EROGENOUS ZONES. In men, the *penis**, *scrotum** and *perineum** are prime erogenous zones. In the female, it is the external genital organs, collectively known as the *vulva**. In particular, the skin over the pubic bone which is covered with hair (*mons veneris*) and the outer lips of the vulva are very sensitive to stimulation, as is the area between the anus and the vulva (the female perineum). The most sensitive part of the female sex organs and the base of orgasmic response is the *clitoris**, situated at the front of the vulva between a fold of the inner lips called the hood. The clitoris is capable of erection like the penis. In either sex, the area around the anus is sensitive and is capable of producing sexual arousal.

A lover tries not only to discover the zones which produce arousal but also what type of stimulation—light or heavy touch, kiss or lick—of various places produces response.

Drugs and Sex

Various aspects of sexual behaviour and sexual response may be affected by drugs. Some drugs act on the part of the brain that controls sexual desire thereby modifying *libido**. Other drugs act on either the nerve pathways between the brain and the sexual organs, or on the blood supply to the sexual organs which influences their response to sexual stimulation. It is difficult to say exactly what sexual effects various drugs have. The actual effects of a drug depend upon several factors such as the dose taken (whether once or long-term) and the health and condition of the patient before the drug is taken.

Sexual effects of drugs may occur as side effects when a drug is being used to treat a specific illness. Some men, for instance, complain of impotence when they are being treated for high blood pressure, because many of the drugs used in its treatment interfere with the nerve pathways responsible for erection and ejaculation. Sometimes a drug is prescribed for its sexual effects. *Clomipramine,* used in the treatment of depression and other psychiatric conditions, can delay ejaculation or cause impotence; it is sometimes used to treat severe cases of *premature ejaculation**.

The effects of drugs on sex are better understood in men than in women because male sexual functioning is easier to study. Drugs that act on the brain are called *centrally acting drugs* and those that act on the nerve or blood supply of the genital organs are called *peripherally acting drugs.* Centrally acting drugs may affect both sexual desire and sexual performance, whereas peripherally acting drugs usually only affect sexual performance.

The SEX CENTRE, or part of the brain that is responsible for sexual desire and which initiates sexual functioning, may be stimulated causing an increase in sexual desire or it may be depressed reducing sexual desire. The search for a drug that will selectively stimulate the sex centre without affecting other parts of the brain (a true *aphrodisiac**) has so far been unsuccessful.

The sex centre of the brain is sensitive to the male sex hormone (androgen). The administration of androgens may enhance sex desire in both men and women, and either natural or synthetic androgens are sometimes prescribed for this effect. Androgens are not without side effects and will cause,

the development of male features if taken over long periods of time.

If a drug is taken that prevents androgens from stimulating the sex centre, sex desire diminishes and may be completely abolished. One such drug (*cyproterone acetate*) has been used to suppress the sexual desire of male sex offenders. *Cyproterone acetate* blocks the action of androgen directly. Other drugs may interfere with the stimulating effect of androgens by reducing the body's own production of them. Such drugs are the female sex hormones or estrogens, cortisone derivatives (used in the treatment of allergic and inflammatory conditions), and *spironolactone* (used in the treatment of high blood pressure and water retention).

Drugs such as the amphetamines and cocaine stimulate the brain and may enhance sexual desire when taken intermittently, but prolonged usage decreases sexual desire and impairs sexual functioning. The hallucinogens (LSD and marihuana are prime examples) sometimes enhance sexual desire and sexual functioning, but more frequently have the reverse or no effect on sexuality.

A new drug (L-Dopa) that is now being used in the treatment of Parkinson's disease has been reported to increase libido. This drug works by interfering with the mechanism which controls the influence of one part of the brain on another part. Another still experimental preparation works in a similar way and may eventually prove to be an effective aphrodisiac. It is called *parachlorophenylanine* (PCPA for short). In tests on animals it has been shown to increase sex desire.

*Stress and depression** and anxiety may have inhibiting effects both on sexual desire and performance, but administration of psychotherapeutic drugs may restore normal sexual functioning. It is doubtful whether such drugs have any direct central effect on sexuality, though many do alter the sex hormone production of the body. In fact, some of these drugs can cause a male to develop breasts that actually produce a fluid similar to that produced by female breasts in the early stages of lactation. Many of the drugs used in the treatment of depression, anxiety and other psychiatric conditions affect the passage of nerve impulses to the genital organs and can cause disturbances in ejaculation.

Sedatives such as the barbiturates and narcotics such as heroin and morphine reduce sex desire and may impair sexual functioning by causing general

depression of the brain. Impairment of sexual performance has also been reported as a side effect of *antabuse,* used in the treatment of alcoholism. Some preparations used to reduce appetite also reduce libido, but one such drug sometimes increases sex desire in women.

Not only the sex centre of the brain but also the genital organs are stimulated by male sex hormones. In the absence of adequate androgen the penis fails to grow and the secondary male sexual characteristics such as the beard and deep voice do not develop. If androgens are administered to females they develop these male characteristics and the clitoris enlarges. Female sex hormone (estrogen) is responsible for the development and maintenance of the secondary female sexual characteristics. After the *menopause** when the production of estrogen is greatly reduced, the female sexual organs get smaller, the lining of the vagina gets thinner and lubrication fails. Taking estrogen at this time of life helps to maintain the female genital organs in adequate functional order.

Sexual functioning involves three phases: EXCITEMENT, with erection of the penis in the male and LUBRICATION and swelling of the vulval area and organs in the female; EJACULATION in the male and, finally, ORGASM in both sexes. Each of these phases is under different nervous control and may be impaired by different drugs. Preparations that block the parasympathetic autonomic nervous system like *atropine* and *propantheline* (the latter is used frequently in the treatment of peptic ulcer) may cause a failure of erection. Drugs that block the sympathetic autonomic nervous system such as *guanethidine* (used in the treatment of high blood pressure) may inhibit or delay ejaculation. (The use of drugs that have this property in the treatment of patients with premature ejaculation has been mentioned.)

Strychnine, a poison which used to be incorporated in small doses in tonics but is now rarely employed in medical practice, has the property of facilitating the passage of nerve impulses in the spinal cord and can accelerate the reflexes involved in sexual excitement and orgasm. It is currently incorporated in a preparation known as Potensan Forte which is marketed, on prescription only, for the stimulation of libido and sexual response. *Amyl nitrite*, a drug that is used for the relief of angina is reputed to enhance orgasm—but it produces a distressing headache as well.

Alcohol and Sex

Alcohol is not a sexual stimulant. It can, however, have an indirect *aphrodisiac** action. In small quantities alcohol produces relief from stress, anxiety and fear. For a large number of people sex is shrouded in fears and anxieties which inhibit their sexual performance and may even cause sexual inadequacies such as impotence and the avoidance of sexual intercourse. By reducing anxieties, alcohol removes the inhibitions that may preclude normal sexual functioning. Because anxieties are relieved, small doses of alcohol often cause a temporary enhancement of sexual desire and may greatly assist a couple's sexual adjustment. Some doctors recommend a glass or two of wine or a measure or two of spirits to be taken before attempted intercourse for all manner of sexual difficulties, but now that there is a better understanding of the causes and treatment of sexual problems, there is little in favour of this line of treatment.

The effect of alcohol in relaxing inhibitions is widely used by men as an aid to seduction. Many a sexually eager male has coerced a female into submitting to his sexual demands by plying her with alcohol—it is surprising how much some women will unwittingly drink while engaged in romantic conversation. While in a carefree, inebriated frame of mind produced by alcohol, a girl or woman might take chances that she would not otherwise take. She might forget to take contraceptive precautions, and if she was using oral contraception she might not remember to take a pill while under the influence of alcohol. Many unwanted pregnancies are started while women are under the influence of alcohol.

When alcohol in larger doses is taken, there is a general depression of behaviour, including depression of sexual desire. The reflexes of the body become retarded with the result that capacity for normal sexual function is diminished and is eventually abolished altogether. As Shakespeare wrote in *Macbeth*, drink 'provokes the desire but it takes away the performance'. Alcohol appears to affect the sexual performance of men more than it does women. This is because when a male fails to achieve an erection the act of sexual intercourse is impossible. When a woman's sexual functioning is disorganized, with few exceptions, intercourse is still possible. Under the influence of excessive alcohol consumption, the ability to achieve and maintain an erection is impaired and ejaculation may be severely delayed or abolished. It is not uncommon for a man who fails in sexual intercourse while under the influence of alcohol to develop a continuing sexual inadequacy because of his fear of sexual failure long after the direct effects of drink have worn off. Thus even an occasional binge could decrease a man's sexual ability.

Chronic over-indulgence of alcohol may lead to disruption of both sexual desire and sexual functioning even before the stage of true alcoholism is reached. Prolonged heavy drinking produces several medical complications which themselves may cause failure of sexual ability. An alcoholic frequently neglects to eat a balanced diet and early on may become deficient in vitamins (it is known that adequate vitamin intake is essential for satisfactory sexual functioning). The combination of the direct toxic effect of alcohol and vitamin deficiency in a chronic alcoholic will cause such illness as cirrhosis (degeneration of the liver) and peripheral neuropathy (degeneration of the nerve tracts), both of which are detrimental to sexual performance. Frequently, impaired sexual activity does not improve when the alcoholism is treated. In fact, one drug used in the management of alcoholism, *disulfiram (antabuse)*, has been reported to occasionally cause *impotence**.

Dancing and Sex

In different human cultures around the world, dancing has deep sexual significance. In our own society dancing has two roles. It may form an important part of courtship and *foreplay**, but it may also be devoid of obvious sexual significance and be a social recreation—one of the few occasions where close body contact is permissible in an essentially non-sexual activity.

Many of the older forms of dances such as the waltz and the foxtrot and the modern 'smooch' or cheek-to-cheek dancing involve very close body contact with the more sexually sensitive zones of the body being pressed closely against the partner. The faces are close together allowing freedom to kiss both the lips and the neck. The body contact extends to the genital areas of each partner which are pressed firmly together.

Some modern popular dancing is more or less devoid of body contact between the partners. The sexual stimulating aspects of these types of dances are the movements which frequently mimic the body movements that occur during sexual intercourse. Such dancing is accentuated by clothes in current fashion which show the outline of the dancers' genital organs and *erogenous zones**. The rhythm of the *music** adds further eroticism to the dancing.

Tomi Ungerer

Biological Rhythms

Life is strangely and strongly rhythmical. This applies to plants and to animals at all stages of evolution— from the most primitive single-celled organism to the complex human being. Many of the rhythms of life are determined and controlled from within the organism by so-called 'biological clocks'. Other rhythms are controlled by factors in the outside environment such as the moon, tides and changes in light and temperature.

In humans there are numerous biological or life rhythms all going on at the same time, each at its own rate. There is the rhythm of the heart muscle, contracting and relaxing at an average rate of seventy-two beats per minute. Slower than this is the breathing cycle, about sixteen times a minute (this rhythm can be easily overruled by voluntary effort). There is the daily (or circadian) cycle of activity and sleep, and from puberty until menopause the monthly female cycle of about 28 days of egg production.

Recently there has been more and more scientific research into what are call BIORHYTHMS—these are three internal cycles which influence human beings from birth to death. The physical cycle concerns high and low points in physical health and activity and takes twenty-three days to complete. The emotional cycle which governs all of the processes of mind and imagination takes twenty-eight days to complete. There is some evidence to suggest that the sex of children may in some way be determined by conception taking place at different phases of the emotional cycle. Then there is the thirty-three day intellectual cycle which governs memory and knowledge and the logical functions of the mind. Study of biorhythms has tried to assess how people function at peak and at low cyclical periods and also how they fail to function when cycles are at a 'critical period' or change from high to low.

In a large majority of animals, sexual activity in both sexes is controlled by biological rhythms which may be influenced by environmental factors. A bitch will only accept a male dog during the period of heat (estrus) as it is called. This is the time, which occurs about twice a year, when an egg is being expelled from the ovary. The male dog is rather like man (and woman) in that he is capable of copulating at any time—

his sexual activity is not, as far as we know, determined by a biological cycle. This is not true of all male animals.

Although a human woman is capable of copulating at any time, the rhythmical, approximate monthly cycle of menstruation means that she is fertile on some days of the month and infertile on others (*Rhythm Method**).

These changes result from the fluctuations in the amount of various hormones circulating in a woman's blood.

There have been many studies carried out to see whether women become sexier at one time of the monthly cycle rather than another, but the results are not convincing one way or another. A large number of women become emotionally depressed or tense during the week or so before the bleeding period and this is known as pre-menstrual tension. There is usually a small gain in weight during the cycle. The combination of pre-menstrual tension and weight gain makes some women feel unsexy around the time of their period, while others report greater desire.

Unlike women who usually release only one egg each month, men continuously produce sperm. Many research workers have looked for cyclical patterns in a male's reproductive function, but none have been found. However, male sex hormones which can be measured in urine samples fluctuate on a fairly regular monthly basis (in fact, a twenty-eight day cycle) and industrial psychologists have studied regular fluctuations in men's emotional patterns and a twenty-eight day cycle has also been discovered. In both sexes there is a daily cycle of changes in hormone production. The steroid hormones, for example, which include the male sex hormones, are produced in greater quantities in the morning (usually between seven and nine o'clock) than at any other time of the day. There is, therefore, some reason to suggest that people's sex drive might be more active in the morning than at other times of the day.

An interesting biorhythm exists in men during sleep. The penis becomes intermittently erect and flaccid. This is caused by changes in the activity of a particular portion of the brain. The periods of erection are associated with rapid movements of the eyes which gives this particular phase of sleep the name REM (rapid eye movement) sleep. Since most people wake up during a phase of REM sleep, this probably accounts for the fact that a majority of men awake with an erection (*dreams**).

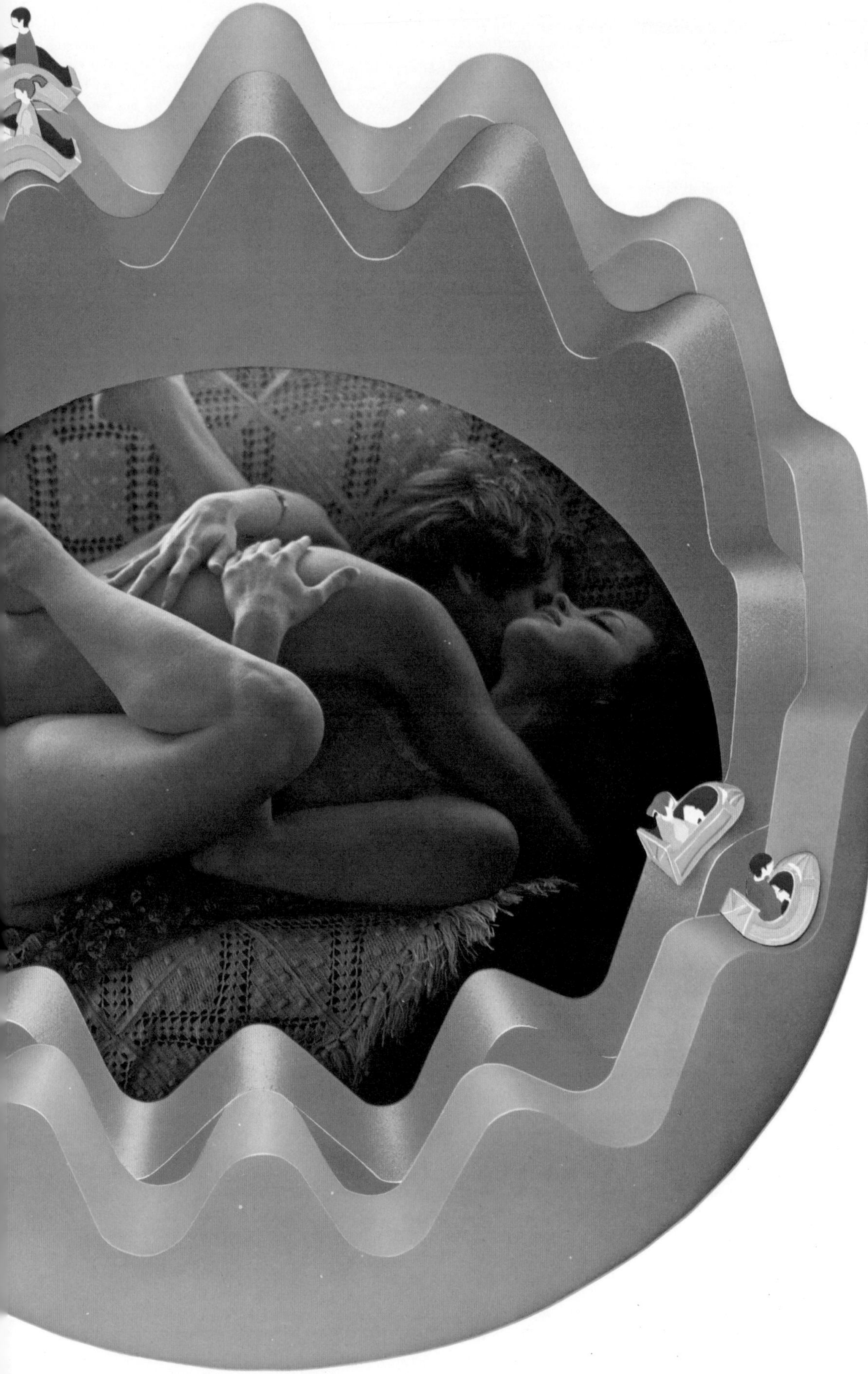

Fitness

An engine that is not serviced regularly and kept 'tuned up' does not function as well as it might. Similarly, we can only expect to get the best performance out of our bodies if we keep them in tune. Athletes know this. To perform well in sports events, athletes have to be really fit physically and fully prepared for physical exertion. This is equally true of sexual response and performance. Although love making should not be regarded as an athletic contest, at a physiological level the difference between sexual and athletic exertion is not very great. We cannot hope to obtain optimum sexual performance unless we keep our bodies fit and healthy.

Acute illness and chronic ill health often result in loss of interest in sex and impairment of sexual functioning. In rare cases of high fever there may be an increase in sexual desire, but no enhancement of performance. Psychiatric disturbances are frequently also accompanied by altered sexual responsiveness. Even mild depression may result in loss of sexual interest and is a frequent cause of female inability to reach orgasm.

The act of sexual intercourse for the male, and to a lesser extent for the female, involves the expenditure of a considerable amount of energy. There are various conditions which may make a person physically unfit to perform at their best or even to enjoy sex. Overweight and obese people may not enjoy sex to the full or may not perform to their satisfaction. The more overweight a man is, for example, the more quickly he will tire and the more rapidly he will get out of breath. He will thus find it difficult to prolong intercourse to a satisfactory conclusion. Some very fat men have been known to avoid sexual intercourse because they are just too unfit to complete the act without distress even though the desire is present. Obesity may cause other physical problems which themselves may impair sexual performance—high blood pressure and disease of the arteries are just two examples.

The need to control obesity leads on to the importance of diet in healthy sexuality. To keep fit it is essential to go easy on carbohydrates, particularly white sugar and white flour. But even a strict reducing diet must include an abundance of vitamins and mineral salts, such as are provided by fresh fruit, vegetables and wholemeal bread. Deficiency of vital trace elements may quickly and insidiously reduce fitness, causing loss of sexual desire and impairment of sexual ability. While on the subject of diet, drinking of *alcohol** should be mentioned. Alcohol in limited quantity tends to increase sexual desire, but may reduce sexual performance. Heavier drinking seriously affects physical fitness and eventually destroys sexuality.

Regular exercise is essential in both controlling obesity and maintaining fitness of heart and body. Muscles soon get soft and flabby if they are not vigorously used. Without exercise a person will be OFF-FORM more than on form in sexual performance. 'Keep fit' exercises are widely publicized and any program to keep fit should be selected to exercise the whole body, fully flexing joints and spine. Exercise should be followed as a regular routine, and medical advice should be sought if there is any history of illness or general debility to begin with. Particular attention should be paid to breathing exercises, aimed at developing breathing from the diaphragm so that vigorous love making will not be hindered by shortness of breath. Smoking tobacco in any of its forms can also cause shortness of breath as well as general ill health. Although in the past, smoking had some reputation as a sexy thing to do—it isn't. The resulting bad breath, coughing, spluttering and serious threat to health do not aid sexual performance or attraction.

Sexual pleasure can often be enhanced by developing various muscles that play a specific part in love making. One way of doing this is to carry out regular exercises that develop, tone and strengthen the pelvic muscles (these are known as Kegel or pelvic-floor exercises after the doctor who first invented them). Not only will such exercises tone up these muscles but very frequently they will help make a person more aware of the sensations that can be developed in the pelvic area during intercourse (*muscle consciousness**). Many doctors give patients who complain of loss of sexual feeling these simple exercises to do:

First, tighten the muscles that control the anus. This can be helped by imagining that you are gripping a thin object such as a pencil in the back passage. Grip it as tight as you can in imagination, then hold that tension for six seconds or more and then relax—tighten again, hold and relax. Next, exercise the muscles in the front of the pelvis, at the outlet of the bladder. Imagine that you have just started to pass urine and must stop the stream—tighten up these muscles very hard and hold the tension for six seconds or more, then relax. Both these exercises, repeated about six times in succession, should be performed as often as you can remember to do them.

Good general hygiene is, of course, very important in keeping fit. One 'must' is regular dental attention to avoid, among other things, gum disease and bad breath—an obvious 'turn off' during love making. Clean skin and hair and a daily bath or shower are very important in keeping fit and healthy. Short, smooth, clean finger nails and toe nails are other necessities for the successful lover.

Men and women who are physically healthy and fit often have a more relaxed frame of mind—a great aid to love making—than those who are off-form.

Randy

During periods of intense sexual desire a person is described as being randy or sometimes RAUNCHY. Interest in sex and the desire for relief from sexual tension are biological phenomena. The so-called sex drive which directs a person to seek a sexual partner and ultimately to obtain sexual satisfaction is very powerful. The sex drive is initiated in certain areas of the brain under hormone stimulation (*drugs and sex**). The basic sex drive in humans is modified and restrained by social circumstances.

In the majority of animals sexual activity is confined, by cyclical variations in hormone production, to those times, known as the estrus or oestrus, when the female animal is ON HEAT, that is to say, when she is fertile. In this way copulation (the animal equivalent of sexual intercourse) is restricted to a biological role of producing offspring. Humans are, in general, different. The majority of healthy, normal men and women have almost continuous sexual desire and are physically capable of having sexual intercourse at any time. At certain times, however, the desire may be stronger than at others making a person more lustful and more amorous. Medical researchers have tried to relate changes in a woman's sexual interest and responsiveness to different stages in the menstrual cycle, but the results have not been convincing.

Yvette Santiago Banek

Sign Language

Almost every species of animal has its own system of non-verbal communication which is employed during *courtship** and *foreplay**. Sign language has evolved in human sexuality too. The partners in every relationship spontaneously develop their own system of sexually significant signs and gestures (which are usually completely incomprehensible to a third person) so that their emotions, desires, likes and dislikes can be conveyed between them without the utterance of a single word. BODY LANGUAGE is a fairly recent phrase for bodily gestures and motions which communicate feelings and emotions, both sexual and non-sexual.

There are other gestures of sexual significance which are more widely recognized—even between people who do not speak the same language. The two finger 'V' sign with its vulgar connotations is well recognized. Non-verbal requests for sexual intercourse are the movement of the tongue gently along the margin of the upper lip and sometimes making a circular movement on the palm of a partner's hand with a finger while holding hands. A simple gesture is squeezing a loved one's hand three times in succession to indicate the three syllables of 'I-love-you'.

There is another aspect of sexual sign language which is much more subtle. We mimic features of sexual arousal in our everyday life which are, unknowingly, aimed at inviting interest from the opposite sex. The use of eye shadow and other facial cosmetics artificially makes the face appear as it does during sexual *arousal**—with flushed skin and lips and accentuated eyes. The *advertising** business exploits this to a very great extent, employing sexual sign language to entice prospective buyers, just as a person in search of a sexual partner does.

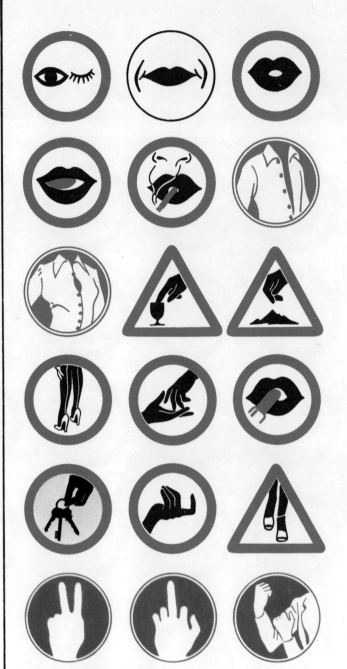

Opposite page *SM and gay codes for sexual preferences and roles:*

1, 3 *passive role.* 2, 4 *active role (Red) fist-fucker: 5 active, 6 passive. (Blue) anal sex: 7 active, 8 passive. (Light blue) oral sex: 9 active, 10 passive. (Yellow) urolagnia: 11 active, 12 passive. (Brown) coprophilia ('scat'): 13 active, 14 passive. (Mustard) 15 needs big penis, 16 has 8 in.–plus. (Orange) 17 anything anytime, 18 nothing now.*

(Khaki) 19 military type, 20 likes military type. (Green) 21 hustler selling, 22 trick buying. (Black) flagellation: 23 active, 24 passive. (Gray) bondage: 25 active, 26 passive. 27 SM Slave (left shoulder: SM Master). 28 SM Master (right side: SM Slave). 29 SM Master. 30 SM Slave. 31 SM Slave. 32 SM passive role. 33 SM active role.

Hanging from the belt:

1
2
3
4

Coloured handkerchiefs in back pocket:

5
6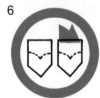
7
8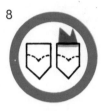
9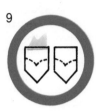

10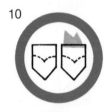
11
12
13
14

15
16
17
18
19

20
21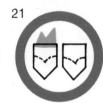
22
23
24

25
26

Rings and chains:

27
28

29
30
31
32
33

Gay Costume Signs

Homosexuality having been so long a taboo subject, a rich costume language has developed, particularly in the USA, which allows one gay person not only to recognise another, but to ascertain what form of sex he or she prefers.

A gold ring is often worn on the little finger but, as a reaction to the effeminate caricature of homosexuals, there is a tendency to 'dress down'. For men, this has resulted, perhaps in over-reaction, in the lumberjack, back-woodsman, or Sierra Club look. Limp wrists are a thing of the past. Muscles, somewhat over-developed in the chest, are worked for.

Levi's are worn with Fry boots, hiking or construction-worker boots, plaid shirts, leather flying jackets, or battle-jacket-styled tops in some other material. There is a generally faded, worn-out look to everything. Jackets end at the waist and some indication of a bulge at the crotch is usual. Underwear is not worn.

In warmer weather, the jacket and shirt are replaced by a tee-shirt or, whenever possible, nothing, and the jeans by cut-off Levi's. A handkerchief can be worn in the back pocket, following a recognized *sign language**. However, the construction-worker or hiking boots are retained and worn with white cycle socks with brightly striped tops. This fashion, and the handkerchief in the back pocket, has caught on in the heterosexual world, and some confusion has resulted about individual preferences.

This costuming is a manifestation of the homosexual's struggle to rid himself of the stereotyped image of limp-wristed effeminacy. It is, of course, a form of cult behaviour, which has been taken to extremes by the leather club members, who often go butch to a sinister degree.

Tom of Finland

Cupid in the Kitchen

Men have always hoped to find food which will increase their virility, and almost every edible substance has, at some time or other, been considered an *aphrodisiac**. There is however, no scientific evidence that suggests that delicacies like oysters, asparagus, truffles or particular herbs and spices do any such thing. On the other hand, the link between sexuality and food is obvious. Few people doubt that eating a delicious meal can be a sensual experience, especially when accompanied by good wine.

Honey has had associations with sex since ancient times, perhaps because pollen contains minute quantities of sex hormones. Ovid in *The Art of Love* advises lovers to try a diet of 'white onions, green vegetables, eggs, honey and the nuts of the pine tree'. Onions and garlic were considered aphrodisiacs —their smell resembles human sexual *odours**. The 4th-century Greek playwright, Diphilus, said the onion was 'undoubtedly capable of stimulating sexual desire'. Truffles, too, had a reputation for arousing passion. The classic French gastronome, Brillat-Savarin, said (somewhat elaborately) that they awaken 'erotic and gastronomic ideas both in the sex wearing petticoats and in the bearded portion of humanity'. Eggs have always been used to provoke desire and they are symbolic of procreation. Byron mentioned them, along with oysters, in *Don Juan*; and Shaykh Nefzawi extols their virtues in *The Perfumed Garden:*

'He who makes it a practice to eat every day fasting the yolks of eggs, without the white part, will find in this aliment an energetic stimulant towards coitus. The same is the case with the man who during three days eats of the same mixture with onions.

'He who boils asparagus, and then fries them in fat, and then pours upon them the yolks of eggs with pounded condiments, and eats every day of this dish, will grow very strong for the coitus, and find in it a stimulant for his amorous desires.

'He who peels onions, puts them into a saucepan, with condiments and aromatic substances, and fries the mixture with oil and yolks of eggs, will acquire a surpassing and invaluable vigour for the coitus, if he will partake of this dish for several days.

'Camels' milk mixed with honey and taken regularly develops a vigour for copulation which is unaccountable and causes the virile member to be on the alert night and day.

'He who for several days makes his meals upon eggs boiled with myrrh, coarse cinnamon, and pepper, will find his vigour with respect to coition and erections greatly increased. He will have a feeling as though his member would never return to a state of repose.

'A man who wishes to copulate during a whole night, and whose desire, having come on suddenly, will not allow him to prepare himself and follow the regimen just mentioned, may have recourse to the following recipe. He must get a great number of eggs, so that he may eat to surfeit, and fry them with fresh fat and butter; when done he immerses them in honey, working the whole mass well together. He must then eat of them as much as possible with a little bread, and he may be certain that for the whole night his member will not give him any rest.'

Visual associations with the sexual organs have often earned a sexy reputation for certain foods, but there is no proof of their efficacy, except perhaps in stimulating erotic ideas in the eaters. Asparagus, carrots and bananas have a *phallic** shape. The succulent, bright red tomato was originally known as a 'love apple', and the small, round, ripe cherry has long since passed into sexual slang. 'To take or eat a cherry' means to deflower a virgin. The banana split has an obvious sexual appearance. A split-open phallic symbol supports two round breast-like scoops of ice cream, topped off with, of course, a cherry. Sea food has a reputation for enhancing sexual desire, possibly because of associations with the love goddess Aphrodite who rose from he sea. It is also obvious that oysters and bearded clams resemble the moist appearance of aroused female genitals.

Red, and especially raw, meat ('steak tartare puts hair on your chest') is supposedly sexy. There is a psychological connection between flesh and blood and the sexual functions.

The maintenance of virility, however, depends on a healthy, well-balanced diet, not on particular foods or particular meals. *Fitness** is more likely to make men and women naturally passionate. Most people get sufficient nutrients and vitamins in their daily diet but it should be pointed out that Vitamin E (or the lack of it) can marginally affect one's vitality. It is contained in wheat germ, which can be obtained in powdered or capsule form.

Tomi Ungerer

Tongue

The tongue is a sensitive organ, especially at the tip, and plays a part in love-making in various ways. Licking erogenous zones can be extremely stimulating, and licking the head of the penis or the external female sex organs (the clitoris in particular) is highly erotic. The tongue can be inserted into various orifices of a loved one's body. In the FRENCH KISS the contact between the lining of the mouth, the teeth and the lover's exploring tongue is particularly arousing for both partners. Putting the tongue into the ear or the vagina is also common during love-making.

Mouth

The mouth is an important feature in human sexual behaviour, both for giving and receiving pleasure. The lips can be used in closed mouth kissing, but more passionate and arousing is the open mouth or FRENCH KISS, particularly when the tongue is used. The mouth can take in parts of the loved one's body—nipples, penis, ear lobes—and even putting fingers into the partner's mouth during love-making can be arousing. The pleasure of oral contact can be enhanced by sucking. Both vigorous sucking, that hurts pleasurably, and LOVE BITES, can be extremely stimulating.

Kiss

Smacking the lips in contact with another person's skin is, in many cultures (including our own), an expression of respect and endearment, but also of passion. Russian leaders hug and kiss their honoured guests, and Frenchmen never receive a medal without the formality of kisses on the cheeks. Kisses range in intensity from a peck on the cheek to deep, erotic mouth-to-mouth contact. Kissing parts of the body other than the mouth, such as the ears, neck and breasts or a partner's genital organs (*oral sex**) can be extremely arousing and stimulating for both partners in a sexual relationship.

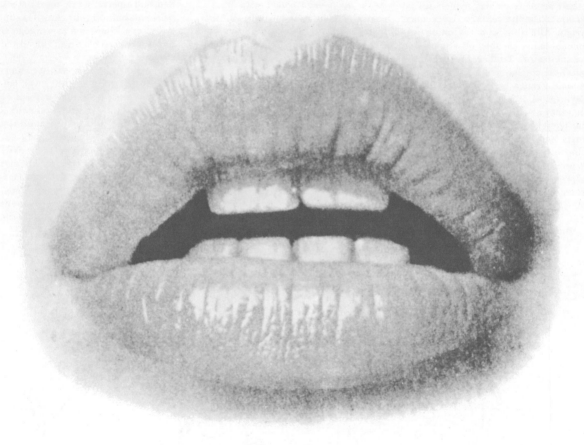

Odours

The sense of smell is intimately related to sexual function. Odour is used as a means of alluring and arousing members of the opposite sex in a large number of animal species. Even with the sophistication of modern man and woman odour still features prominently in sexual behaviour, although the sense of smell now probably ranks second to that of vision. In many primitive civilisations, animal and vegetable concoctions were applied to the human body to accentuate and fortify natural body odours. Custom has changed and it is difficult to assess the significance of natural body odours in present-day human sexuality.

Nowadays, natural body odours tend to cause varying degrees of repulsion between people who are not sexually involved with each other, but they can be sexually stimulating between lovers, especially after the process of sexual arousal has been initiated. Every person has a characteristic body odour. It is known that sexually mature women produce, in a cyclical pattern, the same odourous chemicals, called PHERO-MONES, that female monkeys produce to attract their male mates, but it is doubtful that the human male is responsive to pheromones in the same way as monkeys.

The pendulum has swung from accentuating body odours to taking measures to disguise or even suppress their formation altogether. The market place has become flooded with all manner of toiletries and preparations to prevent the occurrence or detection of SMELLS from all parts of the body. There are deodorant and other BODY SPRAYS, perfumed lotions, scented talcs and both pungent and subtle perfumes. Tissues pre-saturated with deodorant and perfume are widely advertised to prevent 'vaginal odours'. Since the source of one constituent of many perfumes—musk oil—is the sex glands of an animal, it seems unnatural to substitute an animal sex smell for a natural human smell. However, it is said that the fragrance of musk oil closely resembles the odour of the human body, and many people find it highly erotic. *Advertising** stresses the sexual implication and attractions of perfumes, after-shave lotions and other toiletries, but scientific evidence that such scents can cause sexual arousal is not convincing. The attraction of such scents is probably cultural rather than natural.

Music

Music is not inherently a sexual stimulus because it can also have a soporific or a spiritually uplifting effect, but in all cultures it has associations with emotion and sensuality. Music can stimulate the body to movements which celebrate its beauty, health and energy and this is bound to be linked to sexuality in its broadest sense. Since it depends on rhythm, it can easily suggest sexual intercourse. In modern rock music, with its Afro rhythms, this has led to a tradition of sexual mimicry on-

stage which is often reflected in audience responses; both seem to grow from the music. The sadistic, pouting and sometimes savage Rolling Stones act centred on Mick Jagger, the bi-sexual pseudo-decadent act of David Bowie, and most of the celebrated stage acts of modern rock and pop stars are not so much supported by their music as aptly expressive of its content. However different the idiom of the music, this sexually frank response to it is related to the use Mozart (who is noted for sublimity and cool classicism) could make of music: as, for instance, Donna Anna's two great arias in *Don Giovanni*, in which the music portrays sexual hys-

teria, frustration and anguish.

Music can express many moods and, depending on what we expect can induce moods ranging from the gently sensuous—soft music and low lights, as a prelude to making love—to the nearly orgasmic. In the prosecution of the undergound magazine *OZ*, one phase of the trial turned on a review that had commented: 'I'd love to meet a chick who could fuck like *Led Zepplin One* but she'd wear me out in a week.' As part of the scene at huge festivals and concerts, current rock and folk and jazz can take on the power of one more drug and help stimulate audience frenzy that is obviously sexual in energy. But

Richard Strauss already portrayed lovemaking musically in the prelude to *Der Rosenkavalier,* and Ravel's orchestral piece *Bolero* exactly depicts the rhythm of sexual intercourse, beginning at a low point in arousal and building to a climax. Stravinsky's *Rite of Spring* caused riots at its Paris première in 1911. Music-induced frenzy is no new thing, even in what are called 'classical' forms. At its more primitive, the rhythmic power of music supports fertility rites and dances, while in its most sophisticated forms its direct emotionality can be blatant. Passion comes over at its most stirring and memorable when allied to music.

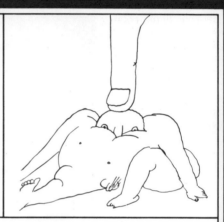

WORRY BLOCKS

Anxieties and phobias that can turn people off.

Stress & Depression

Many things can turn people off. The male clothed only in his socks appears to have this effect on most women. There are a great variety of things like that, many of them personal to the individual. Beards, lack of beards, smells pleasant and unpleasant, picking the nose or clicking the teeth, can all affect some people. The variety of things, actions, and places that have this sorry effect are almost limitless. Their significance can be important or they can be easily corrected. There is always, if not an answer, a remedy.

Stress and depression are rather different, since they cannot be dealt with by simply taking off the socks, avoiding the partner's own special hang-ups, or simply sorting it out. Stress is a word on everyone's lips. It would appear that all of us are constantly under stress. This in one sense is true, so some amount of stress must be looked upon as normal. (This is using the word normal in the statistical sense, which means that normal is what most people are.)

Assuming that most people are under some degree of stress does not mean that stress is always normal. Abnormal stress is either abnormal because of its amount, or because it is present without any apparent good cause. Thus, some people worry much more about their jobs than others and some are tense and anxious in situations most of us would find relaxing. Abnormal stress can have many causes; some causes are sexual, many are not.

Stress, anxiety and worry may in themselves turn one off. Stress, anxiety and worry may not be related to sex, but may be due to other causes. However, if stress not related to sex is present and as a result interferes with sexual activity, an association then does arise. The anxious man who finds himself impotent becomes anxious about this and is even more likely to be impotent the next time he tries. The worried girl fails to make it to an orgasm, and next time may be even more turned off. It must be emphasized that stress, anxiety and depression, while being causes of impotence or frigidity, are not the commonest causes in themselves. This will be discussed later.

DEPRESSION has a general usage and also a technical psychiatric meaning. To most people, being depressed is the same as being fed-up or 'feeling blue'. Psychiatrists use the word to describe emotional illnesses. One symptom of these illnesses is becoming sexually turned off. The illness type of depression may not in itself be related to sex and when it has been successfully treated, sexual activity should return to normal. On the other hand, sexual problems can themselves produce depression in this technical sense. It is of course important that the sexual problems be dealt with.

The most common cause of sexual difficulties is GUILT. One may be aware of one's guilt, or it can work in the unconscious. Sadly, most people are still afflicted with some degree of guilt about sex. Children are still taught to feel guilty about their sexual organs

and feelings. The association between these organs and the equally innocuous orifices of elimination, connects sex with dirtiness.

Guilt and feelings of 'dirtiness', are the great inhibitors of sexual pleasure. INHIBITION is really another word for being turned off from sex generally, or from particular aspects of it. Sometimes the indoctrination is quite open and remembered. More commonly it is not remembered and appears in the mind as a muddled-up mixture of early memories and ideas of morality. CONSCIENCE describes the product of this mixture of early indoctrination and moral teachings. The development of a conscience is obviously important, since it regulates our behaviour towards others and society in general. Unfortunately the development of an individual's conscience can and does result in the production of a variety of sexual hang-ups. When people talk of morals they usually mean matters sexual. Morals are about much more, yet because of indoctrination, sex is over-emphasized, made dirty and so people are pushed into guilt and hang ups. These hang-ups benefit no one and are the product of the hang-ups of the individual's parents and other adult figures in their early life. The hang-ups are carried on from one generation to the next, but can fortunately be dealt with at any time, so finally breaking the chain reaction.

Another group of causes of being turned off are related to false concepts of self and false concepts of normality. For a number of different reasons, some people feel inferior to their fellows. This feeling of inferiority, sometimes described as an INFERIORITY COMPLEX, can affect sexual ability. 'I am no good', tends to make a person no good. It is not that you *are* no good, but the thought is making itself come true. One may not have any great feelings of inferiority, but still develop them about sexual skill and pleasure. Bragging friends and stories of sexual athletes can quickly make us believe that we are not very good at the game. Most of these stories are of course untrue and anyway there is quite a wide range of normal sexual ability. We all have our own level, but expecting much more tends to diminish it. Great expectations that are not realized may block and turn one off. Thus, the man who finds he cannot manage it more than twice an evening may feel inferior and fail to manage it at all next time. The woman expecting an unbelievable experience when reaching a climax and perhaps expecting this very many times during one love making, can be sadly disappointed. This disappointment makes the next time more disappointing, even though the first time was, in fact, a great experience.

Anxiety, fear, worry, depression—all can turn people off, often for reasons unconnected with sex. Failure due to guilt, or feelings of inferiority, or false expectations, can do the same damage and as a result make one more anxious, worried and depressed. In the first case, treatment is needed for the anxiety or depression, while in the second case it will be advisable to discuss the sexual hang-ups with a professional counsellor or therapist.

Frigidity

Frigidity describes a woman who is sexually unresponsive or who fails to reach orgasm. Some men use the word frigid as a term of abuse: 'She's a frigid bitch'—which usually means a woman has failed to respond to a male in the desired sexual way. There are, in general, two types of frigidity: primary and secondary. Primary frigidity, sometimes called PRIMARY ORGASMIC DYSFUNCTION is used for a situation in which a woman has never been able to achieve orgasmic release by any means. *Masturbation**, or manual stimulation of the genitals, and sexual intercourse in whatever position or situation, all fail to produce *orgasm**. Sometimes a woman finds all sexual contact ex-

tremely unpleasant and rejects it—this is the most severe degree of primary frigidity. A dislike or rejection of all sexual contact, and even physical contact, can occur in secondary frigidity or SECONDARY ORGASMIC DYSFUNCTION. This describes a situation in which a woman has experienced orgasm and then subsequehtly fails to do so. Most commonly, orgasm has followed masturbation but does not occur during penetration. Recent studies suggest that a failure to orgasm during penetration is not unusual in females, and it probably is not a sexual dysfunction.

It is important to consider a man's role in the arousal of a female to orgasm. A quick grab and fumble, followed by a lightning sexual encounter is not likely to turn on many women, let alone help them to reach a climax. Inexperienced, nervous and self-cen-

tred men usually fail to arouse their partners to orgasm, but this does not make a woman frigid. The sexual act is a mutual, physical and emotional experience and failure to achieve the desired degree of sexual responsiveness is not something in which the 'blame game' can be played.

Anti-sex indoctrination of children takes many forms—and may substantially contribute to frigidity in women and its friend-in-misery, *impotence**, in men. Because anti-sex indoctrination has been so widespread, it is surprising that such sexual difficulties are not more common. Some children are brought up in a 'no touch' atmosphere, and therefore some women (and men) have never been used to physical contact of any kind. Parents, because of their own inhibitions and hang-ups, may not only have failed to fondle and

Calman

cuddle their children, but also may have actively discouraged caressing, fondling and cuddling by anyone, under any circumstances. Usually such parents have also discouraged, by punishment, a child's tendency to touch its own genitals or to engage in masturbation. Not surprisingly, such children may grow up with a dislike for and feeling of uneasiness about physical contact. With touching, which has any sexual overtones, dislike and uneasiness may change to abhorrence or repulsion. Religious taboos, cultural ideas and beliefs about purity, sin, and right and wrong, as well as sheer ignorance about the facts of life and all sexual matters, play their part in primary orgasmic dysfunction.

Secondary frigidity can be caused in a number of different ways, too. Poor sexual techniques, unhelpful and self-centred partners, loss of interest in one's usual sexual partner, fear of pregnancy and fear of sexually-transmitted disease are just some of the causes, singly or in combination. Emotional hang-ups of many varieties, as well as *stress and depression** can contribute to frigidity. Everyday distractions such as rearing a young family and even unsuitable surroundings for sexual activities can cause periods of sexual unresponsiveness. When both partners have sexual difficulties, a complex emotional interaction may be set up in which each blames the other for their failure in love making. A more usual situation is one of non-communication. Sexual problems are never discussed so that both partners shrink into a world of sexual inhibition and irritation and frustration. Failure to talk about sex is an important factor in both frigidity and impotence . . . it may not be a cause in itself, but certainly makes problems worse and prevents both self and mutual help.

Help and treatment for primary or secondary frigidity depend upon the cause or causes. Sometimes simple advice about sexual techniques—for both the male and female partners—may be all that is necessary. In some cases, *sex therapy** is required, which may take a variety of different forms, from guidance counselling to contraceptive information to *surrogate therapy**. It is almost always possible to help anyone who is frigid.

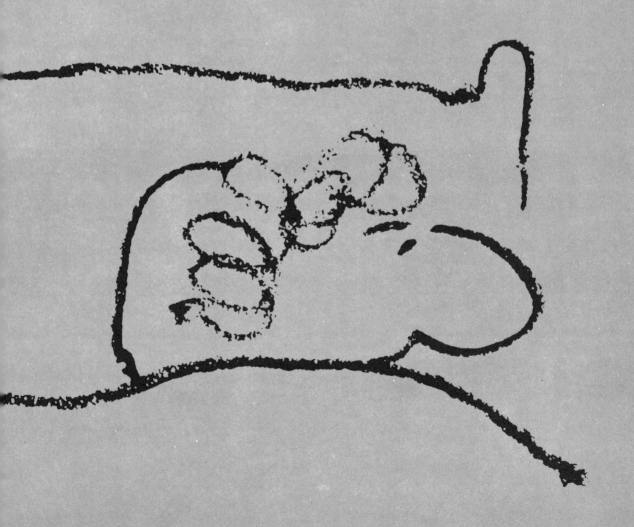

Impotence

This is the inability of a man to achieve an adequate erection to make penetration of the female vagina, followed by ejaculation, possible. There are varying degrees of impotence, conventionally classified by doctors into primary and secondary impotence. The man who has never been able to have intercourse because of failure to obtain an erection suffers from PRIMARY IMPOTENCE. SECONDARY IMPOTENCE is the condition in which a man has previously performed adequately before failure occurs. Secondary impotence is much more common than primary impotence.

The victim of primary impotence has never been able to perform sexual intercourse. He may have, and usually has, achieved erection and ejaculation by masturbation, but fails with a sexual partner. There are many possible causes for this. Excessive shyness, ab-normal concern about the sexual organs (particularly the penis), fear of women and guilt are causes.

There are many similarities in the origins of impotence and female failure to reach orgasm. A family that raises children with the 'no-touching' outlook are liable to produce both inhibited girls and impotent boys. Indoctrination with the belief that sex is dirty, immoral, ungodly and everything nasty too often works. Other factors may reinforce or produce the problem: lack of contact with girls in adolescence, ignorance of what sex is about, coupled with belief in bizarre tales about sex, can all hinder subsequent performance. Some men are afraid of women and others believe that their sex organs, particularly the penis, are inadequate. A man's belief that he has a 'mini' penis, which will not satisfy a woman, blocks his ability to have sexual intercourse almost before he even thinks about trying.

An important factor in producing pri-mary impotence is a catastrophic 'first try'. In this case, a man may have some or none of the problems mentioned, although he is likely to be a little shy and unsure of himself. Because of anxiety, tinged with guilt about the whole business, the first time he tries he fails. It may be a very miserable failure indeed. If his partner is sympathetic and understanding, there may be hope for the next time, but if she is scathing, annoyed or acts out her own feelings of rejection, his next attempt will be even worse. This has been described as the 'fear of fear phenomenon'. It also operates in cases of secondary impotence.

In the past, the treatment of primary impotence has not been particularly successful. One problem was that most men with this problem tended not to have a sexual partner. Thus the only treatment considered possible was psychotherapy and/or drugs. The use of female sex partners in *surrogate therapy** has changed this situation and

Calman

has helped sufferers to become sexually potent.

Secondary impotence is a much more prevalent problem than the primary variety. It particularly affects the middle-aged and the elderly, but young men are not exempt. Guilt, anxiety and misuse of alcohol are common causes. Needless anticipation of waning sexual ability also plays its part. A man becomes anxious and depressed because of work, failure, an unhappy relationship or something else. Because of this depression, with or without anxiety, he becomes impotent. Having failed once, the 'fear of fear' reaction begins. He fails again and again and since he then expects to fail, he does. To add a little confusion it may be that having failed the first time for another reason such as a rekindling of guilt or hostility toward his partner, he becomes depressed and anxious because of this.

Guilt is always lingering around the corner when sexual problems exist.

Consistent sexual success does not destroy it. The married man 'having it off' with someone else, the rekindling of childhood memories, a smell, a tune, a sound, a place can all rejuvenate guilt. A man can become fed up with his partner and as a result become impotent. He fails with her, perhaps repeatedly, tries someone else and fails again, perhaps because of guilt, certainly because of the 'fear of fear'.

Alcohol can play nasty tricks on men. Obviously, alcohol does not *always* take away the mechanism, but it is very likely to do so. For example, a man gets a little drunk, becomes very amorous and then fails. Particularly if he knows about the possible effects of alcohol, the next time he tries, if he is sober, he will probably succeed. However, if he is not aware of the effects of alcohol, 'fear of fear' comes into play. Of course there is always the partner, who suffers as much as the impotent male. If she is his usual partner and understands the 'fear of fear' it may be

dispelled. If she is not understanding, or if the next attempt is made with someone else, the sober attempt may be as bad as the first alcoholic failure. Like the catastrophic first failure of primary impotence, the first failure in secondary impotence can be equally catastrophic.

Impotence is not always an emotional problem. There are physical causes, although they are rare. Alcohol is a physical cause, so are certain drugs, particularly the so-called major tranquilizers, some anti-depressants, and drugs for treating high blood pressure. Diabetes may also cause impotence. It is particularly difficult when tranquillizers and anti-depressants cause impotence, since they are used in the treatment of anxiety and depression, both of which can themselves cause impotence. These conflicting effects can be sorted out and dealt with by a sympathetic doctor or therapist.

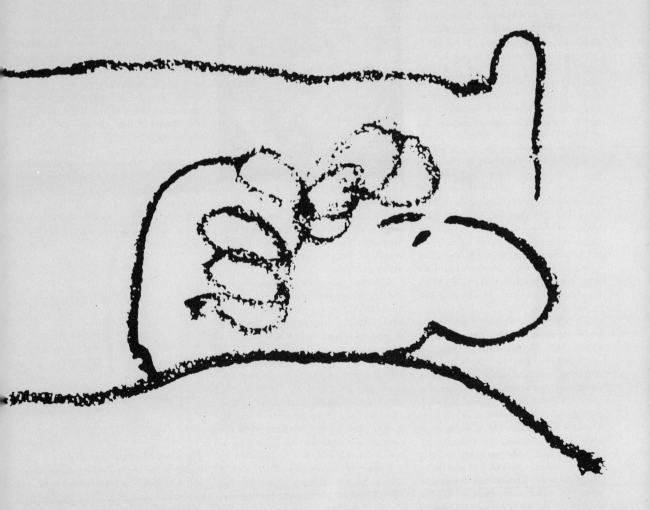

Aging

Aging is used as an excuse and an explanation for all sorts of things that have no real relationship to the aging process. At whatever your age, a whole variety of problems are dismissed with, 'It is due to your age!' Babies, children, adolescents, young adults, the middle-aged and the elderly are all included. It would be foolish, however, to suggest that age is of no significance.

There are many myths about the effect of aging on sex. A sixteen-year-old may believe that anyone over twenty-five has dropped out of the game. A thirty-year-old, viewing a sixteen-year-old as naive and inexperienced, may also view the over-forties as sexless dinosaurs. The view that sex is dirty influences some of this thinking: sex may be all right if you are young, but not once you are old and respectable. Such attitudes about sex and age affect individuals as they get older. The young man proud of his sexual athleticism will later become a middle-aged man and then an old man well past it. Expecting a deterioration in sexual ability can make it happen.

Sexual enjoyment is available to everyone. Aging should not and need not take away this joy. Since sexual activity usually involves two people, two people's prejudices, superstitions and ideas of right and wrong are involved. Thus couples reinforce each other's misconceived prejudices about aging and sex. Both men and women can continue to enjoy, and perhaps enjoy even more, a full sex life up to the time they finally die. Rather sadly, this is not usually the case. Many people withdraw from sex once they view themselves as middle-aged. Aging is one of the great sexual worry blocks. The aging process does affect sexual activity, but the emotional response of individuals and society to aging is the major problem.

A young man is able to produce a more upstanding erection than an elderly man. There is no doubt that the angle between the erect penis and the abdomen is influenced by age. This in itself does, but should not, influence a person's reaction to sexual activity. Aging also delays the establishment of a full erection. Again this is not necessarily a disadvantage or evidence of decay. In fact, older men are usually able to maintain an erection and delay emission more effectively than younger men. An older man, because of his

acquired skill as a lover, is usually better able to provide his sexual partner with a climax than a young man. There is little doubt that once hang-ups, inhibitions and false expectations are thrown out, the older man is sexually favoured. It is equally true that the older woman is also favoured, provided she can rid herself of indoctrination, old wive's tales and her own sexual inhibitions.

Successful, mutually satisfying sexual activity can and should continue from adolescence to the grave. This happy situation is disturbed by many things. Women who do not reach orgasm may disguise this from their partners until they become middle-aged. Once they have passed a certain age then they feel they can reveal this, but explain it away as an effect of aging. A man harassed by many sexual hang-ups also gives in when he becomes

middle-aged, because now he has an explanation and excuse for any problems. Loss of sexual interest and performance is much more likely to be the result of sexual hang-ups than the aging process.

Age can and does reduce the frequency of sexual activity, but should never take it away. Never perhaps is a little strong, since there are age-dependent afflictions and problems that do interfere with sexual activity. These in themselves do not usually take away sexual desire or ability to perform forever, but do interfere. For example, many middle-aged and elderly men have to have their prostate gland removed because it interferes with the elimination of urine. An operation to remove this gland may be followed by a period of impotence. This should always be a temporary phase, but too often becomes permanent. Having had

an operation on a 'sexual' gland, a man who finds himself impotent may believe this is a permanent effect of the operation. If he is told this is only temporary and is encouraged to go on trying to be sexually active, sexual activity usually returns. Women are similarly affected by operations on their sexual organs. Removal of the womb or the repair of a vaginal *prolapse** is often followed by an inability to reach orgasm, which can become more or less a permanent condition. This can be prevented by explaining that this temporary phenomenom will go away in time. If she has no serious sexual hang-ups and is fortunate enough to have an understanding partner, sexual enjoyment is soon restored.

Other physical things that make the myth of loss of sexual activity with age come true include a whole variety of drugs used in the treatment of illnesses that affect older people. Tranquillizers, anti-depressants and drugs used for the treatment of high blood pressure can all affect sexual activity (*drugs and sex**). These effects are usually temporary and depend upon the continued use of the drug. It is important that people are aware of these effects, know that they are almost always temporary and discuss the problem openly with their doctor. If a person is aware that impotence, for example, may be a consequence of some medicines taken in the short term, sex life into old age should not be too seriously affected.

Aging does tend to reduce the pleasurable frequency of sexual activity. This should not mean that age takes away the joys of sex. Free of worry blocks and hang-ups, it is usually possible for men and women to continue to enjoy a full sexual life until this life ends.

The plum blossom against a background of cracked ice, decorating this Chinese vase, symbolizes sexual content in old age.

Premature Ejaculation

Ejaculation which occurs too quickly and too early in sexual activity is called premature ejaculation, and sometimes referred to by its medical name in Latin, *ejaculatio praecox*. It is one of the most common male sexual problems. For some, ejaculation occurs before penetration is even attempted. Thoughts, of course, can produce sexual arousal and some men find that by continuing their erotic thoughts, erection is followed by ejaculation, without any manual or other stimulation of the penis. Others may ejaculate, or come, too quickly after a short period of sexual foreplay; some ejaculate just before, during, or immediately after penetration, managing one or two thrusts before ejaculation occurs. Thus, intercourse may take place in a technical sense in spite of premature ejaculation. The possibility of pregnancy occurring is real. Ejaculation near, or very near, and just inside the vagina can and does result in fertilization and pregnancy.

Ejaculation, at whatever stage in sexual activity, produces pleasurable release in a man. The problem with premature ejaculation is that this pleasurable release is mingled with feelings of inadequacy, failure and anxiety. Premature ejaculation can be as traumatic as impotence.

The nervous and chemical mechanisms involved in producing ejaculation are not fully understood. However, everyone knows that ejaculation can occur without physical stimulation of the penis either in or out of the vagina. Most men have had WET DREAMS or noctural emissions at some time in their lives. This is common in adolescence or any other time in life if a man neither masturbates nor has sexual intercourse. Wet dreams are simply a method of some release of sexual tension. The young, or not-so-young male, who does not have regular intercourse, for whatever reason, and refrains from masturbation, will have a wet dream sooner or later. There is nothing abnormal about this, any more than there is anything abnormal about masturbating.

A wet dream may occur as part of a sexual dream, or one may occur during sleep without an individual being able to remember any kind of dream, sexual or otherwise. Sometimes a dream is odd, bizarre, or sexually disturbing.

For example, the wet dream may result from a sexual dream which may appear very perverted to the individual having it. Again this is not necessarily abnormal in any way, but can cause the individual considerable anxiety and because of this may warrant him seeking professional advice.

Some complicated theories have been evolved to explain premature ejaculation which may or may not be true. Understanding them and accepting them does not really help the victim, neither apparently does psychotherapy of whatever type. Some doctors advocate the use of either one of the major tranquillizers, technically known as *thioridazine,* or one of a group of antidepressants described as *monoamine oxidase* inhibitors. These drugs can

Aubrey Beardsley

delay ejaculation and hence make intercourse successful. However, they only work, *if* they work, while they are being taken. Once a man stops taking them, premature ejaculation returns. They also produce side effects and carry certain dangers. This applies particularly to the monoamide oxidase inhibitors.

There are two much more effective and successful methods for dealing with this problem. Both depend upon an understanding and helpful partner. One method known to many women, probably since the beginning of human existence, is simply accepting the first failure by the man and then going on to stimulate and encourage him to try again. Having had a premature ejaculation and then attempting intercourse

within a reasonably short time, helped by a sympathetic and sexually-stimulating partner, often results in 'second time lucky'. If this is repeated the man becomes progressively more confident. *Surrogate therapy** has proved helpful.

The other method, which is the one most therapists recommend, is described as the 'squeeze' method. The couple first has to discuss, understand and accept the existence of a problem. The woman then has to play an active role in stimulating the man's penis. In the normal course of events, premature ejaculation would usually follow, but if at this stage she applies firm pressure (lasting for three to four seconds) to the penis at the point of the corona's ridge with the thumb beneath the penis and two fingers on the upper side, ejaculation will be prevented. Further stimulation can then occur, followed by a further period of pressure. This can be continued until the couple gain confidence in controlling the ejaculatory response. Finally, penetration and intercourse takes place to the couple's mutual satisfaction. Sometimes it is necessary to withdraw the penis during intercourse and again to apply pressure if ejaculation is about to occur prematurely. It appears important that the pressure is applied by the partner, for if the man applies it himself, it does not seem to work.

Castration Anxiety

Castration, or removal of a male's testicles, has been used in the past as a punishment, as a method of preventing boys' voices from deepening at puberty and to ensure that harem guards did not seduce their charges (*eunuchs and castrati**). It is now used in rare cases as a treatment for habitual sex offenders.

The idea that boys and men may suffer from castration anxiety was popularised by *Sigmund Freud**. His theory was that towards the end of his third year a boy became interested in his penis which gave rise to feelings of sexual attraction towards the mother and feelings of jealousy or resentment of the father (the well-known OEDIPUS COMPLEX). Freud claimed that castration anxiety arose because the boy imagined that his illicit desires might be punished by his father castrating him. This may be the origin of some men's anxiety over possible loss of the genitals. Certainly the fear can block satisfactory sexual activity.

Sex Aids

Anybody who is suffering from disinclination for sex need not despite the numerous aids offered for sale by sex stores and mail order advertisements. The principle types of sex aids on the market are described in section 26, under 'In the Sex Store'. Experimenting with some of these may in itself precipitate a revival of sexual interest that a person thought had died away. From the point of view of a sexual mate, showing that the other partner is bothering to do something about his or her difficulty can also stimulate that mutual warmth of feeling that can help to regenerate dormant sexual responses.

If more sex aids seem to be for male than for female use, it is due partly to the commercial reason that most customers who are likely to enter a sex store are men. However, mail order services are available and there is no reason for women to find it more difficult than men to obtain the articles which they think might help themselves or their partners.

A key to the various items (right) *appears on page 286*

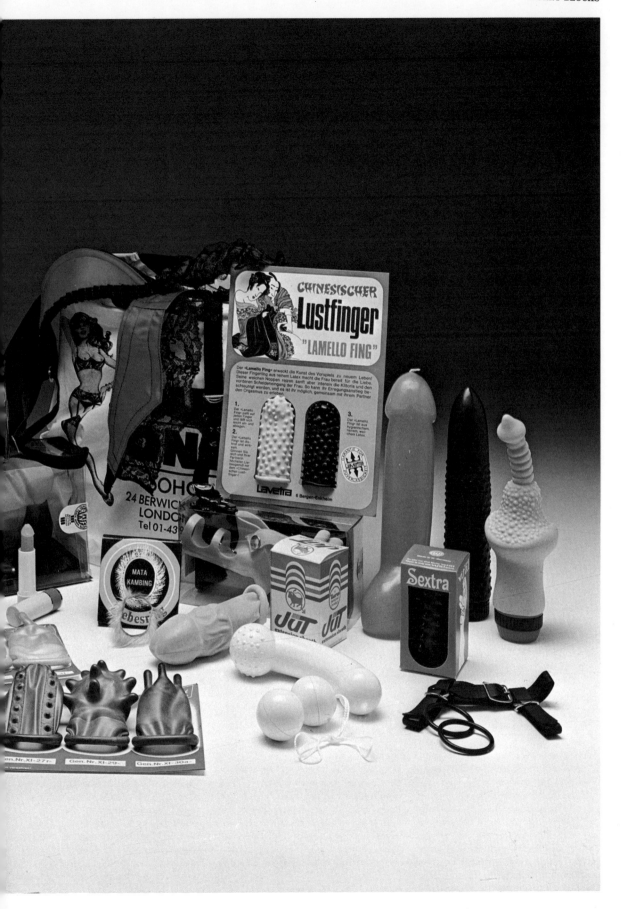

Sex Therapy

There is a number of ways of treating and helping people with sexual problems and disorders. These include treatment with drugs, psychotherapy, medical and lay counselling, *surrogate therapy** and self-help discussion groups and workshops where men and women explore together the whole area of human sexual consciousness. Sex therapy as a field of expertise is in its

infancy and new techniques of helping in cases of sexual dysfunction are being discovered all the time.

Until fairly recently the three most popular forms of sex therapy were counselling (medical and lay), psychotherapy and the prescription of drugs. Drugs used by the medical profession for various sexual problems (*drugs and sex**) include tranquillizers and sedatives which are normally used to damp

down anxiety and anti-depressants, which, as the name suggests, counter depression which may affect sexual response and performance. There is little scientific evidence to suggest that claims made for specific drugs to treat actual sexual dysfunction (for example, *impotence**) have much effect. It is also doubtful if any drug therapy really can 'cure' sexual problems unless there is an underlying mental illness such as depression. Psychotherapy may help some people to understand their sexual problems and thus help them to help themselves, but the process takes a long time and may not work in practice. *Counselling** is a less intensive process of talking about one's particular problems; as with psychotherapy it may help some people to see their problems in a new light and thus help them help themselves.

Sex therapy, which does not include doing anything of a physically sexual nature, has been likened to trying to

teach someone to play the piano without even seeing the instrument. *Masters and Johnson**, and Martin Cole in Great Britain, are perhaps the best-known practitioners of practical, physical sexual therapy, a type of treatment which grew out of the psychological treatment called behaviour therapy. In this it is assumed that all behaviour is simply learned and can be unlearned and replaced by more satisfactory behaviour. In essence, this kind of therapy for sexual dysfunction consists of a two-week programme (usually) in which a patient is helped to develop a sexual relationship with another person in slow stages which culminate in a mutually satisfying sexual success. The obvious choice of sex therapist may appear to be a patient's natural partner, married or otherwise, but this is not always the case. *Surrogate therapy** is then employed in which a surrogate, or substitute, sexual partner helps the patient to achieve a satisfying sexual performance. Sex therapy of a physical nature is reported to be the most successful of all forms of treatment for sexual dysfunction.

The need for sex therapy has seen, especially in the USA, a burgeoning of techniques which help people with psychosexual problems. Many groups and organizations specialize in various forms of *sex education** and generally explore human sexuality as a form of therapy. There are special groups interested in touching and body sensitivity, in play and family therapy, in Gestalt therapy, in sexual attitude restructuring and so on. All these are, fundamentally, self-help groups.

Today, many general hospitals and colleges and universities have special sex therapy units or clinics which treat singles or couples. The Human Sexuality Program at the University of California School of Medicine (San Francisco), for example, is currently studying the whole field of sex therapy, engaging in widespread research and trying experimental techniques. Slowly, the general public is becoming aware of new sex therapy techniques as the media reports on the work of scientists and researchers and the setting up of new clinics and workshops dealing with problems of sexuality. The advantage of such clinics is that a whole range of specialists is available for treating sexual dysfunction, from therapists and psychiatrists to gynecologists and surgeons. Consultations on sex problems are backed up by expert and readily available medical help.

8

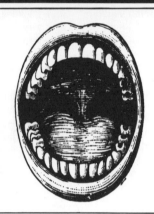

ORAL SEX

Mouth and tongue caresses that bring the closest loving partnership.

Oral Sex

This means quite simply the use of the lips, the tongue and the mouth and cavity of the throat in love making. Oral sex is one of the most intimate of all the physical acts possible in a human relationship. In spite of the amount of publicity that has been given to oral sex in recent years, there is in fact nothing new about it. It has been known and practiced throughout the ages.

The mouth and tongue are exceedingly sensitive organs. The tip of the tongue is one of the most sensitive parts of the body. A small child repeatedly puts things in its mouth, not in order to taste them but to 'feel' them with its tongue. Furthermore, the mouth is a body orifice or opening, and as such it features strongly in pleasurable sensations, particularly those of a sexual nature. The shape of the mouth is profoundly attractive because of this—which is one reason why women emphasize the area with lipstick or gloss. That the mouth bears some resemblance to the vaginal opening may be partly responsible for its powers of attraction. However, women are attracted by a masculine mouth or by mobile and smiling lips—so there is a satisfying emotional appeal in seeing lips, too.

The sensitivity of the mouth area and its flexibility has brought the *kiss** into prominence. As people grow up already aware of the great enjoyment that the giving and receiving of oral contact in the form of sucking and kissing can yield, it is a normal sequence that in love play which is abandoned and unrestricted, there will come a time when it will seem quite natural to kiss a partner's body and genital organs. Lovers moving together in the changing embraces of their sexual play will clearly be attracted to the penis or the vagina. Both feel unusual to the touch, are interesting to look at and pleasant to caress. They have an arousing *odour** which appeals to the sense of smell. Sooner or later, kissing the partner's sexual organs becomes irresistibly attractive and almost inevitable. Perhaps hesitantly to start with, but later with increasing fervour, kisses lead to more voluptuous licking and sucking movements. The penis is taken into the mouth by the female; the lips of the vulva are parted by the male who explores the labia with his tongue and inserts it into the vagina. The free application of saliva on the clitoris produces a slippery, sliding friction which raises the level of stimulation. Perhaps individually or perhaps together, there is a working of the mouth and lips around the aromatic and visually aroused genitals of the partner (*erogenous zones**). Skilful oral sex can lead to orgasm in both partners.

Not infrequently a person will prefer oral sex to any other kind of sexual activity. More often than not, the preference is for receiving rather than giving pleasure orally. Although a man's tongue is narrower and far shorter than a penis, and although a woman's mouth is not as deep as the vagina, there is a compensation in the vastly greater muscular strength and dexterity of the mouth and tongue. Not only can the lips feel and be felt in their movements, but the mouth orifice can be tightened far more than the vagina. Additionally, a man's flexible, muscular tongue tip can seek out sensitive areas for stimulation that would be inaccessible to the blunt probings of his penis, and his lips can suck at the clitoris. A woman's mouth can offer the subtleties of what can be thought of as a 'mobile', active kind of vagina to the penetrating penis. It can also produce suction, a technique that is possible but rarely achieved with vaginal muscles (*muscle consciousness**).

Clearly, in oral sex there is a need for immaculate hygiene. Washing with soap and water before beginning love making is not only a courtesy to one's partner, but also decreases the likelihood of spreading any bacteria which may be present on the genitals from previous urination or bowel movement. Soap and water will not destroy any natural, pleasant odours arising from the genitals during sexual stimulation.

Fellatio

Fellatio (from the Latin *fellare*, 'to suck') is the sexual activity in which a woman takes a man's penis into her mouth and stimulates it by licking or sucking or kissing to produce male sexual arousal and orgasm. Fellatio is also known, especially in American slang, as *sucking off, giving head* or, more popularly, as a *blow job* (in spite of this term, the penis should never have air blown into it).

Fellatio follows on naturally from other kinds of *foreplay**; it can be used initially to stimulate a male erection and arousal prior to full intercourse, or to produce arousal and orgasm or, without intercourse taking place, to stimulate the male when his erection has subsided after prolonged foreplay and concentration on stimulating his female partner or, after orgasm and a suitable resting time has elapsed, to restimulate a man for further sexual activity and possible orgasm.

The method of fellatio will vary according to the techniques and the desires of both partners. Certain broad categories of fellatio are generally recognized. Kissing and licking of the glans, the penis itself and testicles is known as PENILINGUS. The lips and mouth may be used in a light, sensitive fashion to stimulate the surface of the male genitals (which are made sensitive by the hairs that grow on the genital skin covering). Alternatively, kissing and licking may be accompanied by nibbling movements of the lips and teeth (used gently) moving around the glans and up and down the shaft of the penis, over the scrotum and around the perineum.

Another method is IRRUMATIO, in which the penis makes in-and-out penetration movements into a woman's mouth, similar to those of vaginal intercourse. A woman's mouth may remain still while the penis moves, or may exert suction, or she can move her head in rhythm with the penis which simulates the active movements of two bodies in intercourse. A variation on this method is called DEEP THROAT. A few women are able to overcome the reflex reaction to vomit when something is thrust into the throat passage, and can thus accept partial penis penetration. This specialized fellatio technique is rare because of the physical structure of the male and female bodies (a woman's nose may be so closely pressed against a man's pubic hair and bone that she is unable to breathe!). For acrobatic couples who can overcome the obvious difficulties, deep throat may have an exciting novelty value.

There is little danger in fellatio, unless a woman bites the sensitive male genitals too hard, causing him pain. Semen ejaculated into the mouth or even swallowed is harmless; it has a faintly salty, pungent taste. Breathing it into the larynx or lungs may be a potential danger, as would breathing in any foreign substance, but this does not ever seem to have been described.

All in all, fellatio is a special method of achieving male arousal, as well as an exciting way to avert sexual boredom between regular partners, and a useful technique when intercourse is not desired. Obviously, fellatio should not take place if one or the other partner has any symptoms of sexually-transmitted disease or feels that there is any likelihood that exposure to such infection may have occurred. Remember that sexually-transmitted diseases such as *gonorrhea** can incubate rapidly in the throat.

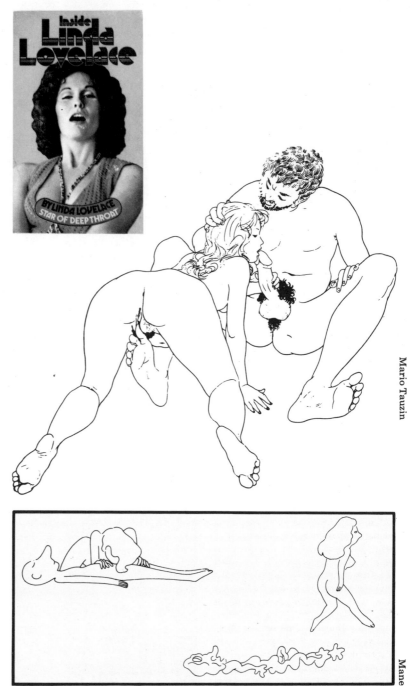

Mario Tauzin

Mane

Cunnilingus

(From the Latin *cunnus*, vulva and *lingere,* to lick).

Oral stimulation of the female genitals is called cunnilingus. It is sometimes called *cunnilinctus* or *cunnilinctio* and generally includes kissing or licking of the anal region which is known as ANILINCTUS.

The vulval odour, the so-called *cassolette*, contains chemicals that have the power to unleash in men a tremendous sexual response. For this reason, although sensible hygiene is required, a woman should never wash away all her natural scent with perfumed soaps and vaginal deodorants immediately prior to sex. Providing he is not inhibited (by himself or his partner), a man will thus be drawn towards the vagina and will attempt to put himself in a position to become aware of the scent. There is also a strong visual voyeur appeal in being able to see the female genitals close up. As part of *foreplay**, body kisses lead steadily and naturally toward the genital area.

When a man is stimulating his partner by oral sex, and his head is buried in the vulval area, some practical problems can arise. The first is difficulty in breathing. When his tongue is thrust into the vagina, his nose is pressed against his partner's skin or into her pubic hair. A woman's thighs should be well parted as cunnilingus takes place in order not to make her partner's efforts to stimulate her more physically difficult. If a woman accidentally grips a man's head too tightly between her thighs, it can be painful. Some men wear glasses, and, at the risk of appearing comical, they may prefer to keep them on during lovemaking as seeing the actual physical arousal of a partner's genitals can be very exciting.

A common position for a woman to enjoy cunnilingus is by kneeling astride her partner's head and facing his feet. The effect of this position is almost as if she were kissing his lips with her vulval lips. This is fine, but cannot be prolonged, as a man will soon get a stiff neck from the effort of holding his head erect enough to participate actively while in this difficult physical position.

A good position is for a woman to lounge back on a chair or bed, with her thighs widely separated and her vulval area extended well out over the edge, while making sure her back is comfortable, perhaps supported by a pillow. Her partner can then sit on the floor and nuzzle her deeply and still be comfortable. Should she be standing up, it is much harder for the male to reach her with his tongue or do anything more than kiss the most forward parts. If a woman prefers cunnilingus in a standing position, it is best for her to stand with her legs far astride and almost over his head. He can sit and lean back on his hands facing up toward her. As he is using his hands for support, it helps for her to part her vaginal lips for him.

One of the best positions of all is for a woman to lie flat on her back with her partner kneeling astride her head and facing her feet. He pulls up her thighs and parts them by keeping his elbows behind and between her knees. This position lays the entire perineal area open. He can easily press his tongue flat on the vulva, moving it gently for small distances in all directions. Broad, sweeping licks across the area are stimulating too. According to the request of his partner or their mutual experience, he can use licking movements of the tongue-tip or nibbling lip movements all over the area and especially around the clitoris, while as a woman becomes sexually aroused he can gently suck on the area of the clitoris increasing the sucking movements as her orgasm approaches.

Many men will have experienced their partner not being particularly aroused by cunnilingus. Various reasons for non-arousal by such a highly erotic technique (if performed by a skilled lover) include the fact that most of the sensation of a saliva-coated licking tongue will be lost as a woman's own natural lubrication increases. Also a thrusting and licking tongue may not sufficiently stimulate the clitoris to bring a woman to orgasm. Sucking technique can skilfully bring on orgasm as a woman's lover will discover with practice. Probing movements of the tongue as far up and down the vagina as possible is another technique to be used, as is hard side to side pressure of the tongue against the walls of the vagina.

Robert Stanley

Soixante-Neuf

This is French for the number 69. The numerals symbolically represent two people lying curled together head to toe—a position that allows mutual oral sex. The widespread practice of '69' is an extension of the much sought-after simultaneous orgasm: couples wish to give pleasure to each other, receive pleasure themselves and achieve orgasm at the same time. As a change from more routine sexual practices, enjoying the sight, flavour and aroma of the genitals while achieving orgasm is very exciting.

Not all partners find it easy to engage in oral sex at the same time. Gentle '69', with the couple lying on their sides facing each other, works best when both people are of much the same height. More vigorous play, especially where they have markedly different physiques, becomes more difficult except for the very agile. Despite some limitations, mutual oral sex can be a enjoyable part of love play, and can lead to intense mutual orgasm.

9

POSITIONS

Change and variation within the
scope of average partners.

Positions

Humans are the only 'higher animals' to make love face-to-face habitually, but that is not the only possible way. Human anatomy is such that the body can be twisted into a considerable number of positions for any physical activity, including sex. Furthermore, people's curiosity, adventurous impulses and desire for variation encourage experiment. At many other times and places, men and women have favoured different positions for sex—face-to-face sex has not always been the choice.

There are hundreds of books which dwell at length on the pros and cons of different sexual positions. One of the most famous is the KAMA SUTRA, an ancient Indian treatise on the arts of civilized living, including love. There have been claims that there are far in excess of a hundred different positions possible, but many of these are so complicated as to be hardly worth trying. Others are frankly uncomfortable or downright dangerous for people with delicate limbs, arthritic joints and so on. A large proportion of the variations in position only differ from each other very slightly, depending on the placing of fingertips or direction of the lover's gaze.

Whereas a few couples may seek repeated new ways to have intercourse, the vast majority are contented with one or two positions with only occasional departures to more exotic techniques. The important thing is to try different positions and discover which ones both partners enjoy most.

The two most widely known positions for sexual intercourse are: the familiar so-called 'missionary' or face-to-face position and the rear entry position. Either can be performed with the male or female on top. Face-to-face intercourse with the woman supine or lying on her back is a popular choice for a large majority of people. One reason for this is conditioning . . . it is what they are used to, it feels right, natural and safe in its familiarity.

Just as important is that in this position the hard ridge of pubic bone across the male abdomen above the root of the penis presses against the area surrounding the clitoris. The wiry male pubic hair is crushed against the female pubic region. In and out movements of the penis alternatively pull and relax the labia majora and with them the hood of the clitoris. This combination

of pressure and pulling can stimulate the nerves which arouse the clitoris, and eventually bring on a woman's orgasm, while the suction of the vagina on the penis provides stimulation to orgasm for a man. To increase female pleasure further during intercourse, one or other partner may reach down and draw the clitoral hood back. As the woman approaches orgasm the man can support himself by his feet and hands and gently rub his pubic bone region over the area of the clitoral shaft which greatly increases stimulation for both.

There are other advantages of face-to-face intercourse. The breasts and nipples (of both partners) are available for stimulation. Heads are close for intimate conversations, although vision tends to be limited and with couples to whom this is important it is better to move a little further apart. If a man gets up onto his knees and spreads a woman's legs apart, her genital *odour** can be appreciated. A pillow or two under the woman's head and shoulders gives her a better view too. One placed under her hips or the small of her back varies the angle of her pelvis and thus the direction of penetration. The man, too, can make his penis touch different areas of the vagina by angling his hips. He can also grasp the root of his penis by hand and direct its pressure.

The alternative position with the woman on top, while still facing her partner, may be welcome if a man is very heavy or after surgery or illness if deep penetration is unwelcome. Also, when a woman is on top she has control of timing and depth of penetration. She can also position her clitoris in the most advantageous spot to achieve orgasm and control rubbing of the clitoral area. Additionally, a woman can stimulate her own clitoris at the same time, or the man can do so while penetration is taking place. The man is able to reach around and caress her buttocks, as well. Many women are only able to achieve orgasm in sexual intercourse while on top because of the angle of stimulation of the clitoral shaft and hood. This is not unusual.

The alternative to face-to-face intercourse is known as FLANQUETTE. Instead of the man's legs being between the woman's, they are astride one of them. Correspondingly hers must be astride one of his. One apparent benefit of this position, apart from novelty, is that different areas of skin, in particular the inner surfaces of the thighs, come into contact with the partner's skin, and partners are able to caress

and stimulate different body areas. The angle of entry into the vagina is also different.

The other main group of intercourse positions involve entry from the rear. These positions are called CROUPADE. Rear entry of the penis into the vagina can be effected with the woman standing, touching her toes, kneeling, lying or the man sitting astride her. The male should bear in mind certain essentials in each instance. If a standing position is used, a woman will need steadying so she does not fall; if touching her toes she is even more likely to overbalance. While kneeling, it is a temptation for a man to rest his weight on her, which could be uncomfortable or hurt if her back is not strong.

A rear entry position is the nearest human method to the copulation of many animals in nature. A man can watch the actions of his penis while intercourse takes place, which can be highly arousing, and he is also able to fondle her breasts easily. The degree of penetration is perhaps greatest of all in a rear entry position—but it is wise for a male to be careful, as overdeep penetration can hurt a woman, especially if the angle of thrust is not straight and the penis presses on one or the other of the ovaries. Also the jarring effect of deep thrusting can reduce a woman's excitement level as she approaches orgasm even while increasing a man's. For a woman, the rear entry presents certain drawbacks besides the supporting of a man's body weight. The clitoral area is not stimulated, but her partner can redress this by gently massaging her during intercourse. She, in turn, can reach back between her own legs and fondle his testicles.

Rear entry can be effected with the man flat on his back and his partner lying on her back on top of him. Depth of penetration is limited, and thrusting movements of the penis are almost impossible, but a woman can contract and release her vaginal muscles to stimulate his penis. As a woman reaches a higher level of excitement and arches her back, his penis can easily slip out of her vagina. However, the position is warm and intimate for lovers, as the male can put his arms around her whole torso or fondle her breasts and genitals with ease.

An alternative rear entry position is called CUISSADE. The difference is that the man is astride the partner's thighs instead of being between or astride them both. Again, the penis enters the vagina at a different angle and different

skin surfaces can be touched and caressed.

Other far more exotic positions exist. There are positions in which the standing man supports his partner with her legs around his waist. She may lean over a bed or lie on her side or they can both sit in a chair. He can vary the angle of penetration and the positions of his limbs. However novel these positions may seem, they are only variations on the main face-to-face or rear entry positions, and not basically different ways of having intercourse. There are, of course, some special variations on intercourse positions which are both enjoyable and helpful for those who have some illness or disability (*disability and sex**).

There is no English equivalent for the French word POSTILLIONAGE meaning to insert the finger in one's partner's anus during love play or intercourse, or on one's own while masturbating. The practice is common to both men and women. To a lot of women, it is powerfully erotic immediately before or during orgasm. In some cases just the tip of the finger is inserted, though true postillionage implies in and out movements and rotating the slightly curved finger well inside the sphincter, and friction on the sensitive interior walls. Though fewer men than women find postillionage particularly exciting, if a finger is inserted far enough into the male rectum it can press forwards against the prostate gland. This is usually a more stimulating process and can cause ejaculation.

If a woman expresses a wish for postillionage, and this is unacceptable to the partner, she can do it for herself. Alternatively a small vibrator can be used, or, it may be found that firm pressure just in front of the anus will suffice. Finger nails should clearly be smooth and short, but even so they will become contaminated by feces and thorough scrubbing afterwards is essential.

Positions

CAPRICORN — aware

TAURUS — creative

LEO — FRIENDLY

LIBRA — PROFESSIONAL

SCORPIO — CAUTIOUS

PISCES — PROVIDER

Kama Sutra

The most famous—and earliest—classified description of coital variations is contained in the Sanskrit classic called the KAMA SUTRA ('Love-Doctrine'), dating from some time in the first five centuries AD and based on still older writings. Much of the text deals with advice on general social conduct and marriage, but its title has become synonymous with 'positions'. The part that deals with sexual practices discusses the size of genitals, touching, kissing, scratching, hitting and sounds, as well as how to vary positions. The central passages dealing with the latter are reproduced here, in the translation by Sir Richard Burton (1821-1890):

Man is divided into three classes, viz. the hare man, the bull man, and the horse man, according to the size of his lingam. Woman also, according to the depth of her yoni, is either a female deer, a mare, or a female elephant.

There are thus three equal unions between persons of corresponding dimensions, and there are six unequal unions, when the dimensions do not correspond, or nine in all.

The Deer-woman has the following three ways of lying down:

The *widely opened position*
The *yawning position*
The *position of the wife of Indra* (Indrani)

When she lowers her head and raises her middle parts, it is called the 'widely opened position'. At such a time the man should apply some unguent, so as to make the entrance easy.

When she raises her thighs and keeps them wide apart and engages in congress, it is called the 'yawning position'.

When she places her thighs with her legs doubled on them upon her sides, and thus engages in congress, it is called the position of Indrani and this is learnt only by practice. The position is also useful in the case of the 'highest congress'.

The clasping position is used in 'low congress', and in the 'lowest congress', together with the 'pressing position', the 'twining position', and the 'mare's position'.

When the legs of both the male and female are stretched straight out over each other, it is called the 'clasping position'. It is of two kinds, the side position and the supine position, according to the way in which they lie down. In the side position the male should invariable lie on his left side, and cause the woman to lie on her right side, and this rule is to be observed in lying down with all kinds of women.

When, after congress has begun in the clasping position, the women presses her lover with her thighs, it is called the 'pressing position'.

When the woman places one of her thighs across the thigh of her lover it is called the 'twining position'.

When a woman forcibly holds in her yoni the lingam after it is in, it is called the 'mare's position'. This is learnt by practice only, and is chiefly found among women of the Andhra country.

The above are the different ways of lying down, mentioned by Babhravya. Suvarnabha, however, gives the following in addition:

When the female raises both of her thighs straight up, it is called the 'rising position'.

When she raises both of her legs, and places them on her lover's shoulders, it is called the 'yawning position).

When the legs are contracted, and thus held by the lover before his bosom, it is called the 'yawning position'.

When only one of her legs is stretched out, it is called the 'half pressed position'.

When the woman places one of her legs on her lover's shoulder, and stretches the other out, and then places the latter on his shoulder, and stretches out the other, and continues to do so alternately, it is called the 'splitting of a bamboo'.

When one of her legs is placed on the head, and the other is stretched out, it is called the 'fixing of a nail'. This is learnt by practice only.

When both the legs of the woman are contracted, and placed on her stomach, it is called the 'crab's position'.

When the thighs are raised and placed one upon the other, it is called the 'packed position'.

When the shanks are placed one upon the other, it is called the 'lotus-like position'.

When a man, during congress, turns round, and enjoys the woman without leaving her, while she embraces him round the back all the time, it is called the 'turning position' and is learnt only by practice.

Thus, says Suvarnabha, these different ways of lying down, sitting, and standing should be practised in water, because it is easy to do so therein. But Vatsyayana is of opinion that congress in water is improper, because it is prohibited by the religious law.

When a man and a woman support themselves on each other's bodies, or on a wall, or pillar, and thus while standing engage in congress, it is called the 'supported congress'.

When a man supports himself against a wall, and the woman, sitting on his hands joined together and held underneath her, throws her arms round his neck, and putting her thighs alongside his waist, moves herself by her feet, which are touching the wall against which the man is leaning, it is called the 'suspended congress'.

When a woman stands on her hands and feet like a quadruped, and her lover mounts her like a bull, it is called the 'congress of a cow'. At this time everything that is ordinarily done on the bosom should be done on the back.

In the same way can be carried on the congress of a dog, the congress of a goat, the congress of a deer, the forcible mounting of an ass, the congress of a cat, the jump of a tiger, the pressing of an elephant, the rubbing of a boar, and the mounting of a horse. And in all these cases the characteristics of these different animals should be manifested by acting like them.

When a man enjoys two women at the same time, both of whom love him equally, it is called the 'united congress'.

When a man enjoys many women altogether, it is called the 'congress of a herd of cows'.

The following kinds of congress—sporting in water, or the congress of an elephant with many female elephants which is said to take place only in the water, the congress of a collection of goats, the congress of a collection of deer—take place in imitation of these animals.

In Gramaneri many young men enjoy a woman that may be married to one of them, either one after the other, or at the same time. Thus one of them holds her, another enjoys her, a third uses her mouth, a fourth holds her middle part, and in this way they go on enjoying her several parts alternately.

The same things can be done when several men are sitting in company with one courtesan, or when one courtesan is alone with many men. In the same way this can be done by the women of the king's harem when they accidentally get hold of a man.

The people in the Southern countries have also a congress in the anus, that is called the 'lower congress'.

Thus ends the various kinds of congress.

10

ORGASM

The phases of male and female climax explained by recent research.

Intercourse

The physical act of two bodies being joined together by the genital organs is called intercourse or *coitus*. In human beings, it has two main objectives which may exist together or singly: starting a pregnancy and for purposes of enjoyment. There are a number of stages to the act, but they may all be included in the statement that there is a steady increase of emotional and physical excitement during which the sexual organs become physically prepared for intercourse, followed by a period of actual contact, during which the male sperms enter the female reproductive system.

The basic process of intercourse is a simple one. Increased blood supply to the penis makes it rigid and larger than before. At the required moment, the woman positions herself conveniently and makes the opening of the vagina available. The penis is inserted into the vaginal cavity. There is then a period of friction, at the end of which small containers of semen in the male body contract and, with the aid of muscles, are forced out of the penis and into the vagina. Intercourse is then finished, the couple separates and the sexual organs return to their normal condition. This uncomplicated, fundamental physical act is, however, made much more complex by the atmosphere of emotional enjoyment surrounding it.

When animals have intercourse, we tend to think of it as a simple procedure and often use the word COPULATION. Even in animals, however, there is often some apparent show of pleasure and enthusiasm. Certainly, there is often a great deal of preparatory courtship and love play. With humans, the latter are vastly increased. Not only are there the primitive sexual urges operating, but the act of intercourse and everything leading up to it, feels—or should feel—pleasant. Indeed, if sexual play and sexual intercourse do not seem pleasant to a person, then something is most surely wrong somewhere. All too often, the trouble with sex in a relationship comes from its sense of unadventurous sameness. As with any enjoyable sensation, people will naturally develop preferences for certain parts or aspects of the sexual act. For the most part, however, couples develop a fairly routine sexual process and this may well rob the occasion of any sense of thrill or importance.

Couples frequently restrict intercourse in such a way as to reduce it to the animal level. The man feels intercourse is his regular need and right. The woman feels it is a comfortless duty. If there is no attempt made by the partners to look nice, to develop a pleasing style, or to explore the many possibilities of a warm sexual relationship then the act of intercourse becomes a mechanical process lacking warmth or reward (*boredom**).

The anticipation of sexual intercourse can be a stimulating source of emotional strength. It can even provide a secure foundation upon which to cope with the day's business. The warmth and comfort of a deeply involved episode of love making and sexual intercourse have no equal. If it is to be so, there are two intrinsic rules to follow. The first is to aim to please your partner as much as youself. Learn what he or she likes best. Does she like slow, deep thrusts of the penis or short, fast ones? Does he like it best when he is on his back or doing it from behind on his knees? Try to tell each other the best things and encourage them. The second rule is to do what you like but not what you do not like, where possible. Clearly one partner may do some things that are not stimulating to himself or herself, just to give pleasure to the other partner, and in that way may get to like the same things together.

Lubrication

Within seconds of starting sexual excitement, the vaginal walls begin secreting a liquid which acts as a natural lubricant to the movement of the penis, converting a rough, uneven rubbing into a sliding, smooth penetration. Some women may not lubricate naturally because of hormonal changes during and after the menopause or while they are on a contraceptive pill or because of a lack of sexual excitement or because the penis has been inserted before excitement has been enhanced by foreplay. Lack of lubrication makes sexual enjoyment almost impossible for both partners, and if more prolonged and effective love play does not help, a substitute lubricant should be applied to the penis or outer and inner vaginal areas. Saliva is the simplest kind to apply, but it can increase the chances of a yeast infection or *moniliasis**. Vaseline or petroleum jelly is good but messy, but, as it deteriorates rubber, should never be used with a rubber condom or a diaphragm. Nivea cream is effective, but can soil clothing. K-Y jelly is waterbased and very suitable, although it tends to dry after a few minutes' application. Abolene cream or birth-control foams, creams and jellies are also good lubricants.

Muscle Consciousness

Around the opening of the vagina is a complex network of muscles. Within the vagina are the pelvic floor muscles which support a woman's internal organs below her rib cage. The vaginal muscles contract spontaneously around a penis or a finger and also during sexual excitement. A woman can learn to contract and release her vaginal muscles consciously. KEGEL (OR PELVIC FLOOR) EXERCISES were developed by Dr. Alfred Kegel, a California physician, as a training programme in muscle consciousness. The exercises involve the same muscle movements as are made when one starts or stops urinating, but are practised until contractions are stronger and can be kept going for longer periods of time. They can help prepare for childbirth, reduce incontinence, resist *prolapse** of the womb and strengthen female orgasm. Male pleasure is increased as well, by firmly gripping the penis as orgasm begins. Instruction in pelvic floor exercises can be obtained from childbirth groups or clinics. Masturbation with *vaginal balls** can aid muscle control.

Sounds

Some people make love in silence, others make a great deal of noise. Making love involves doing things that, in other circumstances, would be thought of as unacceptable behaviour. Part of this sex-induced release from inhibitions may be making various sounds and noises and the use of certain words and phrases. Love sounds often have a primitive or animal-like quality—grunts, gasps, moans or groans. Words used may range from sweet talk to *taboo** words. Sounds and words can be a great encouragement, and are a subtle expression of pleasure or preferences in a partner's sexual techniques. However, extraneous sounds, such as voices on a radio or television, or those produced by a squeaky bed do not usually enhance love making.

Satisfaction

The successful completion of sexual intercourse gives each partner a feeling of relaxation and pleasure that adds up to an overall sense of satisfaction. The deliberately encouraged *arousal** of sexual emotions and tensions reaches a peak and is then thoroughly satisfied by intercourse resulting in orgasm. Then, for a time, the ever-present pressure induced by the sex urge is in

abeyance. Much of a person's day-to-day feelings of competition, aggression and even routine effort are in fact thinly disguised sexual tensions. After a deep and rewarding period of sex play and intercourse these are, for a time, reduced in intensity. The physical efforts of sexual intercourse are considerable. The entire body—the circulation, respiration, nervous system and muscles—has been at a high energy output level, and it therefore becomes

exhilarated but tired. After-sex satisfaction can offer lovers such an unequalled phase of real peace and relaxation that they may sink immediately into a sound sleep without more ado.

However, they may often experience what is sometimes called the AFTER GLOW. This is a stage of physical and emotional warmth and love. The tired bodies lie together, perhaps just touching hands, perhaps still locked in the last fierce position of orgasm. The body processes subside. The breathing stills, the heart slows down, the penis and

the vagina relax. A couple may talk, perhaps reminiscing or, if married, discussing family matters. Sometimes they may discuss their recent love making. They may laugh and joke or they may say nothing and just enjoy lying together thinking their own thoughts and hearing the gentle breathing of the loved one beside them. The after glow brings a feeling of being in tune with one another, and perhaps this aspect of the joining of human bodies marks the

existence of love.

Even comparative strangers can experience a feeling of satisfaction. They may be able to talk and get to know one another better during the after glow phase when so many human barriers, personal and social, have just been lowered. Casual lovers may not experience the magical depth of satisfaction that comes to two people who have a long standing love and friendship for each other, but they certainly experience the after glow of warmth, relaxation and pleasure which follows naturally after orgasm.

Immediately after the completion of sexual intercourse, most people go through a stage of total disinterest in sex. When a man has experienced orgasm he will undergo a totally non-reactive phase when nothing stimulates him sexually. In rare cases, it may even be painful to touch the penis at this time. This stage lasts in a young man on average about 15–30 min. After that, re-arousal is much easier, especially if the woman is a skilled lover. Very few men can proceed to a second orgasm very quickly after the first. Perhaps a quarter of all young men can do so, but almost none over the age of around forty or forty-five years. Satisfaction from sexual intercourse is more profound for an older man in the first instance.

Women, conversely, in greater proportion can experience double, treble or multiple orgasms. In this phenomenon there is not such a non-reactive phase as in men, and as the excitement level of orgasm subsides to the PLATEAU PHASE just prior to orgasm, a woman can be brought to a new orgasmic peak if she is stimulated. For some women, it is irritating or even painful to have the clitoris stimulated immediately after orgasm.

No man should feel diminished by his female partner's natural ability to have repeated orgasms. He should not feel that he needs to compete because physically he is not equipped for rapid multiple erection and ejaculation. On the other hand, no one should regard a woman as a nymphomaniac because she enjoys multiple orgasm. The essence of a contented relationship is for partners to please themselves and each other to the best of their natural abilities. Sometimes the needs, abilities, and even the techniques will coincide. It is additionally satisfactory if they do. If not, it is a reflection of their love and understanding to effect a compromise. It is all a question of balance. (*Person to Person**.)

Female Orgasm

The female orgasm is in many ways similar to that of the male. It is usually, but not always, centred in and around the genital organs. Women can achieve orgasm from stimulation of various parts of the body especially the nipples and the mouth. Even so, most report that they also have sensation in the vagina, and can masturbate at the same time—if not with the hands, then by pressing the thighs together, contracting the muscles in that area and moving.

In the female, four quite distinct phases are involved in the process of orgasm. (They also exist, but are less distinct, in the male.) The phases are *excitement, plateau, climax* and *resolution*. The EXCITEMENT phase, as the name suggests, is that of a steadily mounting sexual awareness. The genitals are being prepared for subsequent stages. A series of nerve impulses from the highly sensitive tissues in the genitals enter the nervous system and pass up through the spinal cord to the brain. The brain, where all bodily sensations are assessed, in return records an emotional feeling and directs a response. Gradually an extra amount of blood is pumped into the walls of the vagina, into the vaginal lips, inner and outer, and especially into the clitoris. These all become swollen and tend to bulge and become pinker in colour and warmer to the touch. In this condition they become still more sensitive to stimulation. At the same time, other bodily functions react. There is faster breathing, an increased pulse rate, a reduced awareness of other stimuli like noise, disturbance, cold or uncomfortable surroundings. The entire action of the body becomes engrossed in and obsessed with the sexual approach to orgasm. Involuntary movements, writhing limbs, jerking muscles, gasps, grunts, groans are all to be found in some women. This phase corresponds to erection and mounting excitement in the male.

Usually what is called a PLATEAU phase is then reached. In this there is little, if any, increase in excitement. The women has reached a level at which, for a while, she remains. She is largely oblivious to her surroundings and is closely, and indeed perhaps totally, involved with her sexual emotions and little else. Involuntary movements continue but respiration and pulse rates do not go on increasing.

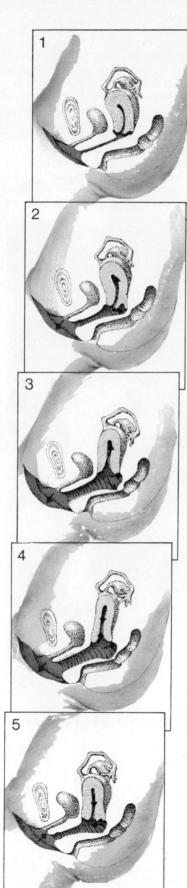

They may actually reduce a little. During this phase, couples who are experienced may separate and re-join in a variety of different positions, or may alternate periods of oral sex, hand and tongue caressing and so on. This is a phase which most people find the most rewarding. With practice, it can be prolonged for as long as is wished, but there is nonetheless a strong instinctive tendency to rush forward to the next phase. While this may be good on some occasions, it is not to be compared in general with the rewards of long and skilled plateau-phase love making. It is harder for the male, although he, too, can contribute. Success depends on becoming familiar with the approach to the next phase and developing techniques of holding back.

Eventually, the next stage arrives. This is the orgasm itself or CLIMAX phase. Quite suddenly, all control is lost and the process becomes involuntary. The muscles in the genital area contract powerfully and usually in a series of jerking convulsions. Other body muscles, especially in the abdominal wall, do the same. There is a peak experience of emotional thrill, the breath is held and often the face is contorted. This phase coincides in feeling but not necessarily in time with *ejaculation** in the male, and is popularly referred to as 'coming'.

Finally, there is the RESOLUTION PHASE when excitement and blood engorgement steadily reduces. Commonly, too, there is a relaxed and languid period when feelings of affection and companionship tend to supersede the sexual longings. At this stage, many women can be re-excited to start the cycle again. Most women can experience more than one orgasm; it is mostly a matter of motivation and practice. There is no truth in the idea prevalent among men that at orgasm women also ejaculate 'juices'. There is a *lubricant** that is secreted from the walls of the vagina, however, and sometimes this is enough to be noticeable to a male partner.

Much confusing nonsense has been talked about a supposed difference between vaginal and clitoral orgasm. The distinction is pointless, as most women do not notice a difference. Occasionally, a woman has a preference for orgasm centred around vaginal stimulation or conversely around clitoral.

1. Normal 2. Excitement Phase
3. Plateau Phase 4. Orgasm
5. Resolution
⟵⟶ expanding or contracting

Erection

In a sexual sense, erection is the conversion of the penis from its normal condition to one of readiness for sexual intercourse. In the absence of sexual arousal, the penis is in a state of softness and relaxation that is called FLACCID. Then it is small and drawn back close to the body in the groove between the tops of the thighs. There, together with the testicles, the penis lies in a partly protective hollow. It is able to move freely as the body moves and is not cumbersome or vulnerable to injury. In its flaccid condition, the penis is unable to penetrate into the vagina as it is not firm enough to thrust aside the lips and walls of the vagina, and is also not usually long enough for insertion. In very cold conditions the flaccid penis may shrink to little more than a wrinkled tassle of skin not much more than an inch long. An average size would be about 2½ to 3in.

Erection is the stage of sexual arousal in the male which corresponds to the EXCITEMENT PHASE in the female (*female orgasm**). Under the influence of increased sexual and physical arousal, the blood supply to the penis increases. There are three areas of tissue in the shaft of the penis that rather resemble a sponge. These always contain some blood, but as erection takes place more and more blood is pumped in. The holes in the spongey tissue become engorged with blood and swell up to double their normal size or more. This increased blood content also has the effect of stiffening the shaft so that the penis eventually becomes one long and rigid shaft standing out from the body. At the same time the glans, the pink-coloured head of the penis, is also increased in size. Along with the greater blood supply into the penis, some of its vessels contract so that blood cannot easily flow out of the penis and back into the body. The result is full erection and readiness for sexual contact.

Once the penis has reached its full size the couple can position themselves for the penis to be pushed into the vagina. The penis will be long enough to span any gap between them. Initially, as intercourse begins, the penis parts the outer and inner vaginal lips (the labia majora and minora) and dilates the muscles that surround the orifice of the vagina. The very opening of the vagina is known medically as the INTROITUS and the insertion of the erect penis into it and up the vagina proper known as INTROMISSION.

There is a concern and interest among men—and sometimes women—about the entire matter of penis size. Somehow or other, a large penis is supposed to mean a greater sexual capacity and ability to satisfy women. This is a total fallacy. Undoubtedly there are women who find a large penis attractive and some probably obtain a greater degree of sexual pleasure from being penetrated by a large penis. The main appeal would obviously be visual, as there are few if any women who could actually distinguish between a six-inch long and a seven-inch long penis when it was inside of them. Still, many men irrespective of the size of their penis would wish it larger, but that is a matter of competition between males rather than actual satisfaction of women. Methods of enlarging the penis are almost always unsuccessful. Drugs have proved a complete failure.

Ejaculation

At the peak of sexual excitement, called orgasm, the adult male usually effects the sudden discharge or emission of semen from his penis. This is the phenomenon of ejaculation.

During the mounting sexual pleasure of intercourse, the penis doubles in size and is converted into a strong, bone-like projection, rigid and swollen, and capable of considerable thrusting, even if necessary, into an unyielding vagina. In the days and hours preceding intercourse sperm produced in the testicles have passed along tubes to be stored in special sperm sacks called *seminal vesicles**, near the base of the bladder. The sack walls produce extra fluid which, added to the sperm, constitutes semen. While sex play is going on, the sensations from the stroking of the penis added to emotional arousal and the other sexual sensations from the different parts of the body, induce a number of things to happen.

Semen from the sacks is steadily forced into the innermost end of the pipe (urethra) through the penis. This quantity balloons the urethral wall out perhaps to double or treble its usual dimensions. The feeling produced by the stretching walls is intensely enjoyable. Throughout this phase, the experienced lover is in absolute control. He will be able to press on to an uninterrupted swift climax, or retard the sensations in order to prolong this tantalizing and thrilling stage.

Eventually, however, if the tension is allowed to mount, the man reaches a point of no return and reflex takes over. (A reflex is a body response controlled by nerves from the spinal cord, instead of from the brain; as such, it is automatic and not under the control of the will.) From the moment the reflex starts, the whole of the subsequent action is programmed and the man cannot interrupt it. Suddenly, the entire musculature of the area around the base of penis starts to undergo waves of contraction. Excitement, physical and emotional, reaches its apex. There is an overwhelming feeling of approaching climax. All feelings like discomfort, guilt, shame and other possible unpleasant associations are blotted out from the mind. There is an over-powering and ever-increasing concentration on sexual involvement, thrusting, jerking and convulsively pushing the penis forward and upward into the vagina.

Progress becomes a breathless rush. Again, completely by reflex, the muscles around the urethra contract in a series of about six or so violent spasms. The semen pooled in the urethra is subjected to these spasms like a number of sudden, grasping pressures. It is forced, rushing up the urethra to its opening, to be spurted out as white droplets or a tiny stream. The mixed feelings of pleasure, of the hot semen gushing up and out, the repeated contractions of the inner muscles and the overall feelings of intense excitement, constitute the orgasm, culminating in the ejaculation of semen.

The time needed for ejaculation to be reached is variable. Under extremes of excitement, or when there is only a poor degree of control, ejaculation can easily be accomplished within thirty seconds. At other times, when skill is used or excitement levels are low, it can be postponed until the end of a half-hour session. Theoretically, there is no reason why it should not be delayed even longer. In fact, the really long sexual sessions that have been bragged about are surely the product of a vivid imagination: soreness of the penis and the uncomfortable slight swelling of the testicles tends to result in a bout of sexual activity being limited to within an hour. The amount of semen ejaculated is usually between .07 and .21 fl oz (2–6 ml). (.20 fl oz or 5 ml is a teaspoonful). Subsequently ejaculations are of much smaller quantities. The subsiding of the penis after erection back to its resting or flaccid state is known as DETUMESCENCE.

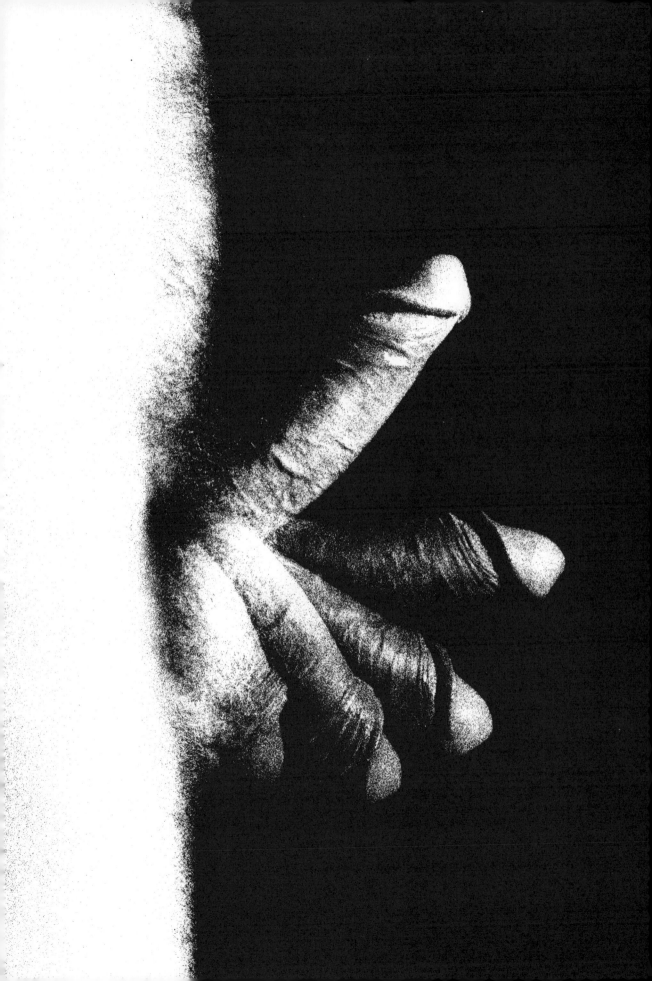

Orgasmic Response

Orgasm, the peak excitement of the sexual act, is also probably the most extreme form of associated emotional and physical elation known to humanity. It has always held a unique fascination. Sadly, until the last two decades, public discussion of the topic was almost impossible. Even in learned and scientific circles some subjects were taboo. Today it is still difficult for many people to be frank about sex.

It is essential for the advance of learning that sex should be studied in detail. Yet for anyone, even a dedicated doctor, to be involved in such studies, is often to attract professional and public disapproval. Some courageous

urement. Myths and legends abounded. Did orgasm cause fatigue and weakness? How many times could or should people experience it? How do people reach orgasm? Is it the same mechanism for men as for women? How do orgasmic faults lead to sexual problems and vice versa? What are the pros and cons of simultaneous orgasm? What happens to the body chemistry during orgasm? How can problems be overcome and sex lives improved? In other words there was no apparent limit to the study field of orgasmic response, so sparse was the scientific knowledge on this subject.

Research teams began by conducting in-depth interviews about sexual habits, but there was a weak spot. In sexual discussions, more perhaps than in anything else, people tend to conceal

assembled that could be inserted into the vagina. They could film the wall of the organ and also the opening in the neck of the womb during orgasm. Other instruments could measure the amount of fluid produced as lubrication by the countless tiny glands in the vagina. Everything was tested, from the best ways to increase the lubrication to the actual chemical composition of the fluids. All other body functions were monitored, often by instruments wired on to the body.

Brain waves, heart beats, pulse, blood pressure, breathing rates, temperature and the blood chemistry were continuously recorded through varying periods of sexual activity. Even the things that cause attraction and the start of excitement were tested. Miniaturized telemetry instruments con-

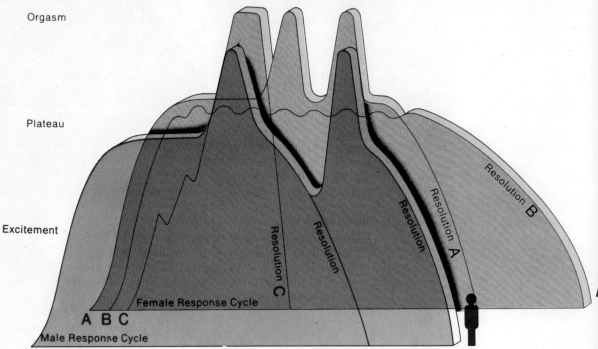

pioneers, like Kinsey, and the sex study team of Masters and Johnson, have dared to run the risk.

One of the things that needed to be studied in extreme detail is what is known as orgasmic response. This is the precise way in which the various bodily processes and systems react to sexual stimulation, and join the crescendo of excitement that culminates in orgasm. Much was already known about it, but they were individual observations. No one really knew whether his or her particular responses were unique, similar to, or identical with, anyone else's. Not only could they not talk about it, but there was no known method of assessment or meas-

what they think are disagreeable truths. They are likely to brag about their abilities and to indulge in wishful thinking. So results when put down on paper were far less than 100 per cent reliable. Next came the process of watching people in their sexual activities, at first while they masturbated themselves, then each other, and eventually during sexual intercourse. Photographs and films were made using infrared lighting of which the experimental subjects were unaware. Real knowledge about sex and orgasmic response at last began to be collected.

Subsequent stages of investigation meant the construction of highly specialized equipment. Tiny cameras were

firmed the somewhat cruder findings of Masters and Johnson. Cheesecake and beefcake pictures, pornographic stories and films, ways of giving and receiving sexual stimulation and so on were studied. Outside factors were discovered, like the way unnoticed smells of the sexual organs, when introduced into the atmosphere in tiny quantities, can initiate the phases of orgasm. Already we know there are basic processes in orgasmic response. Certain phases and sequences are common to most people, but, as with almost everything else, there are aspects of detail in which the orgasmic response experienced by each one of us is very individual.

11

PERSON TO PERSON

Needs from the emotional side of
a physical relationship.

Tenderness

The most rewarding form of any human activity is one that draws on the whole of the human personality. Human loving is a total personal experience, evoked and enriched by the need to share, and by the quality of the sharing.

The longing to share nearness and tenderness, to be close, to see the wanted one if only for a minute—these are the universal yearnings of lovers, celebrated equally by Shakespeare and pop lyrics. Gentleness is one of the sexiest of qualities; it carries proof of how precious the other is. For the same reason, each partner seeks to give, and to receive, tokens of affection: a kind thought, a touch, a gift, a kiss. Every sign of kindness and caring is treasured, and every evidence of their lack is experienced as a hurtful rebuff.

Tenderness in loving is not sentimentality. It is deeply rooted biologically. Animals frequently show great tenderness towards one another. They will snuggle close, nuzzle, touch, cuddle and carefully groom one another. Some animals and birds pine for absent mates and go into ecstasies of delight upon reunion. In human beings these propensities are, of course, more highly developed, manifesting themselves with greater sensitivity, awareness and imagination.

In our society, there is still to be found a fear of feeling, 'a taboo on tenderness'. Inhibition of feeling is a serious obstruction to happy love. Consequently, lovers have to find out how to enter each other's inner worlds so that feelings can be fully shared and, if necessary, adjusted to each other's. This is obviously possible only in a context of trust. People will not reveal themselves fully to those in whom they lack trust. Trust and love are very closely related.

COMPATIBILITY is the temperamental capacity to live and grow together. A person may feel attracted to another in an absorbing and exciting way, but a short period of living together may bring out incompatibilities that gradually weaken and, finally, sever the bond. Compatible partners battle it out and come to a better understanding of one another as a result. Incompatible partners bicker endlessly and grow steadily further apart. Compatibility also has a physical dimension, but today serious physical incompatibility is likely to be discovered prior to marriage. Absolute physical compatibility from the start is a rare bonus.

COMMUNICATION between partners is basic to generating good love relationships and the development of mutual compatibility. Many people however, find it extremely difficult to discuss their love life with partners. This is to some extent a hang-over from the sexual inhibition of earlier times, but it is also the outcome of shyness over the intimacy of sex. This shyness is exacerbated by the widespread anxieties concerning sexual performance. Partners are afraid that any comment about the other's loving will be interpreted as a criticism of skill, or a charge of ignorance. Small irritations can be left unresolved and may, in time, grow into big frustrations. Postponement of discussion is always a risk to future relationships because, sooner or later, one of the partners is likely to protest about a long-standing frustration, to the horror of the other partner, who may feel diminished and angry by the thought of the back-log of displeasure. No one 'knows it all' where sex is concerned. What delights one partner may fail to stir another. The only way to find out what pleases, and what does not, is to talk about it, or gently to steer hands to where caresses are desired. Such simple requests as 'You must tell me what you like' and 'If I do anything you don't enjoy, just tell me' are a great help in ironing out uncertainties. The reply may well be 'I love everything you do', but the way is opened for an occasional word that can do so much to maximize physical relationships.

Communication out of bed is also important. When feelings, attitudes or ideas are definitely affronted by something the partner does or says, the matter should be raised at once, or quite soon after. Feelings may be a little hurt but nothing like as much as if the issue is allowed to fester. Some people are inclined to nurse a grievance against their partners rather than to share it with them. Such behaviour can deeply impair a relationship.

But communication is not only for negative issues. Appreciation is the nourishment of love. 'What a gorgeous meal!' 'You look lovely!' 'Thank you for calling me today' and a hundred other remarks guard against any feeling of being taken for granted.

HUMOUR is both an enhancement of the love relationship, and a safeguard against embarrassment. Human loving should always be treated as significant, but should not be solemn. On the other hand, anything flippant can turn people off. The humour of lovers should always be light-hearted—laughing with, not laughing at. Humour and ridicule are very different things; the former builds trust, the latter destroys it.

If it might be said that passion is the flowering of love, then tenderness, caring, affection and trust are its base and nutrients. Passion comes and goes, person-to-person warmth and communication grow stronger when the relationship is right.

Facing Facts

Human loving hovers on the border between fantasy and reality. Dreams of being, or finding, the perfect lover conflict with the realities of human imperfection. Conversely, shaky confidence and dreads about personal inadequacy can vanish in the mutual warmth of understanding love. There are no perfect bodies, no super-lovers. What certainly exists is the need to give and to receive love. These are real needs, which can be answered in reality. The quest for sexual fulfilment is really the search for a relationship in which fantasy can be replaced by delight in one another as each actually is.

Simulation

The achievement of a satisfying orgasm by both partners whenever they make love is so over-emphasized today that it can lead to one or the other making a charade of having been more fulfilled—complete with sound and action—than is actually true. 'Faking it' can be meant kindly, but it involves risks. Sexual relationships should be frank. Once pretence enters in, it can lead to snags. Vitality and virility, and even desire, fluctuate. Failure to achieve orgasm or even erection on a particular occasion is of no real consequence. Lovers need to accept the ups and downs of sexual performance.

Aggression

If human beings did not have the urge to express themselves, we would be a race of nonentities. We have to attack life boldly if we are to make any ground at all. Inevitably this brings us, at times, up against others and up against situations. To help us deal with such conflicts we have in our brains what might be called an area of aggression. If we feel challenged, threatened, block-

ed, or belittled by others, or if circumstances or people frustrate us, then this button is touched, arousing hostility and anger. This is nature's way of bringing us to a pitch when we can act against what is obstructing us, or threatening us. The antithesis is the flight response—to get out of range of the threat.

We should accept our feelings of hostility and anger without guilt. To repress aggression because we are ashamed of it may lead to devious,

unconscious ways of expressing hostility and may produce neurotic symptoms. The pet lover who declares that people who are unkind to animals should be flogged without mercy is a classic example of this. A child crushed by a dominant parent may turn into a well-behaved child who gives away his tensions by biting his nails ferociously.

FRUSTRATION is particularly likely to produce an aggressive response. A curious propensity of frustration is that it often leads to transferred aggression. A man who has had a bad day at the office may take it out on his wife and children when he gets home. Or the arrival of annoying news in the mail may make a person bad-tempered. If it is not possible to attack the source of the frustration directly, anyone or anything near at hand may bear the brunt instead. Should he decide to write a strong letter as a riposte to the unwelcome news, the bad temper may clear away immediately.

Some members of society feel frustrated by society itself, and release

their aggression on it by attacking, or ouraging, society in a variety of ways. Modern urban societies are very likely to frustrate young males by denial of personally fulfilling objectives and outlets. Thwarted young men turn to collective acts of violence.

Juvenile vandals or football hooligans ease their everyday sense of frustration at the expense of the environment or of innocent bystanders in random violence. Others who band together like the HELL'S ANGELS, prefer to ritualize their violence, but are often not so sinister as they try to look. Their sado-masochistic paraphernalia of black leather and chains may be less of a threat to society than a protective covering for the wearers' sense of inadequacy.

The cult of group *rape** or a GANG BANG appeals to Hell's Angels and similar male cliques because most of the members are insecure adolescents, who are actually rather frightened of women. They can support each other in ravishing their victim, whom they may select because she is too frail to threaten their self-esteem. Their attack upon their victim may be a measure of their frustration at their own inadequacy or ineffectiveness, and also an act of hostility against women in general because they feel that women represent a threat to them.

Aggresion also has a positive role in sex and love. Equality of the sexes does not take away the urge of men to capture and conquer, or the need of women to feel possessed. Part of the role of a woman is to stimulate and provoke her lover into the passionate response she needs for her own fulfilment. A woman can, and should, play an active part in love-making, yet the male is the one who enters and the woman is the one who is entered, so that a certain primal element of 'male dominance' will still be present, however understanding and reciprocal loving becomes. The mixture of dominance, acceptance and reciprocity in all this will depend on the individual natures of the lovers, and their sensitivity to one another's needs.

Accepting, and dealing sensibly with one's own and others' aggressive feelings and behaviour is a crucial aspect of good relationships, including good love relationships. This negotiation will often happen gently but may become quite robust. Lovers sometimes have furious quarrels which can clear the air whereas repressing bitter feelings can lead to accumulating resentment and finally, hurtful anger.

Jealousy

Jealousy indicates an inability to share the loved person, or any aspect of the loved person, with anyone else. It is, therefore, closely related to POSSESSIVENESS. If a person feels very possessive about a partner, or a child, any sign that the wanted individual is not entirely theirs is sensed as a hurtful rejection. Jealousy and possessiveness are highly self-centred. Behind both of them lie insecurity and lack of self-confidence which are likely to have their roots in early experiences and relationships.

Everyone has twinges of jealousy at times but, at its most intense, jealousy can dominate a personality. In this form it works against its own goals because the object of jealousy is likely to resent the claims upon him or her and the limitations imposed by the jealousy on his or her freedom. Jealousy, which aims to bind, may drive the loved one away.

The best way to deal with jealousy is to accept it, admit it, but to guard against its becoming dominant, that is to seek to keep it in reasonable bounds. If it grows dark and deep and persistent and gets out of control—as in Shakespeare's Othello—then there is likely to be some acute inferiority or lack of perspective in the personality concerned. To reduce this to an acceptable level may call for professional assistance, but frankness and discussion between partners in a relationship can also help to get jealousy into perspective.

Jealousy involves unreal expectations about another person and is often particularly acute in association with *infatuation*. This is a compulsive commitment not so much to another person as to what that person is imagined to be. The loved one then becomes a symbol for all that is wonderful and desirable, and to share any part of him, or her, with another or others, seems an unendurable loss.

In recent years the attitude to jealousy has changed somewhat. It has always been recognized as a powerful, and sometimes dangerous emotion, but whereas jealousy was formerly regarded as an inevitable aspect of a loving relationship—even its protector—the modern approach is that jealousy reveals a psychological immaturity in a person's emotional response which should be outgrown as far as possible.

liness is rare, but in a mass society it is one of the commonest sources of unhappiness at any age.

Situational loneliness is the outcome of circumstances: the only child living in isolated conditions; the divorced woman with young children who has no opportunity for social life; the elderly person living alone; and many other cases. *Psychological loneliness* arises from personality traits or conflicts. For example, very egocentric people are unlikely to keep friends easily; aggressive, dominant life styles and excessive affectation tend to drive people away; or an individual may find his interests and attitudes make him the odd man out—for instance, the sensitive, introverted child—or wife—in a toughminded, extroverted family.

The antidote to feelings of loneliness is always the same—to develop stronger links with society. This may involve doing something positive about one's circumstances, reexamining one's life style, or seeking out activities with people of similar outlook and interests. This is easier said than done, but loneliness should be treated as a problem to be solved rather than as a hopeless fate.

Sexual loneliness—lacking a close, warm friendship with a person of the opposite sex or, in the case of homosexuality of the same sex—is a special case of loneliness. Marriage bureaus and various contact services, including 'lonely hearts' advertisements, exist to help bridge the gap. Alert entrepreneurs, aware of how many sexually lonely people are around in the big cities, have created the 'singles' bar' which profitably provides opportunities for customers to get together without any responsibility on the part of the owner.

SHYNESS can be appealing if it is the outcome of genuine modesty but, if at all acute, it becomes painful to the sufferer and an embarrassment to the person subjected to it. It may be the outcome of a profound sense of personal imperfection as compared to others; it may also be the result of a general inhibition about interpersonal relationships or physical contact. Voluntary techniques of social training, like group therapy, can help individuals with social problems towards more outgoing relations with others.

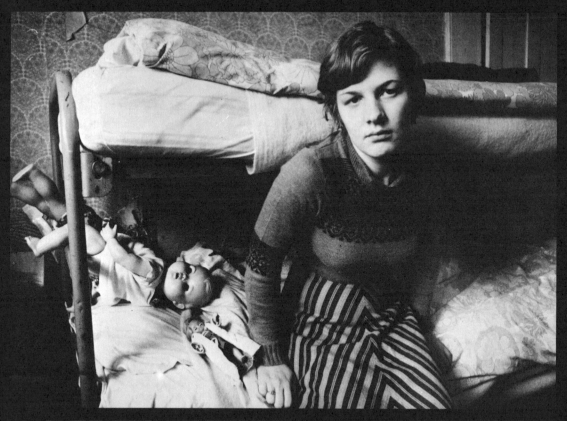

Permissiveness

The ideal of sexual permissiveness rests on the conviction that the sexual impulse is natural and good, and that it would raise the quality of sexual experience if men and women were free to make love as they fancied, with no controls other than human values and good sense. It is opposed to the regulation of sex life by religious sanctions or restrictive laws.

There is a long history behind today's relative permissiveness (mainly in the advanced western countries) and at different periods sexual repressiveness has been less heavy than at others. 'Free Love' began to be discussed and defended by intelligent writers and educationalists during the 19th century, notably by the French feminist writer George Sand, and later by George Bernard Shaw, H. G. Wells and Bertrand Russell.

Before the liberation of love life could occur it was necessary that women should enjoy equal status with men, and the drive for the emacipation of woman has always been a part of the movement towards greater sexual permissiveness. Since the Second World War, progress towards sexual liberation has been rapid. It has partial social acceptance in the form of legislative changes; the legalization of abortion, of homosexuality between consenting adults, and easier divorce.

The current difficulty is how the attained degree of permissiveness is to be used. At one extreme is the attitude that anything goes—the more sex of any kind the better. At the other—that sex is a profound human experience which, although it should be freed from prudish inhibitions and restrictive laws, cannot be treated casually without destroying its potential for fulfillment and happiness. An intermediate position is that sex is, among other things, a form of recreation which can and should bring happiness and pleasure to people without necessarily involving deep commitments. This is FUN SEX, light-hearted but not depersonalized, since pleasure is clearly not possible without one partner being *turned on** by the presence of the other.

As people vary greatly in their sexual needs, capacities and attitudes, there can be no universal 'right way' governing sexual behaviour. Nevertheless some general principles such as concern for one another, mutual respect, and care for the future generation are needed if misunderstandings, exploitation and unhappiness are to be avoided.

12 S.O.S

PROBLEM LETTERS

Write-ins and phone-ins as ways of helping people solve their problems.

Problem Letters

Each year, hundreds of thousands of people write letters to advice columnists in newspapers and magazines, seeking for help with personal problems. No one has ever actually counted how many people in the world seek guidance of this sort via the media, but it is obviously an awe-inspiring total, if the experience of the best-known writers in this field is a guide.

Why are such pleas for help made to these writers—most of whom are female? After all, in the social services of all advanced countries there is plenty of help available. A person in trouble can turn to doctors, school counselling services, family planning organizations, marriage counsellors (available to anyone who seeks their help, whether they be married or single, young or old, male or female), the various telephone befriending services, and so on.

There are many reasons, one of which may sound like a contradiction. The people who write these columns are both very, very familiar, and yet totally anonymous. Their photographs appear over their columns, and they may appear on television or on radio so the reader feels that this is someone they know intimately. Yet, at the same time, this person does not know the reader personally. A letter describing the most intimate details could be written to one of these women one day, and the writer could come face to face with her the next day and not be recognized.

That is why so many people feel they can confide in these columnists. It is often easier, especially for the young, to tell a familiar stranger about masturbation anxieties, say, than to face their own doctor across his desk and look him in the eye while talking about it.

Everyone knows that people ought not to be embarrassed with their doctors. We all know there is no need to be ashamed of any aspect of human need or behaviour—but knowledge doesn't alter emotions—and the fact is many people still feel that way.

Another reason for journalists being chosen to give help on sexual matters is that so many of them make it clear they are unshockable, they do not make judgments and they offer their help unconditionally and never, never pry or try to force anyone to do anything they don't want to do. A doctor may tell an individual to go to a hospital or try to insist on uncomfortable treat-ment. Journalists cannot do that, and readers know it.

So, that is why many of the letters are written. But *what* is written? A large group of readers want help on sexual matters. Despite attempts made in recent years to offer *sex education** in schools, there are still vast areas of ignorance which cause people much anxiety. For example, what sort of sexual behaviour is normal? What does masturbation do to you? Can love bites or hickeys cause cancer? Is circumcision necessary? Why is my penis this size and shape? Why have I grown little 'flaps' on my crotch? Why don't my breasts look like the ones in magazine pictures? What sort of contraceptive do I need? Why can't I get pregnant? What can I do about my homosexuality, transvestism, fetishism, and so on.

Closely tied up with these searches for information and reassurance is what could be called the health education aspect. People want to know why their periods aren't as regular or comfortable as they should be, what to do about VD, pubic lice, assorted aches and pains which seem to be coming from the sex organs, guidance and advice on pregnancy and childbirth, on children's development and on healthy sex education for the young. The list is considerable.

Who writes these letters? It used to be thought that only 'working-class' or 'ignorant' people would write to the 'sob sisters'. That 'middle class' intelligent people had no need of such help. In fact this is not true. The letters come from every class, every age group, both sexes. Doctors' wives and lawyers' children seek guidance just as much as labourers' sons and cleaning women's husbands. Men write fewer letters than women, but more and more are turning to them. On average between a quarter and a third of the letters come from the male of the species, and the figures are rising.

How are they answered? That is an important question, and difficult to answer with total accuracy, as the personalities of the columnists vary, and obviously must affect their points of view. One of the best known ones has herself been psychoanalyzed and so will have a psychoanalytical attitude which affects her work. Another used to write for a very outspoken magazine which specialized in rather way-out sexual problems and her approach is therefore affected by this experience. Yet another was a trained nurse and midwife before becoming a journalist, so her medical background obviously colours her replies.

Yet despite this, the 'sob sisters' are in remarkable sympathy with each other. All of them are friendly and unshockable, don't make moral judgments or push a particular religious or political point of view. All of them will pass readers in need of individual counselling or medical care to the right sort of counsellor. All of them recommend the same sort of books for those needing to 'cure' sexual ignorance, mention the same helping organizations, offer the same commonsense approach. All of them have access to specialists in all sorts of subjects, medical, psychological, sexual, legal, and social to make sure they get the best sort of up-to-date information that is available.

Many people have questioned, over the years, whether the 'sob sisters' do a necessary job or not. Some have suggested that the reason they get so many letters is not that people can't find answers anywhere else, but that newspaper editors and publishers have a cynical awareness of the selling value of other people's sexual problems. But, in fact, this accusation can be denied. While it is true that a page of sexual and emotional questions and answers will be very popular with readers, and a well known and trusted advice columnist attracts new readers, the fact is that every newspaper and magazine which takes its advice column seriously (and fortunately the majority of them seem to do so) invests far more in time and money in offering a backup service to the readers than they every make in return.

Another accusation hurled at problem pages is that they encourage people to be *voyeurs** and find pleasure and kicks in reading about others' problems. Suppose that were true? It does no harm to the readers—and some of them may, and almost certainly do, obtain considerable help and advice for their own problems by reading those of others. And if there are people who need advice columns as a sort of fetish object—well, what harm is done to anyone if it is provided for them?

Finally, one important point must be made. Even newspapers and magazines which do not run advice columns as such still get letters asking for information, help and advice. Ever since magazines were first printed, several hundred years ago, this has been the case, and it is because the letters come in that editors find it necessary to publish the pages at all.

Q Can you answer a problem from a boy whose sister reads your magazine? I've had several girls interested in me, and I've been interested in them, but have never taken them out because of my problem—I do not know how to kiss. I am just as friendly with girls as I am with boys, and have been a very close friend to one girl, so I'm not afraid of them. When I say I do not know how to kiss, I'm talking of mouth-to-mouth kiss, I'm talking of mouth-to-mouth kiss, I'm talking of mouth-to-mouth kissing and its variations (tongue kissing). Please do not say that when the moment comes it will happen naturally—all the magazine problem pages say that! When the moment does come, I want to be sure.

A When a mouth is on a mouth neither should be opened wide as if for biting an apple, but both should be parted and slightly pouting as if to receive a teaspoonful of honey. Tongues are for tasting the lips around the inner edge, the teeth (slightly metallic), and for investigating *gently* the inside of the other mouth and the other tongue that will probably dart out to meet it. The pace of kissing hots up, but, honestly, at the risk of sounding like a "problem page", your mouth *will* know what to do. Kissing is really nice. Be a good lad, won't you, and get some practice in before the big game?

After the birth of our third child, my husband bought me tickets to visit my family in Ireland. But when I arrived he rang and told me not to come home because he'd met someone else and wanted me to divorce him. I came back to try and sort things out, but I'm up against a stone wall. I've tried everything to save our marriage because, quite apart from loving him, I'm a Roman Catholic and don't believe in divorce. This woman is plain and though I don't have much money to spend on clothes, what I want is a bit of feminine advice on how to win my husband back.

Your husband sounds pretty set on what he's doing and I doubt if the Dance of the Seven Veils would move him in his present state of mind. You can't win him back by being enticing because you don't know (or you haven't said) why it was he strayed. If you know what's gone wrong in the marriage, then you have a chance to put it right. But even so, that's a two-sided effort and you have to persuade him to work at it along with you.
The Catholic Marriage Advisory Council at 33 Willow Place, London SW1, might be able to give you some support through this worrying time and to look after your best interests with regard to your children and your future.

Q Do you know the earliest legal age I can get the pill without my guardian's consent, and how do I go about it? I don't want to ask my doctor.

A There is *no* legal age limit, but the doctor concerned will take your age into account when deciding whether or not the pill is for you. There has been much speculation lately as to the desirability of putting very young girls on the pill before their regular menstrual pattern has established itself. Whatever your age, you can go to your local family planning clinic (the address is in the telephone directory) for immediate and confidential expert advice.

Pregnancy Spoiled Sex

I am twenty-one years old, have been married for three years and have a one-and-a-half-year-old son. My husband and I engage in oral sex as well as regular intercourse. Before we were married and six months after marriage I climaxed every time we would have sex. But after I became pregnant it became harder and harder to climax. We've tried different forms of sex and positions. We have even registered in different hotels under assumed names, and he would then pick me up as a date. He bought me a vibrator. The problem is I can climax within two minutes if I use the vibrator or if I masturbate, but not with my husband. Should I see my doctor about this? My husband is very considerate towards me and takes his time and concentrates on helping me climax, but with no luck.

Since you have no trouble climaxing during masturbation, and had no trouble prior to your pregnancy, the difficulty may lie in your feelings either about pregnancy or about your relationship to your husband. Sit down with your husband and examine your feelings about your first pregnancy and childbirth and any possible secret fears you may have about repeating the experience. Ask yourself how you feel about your husband's role in child-rearing and his response to you during your pregnancy. Try to separate the issue of sex from the issue of pregnancy. Evaluate your present method of birth control with an eye to determining if *you* feel safe and secure in this method. It is not at all unusual for women to have some unexplored fears about the pain of childbirth or the physical changes caused by pregnancy, and these will often surface after a first child

---

Complains of Size

I am twenty-five and when my wife and I start intercourse my penis is about five and one half inches long. My wife doesn't have any trouble taking me but the longer we go the bigger my penis gets until it's a full nine-and-a-half inches. Then my wife can't stand it any longer and I have to withdraw. Is there anything I can do about the size of my penis because it's ruining our sex life. It's also embarrassing when I wear tight pants or go swimming. Please give me some kind of advice.

That's a switch. Most men write in wanting what you're complaining about. Our urologist consultant says that once a penis is erect it doesn't grow any more and humorously wanted to know if your nose also grew four inches when you wrote this letter? Assuming some exaggeration in your figures, you and your wife may still have legitimate difficulties with the size of your penis during intercourse. There are positions during intercourse that would make your size less uncomfortable for her. If she is on top and straddling you, she can better control the depth of your thrusting. If you both face each other on your sides, the thrusting will be limited.

POSITIONING PROBLEM ♀
My man and I have been together for five years, and I really like having sex with him any way he wants it.
My problem is that when I'm on top I can never get my body to move as well as when the man is on top of me. What can we do to make the position better? Also, is there any way to have anal sex with me on top?

Miss O.P.,
Penrith

You can exercise a good deal of control in the "female superior" position by kneeling astride your lover, with your weight supported on your hands as well as your knees. It is usually more pleasurable to slide back and forth along the penis, rather than sitting and going up and down, which can force the penis into an unnatural and uncomfortable position.
To be on top during anal intercourse, try squatting over your man, facing his feet. You can control the thrusts in this position, but you need strong legs and a good sense of balance. You could try anal intercourse while seated on a stool, positioning yourself on your lover's penis, your legs firmly planted on the floor, and your weight supported on his knees and thighs.
Both of these positions could become painful for the man if his penis were bent too far in the wrong direction, such as toward his toes in a sudden rapid movement, so I would advise you to be gentle with your man.

Useful Addresses

General Sex Information and Counselling

SFSI (San Francisco Sex Information)
Box 99054,
San Francisco, CA 94109,
Tel: 665-7300
(hotline 3-9 pm, M to F)

CSI (Community Sex Information Inc)
380 Second Avenue
New York, NY 10019
Tel: (212) 982-0052 (hotline)

CSI
Box 47
Waban
Mass. 02168
Tel: (617) 232-2335
(hotline 11 am-8 pm, M to F)

Sex Information Service Program
Newport
Rhode Island
Tel: (401) 849-2304 (hotline)

United Hospitals of Newark
New Jersey
Tel: (201) 484-8000 Ext. 581
(hotline 11 am-8 pm, M to F)

ACME
403 South Hawthorne Road,
Winston-Salem
NC 27103.

Resource Center for
Human Relations,
Oakland, CA
Tel: (405) 653-8901

Birth Control, Pregnancy, Abortion, etc.

Family Planning Services,
BCHF Health Services
Administration,
DHEW,
Rockville
MD 20852

Planned Parenthood Federation
of America Inc.
810 Seventh Ave.,
New York, NY 10019 (head office)
Tel: (212) 541-7800.

National Women's Health Coalition,
222 East 35th Street,
New York, NY 10016
Tel: (212) 986-3880/685-0981

National Women's Health Coalition,
1627 Pontius Avenue

West Los Angeles,
CA 90025
Tel: (213) 826-0818

Sex-Related Diseases

New York City Health Dept
Tel: (212) 269-5300 (hotline)

Homosexuality/Bisexuality

Gay Community Service Center,
1213 N. Highland,
Los Angeles
CA 90017
Tel: (213) 464-7485

Gay Parents Legal and Research
Group
Box 82,
Mountain Terrace
WA 98043

Rape

Rape Crisis Center,
Bay Area
Women Against Rape
PO Box 240,
Berkeley, CA 94701
Tel: (415) 845—RAPE (hotline)

Women Against Rape
150 Amsterdam Avenue
New York, NY
Tel: (212) 877-8700

General Sex Information and Counselling

Grapevine
296 Holloway Road,
London N.7
Tel: 01-607-0935

Help Advisory Centre,
10 South Wharf Road,
London W.2
Tel: 01-402 5233
(hotline, 11 am-7 pm, M to F)

Gentle Ghost Help,
Advice & Information
33 Norland Road,
London W.11
Tel: 01-602 8983
(hotline, 10 am-6 pm, M to S)

National Marriage Guidance Council
Herbert Grey College
Little Church St
Rugby
Tel: 0788 72341

The Association of Sexual
and Marital Therapists
79 Harley St.
London W.1
Tel: 01-935 0616

Institute of Psychosexual Medicine
c/o Family Planning Association
27-35 Mortimer St
London W.1
Tel: 01-636 7866

London Youth Advisory Centre,
31 Nottingham Place
London W.1
Tel: 01-935 1219/8870

Birth Control, Pregnancy, Abortion etc

Family Planning Association
27-35 Mortimer St.
London W.1
Tel: 01-636 7866

Brook Advisory Centres
233 Tottenham Court Road,
London W.1 (Head Office),
Tel: 01-580 3424

British Pregnancy Advisory Service
Second Floor
58 Petty France
London S.W.1
Tel: 01-222 0985

London Pregnancy Advisory Service
40 Margaret St
London W.1
Tel: 01-409 0281/4

Sex Related Diseases

NHS Information Service
Tel: 01-246 8072
(Clinics listed under Venereal
Diseases, London Telephone
Directory)

Homosexuality/Bisexuality

Gay Switchboard
5 Caledonian Road,
London W.1
Tel: 01-837 7324 (hotline)

Friend
47 Church St.
London N.W.1
Tel: 01-359 7371
(hotline, 7.30-10.00 pm)

Rape

Rape Advice Centre
Box 42
London N6
Tel: 01-340-6913
(hotline, 01-340-6145)

13

WORDS & GRAFFITI

The other language of sex: everyday bawdy, and the scribbling on the wall.

Bawdy

Sexual encounters sometimes involve
the temporary breaking down of social
barriers. During sexual arousal, many
people like to say words and phrases
that they might not use in their everyday language. This use of so-called
'dirty' language, called COPROLALIA,
can be pleasurable and a substantial
release of inhibitions, providing one's
partner is not offended.

Drawing or writing offensive materials in public places is called
COPROGRAPHY and is often another form
of releasing inhibitions. It verges also
on sexual provocation, since secretly,
most graffiti artists are hoping to draw
attention to themselves and their sexual needs without the risk of losing
their anonymity. Some of the more
humorous obscene graffiti seen in public toilets seem, however, to be the
result of sheer inspiration sparked off
by something that has been written
there previously.

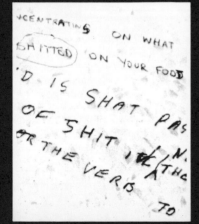

to commit ADULTERY
to have some on the side,
to sly poke, to two-time,
to have a back door affair,
to run around, to play around,
to put the horns on (her
husband), to have a slice,
to yard, to horse, to cuckold
(the husband)

ANAL INTERCOURSE
buggering, bumming,
butt-fucking/butt-hanging,
arse/ass-fucking,
corn-balling, corn-holing,
back scuttling, Greek culture,
bending some ham, goosing,
browning it, fist-fucking,
bottling, moon shot,
stern job, one up the bum

ANILINGUS
arse/ass-licking,
rimming/reaming,
cleaning up the kitchen,
blowing some arse/ass,
smearing somebody's tuna,
taking a trip to the moon,
rim shot, ring job,
tongue sandwich

ANUS
arse/ass, arsehole, back door,
brownie, bum, bumhole, bung
hole, butt, shitter, crapper,
ditch, back passage, manhole,
mustard pot, nooky, Khyber,
duff, old dirt road

BISEXUAL
AC/DC, two-way, ambi,
bi-lingual (oral sex),
bi-minded, double-gaited,
switch-hitter

BREASTS
boobs, bosom, bust, cans,
chabooms, chest, knockers,
tits, Bristols, Manchesters,
norks, melons, brown eyes,
headlights, grapefruits,
hammocks, muffins, Vaticans,
lungs, jugs, udders

BUTTOCKS
rump, arse/ass, rear, cheeks,
bum, butt, can, prat,
haunches, buns, backyard

CLITORIS
clit, button, bud, goalie

CONTRACEPTIVES
Condoms: rubbers, French
letters, cum bag. Caps: Dutch
cap. Coitus interruptus:
Vatican roulette. Rhythm
method: papal prerogative

COPROPHILIA
pound cake

to COPULATE
to fuck, to screw, to hump, to
lay, to stuff, to have a bunk
up, to shaft, to make, to
poke, to service, to root, to
ball, to bang, to shag, to
roger, to charva, to pump, to
have it up/off/away, to knock,
to score, to swive, to do
it/me, to know, to jump, to
rut, to get one's leg over, to
dip the wick, to have a bit of
the other, to roll in the
clover/hay, to get it off/on/
yours

COPULATION
beef injection, nookie

CUNNILINGUS
cunt sucking, Frenching,
eating/out, going down, eating
at the Y, muff diving, clam
diving, tonguing, plating,
licking, blowing, pussy
nibbling, box lunch, head job,
breakfast in bed
cake eater, cat lapper

EJACULATION
cuming (coming), dropping a
load, shooting, making it,
getting your rocks off,
shooting one's wad, dumping
the ashes, shooting the juice,
spending, coming off, shooting
one's load, spunking

ERECTION
hard on, stand, horn, rise,
lead in the pencil, upper,
rod, big brother, bone on,
at full strength

FELLATIO
cock sucking, blow job, BJ,
head job, deep throat, sucking
off, doing down on, nob job,
Frenching, plating, basket
lunch, copping a joint, Derby
picnic, Hoover
blow-job artist

HOMOSEXUAL FEMALE
dyke, lesbian, bull dyke, butch dyke, deisel, radish, sapphist, gay, femme, Amy-John, bull dagger/bitch

HOMOSEXUAL MALE
faggot, fag, queen (closet, drag, wrinkle, chicken), fairy, fruit, pouve, nancy, poof, poofter, radish, daisy, queer, auntie, Nellie, fem, belle, swish, latent, bender, woofter, brown-hatter, pansy adj.: gay, bent, camp

IMPOTENT
limp, droopy, at half mast, with no money in the purse, with brewer's droop

to LUST AFTER
to fancy, to be horny for, to lech after, to be randy for, to cream one's jeans over, to be in/on heat for, to be hot to trot for

LUST
charge, hot pants, hot nuts

to MASTURBATE
to wank, to jerk off, to beat off, to toss off, to beat the meat, to choke the chipmunk, to diddle/flog the poodle, to jerk the gherkin, to knock oneself off, to wack off, to bash/beat the bishop, to milk, to jill off, to play solitaire, to pound the pud, to pull the pudding, to do it yourself, to punish Percy in the palm, to have one off the wrist, to touch oneself up

MASTURBATION
finger job, pocket pool, hand jive, hand shandy, wrist job J. Arthur Rank, Jodrell Bank,

MENSTRUAL PERIOD
curse, rags on, dog days, red sails in the sunset, (to have) the painters in, flying bravo, holy week, blob, jam sandwich, wrong week, (to be) on

MINORS,
chicken, jail-bait, San Quentin quail, quail

Seducer of MINORS,
cherry picker, cradle snatcher/robber, chicken farmer

ORGY
group grope, daisy chain, gang bang, gang shay, love-in, circus, cluster fuck

PENIS
cock, prick, dick, dong, prong, pecker, willy, will, Peter, pistol, Percy, tool, rocket, rod, joy stick, meat, machine, gun, hot dog, pud, shaft, stick, sweet meat, wand, wanger, wee wee, wiener, Johnny, John Thomas, organ, one-eyed trouser snake, bishop, skin flute, Hampton Wick, poker, pole, canary, dingus, hammer, Mickey, member, one-eyed monster, putz, winkle, old man, plonker, nob

PREGNANT
in the club, up the duff, knocked up, (has) a bun in the oven, (has) broken an ankle, up the spout

PROMISCUOUS PERSON
easy lay, easy make, scrubber, swinger, dead cert, walk in, old banger, anybody's

to be PROMISCUOUS
to put out, to have a rabbit habit

PUBIC HAIR
fuzz, bush, fur, thatch, thicket, short and curlies, muff, pubes, beaver, jungle, pussy feathers, cotton, Fort Bushy

SEMEN
spunk, juice, cum (come), load, seed, cookies, goo, wad, cream, oats, baby food, jism

SEX-RELATED DISEASES
Syphilis: pox, siff, jungle rot, old Joe
Gonorrhea: clap, dose, Cupid's itch, Venus's curse, morning dew, head cold, red light receipt

Pubic lice: crabs, social dandruff, love bugs, crotch-bunnies/crickets, beattie and babs
Genital herpes: cold sores
Chancroid: soft sore
Candidiasis: thrush
Scabies: the itch

SEXUAL POSITIONS & VARIATIONS
dog style, boating, 99, 66, 69, wall job, riding St George, numbers game, one-man band, Roman position, wheel-barrow job, knee trembler

TESTES/TESTICLES
balls, bollocks, knackers, marbles, bags, family jewels, basket, groceries, lunch, orchids, jumbucks, pills, goolies, nuts, cobblers

TRANSVESTITE
TV, drag queen, paint queen

TRANSSEXUAL
TS, Swedish number

UROLAGNIA
golden showers, Boston Tea Party

VIRGIN
canned goods, cherry

to deflower a VIRGIN
to punch the ticket, to take the cherry, to blaze the trail, to christen

to lose one's VIRGINITY
to fall off the apple tree

VAGINA & VULVA
cunt, slit, crack, hole, pee-hole, coozy, pussy, twat, bearded clam, fanny, quim, box, doughnut, snatch, beard, beaver, brownie, cherry pie, cooch, fern, fur-burger/ pie/ sandwich, gash, muff, poon tang, tail, nook/nooky, happy valley, trench, snapping turtle, Y, minge, money-box, mousetrap, jelly roll, garden, hatch, promised land, rattle snake canyon, scratch,

VOYEURS
peep freaks

Censorship

Censorship has been studied intensively in the Presidential Report of the Commission on Obscenity and Pornography (1970) and in the British Arts Council Report (1969), and both found that censorship for adults could not be justified logically or socially. The Arts Council Report has been ignored, with the result that in Britain 'there is no more effective censor than uncertain law'. In the USA, President Nixon condemned the Commission's Report for 'its morally bankrupt conclusions'. Arguing a familiar *non sequitur*, he said that if it were true 'that the proliferation of filthy books and plays has no lasting harmful effect on a man's character . . . it must also be true that great books, great paintings and great plays have no ennobling effect on a man's conduct. Centuries of civilization and ten minutes of common sense tell us otherwise . . . American morality is not to be trifled with'. Campaigns by Motorede, Morality in Media and Citizens for Decency through Law groups in America and by Lord Longford, Mrs Mary Whitehouse and followers of the Festival of Light in Britain voice concern at possible harm for a 'permissive' society. However, in the words of a 1966 report by the Danish Forensic Medicine Council concerning pornography under Denmark's penal code: 'as far as the Council is aware, no scientific experiments exist which can lay a basis for the assumption that ..."obscene" pictures and films contribute to the committing of sexual offices by normal adults or young people'.

Firm evidence of unchallengeable objectivity of the harmful influence of pornography would be widely publicized, perhaps resulting in more explicit censorship than even the decency campaigners demand. But compared with the harm that imposed censorship can do to people's self-respect and the process of personal maturing, the imagined risks to children from the free circulation of pornography among adults seem negligible. In his book *The End of Obscenity*, Charles Rembar remarks: 'The true censor has objectives beyond the masking of the erotic and the indecent. The end in view is an established principle of suppression, available anywhere in the world of the mind'.

Paradoxically, censorship creates a black market in the banned material, and there is no stronger stimulant of sex than the effort to suppress it.

Graffiti

VOTRE TRANSISTOR AU RÉGIME WONDE

CHEWING GUM MAY

MARCA INTERNACIONAL

14

BIRTH CONTROL

All the means available for freeing
sex from conception.

Contraception

Contraception, or birth control, has been used throughout the world for centuries. In ancient Egypt, for example, primitive methods such as camel dung *pessaries** were used and the *condom** or FRENCH LETTER has been in use since the 18th century. In the last fifty years, a revolution has taken place both in the variety of contraceptive methods available and in the number of people wishing and able to control their own fertility. Contraception is essentially the prevention of fertilization of the ovum by sperm, in the Fallopian tubes (which connect the ovaries to the womb). With each male ejaculation roughly 40 to 300 million sperm are released into the vagina, of which millions will reach the entrance of the womb, and thousands the Fallopian tubes. Contraception can work by presenting a barrier to the sperm (diaphragm or condom), by killing them (spermicides), preventing ovulation (the contraceptive pill), or a combination of these methods (*Table of Choices**).

The first birth control clinics were opened in the US in 1916 and in Great Britain in 1921; there was initially much hostility to family planning. Changes in society, a greater say for women, the work of pioneering organizations and *sex education** programs have all helped spread information on birth control. However, the young still do not receive all the information or services required and this is partially due to the laws, medical practices and school policies as well as patterns of public morality which often refuse to accept the facts of human sexuality.

The methods of contraception available in the table of choices can be split into two categories—medical and non-medical. The medical methods need prescription and supervision by a doctor and/or a nurse, while the non-medical methods can often be bought over the counter from a variety of retail outlets. In general, the medical methods are considered to be more effective, but with regular and practised use the effectiveness of other methods is high.

The vast majority of people find a method of contraception that suits them and their partner and stick to it until such time as they wish to have a baby. Some are not quite so lucky and may have to try several methods before finding the one that suits them

best. Research into new methods is being carried out continuously and in the next decade advances might include a pill for men. Other products for women being researched or tested include a surgical implant of capsules placed under the skin containing hormones which are released throughout the year; a form of *IUD** which releases a hormone throughout the year; a 'stick-on pill' releasing hormones for absorption through the skin; and an injection to suppress ovulation which is effective against conception for nearly three months. All these will widen the table of choices and help make contraception an even more accepted part of modern living.

Today, it is generally considered a sign of responsibility to accept and use contraceptives and irresponsible to conceive an unwanted pregnancy. Yet in spite of this, there are thousands of 'accidental' pregnancies every year. Some of these fortunately end up as wanted and loved children; others are not so fortunate and become a burden for their single parent or parents. Some

pregnancies end in *abortion** or termination which can be emotionally upsetting for a woman and, as with any operation, a shock to the system. Prevention is better than cure and it is exceptionally important that birth control be universally available.

Family planning or planned parenthood are other phrases for birth control or contraception, although family planning associations and clinics deal with the whole range of sexual matters and associated problems, not just birth control. These include sub-fertility and infertility, psychosexual counselling, testing for cervical and breast disorders and generally checking a woman's health and well-being.

People wanting to know where their nearest clinic is should look in their local telephone directories or call a local government health or welfare department. Your local GP will be able to advise on contraceptives and doctors are listed in telephone directories too. A young person might prefer a family planning clinic as being more anonymous than the family doctor.

TABLE OF CHOICES

Method	Type	Available from	Theoretical Effectiveness
Oral contraceptive Pill (combination)	Medical	Family planning clinic/GP	Virtually 100%
Oral Progestogen (Progestin)	Medical	Family planning clinic/GP	98%
IUD	Medical	Family planning clinic/GP	98%
Diaphragm & Spermicide (barrier)	Medical	Family planning clinic/GP	96%
Condom & Spermicide (barrier)	Non-medical	Family planning clinic across the counter	96%
Spermicide (foams, gels)	Non-medical	Family planning clinic across the counter	60–90%* (not recommended for use on their own
Rhythm Method (calendar)	Non-medical		75%
Coitus Interruptus	Non-medical		
Sterilization			
female	Medical	Hospital	Virtually 100%
male	Medical	Family planning clinic/ GP/Hospital	Virtually 100%

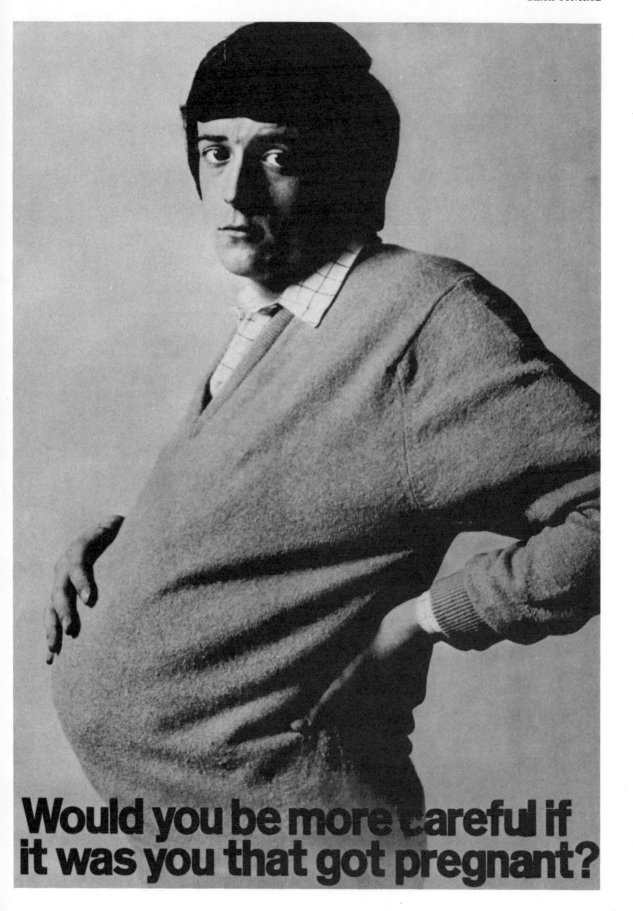

Would you be more careful if it was you that got pregnant?

The Pill

The pill, or oral contraceptive, is the most effective known method of contraception. Its introduction to the public in the 1960s revolutionized contraception. Contraceptive pills are now used by more than 50 million women throughout the world.

The COMBINED PILL, which is the commonest type, is composed of synthetic forms of two female hormones, estrogen and progestogen. By taking the pill in 28-day cycles (21 or 22 pills followed by seven or six pill-free days, respectively), these hormones induce a physical state mildy similar to pregnancy. The combined pill inhibits ovulation, alters the lining of the womb so that the implantation of the egg is prevented, and keeps the mucus plug at the entrance to the cervix or neck of the womb dry and stiff, making it difficult for sperm to pass through. As a result of these changes in the body, the pill provides almost 100 per cent protection from unwanted pregnancy. The combined pill (which comes in low dose, medium dose or high dose forms) has to be taken every day at about the same time. A woman just beginning to take the pill should also use some other form of contraception for the first 14 days to allow her body to adapt to the hormones, and the pill to build up its protection. Thereafter, at the end of each pack of pills she will take a break for either six or seven days (depending on the pill). During this time she will experience withdrawal bleeding similar to a menstrual period.

The other type is the progestogen-only pill which does not contain the hormone estrogen. This pill, which is taken continuously, acts on the body in a different way. It may or may not prevent ovulation, depending upon the woman, but its main action is to alter the balance in the secretions found in the cervix. This pill does not carry the risk of thrombosis associated with the combination pill. Doctors will often prescribe it for mothers who are breast-feeding as the estrogen content in the combination pill dries up the mother's milk and for those who may be at risk from thrombosis (blood clots) or who have had a previous thrombosis but want an oral contraceptive.

It is important not to forget to take the pill as this interrupts the build-up pattern of the hormones and may, apart from being the cause of accidental pregnancy, cause unexpected bleeding. Most containers of pills have the days marked on the back as a memory aid. If the pill is forgotten it is best to consult your doctor as soon as possible. Some pills can be taken up to 12 hours after the usual time, but caution is needed in the case of the newer low-dose pills and a doctor should be consulted if you are in doubt. If sickness or diarrhea occurs within two hours of taking a pill, it is wise to take other contraceptive precautions as well for the next two weeks or until the next menstrual period.

There are women who cannot take the pill for medical reasons, which may include diabetes, liver complaints, high blood pressure, a history of thrombosis or bad migraine attacks. There are women who, having started the pill, find it does not suit them as its side effects can cause depression, headaches, weight gain, vaginal discharge and sometimes a lessening of sex drive. These symptoms can sometimes be helped by changing to another type of pill. Women who wear contact lenses may, in some cases, need their lenses refitted. This is because, in some women, the pill alters the balance in the retention of fluid which may also affect the amount of liquid present at the front of the eye. The most dangerous side effects of the pill are thrombosis and raised blood pressure, which are uncommon. However, if a woman experiences pain or a changed sensation in her legs or arms she should consult her doctor. Modern contraceptive practice is tending to stress that very low dosage combined pills containing 30 micrograms of estrogen are preferable. Recent reports have confirmed that women over the age of 35 are at a higher risk of the serious side effects, especially if they smoke cigarettes and have been on the pill for five years or more, and these women are advised to discuss this with their doctor and possibly to consider alternative methods of contraception.

For most women, however, the pill—apart from being a reliable method of contraception—improves their health and well-being in other ways. Heavy periods and the associated discomfort disappear, skin complaints are often helped, the pre-menstrual problems of irritability and tiredness are lessened and it has also been suggested that the pill may protect women from breast tumors. Many women feel an increase in their sex drive once the fear of pregnancy has been removed.

As with all medical methods of contraception, to get the pill you have to see a doctor. Either Planned Parenthood or family planning clinics or a GP will be able to advise a woman as to what pill is likely to be best for her. A doctor or clinic will usually prescribe three or six months' supply at a time. When the woman returns for a fresh supply the doctor should check her weight and blood pressure. He may give her a pelvic and breast examination and take a pap smear to make sure everything is all right.

If a doctor prescribes antibiotics for an illness, it is advisable to remind him or her that the contraceptive pill is also being taken regularly. This is because it has been found that the drug interaction of some antibiotics with the pill may cause a decrease in the pill's effectiveness. It is usually only necessary to use an added form of contraception if the antibiotic treatment is to be taken over a long period; a few days is probably not enough to alter the pill's effectiveness. If a woman is to undergo surgery of any kind she should remind her doctor that she is taking the pill, as she should stop doing so at least four weeks before the operation.

If after taking the pill for a while a woman decides to try to become pregnant she can stop taking the pill. Most women will be able to conceive immediately. For a few, however, it might take a while for their system to become readjusted to producing eggs regularly and as a result of this, they will not have their usual monthly periods. This is called post-pill *amenorrhea**. For the majority of these women a few months will be long enough for them to readjust but they should, in any case, consult their doctor.

Opposite page
Different types of pill. The pack containing 42 pills (top, left) is a progestogen-only pill and is taken continuously. The two other brands (right and top, right) are combined pills taken for 21 or 22 days followed by respectively seven or six pill-free days. They contain both estrogen and progestogen.

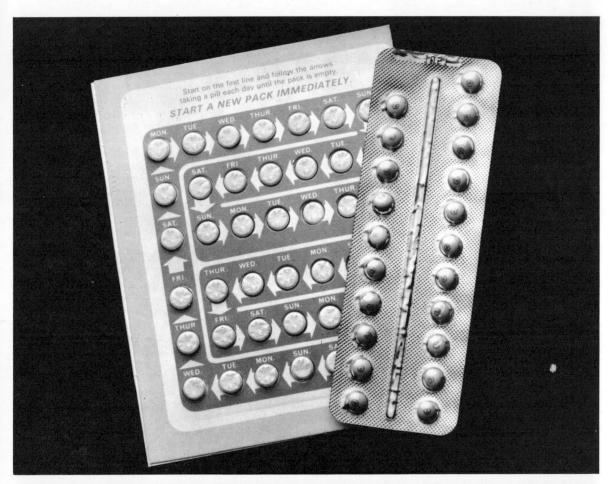

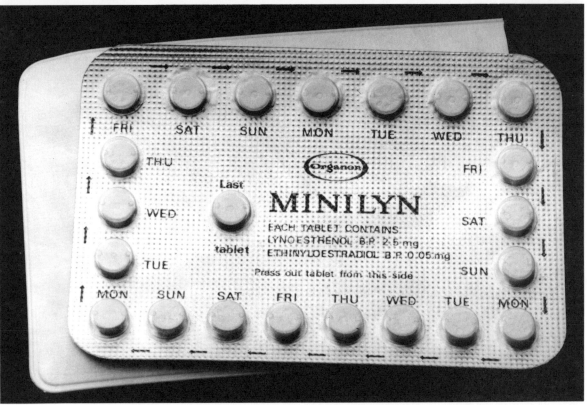

Condom

The sheath is one of the oldest and most used forms of contraception and the only reliable male method except *vasectomy** or male sterilization. Condoms are now manufactured in different colours and shapes; some are specially textured for 'extra sensitivity'. These changes are a far cry from Casanova's era when a sheath made of sheep gut, often tied with ribbon, was a popular form of condom.

If used properly, and preferably accompanied by a *spermicide**, a condom is a very reliable contraceptive with a 96 per cent effectiveness. Regular and practiced use with this method improves its efficiency as both man and woman adjust to the routine.

It is essential for a man to put on a condom before there is any sexual contact with his partner as even the moisture on the tip of an erect penis can carry sperm. A condom should be rolled on gently over the tip of the penis and right down the shaft leaving the last half inch (or teat if there is one) free. In this way the end of the condom catches and contains the sperm after ejaculation. Great care must be taken when withdrawing the penis from the vagina (while the penis is still firm) so as to be sure not to spill any sperm.

The condom should be gripped and removed from the vagina along with the penis. A new condom *must* be used for every act of intercourse.

The use of a spermicide with a condom is advisable as an added precaution and is recommended in case any sperm escape or in the event of a condom tearing or splitting. A spermicide also helps to prevent soreness in the woman's vagina from friction with the rubber, even though most sheaths are already lubricated.

Careful attention must be taken in the rolling on of the sheath so as not to damage it—for instance, ragged fingernails are a definite hazard. Vaseline or grease should never be used to lubricate a sheath as petroleum-based products like these can damage the rubber. Condoms kept in their original packaging in normal dry indoor conditions will keep for up to two or three years, but it is not wise to use condoms much older than this or where the age is unknown. There may be a date marked on the packet telling you a date after which the condom should not be used.

The disadvantage some people find when using condoms is that they can reduce physical sensation and sexual enjoyment by putting a barrier between the penis and vagina. Manufacturers are now using thinner rubber to combat this. Another disadvantage is that it interrupts the mounting emotional climate of sexual arousal.

The main advantage of the sheath lies in its easy availability. Handy pocket or wallet-sized packs can be bought over the counter from pharmacists, barbers and other shops as well as being available from coin-operated machines. They do not need medical supervision or much preparation and have no side effects unless a person is particularly unfortunate and is allergic to rubber.

Condoms have the advantage of giving some degree of protection against sexually-transmitted diseases. Some clinics issue them to patients now as an added safety measure.

Due to the popularity and easy availability of condoms several gimmicky brands are now marketed. Two types on the market which are not satisfactory go under the names of AMERICAN TIPS and GRECIAN TOPS. These do not cover the whole of the penis, just the tip, and could be left behind in the vagina on withdrawal, thus leading to an unwanted pregnancy. Another device which is being sold via the columns of men's magazines is known as a GAMIC GENETIC APPLIANCE. Although repeated requests from the medical profession have been made to the manufacturers, no evidence of safety or reliability has been forthcoming and this product is definitely not recommended.

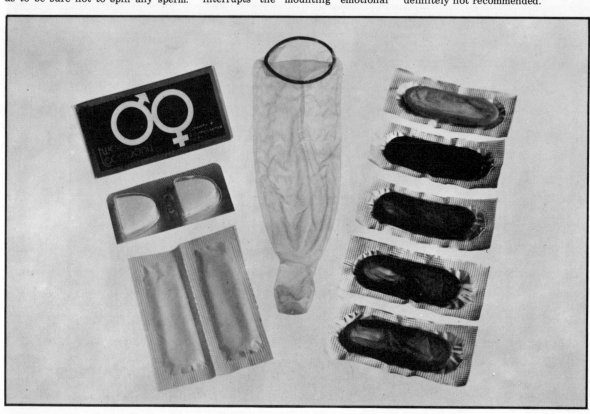

Spermicide

Spermicides are agents introduced into the vagina before sexual intercourse takes place to kill the sperm after ejaculation before they can reach the ovaries. Spermicides come in many forms: *pessaries** (or suppositories), foaming sprays, creams, and gels which are inserted by a syringe and a product called C-film, which is a spermicide-impregnated sheet of film that dissolves at body temperature. It is inserted high in the vagina by the woman or put over the top of the penis by the man before penetration of the vagina.

Spermicides, including C-Film, should not be used alone as a contraceptive method. However, they are effective in combination with other barrier methods such as a diaphragm or condom.

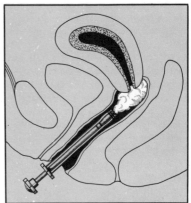

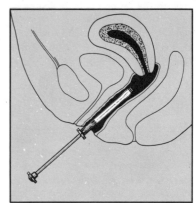

Spermicides, in the form of foams, creams or jellies, can be squirted into the vagina by means of a plastic applicator (left and above). Foaming tablets (top left) which can be pushed into the vagina with the finger, are slightly quicker and easier to use

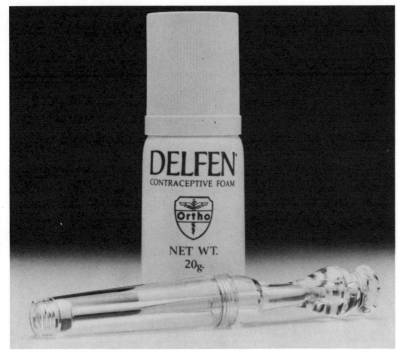

Diaphragm

The diaphragm is also known as a cap. It is called a diaphragm because when it is in position it mimics the barrier or support below the lungs and the rib cage. It gained the name of cap because it sits over the cervix at the entrance of the womb.

There are three different types of diaphragms. The true diaphragm, sometimes called the DUTCH CAP (1), is the most frequently used and consists of a rubber dome fixed onto a supple steel rim. The CERVICAL CAP (3) is designed to fit right over the neck of the womb (cervix) and because of its smaller size is more acceptable to some women. If a young woman has no previous sexual experience, the second type of diaphragm is easier for a doctor to fit. It is more difficult to learn the technique of insertion of a cervical cap, but patience and perseverence pay off. The VAULT or DUMAS CAP (2) is larger and bowl-shaped. It fits across the top of the vagina covering the cervix and is held in place by suction. A plastic variety is available for women who are allergic to rubber. All three kinds of diaphragm, when in position, form a barrier between the womb and the sperm. To complete this barrier effectively, a woman must put spermicidal cream or jelly (*spermicide**) along the sides of the cap before insertion.

If fitted and inserted properly a cap will not usually be felt. At the first visit to the GP or clinic, a doctor or nurse will not only measure and fit the cap but will usually give the woman a practice cap. She will be advised to practise putting it in, wearing it and removing it for about a week. The practice cap cannot be relied on for full contraceptive efficiency and so if sexual relations are going to take place during this time, a man should also use a condom. Medical staff will advise a woman who uses a cap for contraception to come back every six months for a check-up and to be remeasured for fit.

All three types of diaphragm need an initial measurement and fitting to be carried out by a doctor or nurse. Assessing the right size for the cap is very important and if the woman, having been fitted with a cap, gains or loses weight she must go back for another fitting. This also applies if she has recently had a baby and wants to start using a diaphragm again as her regular method of birth control.

The cap is inserted through the

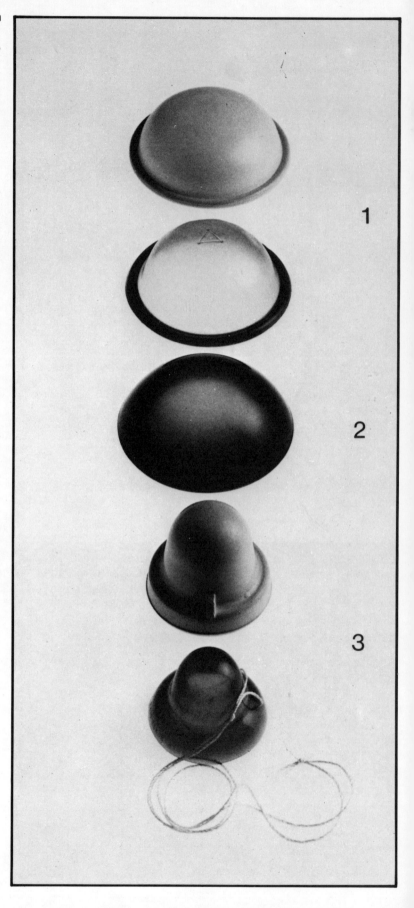

vagina by pushing the rim with a finger. It is pushed right to the top of the vagina and put into position across the cervix. The patient will be taught to feel her own cervix (which feels like a knob at the top of the vagina) and to make sure the cap is in the right position. Some women prefer to use a mechanical inserter which is a fork-like piece of plastic, rather than the fingers.

Although a diaphragm can be put in anytime before making love, if this is

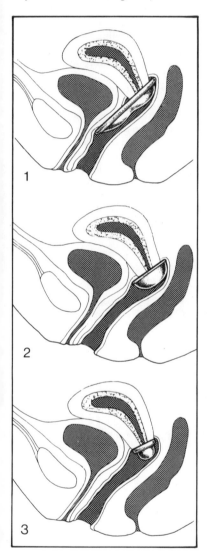

1

2

3

more than three hours before, extra spermicide should be put into the vagina without removing the cap. This spermicide could be a pessary, cream or jelly. The cap should not be removed for at least six hours after the last intercourse. It can be left in longer, but not for more than 24 hours without taking it out and cleaning it. Great care must be taken to ensure that the diaphragm is properly cleaned or the rubber will rot and develop holes in it. A cap should

be rinsed in warm water using only mild soap. Strong soaps and detergents must be avoided as these damage the rubber; so do vaseline or grease of any kind. Preserving powder can be dusted over the cap after cleaning. No cap should ever be stretched over sharp fingernails for obvious reasons.

Some women worry if their periods start while their cap is in position. There is no need for concern as the blood will collect in the cap and may eventually run over if menstrual flow is heavy. The cap can be safely removed at any time and the usual cleaning procedure followed.

Some people do not like the cap because they feel it interferes with the spontaneity of sexual intercourse, but it has the advantage of having no medical side-effects. Used properly with spermicides, it is a very reliable method of contraception and with regular and practiced use its effectiveness is second only to the *pill**.

Pessary

(From the Greek, *pessos,* a pebble or smooth stone.) The pessary is a long established form of contraception and dates back to ancient Egypt. Women have long been aware that inserting some kind of obstruction to sperm into the vagina might prevent an unwanted pregnancy. Some pessaries were so primitive that their success was severely limited, but today we have sperm-

icidal pessaries or suppositories which are used in conjunction with another 'barrier' form of contraception. For instance, used with a *condom** or *diaphragm**, pessaries complete the barrier against invading sperm. For greatest protection against an unwanted pregnancy spermicidal pessaries should not be used on their own. Pessaries are not only used for contraceptive purposes but to treat various vaginal disorders and infections, although these will not contain a spermicide but another active ingredient to treat the disorder.

Inserting a pessary is a simple procedure, just like using a tampon. By using the tip of a finger, the pessary can be pushed up to the top of the vagina. Once in the vagina, a pessary dissolves; some produce a foaming substance. A pessary should always be put in three to five minutes before sexual intercourse to allow it to dissolve completely. As pessaries melt so easily, they should be kept in a cool place before use—and in the refrigerator in particularly hot weather.

Some people may prefer to use pessaries (along with a barrier method of contraception) because they are easy to obtain—they can be bought along with condoms from any pharmacist.

Most women who start on the contraceptive *pill** for the first time will be advised to use condoms and pessaries for a two-week period to act as a back-up method of contraception; this is because the pill takes 14 days (in the first cycle) before it becomes fully effective.

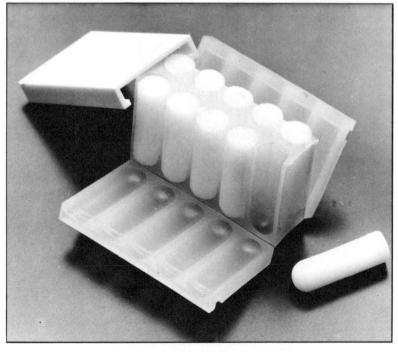

Rhythm Method

The rhythm method is the only method of contraception which is approved by the Roman Catholic Church. Their main opposition to contraceptive methods is that these artificially interfere with the natural course of procreation. Hence this method's other name is 'natural birth control'. It has been in use since the early 1930s when it was known as KNAUS'S METHOD.

The rhythm method essentially consists of determining the time of ovulation in a woman's cycle and abstaining from intercourse during the fertile days before and after. Generally a woman produces one egg per month in the middle of her menstrual cycle. This egg can survive once inside the womb for at least two days. The male's sperm may also survive, once inside the womb, for up to three or five days. To allow for individual variations, several days in the middle of the woman's cycle must be counted as unsafe. If a wo-

man has her period on the average of every 28 days she will probably be safe from the beginning of her period until 10 days later and from the eighteenth day after her period until her next period. Between the tenth and the eighteenth day is the most likely time for a baby to be conceived. The later time in the cycle is safer than the earlier.

Menstrual cycles should always be counted from the first day of one period to the first day of the next. Two ways in which to calculate an individual woman's safe period are known as the calendar method (A) and the temperature method (C). With the calendar method it is essential that a regular and accurate check is kept of the menstrual cycle. To do this the first day of every period should be circled on a calendar and then an accurate record kept of the number of days between each cycle. This must be done for at least six months and preferably a year, before the method can be used properly.

There is a simple formula to work out the safe periods. From the record

on the calendar find the shortest number of days between day one and the start of the next period. Let us say this is 26. Subtract 19 from 26 which leaves seven. Then count seven days from day one of the last period. Day seven is then the first unsafe day. Then from the record find the longest number of days from day one of the period, let us say this is 30. Subtract ten from 30, leaving 20. Then count 20 days from day one of the last period. In this example, day 20 is the last unsafe day. After this the calendar can be marked for each month, circling the first day of bleeding and then crossing out the unsafe days when making love must be avoided.

The temperature method of gauging the safe period is more reliable. A women's temperature usually drops slightly at the time of ovulation (when the eggs are produced), which normally occurs about 14 days before the next period is due. The temperature rises to a high level immediately afterwards. When the temperature has stayed at this higher level for at least three days,

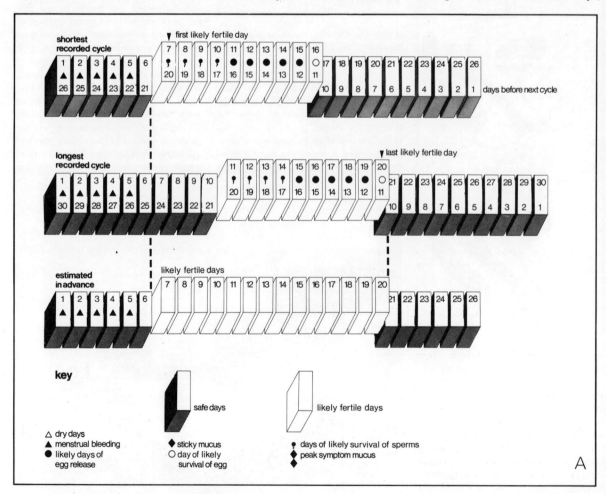

the egg cell is beginning to disintegrate and is unlikely to be fertilized. To keep a check on this method the woman should take her temperature every morning and mark it on a special chart. It is fairly safe to make love on the fourth day after the temperature has risen and remained at the higher level. This method is more trouble than the calendar method but it is probably more reliable. Special charts for both of these methods are available from family planning clinics and from doctors.

It is difficult to be certain of the safe period to have intercourse since ovulation can occur at different times in the month if the woman is ill, upset, has moved to a different climate, or for a variety of other reasons, which could mean that all the calculations become invalid. It also means that love making is limited to very few days each month which may prove unsatisfactory for the couple concerned.

The rhythm method cannot be looked on as reliable for women who have irregular periods. Neither is it reliable for women who have just had a baby,

since it usually takes three or four months for periods to return to normal. For women who are going through menopause or change of life the irregularity of their periods may make this method unsafe although at this time their fertility is low. Those on a diet or taking drugs or pills of any kind likely to upset the delicate hormonal balance which controls the egg release system (ovulation), or those under stress, would be safer using another method.

As the rhythm method is a natural form of birth control, it is understandable that many researchers have devoted their studies to finding more accurate means of assessment. One such method which is presently being investigated is known as BILLINGS OVULATION METHOD (B). This method relies on the woman coming to understand the character of her own cervical mucus or discharge. During different times of the month the secretions (discharge) will vary between 'wetness' and 'dryness'. In the first few days of a woman's cycle she will produce a dry

discharge. The secretions will then become white or cloudy yellow and be slightly sticky in consistency. At ovulation the discharge increases in quantity and has an egg-white type of consistency. Following ovulation the mucus decreases and again becomes cloudy and sticky. At the time before a period the secretions become clear and watery. This safe period is meant to be the dry days after a period and the clear watery phase which comes in the pre-menstrual stage.

With all rhythm methods it is important to stress that calculations or assessments must be accurately carried out and recorded to gain maximum effectiveness, which even then is not too high. Due to the fact that bodies are not fully automated and regulated, the rhythm method which is based on one of the natural *biological rhythms** is unreliable. As famous population expert, Dr. Paul Ehrlich, once said, 'People who use the rhythm method are commonly known as parents'.

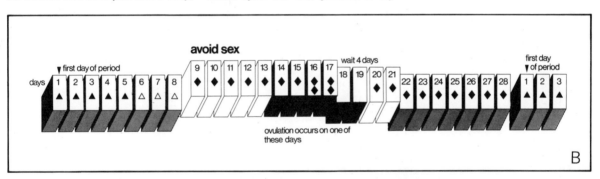

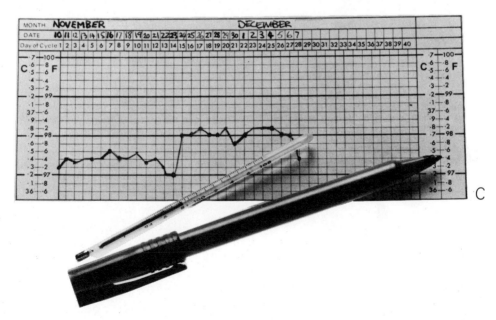

I.U.D.

The abbreviated and most-used term for the *intra-uterine device,* a contraceptive device which is inserted into the womb and remains there for a period of time which varies according to the particular device used. The most common types in use are known as the LOOP (Lippes loop), the COIL (Saf-T-coil), COPPER 7, and COPPER T. The copper devices have made it possible for women who have not had a previous pregnancy to use an IUD, as they are smaller than other devices. There is a new T-shaped IUD available called PROGESTASERT which contains and releases a hormone, progestogen (progestin).

An IUD should be fitted by a specially-trained doctor since the efficiency of the device depends a lot on the skill and practice of the inserter. When a pregnancy is desired, or a change of contraceptive wanted, the doctor can easily remove the device and fertility will be regained. The IUD should not be removed by a woman herself, but she can check that the device is in by feeling for the strings which are attached to it—these fall just into the top of the vagina. The doctor usually checks an IUD once or twice a year.

Doctors will not normally fit an IUD in women who suffer from heavy periods as it may increase this discomfort. Some women find that their body rejects and expels an IUD, but this is very rare once the device has remained in place for three months. Some women find IUDS uncomfortable or painful—if this occurs a doctor should be consulted at once.

The advantage of the IUD as opposed to other methods of contraception is that it is not sex-event related—a woman does not have to remember to put it in or on before intercourse, and once inserted it can be more or less forgotten. In contraceptive efficiency, the IUD, with an approximate 98 per cent success rate, is second only to the pill.

The medical profession is not entirely sure how the IUD works—whether it causes the production of substances which affect sperm or whether it prevents the fertilized egg from implanting itself in the womb is not known for certain. As the IUD is now used by some clinics as a form of morning-after contraception, the latter theory would seem to be more acceptable. An IUD is sometimes fitted not as a contraceptive device but as a support of the womb in cases of *prolapse**.

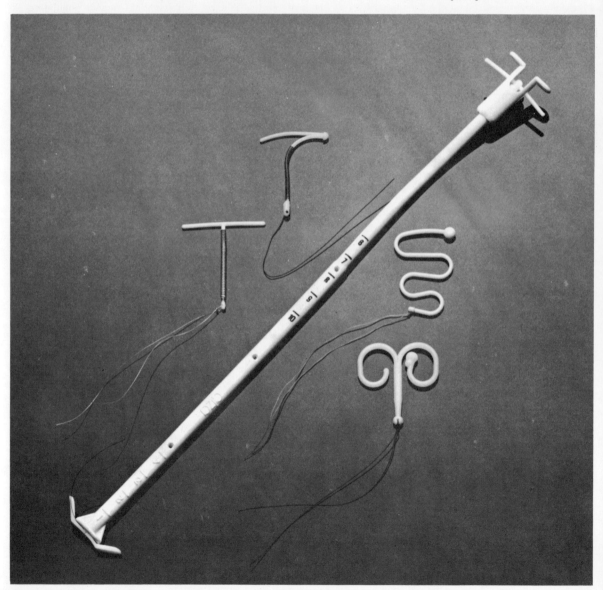

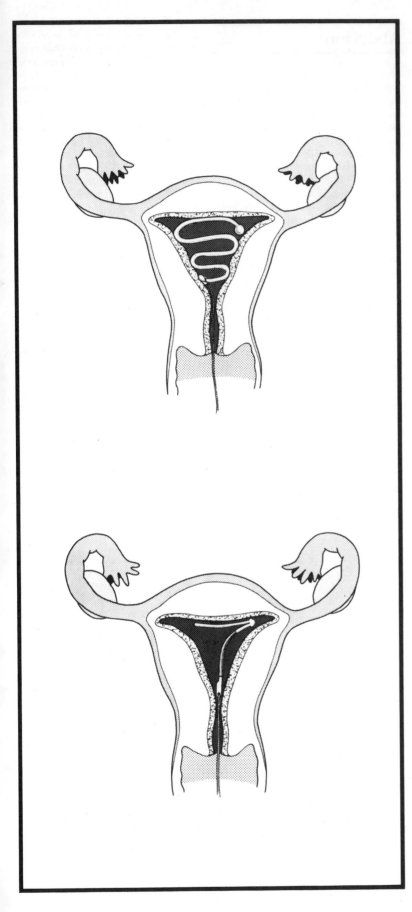

Withdrawal

Withdrawal is a commonly used method of contraception, but one that is rarely recommended. This is because its failure rate in preventing an unwanted pregnancy is high and it can prove extremely frustrating for both partners. Because of its worldwide popularity, withdrawal has acquired a variety of names. COITUS INTERRUPTUS is its formal title and means just that—interrupted sex. However, the method is probably better known as *being careful, taking care of the woman* or *throw outs*. Other terms are *coitus reservatus* (withholding ejaculation), *coitus incompletus* (incomplete intercourse) and *coitus saxonicus*.

In this method when a man feels ejaculation is about to take place, he withdraws his penis and ejaculates outside the vagina. This requires a degree of will power and control not always possible. It is difficult to be sure of the moment of ejaculation and it is important that no drop should be spilled before the man withdraws. Quite often couples may use this method and not let the penis enter the vagina at all, but ejaculate between the woman's thighs. This is very risky as sperm deposited outside the vagina are able to swim up into the womb without the penis being inserted. Also, it is possible for sperm to be released in the fluid lubricating the penis, so that when a man's penis enters the vagina the sperm are already there before he ejaculates.

For some people, using withdrawal as a regular method of contraception may be psychologically damaging. If a person is emotionally insecure or the relationship is in difficulties the stress caused by using this method may prove too great. It can also induce *frigidity** in a woman and *impotence** in a man due to lack of sexual pleasure and fulfilment.

Far left: *common type of IUDs. Lippes loop and Saf-T-coil lie below the long, thin introducer. Copper 7 and Copper T lie above it. The IUD, which is fitted by a doctor, is stretched out into the thin introducer to pass through the cervical canal into the womb. Once there, it regains its original shape. The insertion of an IUD takes about five to ten minutes.*
Left: *Lippes loop (above) and Copper 7 (below) in position.*

Vaginal Douche

Douching or 'washing out' the vagina has always been more popular in the US and on the Continent than in Great Britain. As a contraceptive or birth control method it is not effective, and is not recommended. The theory is that douching washes out sperm from the vagina after sexual intercourse, but in practice it may be used too late or may even help the sperm to reach the womb.

A variety of anti-sperm agents including vinegar (*gonorrhea**), alum, salt, soap and even Coca Cola have been put in vaginal syringes, sprays or douching bags, but it is best not to use any substance or preparation in the vagina unless it is recommended by a doctor.

Morning-After Pill

Morning-after contraception is prescribed in emergencies by a doctor when sexual intercourse has taken place without any precautions against pregnancy. It might be prescribed when a woman has been raped, or when her health might be endangered by pregnancy and she is aware that a condom or diaphragm has failed. This pill consists of a high dose of estrogen, one of the hormones used in the combined contraceptive pill, which induces a menstrual-like bleeding and thus prevents the implantation of a fertilized egg in the womb's lining.

Side effects from the morning-after pill include severe nausea and vomiting; they are not pleasant and this pill is not recommended as a contraceptive. An alternative to the morning-after pill which is now on trial is the MORNING-AFTER COIL. Insertion of an *IUD** after unprotected intercourse has taken place brings on a menstrual period straight away without unpleasant side effects.

Abortion

Abortion is not a method of *contraception** in the true sense of preventing conception but it is a method of birth control. It is often the last resort for women who have accidentally conceived either through contraceptive failure or their failure to use a birth control method correctly or in some cases the failure to accept that a pregnancy 'could happen to them'.

Abortion is now a safe and relatively simple procedure if a woman gets help during the early stages of an unwanted pregnancy. The first step is to make sure that there is a pregnancy by taking a simple pregnancy test which is carried out 14 days after a missed menstrual period. This can be done through most Planned Parenthood or family planning clinics, by pharmacists or your own doctor.

During the very early days of pregnancy a process called MENSTRUAL EXTRACTION can be carried out. The term is usually used when pregnancy has only just occurred and has not necessarily been confirmed. By suction, the contents of the womb including the fertilized egg are removed. SUCTION METHOD can be used up to the thirteenth week of pregnancy, and include vacuum aspiration and the Karmen cannula method. Suction operations are performed under either a local or general anesthetic depending on the length of the pregnancy and the woman

concerned. This technique has been replacing D & C, which is short for DILATION AND CURETTAGE. Otherwise known as a 'scrape', in this method of abortion, the vaginal canal is dilated and the contents and lining of the womb are removed (below). It is often used not only as a method of abortion but as a treatment for women who have suffered from problems with their periods.

Early abortion does not necessarily require an overnight stay in the hospital but after abortion at 12 or 13 weeks hospitalization will be required sometimes for only a day, sometimes for two or three days, depending on the stage of pregnancy. Abortions carried out after 13 weeks are more difficult and carry a greater health risk. They have to be done under a general anesthetic and involve the injection of compounds (called abortifacients) into the uterus which induce contractions and thus expulsion of the fetus.

A new, easier and safer method for very early abortion is undergoing clinical trials now. Called prostaglandin gel, it comes in the form of a pessary which is inserted by the woman herself about four times every hour for a specified period. This brings about womb contractions and induces an abortion, but can only be used in the very early stages of pregnancy. The *morning-after pill** and the morning-after coil (*IUD**) which induce a menstrual-like bleeding are not normally considered to be methods of abortion, since they prevent the implantation of an egg in the womb's lining.

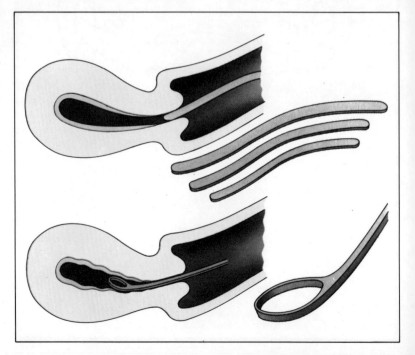

**ABORTION BY VACUUM
ASPIRATION**

1. Sac of amniotic fluid in which the fetus is developing
2. Enlarged womb
3. Cervix
4. Vagina
5. Tube attached to vacuum pump
6. Womb shrinks to normal size
7. Abortion completed

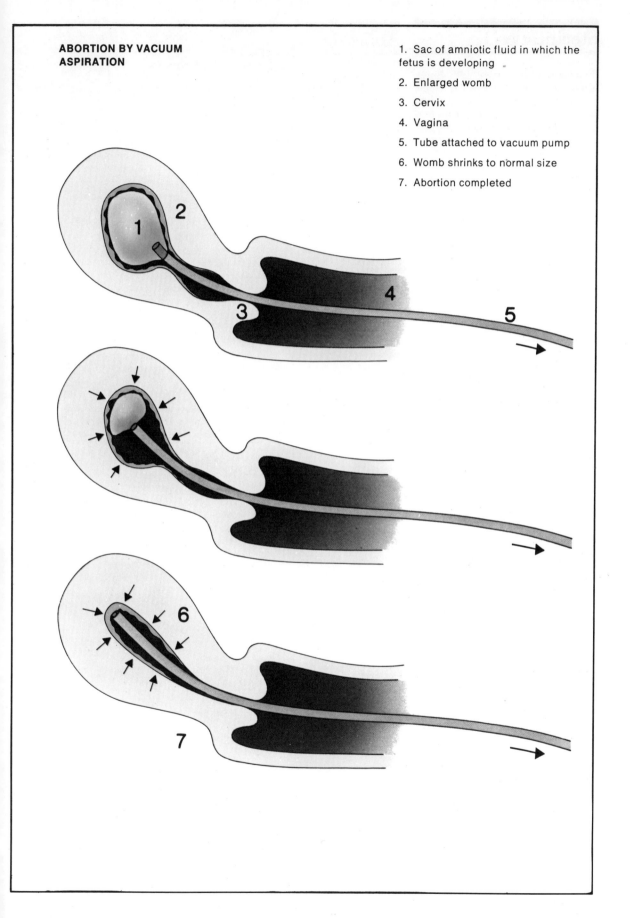

Sterilization

Both male and female sterilization are permanent methods of fertility control rather than just a means of preventing birth. Although reversal operations can be attempted, there is no guarantee of success. Before performing such an operation, a doctor will probably expect to obtain the consent of the patient's partner and will probably talk to the couple and explain in detail exactly what the operation involves. There is no legal requirement for the spouse's consent, but some doctors will not sterilize a woman if her husband objects. If any woman experiences difficulty in obtaining sterilization because of this problem, then she would be advised to seek the help of another doctor or a women's rights group.

Male sterilization, known as VASECTOMY, is a much simpler operation than female sterilization. Vasectomy can be carried out under local anesthetic and does not involve a stay in hospital. It is often carried out in family planning clinics. The technique involves a small incision in each testicle and the cutting and tying of the tubes (vas deferens) which carry the sperm. Neither the sex drive is affected nor the ability to have a full erection after vasectomy. After the operation, another method of contraception will have to be used until the man's sperm count drops to a safe level. A doctor will advise when a man is to have check-ups to determine the sperm level after an operation.

Female sterilization is a more complicated operation because a woman's reproductive system is inside her body. The operation called TUBAL LIGATION involves cutting and tying the Fallopian tubes which carry eggs to the womb. In some cases, the tubes will be completely removed. Access to these tubes is sometimes gained through the vagina, although usually a small incision is made in the abdomen, which will leave a small scar. As this operation is carried out under a general anesthetic and is a more complicated operation than vasectomy, it will mean a short stay in the hospital, normally up to ten days. However, LAPAROSCOPY (female sterilization through a tube or 'scope' inserted into the abdomen) may not require a stay in the hospital of more than forty-eight hours.

When a woman has a *hysterectomy**
or removal of her womb and reproductive organs, the result is complete sterilization too.

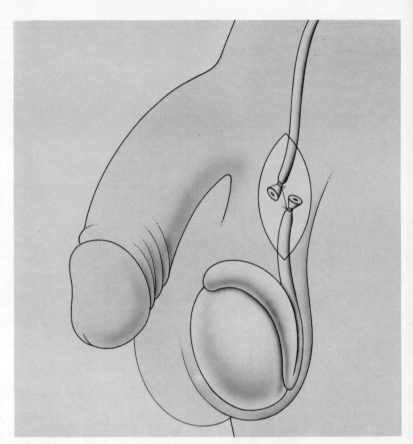

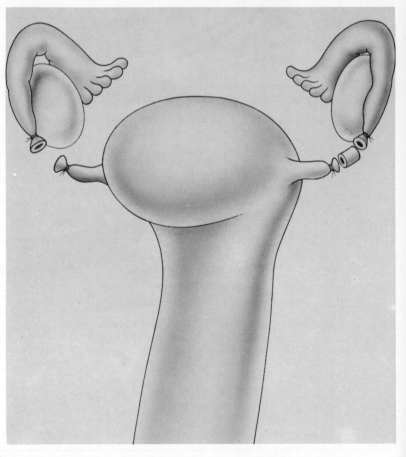

15

Healthy Testicle

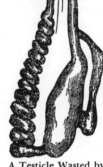
A Testicle Wasted by
Sexual Excess

HEALTH

Defences against and treatments for
the sex-related infections.

Sex-Related Diseases

In recent years, the word 'sex' has come to mean sexual intercourse, rather than gender (male or female). So sex-related diseases are those acquired through sexual intercourse, not diseases which are peculiar to the sex of the individual. There are a dozen or so diseases caught from having sex with an infected person. Many people do not know they are infected and only find out after developing serious complications or after infecting others. The numbers of people with SEXUALLY-TRANSMITTED DISEASES increase every year and result in a huge public health problem throughout the world.

Some countries, such as China and Cuba, claim to be rid of the sex-related diseases. Other countries report a rise in sex-related diseases. About 16,000,000 cases of *gonorrhea** are reported to occur each year throughout the world. (Since a large proportion of gonorrhea infections show no symptoms, the figure may be very much higher in fact.) These include over 750,000 teenagers in the US. In Great Britain since World War II, gonorrhea has increased about 175 per cent in males and almost 500 per cent in females. It affects about one in 1,000 of the population every year.

Gonorrhea and almost all the other sex-related diseases are curable, especially if treated early. It seems strange that the better and more widely available treatment is, the more numbers of cases continue to rise. However, this is because controlling VD or VENEREAL DISEASE is a social problem and concerns sexual behaviour.

Venus was the Roman goddess of love. Venereal diseases are caught through 'venery' or love making. *Syphilis** , gonorrhea and *chancroid** are almost always acquired this way (not from toilet seats). Many other diseases follow sexual relations, close contact without sex or are caught from lavatories, infected towels, and so on. Because 'having VD' has caused so much embarrassment, shame or disgrace for so long, these other diseases are called 'sexually transmitted' or, more correctly, 'transmissible'. They affect one in two hundred of the population. The usage of terms like VD depends upon attitudes to sex. Sexually enlightened people are content with the word 'venereal', while many others prefer to change the language rather than their opinions.

Very many people who are faithful to one sex partner become infected because the partner has 'slept around'. Those who approve of changing sex partners should take note of this. Every case of VD means another case, and another, and so on. That is why tracing sex contacts is so important. The cause of all these diseases becoming widespread is sexual *promiscuity** . A promiscuous person, even while incubating a disease and before symptoms develop, can infect many others who only have very occasional sex away from their regular partners. In some cases of *group sex** there may be no disease until one person introduces it from outside. Then they all catch it.

While probably the majority of people believe in a 'one man/one woman' permanent relationship within marriage, attitudes and behaviour in modern society have changed very much in recent decades. The changes amount to a SEXUAL REVOLUTION. Newspapers, magazines, films and radio bring a greater awareness of sex to everybody. Younger people are more and more involved. Many are physically but not emotionally ready for sex or its possible consequences. The influence of church, school and parents is weaker than it used to be. People travel further from home; tens of thousands of men cross the seas as immigrants or as military personnel, leaving their women at home. The two sexes come into closer contact in factories, offices, schools and colleges. Sex before marriage, including some partner-change, is now accepted by much of society. But people do not accept unfaithfulness in marriage so easily and unmarried couples 'going steady' tend to keep their 'affairs' with other people secret. The PERMISSIVE SOCIETY, however, is ending the double standard where sex is OK for men only. Greater sexual freedom exists for females as a result of safe and inexpensive contraception. A girl with several sexual partners is no longer thought of as a whore. But permissiveness has brought muddled thinking and much distress, especially to adolescents, over the difference between liberation and liberality, between freedom of choice and license in sexual behaviour.

Because the sex urge is very powerful, boys go as far as they dare or are allowed. Girls, seeking love, often have sex to make up for an unhappy home; or because they fear losing their boy friends; or because pressure from their girl friends and the mass media suggest that sex is expected of them. Sex is exploited and cheapened by commerce. *Alcohol** removes self control and more alcohol is drunk today than a generation ago, and by people at a younger age. Additionally, prostitutes are promiscuous by profession. Many male homosexuals lead promiscuous lives. The sex lives of both these groups has added greatly to the amount of sex-transmitted disease.

In the United Kingdom, special clinics exist for the free and confidential examination of all who think they may have become infected (often more than one disease is present). In the United States there are local VD clinics under each state's Department of Health and a national VD 'hotline' telephone number (Operation Venus—1–800–272–2577, which is toll free) will give advice on symptoms and where to find a local clinic. Tests are often free. Some clinics will respect the confidentiality of minors who do not want their parents to receive a bill or to know they may have disease. Planned Parenthood centres in the US will also give aid. No *one* drug will cure all the sex-related diseases. There are no vaccines against syphilis and gonorrhea nor any early-warning blood tests by which to diagnose them. All sex contacts of known cases should be traced if possible, but even this is not enough.

Public HEALTH EDUCATION in matters of sex concentrates mainly on *contraception** and venereal disease. It should warn that the contraceptive pill provides no protection against disease whereas the rubber sheath or *condom** may protect both partners. Responsible teaching about sex-related diseases should include telling people of all the dangers that go with irresponsible sex activity—but should not scare them off sex altogether. It should include advice on simple hygiene like urinating and washing after intercourse with strange partners. It should warn against sex with a second person too soon after the first. This is to allow time for symptoms to develop following a risk. It is better not to wait for these but to go for a test. There may, of course, be no symptoms at all.

The ultimate control of these diseases will only come with a change in sexual behaviour. For this to happen there must be more sex education which deals with personal relationships and making responsible decisions. Really successful sex does not lie in immediate satisfaction wherever it may be found, but in a loving and lasting commitment to one person. In this way lies sexual health too.

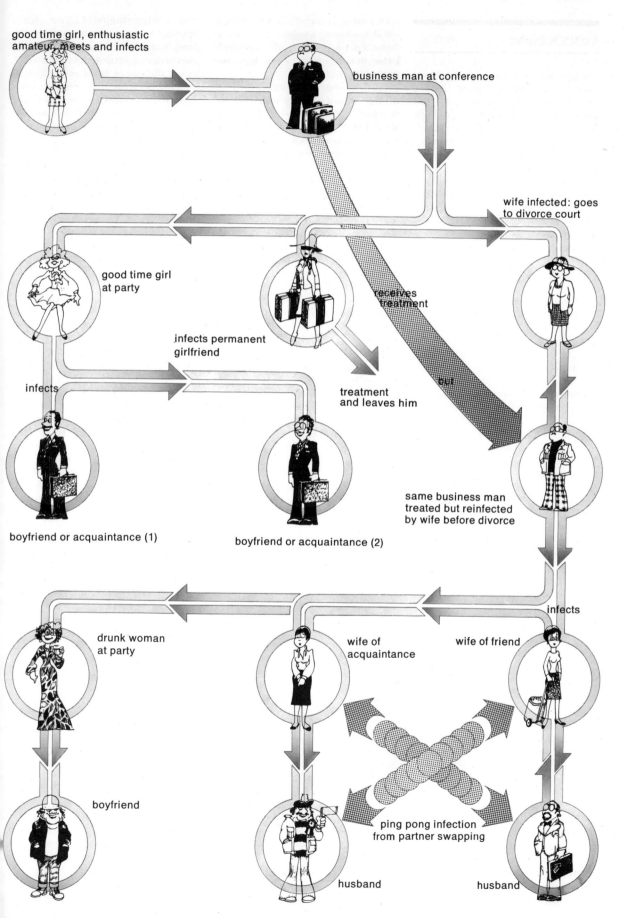

good time girl, enthusiastic amateur, meets and infects

business man at conference

wife infected: goes to divorce court

good time girl at party

receives treatment

infects permanent girlfriend

treatment and leaves him

out

infects

boyfriend or acquaintance (1)

boyfriend or acquaintance (2)

same business man treated but reinfected by wife before divorce

infects

drunk woman at party

wife of acquaintance

wife of friend

ping pong infection from partner swapping

boyfriend

husband

husband

Gonorrhea

Gonorrhea is an extremely contagious sexually-transmitted disease. It has been known since biblical times and occurs throughout the world; no race is immune. The disease's prevalence differs from time to time and from country to country according to sexual customs. Numerically speaking, gonorrhea is possibly mankind's greatest pestilence; it is more common than cases of measles in children. Statistics show that at least about 56,000 people in Great Britain are infected with gonorrhea annually and about 3,000,000 or more in the US. Gonorrhea is spreading at an alarming rate among all ages and all social classes. In law, gonorrhea is a disease which must be reported to the health authorities, but there are serious doubts as to whether this legal requirement accounts for even a majority of cases, as the disease often shows no symptoms. Many countries do not provide statistics.

From health reports, such as they are, gonorrhea affects people in the sixteen to forty-year-old age groups mostly, with a maximum incidence in males aged around twenty-two and in females of about nineteen. Statistically, males outnumber females by three to two, but only about 20 per cent of women show symptoms of the disease. The increase in recorded female infections since World War II greatly exceeds that in males. Nearly one in five females are wives infected by their husbands. Only two per cent of male cases are infected by their wives.

The cause of gonorrhea is a bacterium, the gonococcus (*Neisseria gonorrhoeae*). To remain alive it needs warmth, moisture, darkness, an atmosphere short of oxygen and the right sort of tissue upon which to multiply; it soon dies outside the human body. Suitable tissue is found in the urinary passage (the urethra) of both sexes and in the female cervical canal which runs between the vagina and the uterus. The disease may also commence in the rectum following rectal intercourse or as a result of vaginal discharge reaching the rectum. The throat but not the mouth, may also be infected following *oral sex**. Although gonorrhea is seldom acquired by any other means than sexual contact, in rare cases a female infant may be contaminated by an infected adult who is careless in personal hygiene. An untreated mother may pass the infection to her newly-born baby's eyes as it passes through the cervical canal, producing a condition known as opthalmia neonatorum. Until recently gonorrhea was a cause of blindness in newly-born babies.

The disease mainly involves the genital and urinary passages which become inflamed and discharge a yellowish-white pus. In males the discharge from the penis may be heavy and cause discomfort on urinating. Symptoms develop within about three to eight days of exposure to infection, but the incubation period may extend even to three weeks. A number of males may remain without symptoms (an estimate of from five to 20 per cent is current), and these asymptomatic individuals, as they are called, include those who are in the process of developing the disease. If sexually promiscuous during the symptomless incubation period, infected people can unwittingly transmit the disease to others, and doubtless much gonorrhea is spread in this way.

Females with symptoms usually complain of vaginal discharge which may appear yellowish or discomfort and pain when urinating. This has accounted in the past for some cases of so-called honeymoon cystitis, an inflammation of the bladder (*cystitis**). Some 60 to 80 per cent of female cases remain symptonless, unless complications develop. This is because the female cervical canal is a part of the body that is insensitive. The very short female urethra does not seem to harbour infection either. When inflamed, these areas cause little or no discomfort. The amount of discharge in women with gonorrhea is relatively slight; when present it may go unnoticed in the existing vaginal and vulva moisture. Symptomless females, if promiscuous, will infect others and may not realize they should attend a doctor or a clinic unless an infected partner convinces them they were the source of gonorrhea or a member of the public health or welfare service contacts them, as a result of being informed of the sexual contacts of a known gonorrhea victim. Males or females with throat or rectal gonorrhea will also infect partners.

It is not known how many untreated cases of gonorrhea go on to a spontaneous cure. Though this undoubtedly exists, it is foolish and dangerous to assume that this has occurred in any particular case. Complications all too often follow such a decision. These complications may be local or general, and can be disabling. Local complications of gonorrhea in the male come in the form of acute or chronic inflammation occurring in various glands opening into or near the urethra (Tyson's, Littré's or Cowper's glands), and also in the prostate gland or the epididymis situated in the scrotum behind the testicle). This, if it occurs on both sides of the scrotum, may result in sterility. Chronic inflammation may also lead to a stricture or severe narrowing of the urethra. In the female, gonococci often invade the back passage, even without rectal coitus having taken place. Abscess on the external sexual parts or acute inflammation of Bartholin's glands is not infrequent. The most frequent and serious complication which affects twenty per cent of females with gonorrhea is acute salpingitis (inflammation of the Fallopian tubes which lead from the ovaries to the uterus). Then there is lower abdominal pain, which can often be severe; constitutional disturbance like fever and headache occurs. Peritonitis (a common complication of appendicitis)—an inflammation of the lining of the interior abdominal cavity—may follow with possible fatal results. The Fallopian tubes can get partially or completely blocked. Ectopic pregnancy (the baby developing outside the womb) is a complication of blocked tubes. The patient may then become sterile or subject to chronic miscarriage. Pelvic abscesses may also develop leading to anemia and chronic ill health. Surgical operations are often necessary to help such patients.

The more general complications of gonorrhea involve tissues outside the reproductive system—these are rare and result from invasion of the blood stream by the bacteria. The heart and nervous system, but more especially the eyes may be affected. Feverish illness with skin rashes, joint pains and sometimes septic arthritis are becoming more common, possibly related to undiagnosed and therefore chronic throat infection.

The diagnosis of gonorrhea is first made by finding the gonococci under a high-powered microscope in stained smears (called the gram stain) taken from the male urethra and the female urethra and cervix. Other sites of infection such as the opening of various glands (Skene's tubules, Bartholin's ducts) or the rectum and the throat may be swabbed and the resulting discharge or small bits of tissue put into a special culture media and grown under laboratory conditions for up to two days to determine if the gonococcus is present. The culture test is considered to be very important in female cases of gonorrhea and in asymptomatic men in whom the bacteria may be difficult to find. It is also used with married partners where absolutely no room for doubt must exist in the diagnosis of gonorrhea.

Most antibiotics destroy the gonoccus, but penicillin remains the best treatment when prescribed in the right dosage. Increasing dosage has become necessary over the years in order to maintain a near 100 per cent cure rate. The percentage of strains of gonococci which are partially or wholly resistant to penicillin varies between about 20 and 75 in different parts of the world. Of deep concern is the appearance in 1976 of gonococci which manufacture an enzyme called penicillinase that destroys penicillin and some other antibiotics. These bacteria are completely resistant to penicillin, but other effective preparations are fortunately available.

Infection with gonorrhea provides no immunity against further infection at a later date. Many persons suffer repeated attacks of the disease. There is no vaccine against gonorrhea nor is there any reliable special blood test, but the search for these continues.

Risk of infection from gonorrhea can be reduced by the male sexual partner wearing a *condom**, for vaginal or for rectal intercourse. Spermidical creams, foams and jellies can also be a deterrent to infection. *Lorophyn* vaginal suppositories are of some help in preventing infection. A preparation called *Progonasyl* was developed as a treatment to prevent sexually-transmitted disease and is available on prescription—it is an antiseptic oil used in the vagina. Hygiene will help in prevention of infection. Men should wash with soap and water carefully around their genitals, pulling back the foreskin to wash the glans area. This does not help women much in prevention of infection, but a *douche** of a tablespoon of vinegar in a quart or about two pints of warm water may help. There is a 'morning-after' pill containing a mild dose of penicillin which will help prevent infection if taken within eight hours of exposure; it will not cure an established case of infection, and is available on prescription only. There is some evidence that the contraceptive pill can increase the likelihood of contracting disease.

Lymphogranuloma Venereum

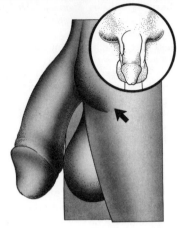

A sexually-acquired tropical and subtropical disease, caused by a virus-like organism called *chlamydia*. After infection, there is a short incubation period before a small painless genital sore appears. (This is rarely seen in women, because it is hidden internally.) Painfully inflamed lymph glands, or 'buboes', develop in the groin soon after. These may become abscesses and discharge through the skin. If untreated, the infection spreads extensively into the pelvic area, causing swelling of the sex organs. Ulceration of various internal organs can occur and sometimes the rectum becomes blocked. These late stages can cause much suffering. Diagnosis is confirmed by blood and skin tests. Sulphonamide drugs and also antibiotics are used in treatment.

Granuloma Inguinale

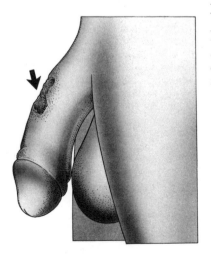

A tropical and sub-tropical contagious disease, rare in other climates, which is possibly sexually transmitted. The sex partner of an infected person often does not acquire the disease. It is caused by tiny organisms called Donovan bodies (*Donovania granulomatis*). After an incubation period of several weeks, painless pimples or blisters appear on or near the sex organs. These turn into chronic, sometimes painful ulcers which bleed and spread extensively to the abdomen, groin, buttocks, crotch or up into the vagina. In extreme cases, the penis may ulcerate away completely. Spread of the infection also occurs under the skin, causing 'pseudo-buboes' (or false lymph gland abscesses). Treatment with streptomycin or tetracycline is effective but may not prevent recurrences months or even years later.

Molluscum Contagiosum

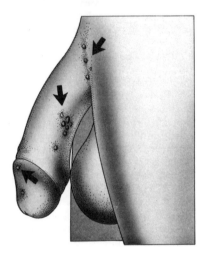

A contagious skin disease, caused by a virus, which can be acquired sexually. After an incubation period of three weeks to several months, hemispherical pearly-white or pink pimples with depressed centres from which cheesy matter can be squeezed are produced. These 'umbilicated papules', as they are sometimes called, vary in size from a pinhead to a lentil or larger. They occur sparsely or in clusters, anywhere on the body. When sexually transmitted, they occur on the penis, scrotum, vulva, thighs or lower abdomen and (after anal intercourse) on the buttocks. The pimples cause no special symptoms unless they turn septic. To cure them, each little lesion has to be pressed out and cauterized separately.

Syphilis

Syphilis is a sexually contagious disease occurring throughout the world that is seldom acquired by any other means than intercourse. It is chronic and can affect any part of the body. At times it may mimic almost any other disease. For months or years it lies dormant and seldom, except in certain late stages, makes a person feel ill. It can pass via the blood from mother to fetus resulting in 'congenital' syphilis. Untreated individuals may sometimes recover by themselves; or they may suffer mild or severe but mostly non-fatal late effects. About 20 per cent of syphilis-infected individuals may die from disease of the blood vessels and heart or the brain and spinal cord.

The cause of syphilis is a spiral shaped microbe called *treponema pallidum* or *spirochoeta pallida,* meaning 'pale corkscrew', which soon dies outside the human body. Provided patients cooperate in treatment with doctors, early syphilis is curable. Syphilis germs are extremely sensitive to penicillin, to tetracycline and some other antibiotics. Injections are given over ten or twenty days. Occasionally second or third courses of treatment are necessary. Proper follow-up is essential, but this need not be for life.

Syphilis spread rapidly through Europe about five hundred years ago, and since that time people have feared catching the disease and have always scorned those who do. After penicillin was introduced in 1943, syphilis was held in check in countries which had effective venereal disease services. But presently, new cases of syphilis are in large numbers in most countries, particularly among homosexual men.

Syphilis germs enter the human body through cracks in the skin, however small, or through the soft lining of the body openings which are involved in sexual activity (the penis, vulva, vagina, rectum or mouth). Syphilis is not caught from toilet seats but from open sores on the infected person in the early or primary and secondary stages or from relapsing sores during the first year of infection. Hence doctors speak of 'early infectious syphilis'. Washing with soap and water will protect doctors and nurses who accidentally touch syphilis infectious matter with their bare hands. In the latest period which follows 'early infectious syphilis' and during the late 'tertiary' stages the disease is no longer in-

fectious. An exception to these general rules is maternal syphilis. An untreated pregnant woman can infect her unborn baby even several years following her own infection.

Early syphilis is diagnosed by observing under a microscope germs in the discharge from a sore. Two or three weeks after a chancre (or sore) has developed, the germs will have entered the infected person's blood stream, so a blood test will show infection at all stages of syphilis.

After an incubation period of approximately two to three weeks (the outside limits are ten to ninety days) a red spot appears on the skin where the germs entered. This becomes a hard painless sore, oozing blood serum but not bleeding readily. It is about ⅜-1¼in. (1-3cm) across. This is the syphilis chancre ('shanker'). Together with enlarged lymph glands in the groin, the condition is now called *primary syphilis* (fig. 1). 95 per cent of chancres are on or near the genitals. They may (fig. 2) occur inside the vagina or inside the anus in homosexual men. Many patients are unaware of these sores and infect others without knowing it. During the primary stage the germs spread all through the body but especially to the skin. After a few weeks to a few months, a widespread rash occurs which does not itch. It may resemble many other skin diseases. (Figures 3, 4 and 5 show the development of a rash which starts as rosy spots, spreading round the body and turning into pimples and then, six to eight weeks after infection, to pustules.)

Moist and highly infectious broad flat warts (*condylomata lata*) may also appear around the genitals (fig. 6). Shallow ulcers in the throat ('snail-track ulcers') may occur which make the saliva infectious (fig. 7). Other symptoms may be present such as enlarged lymph glands and thinning of the hair (*syphilitic alopoecia*). This stage is called *secondary syphilis,* and it lasts many months.

After the appearance of the chancre, a number of protective antibodies develop in the blood. These reach their maximum in the secondary stage of the disease. As a result of these natural defences, which only develop in infected persons but never occur of their own accord, some 50 per cent of all untreated syphilis cases cure themselves. These antibodies also make possible various blood tests by which syphilis is diagnosed.

The other, less fortunate half of syphilis sufferers, after many years of

no symptoms develop *tertiary syphilis.* In some people in this stage, as the defences slacken off, a few of the spiral shaped germs land up in one or another part of the body. The resulting 'inflammatory tumours' may be small or very large. They are called 'gummas' and may cause much damage and disfigurement and occasionally death. In some infected people the brain and/or spinal cord may be involved in Neurosyphilis (*General Paralysis of the Insane* or GPI, as it is called) or a disease known as *Tabes Dorsalis.* These severe late stages often cripple and may eventually kill the patient. Though death from syphilis is rare today, it will become common again if people stop taking the disease seriously. Only the ignorant or stupid laugh it off as 'just a touch of VD.'

In Great Britain and the USA, congenital syphilis has been almost wiped out. Nearly all pregnant women undergo routine blood tests and if these are positive for syphilis, treatment is given in time to protect the child before birth. Untreated syphilitic women may give birth to a dead baby, a heavily infected infant that usually dies, an infant who appears well but develops severe illness early in life, one that develops mild or serious trouble such as blindness, deafness or even GPI in childhood or adolescence or one who shows nothing but a harmless positive blood test for life. Yet others have tell-tale signs of their infection before birth (stigmata) but do not otherwise suffer.

Early syphilis can be cured in nearly every case. Infection can be rooted out in most late cases, but in many of these some damage is beyond repair. Unless treated very early, blood tests (or some of them) will remain positive for many years. Only specialists in venereal diseases are able to decide whether a positive test is dangerous or not. When a patient is inadequately treated, as when he stops going for injections, he may be left uncured *and* defenceless. In this case he is liable to very serious and dangerous relapse. Congenital syphilis is an entirely preventable disease.

Syphilis can be caught a second time, but this only happens when a first attack is treated while the chancre is developing. In these cases, treatment has killed off the germs before defensive antibodies have had time to appear in the blood. When one sex partner is treated and the other is not, syphilis can be passed back and forth from one to the other alternately. This is called *ping-pong syphilis.*

Serological tests for Syphilis (STS)

All these tests have to be interpreted by doctors.
They are NOT simple YES/NO tests.

Screening Tests

C.W.R. (Cardio-lipin Wasserman Reaction)

V.D.R.L.: (Venereal Diseases Reference Laboratory)

Kahn Test

These, and others like them, are tests for non-specific antibodies found in syphilis and various other conditions. Hence the BFP (Biological False Positive) reaction.

R.P.C.F.T. (Reiter Protein Complement Fiscation Test).

A test for anti-spirochaetal antibody. Reacts against syphilitic anti-body and originally reacted against non-syphilitic spinal organisms. Is now almost specific for the former, ie., positive means syphilis.

Any of the above, if positive, suggest syphilis and lead on to verification tests.

Verification Tests

T.P.I. (Treponema Pallidum Immobilizing test).

F.T.A./ABS (Fluorescent Treponemal Antibody – "Absorbed").

The above are tests for specific immobilizing antibody.

T.P.H.A. (Treponema Pallidum Haemagglutinatium Assay). A test for specific agglutinating antibody.

If two out of three of the above tests are positive it really means syphilis now or in the past – but all screening and verification tests are or may be positive in the disease yaws as well.

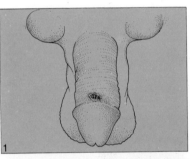

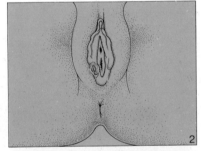

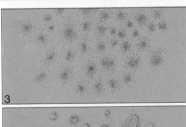

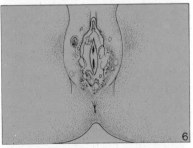

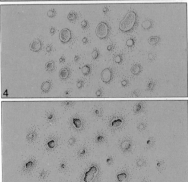

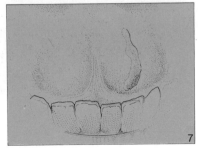

NSU

Non-specific urethritis (NSU) is a disease almost entirely confined to males. More properly called NON-GONOCOCCAL URETHRITIS (NGU), it was originally labeled 'non-specific' because the cause could not be identified. Some cases were later attributed to bacteria which are now known to be normal, non-disease producing germs that live in the male urinary opening. Today the cause is definitely known, in a few cases, for example, *trichomoniasis**. NSU also follows infection higher up the urinary tract. Allergy to vaginal secretions used to be offered as an explanation for NSU, but this idea has fallen from favour. Since the disease usually follows sexual intercourse, with an incubation period of from three to six weeks, it is accepted as being a sexually-transmitted infection, more so as most cases respond to antibiotics.

Opinions differ concerning the role of germs called 'mycoplasmas'. These organisms are often found in the genital tract of both sexes, even when healthy. Most people now accept that the cause of NSU in perhaps the majority of cases if a virus-like organism belonging to a group known as the 'chlamydia' (known as the 'tric-agent'). Growing these organisms on culture plates is difficult and is seldom attempted outside a few research centres.

More cases of NGU, which is on the increase, are recorded annually than are male *gonorrhea** cases. Many of these NGU infections are relapses from previous infections. Unlike gonorrhea, which the disease otherwise resembles, it may relapse several times, causing much distress to the patient. There is mild irritation in the urethra, some discomfort on urinating and a variable amount of penile discharge which is more watery or mucoid and sticky than the discharge of gonorrhea because it has less pus in it.

Local complications are similar to those of gonorrhea but milder. Chronic inflammation of the prostate gland can follow NGU. A few patients also develop skin rashes like psoriasis.

Patients get better by themselves in six weeks to three months, but treatment with pain-relievers and antibiotics help. Treatment of NGU is less satisfactory than with gonorrhea as the relapses and complications show. Penicilin is useless. Tetracycline, if given over several days (10–21) usually suppresses an attack permanently.

Scabies

A very common, world-wide skin disease which is caused by a mite (*sarcoptes scabiei*). The 'itch', as it is also called, is found chiefly among poor, over-crowded families that do not wash often enough. It is a contagious disease and is spread by dirty clothing, towels or bed linen and by close bodily contact. Many cases, therefore, follow sexual intercourse.

The scabies mite below, magnified 56 times, is also called an 'acarus'. It is less than half a millimetre in length and is almost round in shape. It lives and feeds by burrowing into the outer layers of the skin. The female also lays its eggs in these burrows and when they hatch the young mites start fresh burrows. So the disease spreads over the body. Symptoms develop about a month after mites infest the body. The burrows appear as tiny black or white lines with a minute blister at one end where the mite is to be found. The burrows are surrounded by inflamed skin forming oblong red spots. They occur chiefly on the webs of the fingers, the wrists, elbows, armpits and side of the body, the breasts in women and the buttocks in children. In many cases the body is covered with spots all over except for the head. The area of skin between the shoulder blades often escapes, because this area cannot be reached by the hands which carry the mites from one part of the body to another. The genitals are frequently covered with the inflammation, especially in the male. Sometimes, if the disease has been acquired sexually, only the genitals have been affected when the patient first goes to a doctor.

The saliva from the mites and their droppings cause intense irritation. This is always worse when the body is warm, especially in bed. As the rash spreads, the itching may become unbearable. Scratching which makes the spots bleed, and they soon become infected with germs from the finger nails and turn septic. Second attacks of scabies develop more quickly than first attacks. This is because the skin has been made very sensitive to the mites by the first attack.

A less common variety of scabies is 'Norwegian itch' (*scabies Norwegica*). The rash is more widespread and may involve the whole of the body sometimes including the face and scalp. The nails may become misshapen or destroyed. The sores are crusted with dried-up pus and scaly skin. There may be as many as two million mites in a case of Norwegian itch compared with 500 in an ordinary case. Norwegian itch

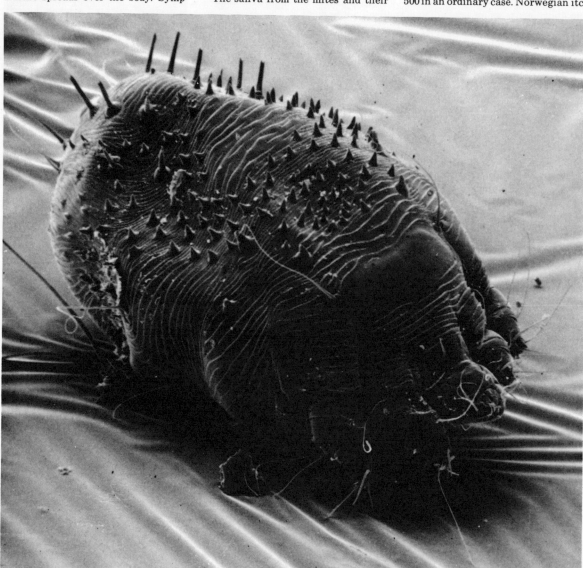

is possibly due to neglect of an ordinary case. In this respect it resembles 'mange' in cats, dogs, horses and other animals.

The mite and its eggs can be removed from its burrow by means of a needle. Although mites can be seen under a microscope, a doctor can often make a diagnosis of scabies from the appearance of the rash. There are various applications for the treatment of scabies (*benzyl benzoate* or *gamma benzene hexachloride* lotions). Patients have a warm bath and scrub all over with soap using a soft brush to open the burrows. After drying, the lotion is applied all over the body from the neck downwards. This can be done by a nurse or by a member of the family at home. Fresh underclothing is then worn. The lotion is applied each night for three nights. A further bath is then taken and another change of clothing is made. Second or third treatments may be necessary at weekly intervals. All underclothing, towelling and bed linen must be laundered. Members of the family and sexual partners have to be examined and treated if necessary.

All adult patients infected with scabies, especially if sexually active, should have blood tests for *syphilis**. This is not only because the two diseases can, and often do, exist at the same time, but because the rash of secondary syphilis may resemble scabies (apart from the fact that it does not itch). If syphilis were mistaken for scabies, the consequences could be very serious.

Genital Herpes

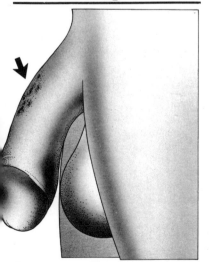

This is a sexually-acquired infection resulting in ulcers, resembling cold sores, on the sex organs. It is caused by a virus (*herpes simplex*) and it is much more common than many types of sexual diseases including *syphilis**. Many cases of herpes follow oral sex, but some sexual partners are not infected. The incubation period is less than a week. Irritating spots and blisters develop into typical shallow painful ulcers of varying size. These may turn septic, but usually heal up within 14 days, although relapses are common. The first attacks are the worst. Careful attention to hygiene is necessary, as no anti-viral drug exists for treatment of herpes. Herpes has not been proved to be a cause of cancer of the cervix, but both conditions are statistically known to increase with teenage sex and promiscuity.

Chancroid

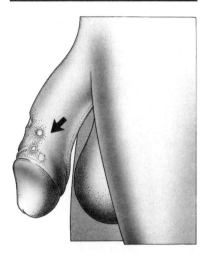

Chancroid, also called soft sores or *ulcus molle*, is a tropical and subtropical disease, little seen in Western Europe or North America. It mostly affects males; women rarely show the symptoms. In European sea ports it can be caught from prostitutes who may have no symptoms. The responsible germ (*haemophilus ducreyi*) is difficult to identify under the microscope. Two to eight days after exposure to infection a soft, tender and inflamed ulcer, which bleeds easily, appears on the sex organs. A succession of fresh ulcers often follow this first sore. These join up and may spread extensively, causing destruction of flesh. The head of the penis and the foreskin may ulcerate away. Neighbouring glands in the groin often develop abscesses, called buboes. Treatment is successful with streptomycin and sulphonamides. Chancroid should not be confused with CHANCRE, the name for the first lesion in *syphilis**.

Genital Warts

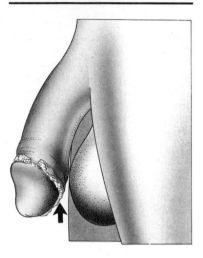

Warts on the genitals or in the vagina are known as *condylomata acuminata*, or more simply as *condyloma*, *vulval warts* or *ano-genital warts*. They are painless, cauliflower-like growths, caused by a virus, and vary in size from a pinhead to a grape. They look like common skin warts, but are softer, and may appear much larger when there are several of them close together. They have no connection with cancer.

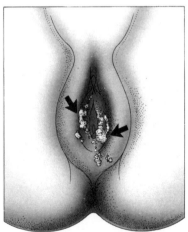

The wart virus can be passed from one person to another by sexual contact, or it can be spread locally by the fingers to the anus. Warts take several weeks to grow, and although they are not a serious medical problem, they can be troublesome for they often recur. Treatment is by application of a chemical wart paint or by cauterization.

Condylomata lata is the name of a separate kind of genital wart, which is syphilitic in origin (*syphilis**).

Candidiasis

Candidiasis or CANDIDOSIS (also called THRUSH or MONILIASIS) is a sexually transmissible infection due to a yeast or fungus called Candida (or Monilia) Albicans, which consists of tiny threads and yeast-like cells or spores. It is easily identified under the microscope. Candida is mostly found in the vagina where it may cause no trouble unless a woman suffers ill health or is emotionally upset. More often it causes moderate to severe inflammation of the vagina and vulva (when it is called vulvo-vaginitis). It occasionally causes 'thursh' in the mouths of babies or seriously ill people. Very rarely it invades the blood stream.

With vulval and vaginal YEAST INFECTION there may be slight discomfort and irritation or intense soreness, burning and ulceration. These symptoms do not depend on the amount of discharge, which varies greatly from watery to thick yellow. Cheesy-white patches appear on the inflamed surfaces which may bleed when they are removed. The buttocks, crotch and thighs are sometimes affected. Because the anus is close to the vagina, many infections come from the bowel where Candida also lives. Infection can also come from borrowed towels or other intimate garments. Women very often are infected from having sexual intercourse and men who are infected nearly always have had sexual intercourse with an already infected person. Re-infections can keep occurring between married couples, known as a 'ping-pong' infection.

In men the fungus gets under the foreskin. There may be nothing more than irritation each time after intercourse with an infected woman, but the end of the penis and the foreskin become inflamed and discharge offensive matter (balanoposthitis). The foreskin may become too swollen to pull back, which is known as phimosis*.

Younger women are more liable to infection when they are pregnant or taking a contraceptive pill. Older women and men are more susceptible if they have diabetes or severe anemia. Some drugs make people susceptible. Tetracycline, for example, kills off normal microbes that hold the Candida fungus in check allowing it to spread freely.

Vaginal candidiasis is treated by suppositories (Nystatin, Amphotericin B) inserted at night. Similar cream is applied to external surfaces. Tablets are taken by mouth for bowel infections. Men should apply the cream externally. Candidiasis is made worse by wearing close-fitting nylon panties or tights. Clean, white cotton pants only should be worn. Personal cleanliness is essential and the genitals should be washed in soap and water after urination or a bowel movement. Sex partners, if infected, should be treated at the same time.

Trichomoniasis

TRICHOMONAL VAGINITIS ('TV') or trichomoniasis ('tric') is a sexually-transmittable infection. It is found in women more often than in men at a ratio of ten to one; possibly 20 per cent of all women are infected at some time. It causes a few cases of non-gonococcal urethritis (NSU*) and is the commonest cause of VAGINITIS or inflammation of the vagina in women.

It is not known how many men and women carry the germs without developing symptoms, but they can infect each other without either showing signs of disease. Women may also become infected from splashings from toilets or from borrowed towels, and female babies can be infected at birth while passing through the vaginal canal. These 'asexual' infections are very rare, however.

The cause of 'tric' is a germ called trichomonas vaginalis, which consists of a single cell and has four little whip-like hairs or flagellae and an undulating membrane like the back of a newt. The diagnosis of trichomoniasis is made by seeing the germ under the microscope where it jerks about in a sample of fresh discharge taken from a patient.

Symptoms follow from a few days to several weeks after intercourse—often after a girl's first experience of sex (trichomoniasis is seldom found in virgins). Some women have only a slight vaginal discharge with TV; others have a heavy white, yellow or greenish discharge which is sometimes frothy and may smell of musty hay. There may also be soreness and itching of the area between the thighs. Intercourse while infection is present can be painful (dyspareunia*) and may cause difficulties between sex partners—one may accuse the other of 'catching VD'. In both sexes trichomoniasis may involve the bladder, causing discomfort and frequency of urinating. TV is one of the causes of honeymoon cystitis*. In males, the organism lives under the foreskin or prepuce of the penis, in the urethra or in the prostate gland.

Trichomoniasis is easily cured by taking oral Flagyl or Naxogin tablets. Sex partners are best treated together so as to prevent reinfection, which is common. Double infections with other sexually-acquired diseases are also common. Gonorrhea is found in about 40 per cent of all female patients with trichomoniasis seen in VD clinics, but in only about five per cent attending other hospital departments or doctor's offices.

Cystitis

Inflammation and infection of the bladder is called cystitis. Diagnosis is clinched by growing the germs which cause the infection from a urine specimen and also by seeing scavenger or pus cells under a microscope. The bladder is very resistant to infection. When such infection does occur, it usually comes from elsewhere—higher up the urinary tract in the kidneys (pyelitis) or lower down in the urethra (NSU*). Infection may result from obstruction to the flow of urine. Causes of obstruction include certain malformations, a stone in the kidney or ureter (leading to the bladder) or in the bladder itself, pregnancy in women and an enlarged prostate gland or a narrowing of the pipe in men. In rare cases, cancerous or other growths inside the bladder, tuberculosis and some tropical diseases may all cause cystitis.

Cystitis causes a necessity for frequent passage of urine, pain on urinating (dysuria) and sometimes blood is noticed in the urine. Additionally the urine is usually cloudy with pus. Treatment of the infection is with antibiotics. Drinking ample water or barley water and simple alkaline medicines are helpful and alcohol is best avoided. Chronic cases and acute cases which do not get better in a few weeks need full investigation. Surgical operations are rarely necessary to remove the basic cause.

The bladder is very sensitive to outside influences—for instance, irritation near the genitals also causes frequent urination and dysuria. Therefore, cystitis can be mistakenly diagnosed when no infection exists. In women, so-called cystitis cases occur four times as often as the real thing, but these are just as distressing and sometimes harder to cure. Often these cystitis-like cases are called the urethral syndrome. Vaginal discharges are a possible cause and easy to treat, but irritation of the vulva (pruritus) may have no obvious cause. Many cases of 'cystitis' occur after a woman's first experience of sexual intercourse—this used to be called HONEYMOON CYSTITIS because it often followed the *honeymoon** period. Poor vaginal lubrication or excessive fondling of the genitals with perhaps not-too-clean hands may cause cystitis after intercourse at any age. This creates much anxiety about general health and interferes with sexual pleasure. Anxiety itself is known to cause bladder disturbances. Thus a vicious circle of anxiety-cystitis-anxiety is created. Treatment of so-called cystitis involves dealing with both physical or psychological causes. Some people have many attacks, but get better quickly without treatment.

Pubic Lice

Pubic lice resemble crabs, as the slang names 'crabs' or 'crab lice' imply. They are blood-sucking wingless insects (*phthirus pubis*), about the size of a pinhead, which infest the pubic hair. The condition is known medically as *pediculosis pubis*. If a person is very hairy, 'crabs' are found elsewhere near the genitals, around the buttocks, the crotch, the upper thighs and the lower abdomen. They may sometimes reach the armpits, eyebrows and eyelashes, but not the scalp. They pass from person to person during sexual intercourse, but may also be caught from infested clothing, towels or bedding. The number of cases is increasing each year, along with other sexually-transmitted diseases. More teenage girls than boys catch 'crabs', but after the age of twenty, men are more likely to have pubic lice.

'Crab' lice clasp hairs with their hind claws, making it difficult to pick them off. They bite into skin in order to feed on blood. This causes itching which results in scratching. Sometimes the bite and scratch marks go septic, causing inflammation of the skin or dermatitis.

Female lice lay about eight eggs (nits) a day and cement them to the root of the hairs. Nits hatch out in about one week. It takes only a few crabs to cause widespread infestation. Patients become aware of crabs by the itching, but they may also see them

moving slowly about. The nits can also be seen, but a microscope is necessary for detailed inspection.

Although 'crab' lice are usually caught through sexual intercourse, other lice which infest the body (*pediculosis corporis*) or the scalp (*pediculosis capitas*) can also be caught the same way. The head variety is mostly found in people who are

careless about keeping clean.

Treatment of lice of any kind is by lotions, ointments and shampoos containing lice-killing substances (*gamma benzene hexachloride*). Most modern preparations are perfumed. For the body, DDT powder may be used. There is seldom any need to shave off the hair, although this is a quick way to get rid of pubic infections.

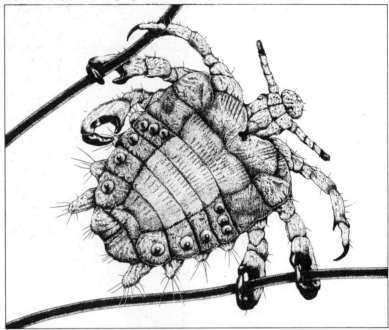

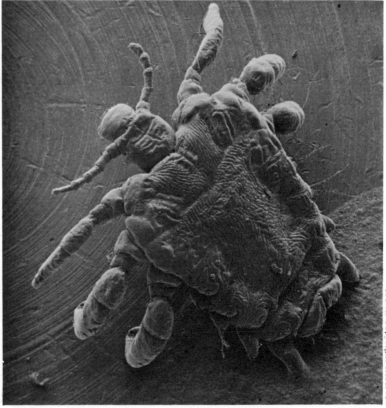

Bidet

A bidet (from the French, for a small horse, pronounced *bee-day*) is an oval basin plumbed for hot and cold running water. A person sits astride it to wash the genitals and anus after sexual intercourse or defecating. Some bidets have a central spray to aid in *douching** the vagina. Douching will wash away semen and vaginal discharge but must not be relied on to prevent sexually-transmitted disease.

Bidets are popular equipment in bathrooms in continental Europe, but are more rare elsewhere. Where sexual attitudes are puritanical, bidets are often a cause of embarrassment or laughter. Bidets can be used for urination, but not for defecation.

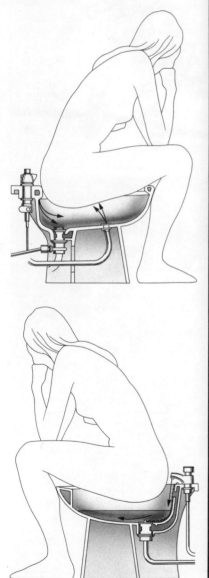

16

SEX FOR ONE

Achieving release from sexual
tensions without having intercourse.

Masturbation

From shortly after birth, human beings begin to derive pleasure from their own bodies. Masturbation, in some degree, starts as soon as a baby becomes aware of the pleasant sensations that are generated in the genital area by gentle rubbing (perhaps when being bathed) and by touching their own genitals (when first beginning to explore the body). From accidental genital stimulation, children graduate to deliberate manipulation of their genitals, which continues intermittently throughout life.

After a more intense phase of masturbation in early childhood, children seem to grow less interested, and there may be a gap of many years when there is no apparent interest in sex in general and masturbation in particular. A revived interest in masturbation occurs at around the start of puberty (age 11 and up), especially with boys, when maturing adolescents start to develop more serious sexual interests and needs. At this time boys often masturbate in groups and girls explore the developing genitals often with a friend.

Masturbation is a kind of preparation for adult sexuality. Young people learn the feel, the smell and the physical sensations of their sexual organs. They see them changing and growing, slowly becoming more mature in appearance. Exploring the genitals and becoming familiar with their sensations is all part of human sex education of an informal kind. In time, it is hoped that adolescents will become adjusted adults with mature and successful love lives. The practice of becoming familiar with and at ease with one's own sex organs can allay much embarrassment and ignorance about one's own sexual processes and arousal patterns when the time comes to engage in sex with a partner.

Masturbation continues in the adult years, as part of a loving relationship between couples and also alone. There does not need to be a 'reason' for masturbating beyond achieving sexual pleasure, but there is medical evidence that masturbation can make an adult a more relaxed, happy, amenable person, better able to cope with the stress of everyday life. This can be particularly so if there is no sex partner readily available, during separations from a regular or marital partner, during illness or pregnancy perhaps, when there is any unwelcome, enforced lack of sexual relations. There is no evidence that long periods of sexual abstinence do any physical good or are character forming.

Masturbation may be especially helpful if a couple have different sexual appetites—the one who has a greater sex drive can help redress the balance in a relationship by masturbating.

Learning different ways to manipulate the penis, the clitoris and the *erogenous zones** to achieve orgasm can help overcome many sexual problems for either a man or a woman. A woman who has a low arousal rate or who is unable to attain orgasm can commonly improve the situation by masturbating, especially in front of a mirror. She can learn the movements and the areas of her genitals which produce sexual arousal and can concentrate on developing this. For a man, too, if he has trouble with reaching his orgasm too soon (*premature ejaculation**) he can practise masturbation as a means of achieving more control.

For a couple to watch each other masturbate is a wonderful way of learning the sexual needs and wishes of a partner. Noticing the movements used while masturbating, the timing and pressure of stroking and other movements and so on can all be put to good use in mutual masturbation during *foreplay**.

People often ask many questions about masturbation: Is it harmful? Do all people do it? Is it immature? How often do people do it? A few short answers will put aside any uncertainties or fears. Masturbation is not harmful if a few simple precautions are taken. Violently pulling the foreskin can injure the penis, so can squeezing its end too hard to bending an erect penis suddenly or too far in the wrong direction. There is an occasional ten-

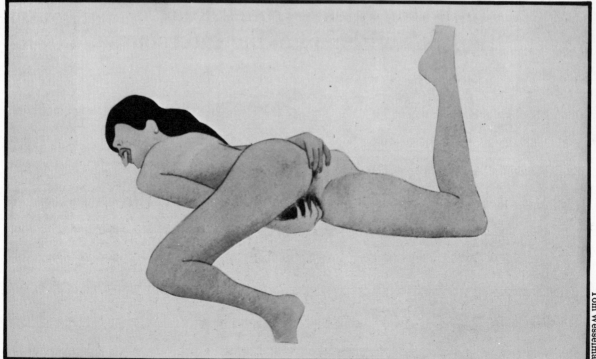

Tom Wesselman

Old Wives' Tales

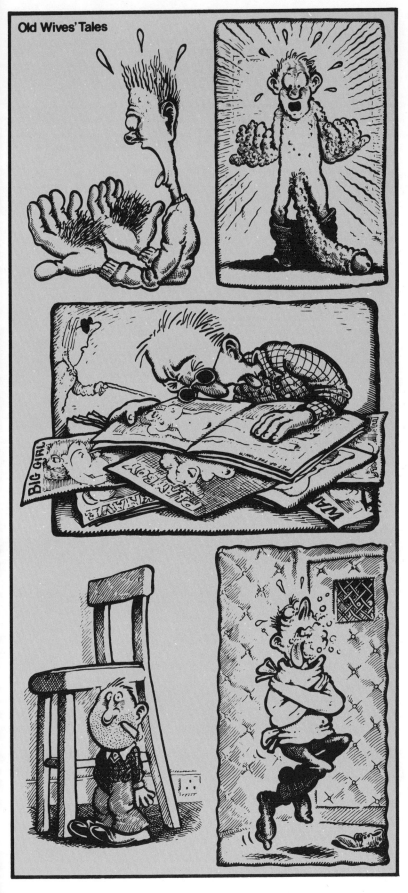

dency for a man or woman to force too many fingers or other objects into the vagina, but using *dildos**, *vaginal balls**, or other softish articles is safe and pleasurable. (Never ever put anything into the vagina which cannot be extracted or any glass object which might break.) People should masturbate together or alone with clean hands and fingernails—germs can cause infections in the sensitive genital areas.

Most people do masturbate sometime, somewhere, somehow (*Kinsey** found out in the 1950s that almost 100 per cent of men had masturbated to orgasm some time in their life and a large proportion of women had too.) Some people may masturbate once a year, once a month, once a week, once or three times a day—how often is a question of personal pleasure and preference. Masturbation isn't just a childish act; it is a mature sexual pleasure too.

There are so many old wives' tales about the dangers and evils of masturbation that they would fill almost a whole book. Actually, anti-masturbation stories should be called 'old doctors' tales' because a long line of distinguished medical men (notable was the Victorian, William Acton) have scared the wits out of generations of people by suggesting horrible results from 'touching yourself' (dementia, blindness, baldness, growing hair on your palms, etc.). It has even been suggested that masturbation is forbidden by the Bible because of the story of Onan who spilled his seed on the ground. Hence, the term onanism came into use for masturbation. However, this Biblical story is more likely a reference to coitus interruptus or the *withdrawal** method of birth control.

Masturbation has been called SELF-ABUSE, but this is without either logical or medical foundation. The terms AUTO-EROTICISM or AUTO-SEXUALITY are more accurate and better describe masturbation. Giving oneself sexual pleasure should be recognized as part of the whole spectrum of enjoyable human sexuality. Masturbation is natural, it is wholesome, it is even instructive and helpful in reducing sexual tensions. 'Know thyself' is one of the important philosophical truths of Western culture. What better way to get to know oneself than through exploring one's own body.

Doll

The ultimate in satisfaction for the man who has no sexual partner is provided by life-size, inflatable rubber dolls. These vary in sophistication according to price, but all offer an artificial vagina and anus, and sometimes a mouth for oral penetration as well. The dolls have female faces, usually with wigs, and large breasts. The arms end in hands but the legs usually have no feet. These masturbatory dummies offer relief mainly to men who are either too shy to seek real-life contacts (*loneliness**) or who are handicapped by a physical *disability**. An elementary version exists in the form of a portable rubber vagina, known rather obviously as a 'sailor's sweetheart'. For women, the equivalent is an inflatable male torso equipped with an erect penis that is stiffened by pumping air into it. Female and male sex dolls have one advantage over human partners: they neither talk nor criticize their lovers' performance.

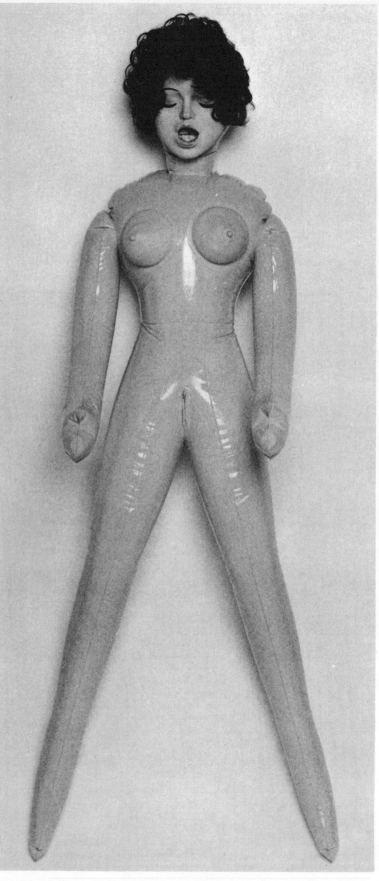

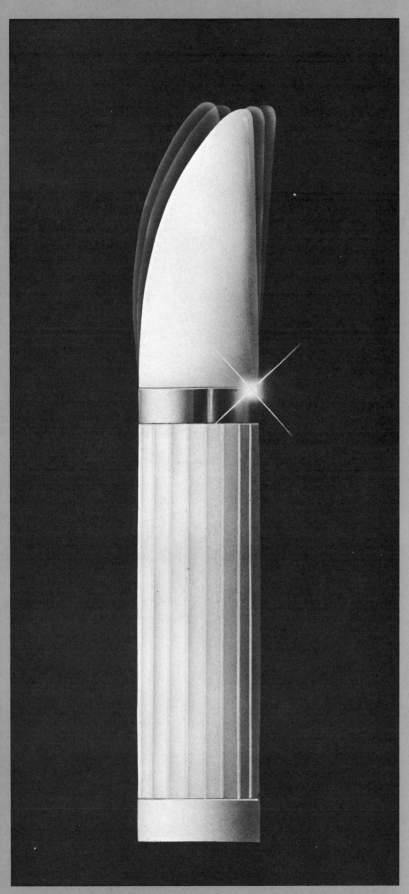

Vibrator

Though often marketed as a device for general muscle massage, a small vibrator is generally used for sexual purposes, as a *dildo** or *clitoral stimulator*. It is enjoyable for women to use while masturbating. In foreplay, a vibrator can be both stimulating and relaxing when it is used to massage the *erogenous zones** and various other parts of the body, such as the cheeks, neck, wrists, armpits or knees.

An ordinary vibrator is a plastic cylinder about 6 to 7in (160–180 cm) long and about 1½in (3.5 cm) in diameter. It is usually tapered at one end and flat at the opposite end. Inside the barrel is a tiny electric motor powered by batteries which effects an up-and-down or gentle side-to-side whirring motion. Some vibrators can be plugged into a main electric current source in the wall.

Vibrators are available in different colours and sizes. Some are equipped with a variety of exchangeable heads— small 3in ones for rectal use (only a small size vibrator should ever be used in the rectum) and larger ones up to 10in around for vaginal use, clitoral and general body massage. Electric vibrating dildos can be partially filled with a warm liquid to imitate ejaculation. All vibrators should be washed in soap and water after use, and there is no danger of electric shock in battery-operated types.

Vibrators generate a warm, pleasant sensation when turned on and pressed against the skin. They can be gently stroked against the glans or shaft of the penis or against the vulval lips or inside the vagina or rectum. They can also be held in place against the genitals and simply left to vibrate. If pressed against the clitoris they can stimulate an orgasm. Vibrators can be used simultaneously, one in the vagina and one in the rectum, but they should not be inserted too roughly or pushed in too far by oneself or one's sexual partner.

Vaginal Balls

The most common kind of vaginal balls are hollow plastic spheres about 1¼in (3 cm) in diameter attached to a nylon cord, which is joined to a waist belt front and back. The one or more spheres are put high up in the vagina (or sometimes into the rectum), or drawn up, by means of the cord, firmly between the vaginal lips. Weights inside the spheres make them move back and forth to provide a pleasurable sensation inside as a woman walks about or sits in a chair rocking back and forth. In masturbation, if the balls are withdrawn just as orgasm approaches, the sensation of pleasure may be intensely increased. Balls containing mercury as the quivering weight inside should never be used. Mercuric salts are highly poisonous and dangerous injury can result.

Various names are given to vaginal balls: Geisha Balls, Ben-Wa, Thailand Beads, Rin-no-Tama. They reflect a probable origin in Eastern Asia, where refined erotic aids made a much earlier appearance than in the West.

BEN-WA Vibra Tone Balls

TWO BALLS: Both consisting of Durable Polished Plastic and both weighted conspicuously, attached together by a fine nylon cord.

"These BALLS are the descendants of the finest "JAPANESE AUTO-MATED MASTURBATION EQUIPMENT FOR WOMEN."

Hundreds of years ago, Japanese Women developed an UNPRECEDENTED technique of "VOLUPTUOUS MASTURBATION" by INSERTING both balls "well into the Vagina."

BECAUSE OF THE "VIBRA" EFFECT CONTAINED WITH-IN THE WEIGHT OF THE BALLS, Immediate "Irresist-able" SEXUAL STIMULATION would occur; transmitting vibra waves of PLEASURE throughout the entire composition of the "VAGINA, UTERUS, LABIA and out-ward to the CLITORIS."

These women could DRIFT continuously FROM ONE ORGASM TO ANOTHER by rolling their hips or by rocking in a chair.

23A–$19.95

23B–FRENCH BEN - WA VIBRA TONE BALL THE TRUE FRENCH CONNECTION

$19.95

It is written that hundreds of years ago, clever Japanese women, developed a tech-nique for masturbating. To relieve her sexual tensions, She reached into a plush case and took out two small, shiny metal balls. These balls were then inserted well into the vagina. The woman would usually lay down, or to become more excited, she would rock in a chair.

BEN-WA GOLD BALLS

23C–Plastic Box – $8.95
23D–Plush Velvet Box – $9.95
23 E–Plush Suede Pouch – $9.95

17

DUO-PLUS

Sharing and multiplying one
couple's experience with others.

Group Sex

Traditionally sex is a personal and private matter. There is no theoretical reason why more than two people should not be involved in sexual encounters, putting aside moral, medical and emotional reasons or objections. Without doubt, for some people, there is a lot of enjoyment to be had from group sex. Certainly the practice of sex in company has increased in the past decade.

Much of the fascination of what is

erotic appeal to be derived from an ORGY, an occasion when several people or even a large group engage in licentious and lewd sexual practices with a succession of available partners. Clearly, *voyeurism** plays a strong part in an orgy's appeal.

Group sex is not necessarily the same thing as *partner-swapping** (which tends to mean two couples exchanging partners on a mutually agreed occasion). For two couples to have sex in each other's company, in a simple exchange of regular partners, is rather a different thing. It can be a warm aspect of friendship, and both couples may find

enough imagination, but an example might be: a woman lies on her back and a man has intercourse with her; at the same time she sucks the penis of another man who is engaged in oral sex with another woman; this latter woman is masturbating another woman who is fellating yet another man . . . and so on and on. CHAIN SEX is another word for daisy chain, but is sometimes interpreted as people having sex with one partner after another in a regular or random sequence.

The so-called GANG BANG is different in that it involves a number of persons of one sex (usually men) having inter-

called group sex lies in its novelty and 'naughtiness' which add a sense of thrill. There is also the attraction of seeing other people naked and of being able to make love to them without the danger of a relationship breaking up or the divorce court looming. In general, group sex appeals more to men than to women. Thus its practice can be a dividing influence between a couple if a woman goes along with it with some reluctance, either to please her partner or for fear of losing him or appearing dull and unadventurous. Nonetheless, there is a great deal of

it a highly instructive process to watch and to be watched, as well as to discuss different aspects of love making. Furthermore, the sexual excitement of seeing others having intercourse, or of having them see you, is a sensation that has to be experienced to be appreciated.

In the frantic search for novelty that goes on in the sex lives of some people, a group sex activity called the DAISY CHAIN has been invented. In this, with some physical difficulty, unlimited numbers of people can have sexual contact at the same time. The actual sequences are available to anyone with

course one after another with a single partner. When coercion and even violence are involved, a gang bang is a particularly horrible kind of multiple *rape**. At other times, with the full agreement of everyone, a woman may permit serial intercourse with one gang member after another.

Quite different is *group therapy**, occasionally used by some psychiatric units in the treatment of sexual and communication problems. Some psychiatrists consider that sexual activities in group surroundings help reduce sexual dysfunction.

Group Sex

Group sex, in general, can cause a number of problems. Foremost is the question of sexually-transmitted disease. Infections like *Candidiasis** or other *vaginitis**, are common conditions, especially in females, which are spread by sexual contact. *Gonorrhea** in females is frequently present with no obvious symptoms and is sexually transmitted. If one infected woman is present in a group sex scene, by the end of the episode several people will have acquired a share of her germs. Without knowing they are infected, they may go on to participate in other group sex, thus spreading infection even further. Men are commonly impotent when they first join group sex scenes. The problem of impotence is that once begun, it can become more and more severe, even occurring in ordinary person-to-person encounters or in stable relations. Also, although people may start group sex with a 'liberal' mind, when they actually see their usual partner in a frenzy of sexual excitement with someone else, deep jealousies can surface which may cause real problems in a relationship. Many people's inhibitions are more real than they thought. To sum up, group sex has little to offer an adjusted couple with a good relationship, except as an occasional diversion. Whether any risks are worth taking is up to the couple.

18

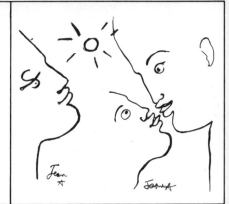

SAME-SEX PARTNERS

Man/man and woman/woman
relationships in the era of Gay
Liberation.

David Hockney (detail)

Homosexual

In its broadest generic sense, 'homosexual' describes any group comprising members of the same sex, including athletic teams, religious orders or a mother and daughter. (The term has nothing to do with the Latin work *homo*, meaning 'man', but derives from the combination of the Greek word *homo-*, meaning 'same' and the Latin-based word 'sex'.)

In contemporary usage 'homosexual' has been loosely and misleadingly applied to individuals who experience same-sex behaviours—loosely, because this usage defines a person purely in terms of his or her sexual orientation, and misleadingly, because *most* persons who have had sexual relations with, or felt a sexual attraction to, others of their own sex, have also experienced sex with or been sexually attracted to persons of the opposite six.

Homosexual behaviour, then, is defined as sexual activity involving persons of the same sex. It can consist of simple touching, kissing, petting, frictation (TRIBADISM, THE PRINCETON OR OXFORD RUB), stroking the genitals, mouth-genital contact, anal stimulation and anal intercourse (for the male, also called SODOMY and BUGGERY). Psychological homosexual reactions consist of an awareness of sexual arousal by seeing, hearing, or thinking about persons of the same sex.

It is difficult for those who are not acquainted with cultures other than those directly under the influence of the Judaeo-Christian tradition to understand fully how inhibited and rigid is this tradition as it has now evolved when it comes to sex. Looking at our Western tradition, anthropologists tell us that we are almost unique in the proscriptions, the anxieties and the rigidities which we have developed in this area.

Homosexuality is found in virtually all species, in all strata of human society, and in all parts of the world. It is as old as humanity itself and examples of homosexuality have been recorded from the earliest times and noted among a great range of peoples. The fact that it occurs among primitive peoples as well as in advanced cultures indicates that it is not the result of cultural decay or degeneration, as some people like to believe. In a study of 76 societies, Ford and Beach noted that in 64 per cent of them some form of homosexual activities was considered nor-

mal and socially acceptable. In the remaining 36 per cent, there was evidence to suggest that even in these more rigid societies, homosexual practices took place in secret. A study of 195 world cultures by Hoch and Zubin showed that only 14 per cent rejected male homosexuality and only 11 per cent rejected female homosexuality. Studies by anthropologists George Devereux and Ruth Benedict only begin to describe the elaborate and often ritualized incorporation of homosexuality into many of the Indian tribes of North America, such as the Mohave, Zuñi and Chukchee. Among some tribes, the shamans, credited with supernatural powers, were often homosexual and referred to as 'men-women' (for example, the Berdache of the Pacific Northwest and the Mujerados of New Mexico). They were accorded high prestige and festivals were given in their honour.

For the half century or more, from the 1860s to 1934, Germany had been the centre of an early and vigorous homosexual rights campaign. Dr. Bankert, a Hungarian, called for a rational approach to homosexuality and himself devised the term 'homosexual' in 1869. Karl Heinrich Ulrichs coined the quaint term 'urnings' (based on *Uranismus*) for homosexuals. He derived it from the Greek word *ouranios*, meaning 'spiritual', and intended it to embody the notion that homosexuals were a 'third sex', a woman's mind in a man's body, and vice versa for women.

Magnus Hirschfeld* who founded the first homophile liberation organization in 1897, the Scientific Humanitarian Committee, also began the Institute for Sexual Science in 1919, as a repository for biological, anthropological, statistical and ethnological data and documentation relating to sexology. Hirschfeld travelled extensively and supporting branches of his homophile group sprang up throughout Europe, including Russia. He even visited China to proclaim the rights of homophiles everywhere. In the United States, this early movement had its first public support from the revolutionary, Emma Goldman, who through her writings and speeches became the first major figure in the USA to carry the issue of homosexual love to the broader public. In May 1933, the books, photographs and documents of Hirschfeld's Institute were publicly burned by the Nazis. The prudery of Stalinism and fascism, and the ravages of the Second World War, wiped out virtually all public traces of the first wave of homosexual liberation.

In America, the Kinsey studies undermined one popular myth—that homosexuality is an obscure phenomenon. Kinsey's data suggested that only about one-half of the adult population in the United States is exclusively heterosexual in behaviour. Using his statistics, 37 % of the adult male population and at least 13 % of the adult female population have some overt homosexual experience to the point of orgasm between adolescence and old age. An additional 13 per cent of the males and 8 per cent of the females react erotically to members of the same sex without having an overt experience.

Contrary to the frequently held notion that all homosexuals are alike, they are, in fact, very diverse. It is more accurate to speak of a variety of *homosexualities* that range from homosexual celibates to homosexual communities, from committed and long-term monogamous couples (sometimes in a solemnized 'gay marriage') to brief multi-partnerships, from the anonymous encounter (or *trick*) to romantic and prolonged courtships. The Kinsey report emphasized that homosexuality, like other natural propensities, exists as a continuum—a matter not of either/or but of degree—that unorthodox sexual practices were not confined to homosexuals but involved heterosexual individuals and married couples as well. In fact, many persons involved in homosexual behaviour are also in heterosexual marriages and/or parents of traditional families.

The Kinsey Report, with its massive data and its affiliation with a major university, plus its unprecedented circulation among the lay public, for the first time put into the hands of the homosexual a weapon with which to launch the battle for equality (*Gay Liberation**).

Many of the myths surrounding homosexuality are falling away, as sex education and sounder research proceed. The illness myth of homosexuals is no longer tenable, and the stereotypes of effeminacy (for males) and the swaggering 'butch' (for females) are being left behind as it is realized that most often there are no 'identifying' characteristics. One of the last myths to go is that the homosexual is likely to be a child molester, or at least a corrupting influence on the young. The facts do not warrant such fears. Child molestation occurs with much greater frequency between an adult heterosexual male and an under age female than between an adult homosexual male and an underage male.

Male Homosexuality

Kinsey's *Sexual Behavior in the Human Male,* although published thirty years ago, is still the classic scientific study in its area. For white males in the American population, the incidence of homosexual behaviour was given as follows:

1 37 per cent had at least one overt homosexual experience between the onset of adolescence and old age.

2 10 per cent were predominantly homosexual for at least three years between the ages of 16 and 55.

3 4 per cent were solely homosexual after the onset of adolescence.

4 18 per cent of all males have as much homosexual as heterosexual experience in their development.

A distinction between heterosexuality and homosexuality is arbitrary, at best. Kinsey's research demonstrates that humans engage in different kinds of sexual activity at different times and in different situations. Therefore we should allow for many phases in the continuum between exclusive heterosexuality and exclusive homosexuality. Modern theorists, like Evelyn Hooker, hold that humans are born sexually malleable and that they have a general sexual predisposition rather than a specifically heterosexual, homosexual or bisexual one. The kind of sexual learning the individual experiences will determine the choice of sexual object. The sexual drive is instinctive; the object of that drive is learned. Kinsey's finding that 37 per cent of the total white male population had had at least some overt homosexual experience to the point of orgasm supports this idea.

Evidence that homosexuality is not merely a substitute for heterosexuality has been found in the behaviour of male primates. They respond readily to homosexual stimuli. Mutual grooming, genital examination, mounting, inversion of sexual role, anal penetration, mutual masturbation, erotogenic play, homosexual orgasm and even oral-genital explorations have been reported, even when heterosexual opportunities existed. Another group of theories is based on the belief that homosexuality develops through severely pathological life experiences. Most of these theories are biased by certain *a priori* assumptions, especially that homosexuality is a symptom of some pervasive disturbance within the total personality and that homosexual interests can

Oscar Wilde with Bosie

Verlaine with Rimbaud

Walt Whitman with Pete

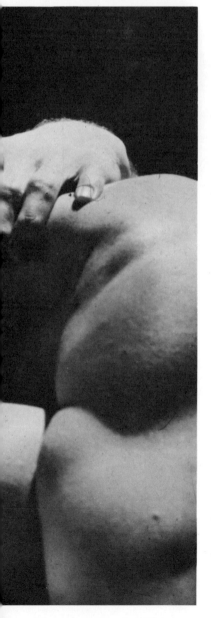

only develop in a context of mental sickness. This bias is supported by theories and perceptions which have developed in a clinical setting, from a population of homosexuals who have already defined themselves as sick, or been defined as criminal by society.

In the learning process, a living organism tends to repeat those experiences which are pleasurable and avoid those experiences which are painful. Yet for a *taboo** activity in our society, homosexual behaviour occurs at least once in 37 per cent of the white male population. Homosexuality (like heterosexuality) satisfies many social, sexual nd emotional needs. Many individuals like, enjoy and love persons of their own sex, and are homosexual not because of hating or fearing members of the opposite sex. Kinsey's statistics show that people move in and out of the gay lifestyle, marry persons of the opposite sex, have children, and at the same time relate in different degrees with members of their own sex.

There is no coherent male homosexual community, but rather a diversity of subcultures. There are cliques composed of long-term monogamous couples who have been together for many decades and do not associate with single individuals. There are cliques of upper-income businessmen who do not go to public gay places like bars, steam baths and restaurants, but stay in their 'closets' by only associating with other similarly closeted persons. CLOSET QUEEN or CLOSET CASE describe the state of mind of a person who hides his or her homosexuality. COMING OUT of the closet is a process involving self-acceptance and, if warranted, disclosure to others.

There is diversity in the nature of gay relationships. Some homosexual men prefer anonymous or one-time sexual encounters, and steam baths and bars provide the opportunity or such contacts. Steam baths are rather like hotels in which a person can rent a small room. People wander about in towels, take showers, go in the steam rooms, pools, or orgy areas, and have sex in pairs or in groups. Individuals may ask others to their room.

Gay bars are a centre for gay men meeting each other in most larger cities and towns. These bars are similar to heterosexual singles' bars, but many emphasize social rather than purely sexual contact.

Currently, the gay movement in America is trying to provide alternative and more personal ways for gay men to meet and relate to each other.

These include their own social and political organizations, community centres in larger cities, student unions, interest groups, free universities, counselling services and health service centres. A major goal of the gay movement is to provide alternatives to the bars, steam baths, parks and other public areas which an oppressive culture has designated as a gay ghetto where homosexual contacts are made.

Anal sex is an important sexual option which many, though not all, gay men enjoy. It is a myth that the partner who receives his partner's penis anally is passive and effeminate and takes a woman's role in the relationship. Masculinity does not exclude enjoying the receipt of anal pleasure, and many partners take turns in giving and receiving it. Anal intercourse is not harmful if engaged in a knowledgeable and sensitive way, with proper lubrication, and anal massage with the fingers before entering. Known by its old English name BUGGERY, or its Biblical equivalent, SODOMY, this kind of intercourse is a criminal offence in many countries and states—even between a man and a woman.

Anal entry with the whole hand is known as FIST-FUCKING, while stimulation of the anus with the tongue or lips is RIMMING or ANILINGUS. The predominant forms of genital sex engaged in by gay men are fellatio and mutual masturbation. FRICTATION is when two men rub against each other face to face, and is also called (depending on one's nationality) the OXFORD RUB or the PRINCETON RUB.

A gay man looking for a one-time sexual encounter (*trick* or *number*) is said to be *cruising*. A men's room which is popular for making sex contacts is called a *tea room*. Holes made in the partitions between men's toilets, through which a man can put his penis for fellatio are called *glory holes* or *suck holes*. A man who prefers underage partners is a CHICKEN QUEEN.

The older style of somewhat effeminate homosexual is an *auntie*. The younger generation of self-affirming gays, with greater inner confidence, who live in a less oppressive climate, may no longer employ the sarcastic wit that is recognizable by gesture and intonation as CAMP. They may call themselves produly by the old terms of abuse, like FAGGOT or QUEER. A more liberating term that has been adopted in place of either 'gay' or 'homosexual' is HOMOPHILE.

A long-lasting relationship between two gays is *gay marriage*.

Homo-erotic Art

Most commonly used in the context of homo-erotic art, this term means the same as homosexual, but is more logically constructed from two Greek words. Homo-erotic art is for gays what pin-ups are for straights. Fine nude physiques, butch faces and well-hung genitals are as standard here as the tit-and-bum and beaver formulas in heterosexual pin-ups.

Popular homo-erotic art has escaped from the hypocritical imitation of classical art which once enabled its themes to be publicly accepted. Photographic studies of nude Neapolitan boys and the slickly erotic neo-classical nudes of Alma-Tadema and Val Prinsep, glorified an 'artistic' ideal. With the frankly homosexual expressiveness of the Arizona cowboys drawn by the American artist known as Quaintance, the pretence could be dropped. The style came up to date in jeans, and had a late, live flowering in the Elvis Presley image. Quaintance's rather sentimental western boys were supplanted by the bike-club style exemplified by the equally pseudonymous Tom of Finland (rumored to be a resident of Sweden). Tom did for gay sex-symbols what Varga had done for girlies, treating the arousing features of male muscle, buttocks and crotches with the same baroque over-emphasis that advertisers give to female bottoms and breasts. More traditionally American in taste, and perhaps a little less erotic, are the drawings of Rip Colt, whose academic draughtsmanship does not inhibit him from hanging his nudes with those disproportionately large genitals that are a 'must' in homo-erotic pin-ups and magazines.

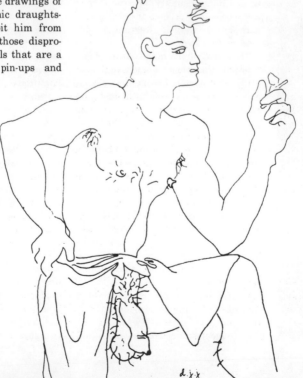

Quaintance

Tom of Finland

Colt

Jean Cocteau

Female Homosexuality

In contrast to the research designed to assess male homosexuals, psychological research on lesbian populations has been scarce. In 1942, Abraham Maslow administered a questionnaire to 139 women about feelings of self-esteem and dominance. The ten women scoring highest on measures of self-esteem and dominance all reported either homosexual fantasies or experiences. None of the ten lowest-scoring women reported either homosexual fantasy or experience. In 1969, Hopkins administered a personality inventory to fifty lesbians and a control group of heterosexual women. She found that lesbians were more independent, reserved, dominant, unconventional, self-sufficient and composed than the heterosexual controls. In the 1970s, Oberstone and Adelman in two separate studies administered the MMPI to separate groups of lesbian and heterosexual women. Differences, where they existed, were insignificant.

Spokeswomen for the lesbian-feminist movement explain their lesbianism as a choice: an emotional and cognitive rejection of the 'patriarchy's' exploitation and devaluation of women, as well as the reclaiming and affirming of women's strength and beauty and the creation of a culture which emphasizes cooperation, conservation and the values of the spirit.

Traditional views seek the causes of lesbianism in psychoanalytic, hormonal/genetic, or behaviour/social learning theories, but Dr. Evelyn Hooker, in her National Institute of Mental Health Task Force report in 1972, wrote: 'diverse forms of adult homosexuality are produced by many combinations of variables including biological, cultural, psychodynamic, structural and situational. No single class of determinants, whether psychodynamic, cultural or biological, accounts for all or even one of these diverse forms'.

Lesbianism as an openly displayed life style occurred only where women had resources to remain financially independent of men, whether thanks to family money, to an independently practiced skill or to a social environment (for example, in countries where welfare benefits are relatively high and accessible). For less fortunate women, it could mean the occasional furtive encounter or a secret second life. For some who were not self-defined as homosexuals, but who hung around gay bars or with gay people, there were the scurrilous names FRUIT FLY or FAG HAG.

In the early 1950s in America, when economic, legal and social sanctions still kept the majority of the lesbian population invisible, Del Martin and Phyllis Lyon formed the Daughters of Bilitis (DOB), a group organized to serve the social, cultural and political needs of lesbians. Their publication, *The Ladder,* first edited in the early days in the movement by Barbara Gittings, was for American and British lesbians, justifiably afraid of disclosure, the only link with an underground with which they could identify. Until the late 1960s, even in metropolitan areas, lesbians met in covert ways, at bars, perhaps at DOB meetings, or by enduring months of testing, veiled allusions if they met in a non-lesbian setting and could not be sure. The risk was discovery and could mean then, as it often does now, loss of job, impugned character, loss of children, career destruction, ostracism by friends and family, perhaps hospital treatment and jail. With this there went depression, anxiety, damaged self-esteem and self-destructive behaviour.

In the 1960s, the women's movement provided, on a grand scale, a context in which lesbians could begin to form positive ideas about their status in society. They saw their oppression as women, and specifically as women who chose not to collaborate with their oppressors. At this point, splits occurred between gay men and women who had previously seen their fates linked by the common oppression of homosexuality. In consciousness-raising sessions, study groups, 'rap' sessions, in National Organization of Women (NOW) and other feminist organizations, lesbians began to find each other, to work with heterosexual women for common political goals, to see themselves no longer as either immoral, sinful or neurotic, and to 'come out' both inside and outside the movement. They formed their own interest groups, and emerged often with an identity separate from heterosexual women's groups and from gay men's groups.

In larger metropolitan areas, lesbians who defined themselves as radical separatists formed living and working collectives. These analyzed their oppression in economic terms, and attempted to live by socialist principles. There are lesbians who share their identity with no one, or only with one lover, and who do not question their status in their culture. There are lesbians who tell friends but not work colleagues about their identities.

The closeness generated between previously heterosexual (usually young) women in the women's movement has created a new type of lesbian—women who, 'came out' through the women's movement, amid the support of their sisters, and with a positive rationale for lesbianism. Kinsey's figures of a one to three per cent lesbian population have probably been outdated by the number of women who have realized their own lesbianism within the context of the women's movement. Lesbians are now more likely to use the courts to challenge discrimination, and although court decisions frequently reflect a heterosexual bias, some landmark decisions have awarded openly lesbian mothers custody of their children and forced employers to make restitution.

The women's movement has also affected lesbian self-images, styles of living and relating. DYKE, long a derogatory word to describe ultra-male-dressing females, has been embraced as their own name by some lesbian feminists. Playing BUTCH (the partner who acts out a masculine role) and FEM (the passive, feminine role), done elegantly with monocles and tuxedos in Paris in the 1920s, and less elegantly by less affluent counterparts in earlier and later generations, has been supplanted among feminists by a more egalitarian, sharing, androgynous way of looking and behaving. Lesbians affected by the women's movement are now less likely to look for a life-long monogamous commitment. Viewing lovers and partners in non-possessive ways, having open relationships or living and relating intimately to more than one woman, is often the preferred model.

Lesbians of today are as diverse as the pluralistic societies to which they belong. They may be radical or conservative, black or white, rich or poor. The may choose motherhood or non-parenthood. They may conceal their sexual identities or be open. They may have many partners, one partner or none. They may be celibate. Their appearance and behaviour may be masculine, feminine or androgynous. They may be content, productive or dissatisfied. They may be gifted or quite ordinary. What these women share is diversity of values, attitudes, experience and economic status, and diversity of reaction to cultural stigma.

Gay Liberation

The first concerted and successful efforts to organize homosexual people occurred in America in the 1950s.

The Matachine Society, an organization for education and fellowship of gay men was formed in Los Angeles, and the Daughters of Bilitis, a parallel organization for lesbians was formed in San Francisco. The social climate in which these organizations could flourish had been created in part by the publication of Kinsey's data and by Cory's book *The Homosexual in America*, which defined homosexuality as a different sexual orientation rather than a disease to be cured.

In the next twenty years, almost 200 homophile organizations sprang up in the USA. A similar proliferation occurred at the same time in Europe. The average group had about thirty active members and rarely existed outside the large cities. Members gave lectures to educate others, and engaged in protests against the hostile treatment of homosexuals in education, business and the media. Counselling for gays was provided, with referral to sympathetic professionals. Money for court cases was collected. Members lobbied against discriminatory laws and the unfavourable categories commonly applied to homosexuals in psychiatric diagnosis.

In the late 1960s, gay people began to link their struggle to other civil rights movements in the USA, particularly the black and feminist movements. The catalyst for this self-definition as an oppressed group occurred in June, 1969, in New York City. A gay bar, The Stonewall, on Christopher Street in New York, was raided by police. Instead of a routine and docile dispersal of the patrons, the gay people gathered outside the bar. A paddy wagon appeared, scuffles occurred, arrests were made. The crowd, charging police harrassment, fought the police. Clashes between gays and police continued for several days. During the week several gay men and women formed the Gay Liberation Front whose slogan was 'Out of the closets and into the streets'. This incident is celebrated annually in larger US cities with a 'gay pride' parade.

During the next seven years a number of gay groups, announcing goals of revolutionary political change, formed in America and Europe. The gay movement today contains significant numbers who see their fate linked to that of other oppressed peoples in the world and welcome the demise of capitalism. Other gay people began to tackle discrimination from inside the system—campaigning as openly gay, and sometimes being elected to public office. Gay people since the 1960s have been less likely to ignore discrimination, and have taken civil rights cases to court.

Gay liberation is for most gay people the growing awareness that second-class citizenship is not a necessary corollary of minority sexual orientation. For a smaller number of gay people, gay liberation is an active struggle against discrimination both within and outside the law.

Paul Hardman, an American attorney and Chairman of the Board of the Pride Foundation, a national educational and legal aid group for homosexuals, cites recent events (1977) as signs of what is to come in the gay liberation movement. For the first time in the history of the US legal system, a lesbian sued the United States Navy and won. Another milestone was the meeting of homosexual rights leaders at the White House in March, 1977, with Ms. Margaret Costanza, assistant to the President in public affairs.

The action of the American Psychiatric Association in dropping homosexuality from its list of mental illnesses is a positive step towards changing attitudes and, eventually, the law. The American Psychological Association's position that homosexuality does not in itself imply any impairment in judgment, stability or general social or vocational capabilities supports the new attitude. In the words of the eminent physician, Dr. Harry Benjamin, in the *American Journal of Psychotherapy*: 'If adjustment is necessary, it should be made primarily with regard to the position the homosexual occupies in present day society, and society should more often be treated than the homosexual'.

Drag

The old theatrical slang word 'drag' is often used by heterosexual people when they mean to describe any man dressed in women's clothes—whether a female impersonator on stage or a *transvestite**.

Strictly speaking, however, drag denotes (apart from the original vaudeville impersonation sense) homosexual men dressing up in spectacular female garments for a 'drag ball' or similar social occasion. In this instance, they are not endeavouring to 'pass' as women, as transvestites do when they go in for one of their periodic bouts of crossdressing. Gay men in drag are deliberately smudging the border line between male and female life-styles. They are even trying to outdo women in the colourfulness and fantasy of their party clothing. A drag ball presents an opportunity for gay men both to satirize female fashions and to indulge in outrageous creations of their own. Thus there are in drag elements of envy as well as of contempt for women.

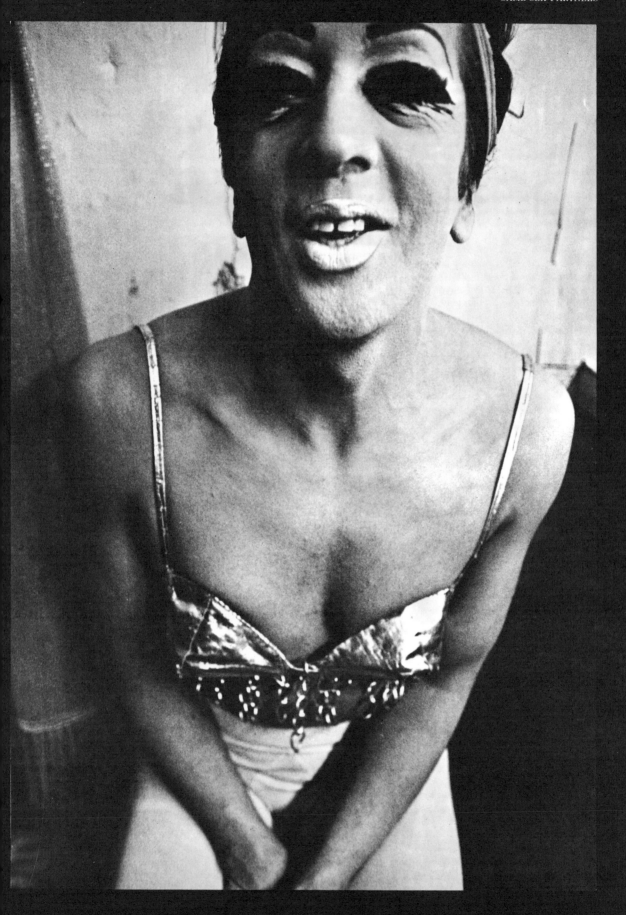

Homophobia

A shortened version of *homoerotophobia*, the term homophobia describes a fear of homosexuals, homosexual behaviour or thoughts, and also a fear of being homosexual oneself. It was coined by Wainwright Churchill in *Homosexual Behaviour Among Males* (1967) and used by George Weinberg in *Society and the Healthy Homosexual* (1972). Kinsey and his colleagues remarked: 'There are practically no other European groups, unless it be in England, and few if any other cultures elsewhere in the world, which have become as disturbed over male homosexuality as we have here in the United States'.

A Harris Poll in 1969 found that 63 per cent of the American population believed homosexuality is 'harmful to American life'. A Gallup Poll, reported in Hyde (1970), measured attitudes held by the public at large about homosexuality. Ninety-three per cent of the populace who were questioned regarded homosexuality as a disease. Simmons (1969) in a representative sample of 134 subjects found that 72 per cent thought homosexual persons to be 'sexually abnormal', 52 per cent thought them 'perverted', 42 per cent thought them both 'mentally ill', and 'maladjusted', 29 per cent thought them 'effeminate'.

Research indicates that people's perceptions are biased in the direction of what they anticipate that they will see. Researchers Kitsuse (1967), Farina (1971), Simmons (1969), and Winslow (1972) have investigated the nature of the homosexual stereotype and a person's reactions to individuals so labelled. The tendency to react to stereotypes seemed to be the general characteristic of certain respondents rather than a response triggered by particular behaviour. Simmons found that the people most likely to think in stereotypes tended to have less education, and that there was an association between intolerance toward ethnic minorities and the tendency to devalue individuals.

Simmons' subjects felt more socially distant from homosexuals of both sexes than from any of 13 other groups, including former mental patients, ex-convicts, political radicals, and alcoholics.

A person who physically assaults men he suspects of being homosexuals is thought by some to be motivated by his own hidden homosexual feelings.

Bisexual

As currently used, bisexual means an individual who loves both sexes and usually acts upon this 'both-sex' orientation for sexual relationships and outlets. In biology, the term describes structures, individuals or aggregates of individuals that possess the anatomy or functions of both male and female sexes. Another older use of the word implied that a person has both masculine and feminine qualities within their single bodies. 'In some ways it is unfortunate', said Kinsey, 'that another

adjective for sexual behaviour is now used as a noun to describe individuals'. He pointed out that his research revealed that 46 per cent of the US population has engaged in overt sex as adults with both men and women. The rest of the population related to only one of the sexes: four per cent homosexual, and 50 per cent solely heterosexual in orientation or experience.

Overt sexual activity with both male and female partners may occur once or at separate periods in the lifetime of bisexual individuals. More closely defined, it means that sexual relations are actively chosen with both men and women. Some research suggests that bisexuals put less psychological investment into their sexual activities and relationships. The differences between men and women in body shape and personality seem to mean little to them as elements of arousal. A partner's congeniality and readiness to cooperate mean much more. Other researches think that the source of a person's bisexuality may be found in their response to personal qualities in others, rather than to their appearance as males or females. The principle that 'opposites attract' is not necessary for sexual stimulation with most bisexuals.

Advocates of bisexuality go beyond sexual behaviour to claim that feeling intellectually, emotionally and physically comfortable with both men and women can be a broader and better attitude to life. It diffuses the polarization of Men and Women and challenges those assumptions of Western culture that appear to be limiting to both men and women, such as competitive action, double standards of morality and rigid sex-role stereotyping and relationship styles, such as monogamy. Indeed in other cultures and civilizations overt sexuality with both males and females is common and often highly prized.

19

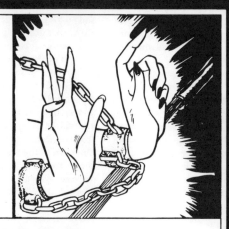

PARAPHILIAS

The varied fetishes and fantasies of the sex impulse.

Deviant

Words like deviant, deviation and perversion are emotionally loaded and difficult to define. Literally, to deviate means to stray or be sidetracked from the established course. In sexual matters, the term is used to describe something that is different from what is generally considered normal. If one is dealing with a measurable condition, like normal body temperature, it is easy enough to decide what is abnormal. The problem with human behaviour, especially sexual behaviour, is that what is normal for one person may be not at all normal for another. Another difficulty is that what is normal in one time and place is not so elsewhere or at a different period.

If normal means the accepted practice of a large part of the population at any given time, one could try to define normal sex for modern Western society on the basis of what happens most frequently. It would consist of mutual attraction, various forms of foreplay all the way from holding hands to fondling the genitals, and culminating in sexual intercourse, probably in a face-to-face position with the man on top. Some slightly less frequent practices, like the rear-entry position, masturbation or oral sex, could be listed among the normal ones (though in Victorian times even these would have been denounced as sinful). Anything else would have to be classed as a deviation. Since, however, there is a much wider spectrum of sexual expression than this, it is more reasonable to describe its many forms as *variations* or by the medical term PARAPHILIAS (meaning alternative ways of loving), rather than attempt to define a standard of normal or abnormal behaviour in sexual contacts.

Sometimes, however, people enjoy sexual variations which do not culminate in the form of intercourse as nature intends it to be, that is to say, orgasm with the penis in the vagina. If couples who masturbate each other or have a mutual oral climax also alternate this with full intercourse, one can still speak of variations. But if a person never has ordinary intercourse and only climaxes with children or animals, or by being whipped and humiliated, the term PERVERSION will be used by psychologists. An exception to this distinction is now increasingly made in favour of homosexual people, whose range of sexual expression cannot, obviously, include ordinary intercourse.

Discussion is made more difficult by the fact that a person's own sexual preferences may feel quite normal, while something another person does may seem odd, unpleasant or even revolting. Equally, many people who do odd things feel there is something the matter with them and seek medical help, only to discover they are not freaks.

No deviation has yet been recorded that is unique to one person, rare though some of them may be. However peculiar, nobody's particular sexual preference is unique, and it could be found somewhere in a list barely reaching 100 known possibilities. No one ever need feel alone with their feelings, and so long as what they do causes no harm to another person, such variations should be regarded as natural aspects of the *libido**.

The mechanisms which produce one or other kind of preference in a person are described—as far as they are yet understood—in the articles under the various headings that follow. In general, it is worth remembering that many functions of the human body are closely wired together through the central nervous system, having in many cases evolved from a common node in the embryo. As a result, parts of the body are often more closely connected with each other in our responses than we realize, and in some individuals more sensitively than in others.

For example, the anus is not a sexual organ, but it shares a network of responses with the genitals, and in some people it becomes a focus of intense erotic excitement. Similarly, the pleasure that comes from being stroked and caressed can be heightened, as the climax approaches, by being scratched or bitten; from this it is a short step to receiving pleasure from painful blows or stripes of a whip in association with feelings of orgasm. These are a few clues to the roots of anal and sado-masochistic 'perversions'.

Occasionally, a person may wish to be 'cured' of a particular sexual preference. Such treatment faces the difficulty that motivation for a real change in the patient's behaviour is seldom high enough—something more radical is involved than swallowing a drug or being listened to by an understanding physician. One method now offered is DESENSITIZATION, based on the ideas of behavioural psychology. This involves excessive exposure to such preferences, or associating the exposure with unpleasant experiences like electric shock or induced vomiting.

It's Your Body! It's Your Responsibility To Take Care Of It!

'If you are considering engaging in sado-masochistic sexual activity, the information that follows will be of use:

● 'The labels people use in describing themselves make clear who will be in control and what kinds of activities are likely to take place: sadist, masochist, dominant, submissive, top person, bottom person, master, slave.

● 'Activities that could take place during an S/M encounter include: verbal abuse, scolding, humiliation, discipline, bondage, restraints, suspension, blind-folding, caging, whipping, caning, birching, fist and/or arm fucking, spanking, branding, the use of hot wax, pissing (also known as watersports and the golden shower), pinching, wrestling, boxing, suffocation by various methods, house cleaning (usually bathrooms), wearing costumes and uniforms (especially boots and leather), wearing rubber, and acts of worship.

● 'Equipment that might be used in an S/M encounter include: ropes, chains, handcuffs, belts, rawhide, hot and cold water, uniforms, dirty underwear, paddles, dildoes, enema bags, hot wax, branding irons, razors, knives, pins, and sandpaper. Custom made equipment is expensive. People in the scene find that best buys can be found in hardware stores. Those that are handy often build their own.

● 'We suggest that beginners experiment with trusted friends. You might very well find that S/M activities are more fun to talk about and to fantasize about than to do. However, there are possible benefits to be reaped even if you don't think of yourself as an S/M person. It can be a way to enact the battle of the sexes in a stylized manner. It provides an opportunity to act out symbolic fantasies. It offers a form through which feelings of guilt over experiencing pleasure can be relieved.

● 'To begin with, you should know what you want to happen and what you don't want to happen. A good way to start is to read some S/M porno books to see what fantasies (if any) turn you on. Write down your fantasies. Make lists of activities that turn you on and activities that turn you off. Exchange this information in advance with your partner(s).

● 'Discuss the details with your partner(s) before actually beginning any scene. Determine in advance how you will let your partner(s) know when you want to stop. We suggest a key word or phrase or an obvious body movement or position.

● 'Above all, remember that it's your body. It's your responsibility to take care of it. Know your limits, and let your partner(s) know your limits. Know how to operate all equipment before using it on a partner. If you are using ropes or other restraints, be extra careful of cutting off blood and/or air for too long a period of time.

● 'Don't be talked into something you can't get out of.'

This advice was compiled by San Francisco Sex Information as a guide for volunteers answering calls relating to S/M.

Calman

Sadism

SADISM, coined by *Krafft-Ebing** from the name of the Marquis de *Sade**, is the emotional condition in which pleasure is derived from inflicting pain of other people. It is not restricted solely to sexual acts though sex tends to feature prominently in sadistic behaviour. It is with sexual sadism that we are concerned here.

From time immemorial there have appeared stories of individuals or groups of invading armies committing the most atrocious cruelties. There is ample evidence that they tended to enter into the spirit of the thing with immense bloodlust and so thoroughly revelled in it . . .

The universal nature of this thirst for cruelty is difficult is explain. Some see it as a progress of the natural rules of competition that exist in all living creatures. To fight, overcome and dominate a cometitor gives the winner better supplies of food, more territory, greater access to desirable females and so on. As humans were capable of intelligence perhaps they not only competed in every way but also took pleasure in competing. This may in part explain the enjoyment of seeing the loser suffer. Being the 'topman' infers a capability of inflicting pain even if that 'pain' is merely psychological 'one-up-manship'.

Whatever the reasons behind sadism, practically everyone at some stage or qther gets a kick out of giving pain. Small children sometimes, torment, torture and kill dumb animals. Gouging out the eyes of frogs, pulling the legs from flies, or daddy-longlegs, pushing pins into pets and the wanton ill use of other animals all fill the records of animal protection societies. Some of it is curiosity. Most of it though is an expression of a built-in desire to be cruel and powerful.

While extremes of sadism are unthinkable to some people under ordinary conditions, there is in everyone a sneaking feeling of sadistic enjoyment. People like reading about sadism. War films, murder, death and horror are sure box office successes. So it is understandable that people get pleasure from a little harmless expression of sadism in their sex play. LOVE-BITES and backs that are deeply scratched in passionate frenzy are minor examples. These can bring fun and pleasure to love making. It must never be taken too far or serious dangers can result.

Masochism

Whereas *sadism** is enjoying giving pain to others, masochism describes the enjoyment of pain received. Both phenomena may be grouped together under the one word that means the deriving of pleasure from the processes of pain, ALGOLAGNIA. Commonly, sadism and masochism operate together and the joint practice of both may be superficially difficult to distinguish. They are then known as sado-masochism (sometimes abbreviated as S/M).

It is difficult to explain the origins of this phenomenon. One theory is that it is an extension into adult life of infantile experiences. The largest part of a small child's world revolves around its relationships with its mother and father. They provide the warmth, the food and the reliability that, to the child represents comfort and security. At the same time, they are authority. Their orders are the law. Their punishment becomes familiar. The association of security and discipline is thus closely forged. The parents also do things that are pleasant. Mother washes the genitals. Father playfully cuffs and slaps or hoists the child to dangerous heights on his shoulders. Again, the connection between danger and possible pain is forged with a strong protector to save one from that pain. If school discipline is very strong, acceptance of discipline becomes a thoroughly ingrained way of life. As an adult, a person reaches the point when he is subjected to little in the way of external discipline. He finds he is giving rather than receiving the orders. And he misses the element of being subject to the security of discipline.

These are the men (and the great majority are men) who seek to have sadistic practices carried out on them. They have learned that these and only these practices can enable them to reach sexual fulfilment and orgasm.

Regrettably this whole area of behaviour is much misinterpreted. Due to lack of comprehension, a man's wife, used to an ambitious and effective husband in ordinary life, does not understand his hankering to be dominated in sex. She declines to cooperate. Her partner feels sexually deprived. Sometimes he will go to expensive prostitutes and brothels who offer the exclusive services he requires. This presents a great danger in itself—possibly of blackmail, a situation which may be even more seductive to the masochist's

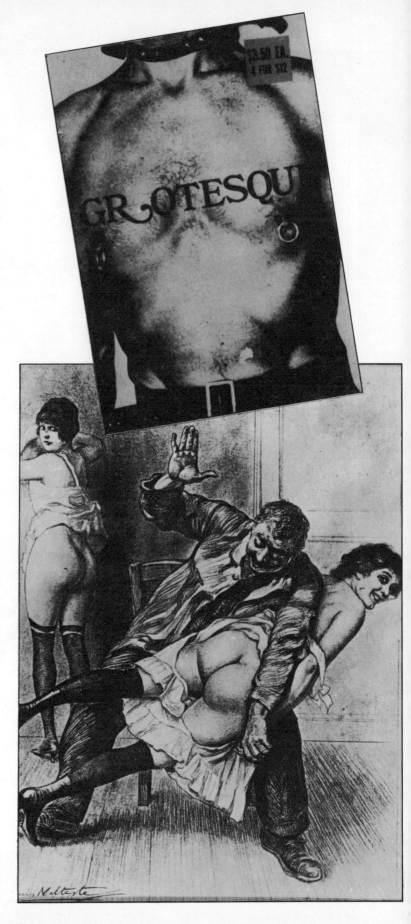

temperament. Scandals in business and political circles which have masochism as their core, are common enough.

Masochism is not entirely confined to men, but it is male masochism that quickly and easily becomes extreme. A man may start by merely seeking a dominant mistress, but the more she represents a cruel and demanding mother/schoolmistress the better. He will offer to be her slave. He will go on to dress in uncomfortable clothing, chains, straps, household aprons or the clothes of a domestic help. He will perform the most menial tasks. The more degrading the work and the more he is humiliated, the better he likes it. To clean the toilet bowl with his tongue, to polish his mistress's shoes, to wash her feet, are a source of delight. She may then 'permit' him to clean the riding crop with which she will beat him after his naked body is fastened by the wrists to a ring in the wall.

Ingenious gadgets like chains, leather thongs and wooden screw-blocks are sometimes wound painfully around the testicles and penis. The manacled and helpless victim is walked over by a girl wearing stiletto heels, and so on.

The most serious risks are run by people who, lacking willing or paid helpers, carry out their own masochistic rituals. Tying themselves up, burning and mutilating their own bodies, and attempted partial strangulations are only some of the personal techniques that so easily go wrong and result in permanent damage or accidental death. A woman may get harmless pleasure from being blindfolded, tied to the bed and tantalizingly masturbated, but for her to subject herself alone to restricting bonds, to the application of painful stimuli to her body, or to devise some apparatus that restricts her breathing, is lunacy.

The man who fastens his throat to the lavatory chain while he masturbates is clearly in danger. Likewise, the person who, living alone, mails a key to himself then uses a padlock and chain to fix himself inside his own front door, so that he can hardly move and must lie perhaps in bitter cold and in his own ordue until the key that can give him release falls through the letter box, is taking absurd risks. Such practices have been recorded and are so dangerous that they should not be carried out. A person who has wishes of this type and to this degree is emotionally disturbed and needs experienced psychiatric help.

Flagellation

Once flagellation was defined as scourging or otherwise inflicting pain on oneself, or sometimes others, as part of a religious discipline to 'subdue the desires of the flesh'. Now it generally means the sexually-motivated practice of whipping or flogging. This change in definition may at first seem strange, but it is not really, for there has always been a close association between religious fervour and the giving or receiving of pain and sexual gratification. From about the 11th to the 14th centuries, the Christian church approved of the use of the whip or scourge as a form of penance. Indeed the idea became so popular that large scale public flagellations were commonplace where partly-clad Christians scourged each other with great gusto. The consolation they derived was interpreted in a religious sense, but there is little doubt that much of it was, in fact, sexual. The acceptance of punishment, especially of a physical type, is closely bound up with *sadism** and *masochism**.

Corrective treatment of a person's behaviour by being whipped or otherwise hurt physically derives from the fundamental human idea that pain received equates with the forgiveness of sins. The guilty willingly accept pain as punishment. This appears as an apology, and so forgiveness results. As a religious concept this has long had its attractions and so has the administration of corporal punishment to transgressors of all kinds. Children in school have always been spanked or thrashed for infractions of school discipline or other misbehaviour. This type of punishment often attracted teachers guilty of DIPPOLDISM which is the beating of children for sexual gratification. There is little doubt today that austere ideals of the benefits of physical correction and religious mortification of the flesh have only been covers for flagellation's true appeal—which is sexual. Known as 'fladge', beatings of various kinds, often in combination with *erotic bondage**, are provided as a service by many prostitutes. This form of sexual release is not uncommon, particularly among the wealthier classes. A well-known example is the English poet Swinburne, who celebrated the delights of the whipping-block in some of his verse and, reportedly, in the anonymous *Whippingham Papers*. Fladge services are frequently advertised by means of euphemisms like 'Discipline', etc.

Erotic Bondage

The complex connections between pain and restraint on the one hand and erotic pleasure on the other, and between the two sides of the *dominance*/submission** coin, are illustrated in the elaborate sex games known as erotic bondage. The basic motives are at least present in everyone, but for those who take it up, a special fantasy can be acted out, with real props, as if they were truly living in a world of slavery, dungeons and torture.

Erotic bondage is available to both heterosexual and homosexual couples, and is frequently offered as a service by prostitutes. A considerable literature of pornographic comics and novels is devoted to the subject, and a recognizable style of graphics is cultivated, which highlights the various fetishes employed in the game. Men who take up erotic bondage often tend to be somewhat passive in their sexual attitudes, and enjoy the chance it gives them to play out aggressive roles.

Physically, many items which massage, or provide pressure and constraint can be erotically stimulating to the wearer. Belts, lacings, wrist straps and neck bands which press against the body act as gentle reminders of sexual interest, and may be seen by others as sensual symbols. Erotic bondage develops this tendency with the use of full-scale equipment consisting of leather, chains, and ropes. Erotic bondage, then, is restraint for purposes of inducing sexual excitement. There is no limit to the ingenuity that can be displayed, but it must never become serious, and certain rules need to be obeyed by both sides.

The actual tying-up process can start at several levels. For those to whom the bondage is a regular and important part of their love play, permanent arrangements are sometimes made. They may already have taken up *body piercing**. By this method, rings can be attached to the nipples, the foreskin, the vaginal lips and so on. To the rings various symbolic buckles or padlocks are attached. Another touch of symbolism comes in the elaborate *tattooing** often in intimate parts of the body. Leather clothes and boots, often with tight restrictive laces and straps, are worn and create images of being tied or strapped for subjugation like a slave. Some people take a delight in concealing the restraining objects under another garment and then going

1. However realistically played out, bondage must only be with the consent of both partners.
2. Never fasten anything around the neck.
3. Never restrict breathing in any way.
4. Stick to knots that are easy to unfasten.
5. Never leave a tied-up person without supervision.
6. Never play bondage games except when you are 100% sober.
7. Agree beforehand to an instant release signal which is always honoured without hesitation.

out. They savour their secret and relish the idea of what they will do when they get home.

Some bondage fans carry things further and fix up elaborate harnesses for each other, perhaps like the halter and bridle of a horse, or perhaps with realistic looking manacles screwed to the walls of a room or a bed. The idea of TRAINING arises frequently. Sometimes it is the man who becomes the horse which must be broken in, or he may be led around by a *cock-leash*, with his hands pinioned behind his back. Sometimes it is the woman who is gagged with a mask that resembles the medieval 'scold's bridle' or BRANK, thus satisfying a common male desire to silence and punish the woman who knows how to wound his ego with words.

When the time comes, one partner may passively accede to the demands of the other and meekly accept being bound as the dominant partner chooses, and where, when and in whatever position. Alternatively, the game may be a struggle to escape domination before being finally overcome and forced to accept the mock degradations planned. The details are all a matter of imaginative personal choice.

Although various materials can be used, many, while looking good, are unsuitable because they can rub and hurt or because they are difficult to undo in a hurry. Ideal is a length of soft 3/8" terylene rope supplied by boat chandlers. It is impossible to break but does not chafe. Once the victim is helpless, he or she, is subjected to teasing, stroking, brushing and sexual exploitation. The writhing limbs add to the thrill, as can such things as blindfolding. The victim can be brought tantalizingly close to orgasm and repeatedly tormented in every imaginable way before climax is permitted, or even deliberately withheld. Numerous ideas are used with personal variations. The victim is obliged to accept what is handed out but the partner must know how far to go. The dominant partner will do all the things the tied-up partner is known to enjoy. Sometimes the denial of such things may be the ultimate thrill. Dildos, gentle spanking, oil massage, talcum powder massage, sex of all kinds, are perpetrated at the whim of the dominant partner. Then they may change places on another occasion.

For those who want to use bondage techniques the boxed rules above *must* be followed under all circumstances.

Exhibitionism

Self-display is a normal and important part of sexual activity for both men and women. It can mean anything from wearing mildly sexy clothing to the mutual undressing of partners during foreplay. Varying degrees of body exposure have been allowed by fashion at different periods, for example, bare nipples or the *codpiece**. 'Exhibiting' and 'looking' are part of the processes of arousal. In the narrow sense, however, exhibitionism means deliberate exposure of the genitals in public for the purpose of sexual gratification, and constitutes a legal offence. This is termed INDECENT EXPOSURE and frequently lands the exhibitionist before the Courts. It is almost invariably a male practice, but some women do deliberately expose themselves, although they usually restrict their activities to seemingly accidental indiscretions, like the unbuttoned blouse or the hitched-up skirt.

Human society, largely under the influence of religion, has surrounded the body, and in particular the genitals, with an aura of privacy and shame, so that a man who shows himself in a natural way is guilty of breaking the law. In spite of this, it is a common practice, and the exhibitionist has become familiarly known as a *flasher*, a term of patient tolerance and even amusement. Most women have, at some stage in their lives, had an experience with a flasher.

Most men who expose themselves are sexually timid. They are shy, withdrawn individuals who have great difficulties in developing any sort of relationship with other people. They are unsuccessful in attracting partners or, having attracted them, are unable to make love to them satisfactorily, and many are impotent under normal sexual conditions. Their purpose in exposing themselves is to produce a reaction of dismay, horror or fear in the unfortunate women to whom the exposure is made, usually when she is alone and in circumstances where there is little she can do to avoid him. It is this reaction which gives him the thrill and can result in an erection or even an ejaculation on the spot. In the classic situation the man, often dressed in a long raincoat and rubber boots (to hide the fact that he wears no trousers), accosts the woman and suddenly holds his coat open, aggressively thrusting his genitals into view. A woman so confronted

can deflate the man if she refuses to be afraid or ignores him. Ridicule is even more successful. It is difficult in the circumstances to say 'Yuk! What a horrid *little* thing you've got' or 'Be careful you don't catch cold' but it is utterly demoralising and discouraging to the flasher.

There is a certain amount of evidence that some women subconsciously seek out the flasher by habitually walking alone in out of the way places, for often one woman will report several such technical assaults on her person.

A man who shows himself naked at a window in public view can also find himself charged with indecent exposure, depending on the circumstances.

Voyeurism

A voyeur is someone who derives sexual pleasure from watching activities associated with sex. Voyeurism can exist at many levels—a voyeur, male or female, may enjoy watching someone undress for bed or may enjoy watching very explicit sex shows. Voyeurism can be both open and surreptitious. It is a difficult phenomenon to assess because at one extreme it is universal and natural, while at the other it can be a perversion (*deviant**). The dividing line

is practically impossible to mark.

The use of visible objects of sexual attraction is encountered throughout nature. Sexual display is one of the most common techniques whereby a creature can secure the attentions of a potential mate (it is, for example, the reason why a peacock has such a fantastic tail). Among human beings there has always been immense care taken to make the body attractive to the eyes of the opposite sex (*fashion**)—that is why men cultivate beards and why women wear lipstick and erotic clothing.

The sexual attraction of watching the unclad human body in a clandestine way is obvious too. To be able to hide somewhere and watch members of the opposite sex undressing is a phenomenon encountered in elementary and primary schools. Slightly older youngsters often go out in groups looking for courting couples to spy on. The visual excitement is often coupled with a desire to know exactly what goes on— children will be unlikely to have had much sex experience themselves.

The all-time popularity of the *strip tease** show is another form of voyeurism—the skilful removing of clothes before an audience is calculated to create sexual arousal. There are both male and female strippers and also dual strip tease acts which frequently simulate intercourse. Topless bar waitresses, go-go dancers and massage girls also pander to voyeurism. So do the multiplicity of sexy magazines and books, especially those using mostly erotic and suggestive photographs of male and female bodies.

Sometimes a person derives such intense thrills from the secret watching of unsuspecting people that he (or rarely she) will creep into the gardens or yards of houses in order to peep into windows. This is the so-called PEEPING TOM carrying out the practice of SCOPOPHILIA which is deriving pleasure from watched human acts. Scopophilia is an extreme form of voyeurism and often brothels offer special viewing facilities such as one-way see-through windows so that customers can watch sex acts being performed.

Sometimes women allow their voyeur husbands to watch them having intercourse with other men, or vice versa. For most couples there is a natural amount of mutual voyeurism in their sexual relationship. This is restricted to displaying themselves in sexy clothing or in the nude as a prelude to and during love making.

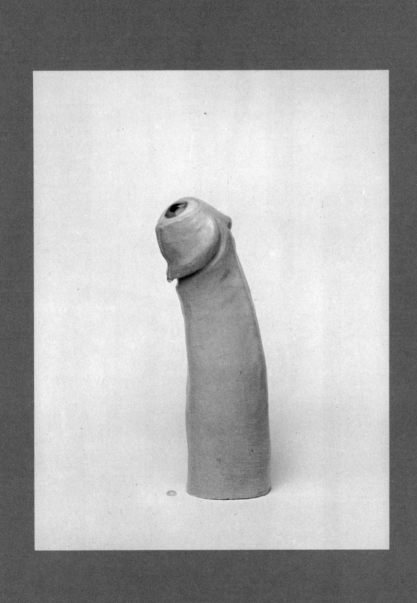

Fetishism

Fetishism is attaching an important sexual significance to an object which is not necessarily sexual itself. Fetish objects may be part of the human body like feet or breasts, or they may be articles of clothing like shiny boots or women's panties. Most people have decided preferences in tastes, colours, music and so on, and it is natural that they should have sexual preferences that excite them, but where a preference becomes a fetish it is hard to say. More men than women seem to have fetishes and some men may be practically impotent except when associating a fetish (for example, a special shoe) with the sex act. In general, the stimulation derived from a fetish adds depth to sexual pleasure.

Rubber & Leather Fetishism

The sexual interest in these materials—generally black and shiny—has not been satisfactorily explained. The cult of studded leather gear implies male aggressiveness, with strongly homo-erotic overtones. On the other hand, rubber fetishes display fetal tendencies, with the emphasis on cuddling up in a dark, moist bag, reminiscent of the womb. Possibly, infant memories of rubber sheets and protective pants contribute to associating rubber with physical pleasure and affection. Elaborate gear is marketed for these interests, such as form-fitting helmets, suits, corsets and tights, with numerous lace-ups. The devoted rubber fetishist delights in dressing up or dressing a partner in them. The smell of the material is also important. Leather and rubber fetishism is usually partnered by *boot fetishism*,* and has obviously close connections with *dominance**, *erotic bondage** and *sado-masochism**.

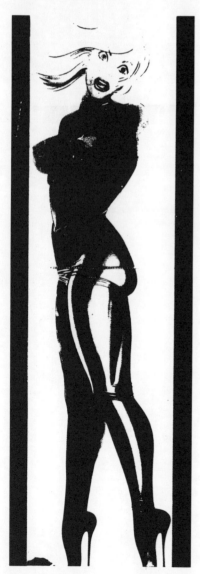

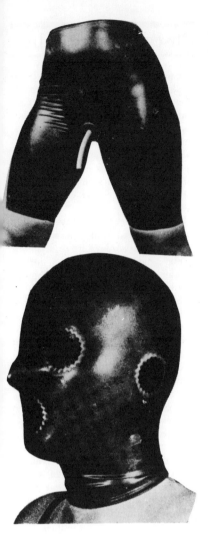

Deformity Fetishism

While concern is growing for the sexual rights of the disabled, there can also be a perverted sexual interest in physically disadvantaged people. Amputated limbs strongly attract some men and, much less commonly, women. A man who feels drawn to an amputee may be compensating for a sense of personal inadequacy, or may get a kick out of the physical superiority he feels he has. Another may find it an opportunity for enjoying female *dominance**—a fantasy of being beaten with a crutch or artificial limb. Very ugly, disfigured or deformed men fascinate some women. A mothering impulse probably combines with the myth of excessive potency in dwarfs and cripples, and compensation may again play a part. These sexual relationships do not exclude real affection and mutual help between people whose needs are balanced in this way (see also *Disability and Sex**).

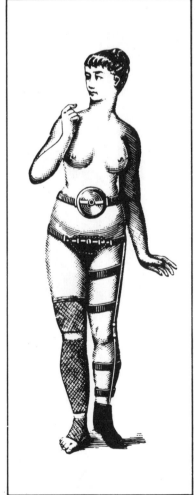

Boot & Shoe Fetishism

Footwear has developed even stronger sexual connotations than feet themselves. In mild forms, most people recognize its fetishistic appeal. The jackboot has an aura of dominating maleness. Conversely, there is a female *dominance** theme in women's high-heeled boots (neatly expressed in Nancy Sinatra's song 'These Boots are Made for Walking . . .'). A sensual, 'undressed' impression is made by female shoes with peep-toes or slingbacks. For male fetishists, a shoe is partly symbolic of a vulva (as the foot is of a penis), and some masturbate with a shoe, or expose themselves in front of women's footwear displays in shop windows.

Foot Fetishism

Babies' feet are almost as sensitive as their hands, and apes use hands and feet with about equal dexterity. An acute foot-consciousness is preserved by many people into adult life. Feelings of sexual excitement can be aroused by having the feet stroked, or by stroking another person's. Tingling in the feet can accompany orgasm. It is not surprising that just the sight or thought of a foot, associated with so many pleasurable sensations, can be erotic. The Song of Solomon hints at their importance: 'How beautiful are thy feet with shoes'. In old China, the daintiness of women's feet was exaggerated unnaturally in the *cosmetic deformity** of footbinding. Feet are also directly involved in sexual play, as when the penis and testicles are massaged between the partner's feet, or a man's toe is inserted into his partner's vagina.

Bestiality

This is the illegal act of human sexual contact with other animals, male or female. More precisely, a morbid sexual attraction for animals is also known as ZOOPHILIA. It is well known that such contacts have taken place from time immemorial. At various times there has even been a belief that copulation with animals conferred some magical power. At other times, bestiality was held to be an abomination. It was also regarded as a rare phenomenon, but this is not the case. It is now known to be far more common than is generally realized.

In general, bestiality takes two forms. In the first instance, there is the rural practice of men having intercourse with farm animals. This occurs among farm workers, for whom there may be a restricted availability of women as sex partners. Unskilled, uneducated labourers have low personal or cultural resistance to such practices as copulation with animals. They are also familiar in their every day work with the handling of farm animals and animal waste. Commonly young cows, donkeys, pigs and sheep are used and less often bitches, mares and goats.

The other group of 'animal-lovers' is to be found among the upper strata of society, and are mostly women. The practice of bestiality at this level is by women who use small dogs trained to perform for oral sex purposes mainly directed at the human vagina. Large male dogs, particularly Alsatians and retrievers, are trained to have vaginal intercourse with their mistresses. Whereas one might expect these exercises to be dangerous, in fact they rarely are. Some animals might claw or bite during orgasm, but as a rule they appear to be gentle 'lovers'. Infection is almost unknown.

Watching human and animal sexual contact can be exciting to a *voyeur**. Magazines exist on the subject and cater especially for those with this particular taste. So-called 'dog films' and other films of animal sex are produced by commerical pornographers.

Obscene Phone Calls

One of the most common of all sexual nuisances is that of the deliberately offensive, or obscene, telephone call. Some are made by youngsters of both sexes simply playing a practical joke, but true, sexually-motivated phone calls are nearly always made by men. Receiving such calls can be both disturbing and frightening, but callers rarely make any other contact with their victims.

Many men lack the courage to speak freely to women, either because they feel inadequate or because they cannot attract a desirable woman into normal conversation. A caller may telephone a particular woman who is sexually attractive to him, often a girl who works in the same office or someone they see frequently such as a neighbour. At other times, if there is no particular woman to whom they attach their fantasies, callers will phone women's organisations who are likely to have women answering the phone.

Frequently the object of a call is to frighten the listening woman which provides a sexual thrill for the deviant. The so-called HEAVY BREATHER will gasp and puff and pant into the receiver . . . perhaps mimicking a state of sexual excitement. Sometimes callers are physically aroused by telephoning, and a fair proportion of men actually masturbate while phoning, sometimes even ejaculating into the telephone mouthpiece. Other men get a satisfactory thrill from saying what they hope will be offensive remarks. They may ask the colour of a woman's underwear or some intimate question about her bust size or the smell of her vagina. Given the chance, callers will often describe in great detail what they would like to do to the listener. (This is a good reason for hanging up the receiver immediately upon receipt of an obscene call.) They may actually threaten to visit the listener there and then. This threat is seldom carried out, even if there is a positive invitation, as most obscene callers are afraid of women.

If a person is commonly troubled by receiving such calls, telephone engineers will arrange to monitor and trace all incoming calls to a specific number. One idea for discouraging obscene calls is to keep a referee's whistle near the phone—a powerful blast on this can give a painful surprise to the offender's ear.

Water Games

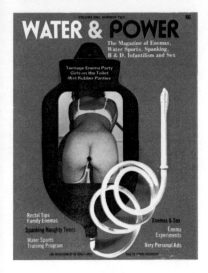

Sexual pleasure can be obtained from water in two ways. One is the sensual feel of soapy or oiled and scented water massaged over bodies, specially the genital and anal areas, during love play. A popular image of this kind of water sex is of lovers bathing together beneath a tropical waterfall. The other kind is the internal douching of body openings. There is a cult among both men and women for the mutual enjoyment of water sensations in the rectum or the vagina by means of ENEMA or CLYSTER treatment. The medical term HIGH CO-LONIC IRRIGATION is often used as a euphemism in advertisements. Massage parlours sometimes cater for both forms of water game, including massage leading to orgasm during masturbation. Special magazines exist for people whose main sexual interest is in the enema cult. The literature harps on infantile features like wet diapers.

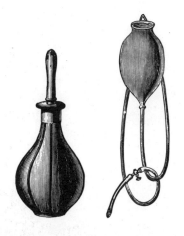

Urolagnia

This is a sexual deviation in which there is an attraction for the urine and urinary processes of the sex partner. As with most deviations, its practice ranges from mild to extreme forms. The attraction may in part stem from the fact that urination involves the genitals and is usually a private act. Thus a sexual partner's urination may be titillating. There may also be a more primitive bio-chemical basis. If an animal urinates at certain spots around its 'territory', the smell of certain chemicals in the urine (or perhaps voided with it) warns off other animals or helps attract mates.

Children play games that involve urine: boys may urinate together or even hold competitions as to who can pee highest or farthest. Interestingly, women and girls seldom urinate in each other's company. Other childhood games involve peeping at others urinating or arranging to be where the sound of it can be heard.

In adult life, people who are stimulated by urine may also contrive to be present or at least close by when someone is urinating. They may attempt to obtain some urine or even clothing dampened or scented with it. These articles are usually sniffed while masturbating. Greater extremes of urolagnia involve persuading one's partner to urinate in such a position that they can be closely watched. There may even be a desire to urinate on (CUNT PISSING) or to be urinated upon (GOLDEN SHOWERS or RAIN), or to drink the urine of the sexual partner. Healthy urine is sterile and there is no harm in consuming small amounts. (Drinking some urine has helped people to survive in deserts in the absence of water.) Many pornographic films contain urolagnic sequences.

Necrophilia

It often comes as a surprise to people to discover that there really are persons who are sexually attracted to corpses. Sexual interest in dead bodies is called necrophilia. A necrophiliac may well have normal sexual relations as well. Most, but not all, necrophiliacs are male.

The bizarre practice of having sexual intercourse with the dead has been known throughout history. It is suggested by some authorities that at least part of the reason for burning bodies or burying them deeply or in solid granite and marble tombs was to prevent their violation in this way. Some societies have taken great pains to preserve bodies intact for a long time after death and there is evidence to suggest that sexual rituals with those bodies once occurred.

It is believed that a necrophiliac likes tenderly dressing the (usually female) corpse's hair, washing the body and caressing it in a familiar manner. Sometimes the corpse is dressed and undressed. Vaginal and anal intercourse and oral sex may take place. In extreme cases of necrophilia, a person may become almost totally indiscreet in the search for dead 'partners' (some necrophiliacs have even attempted to keep the death of a family member secret). Such extremes are known as NECRO-MANIA and usually bring the practitioner into conflict with the law. Some carry out deliberate assaults on the bodies, subjecting them to considerable indignities. Occasionally, wanton mutilations are perpetrated on dead bodies as part of a sex act; this is known as NECROSADISM.

Coprophilia

It is not unknown for a person to have a morbid attraction for excrement—usually, but not always, for human rather than for animal fecal matter. The explanation for this practice, as with so many sexual deviations, is uncertain. In part, it probably derives from the fact that the anus is one of the main body orifices, is very close to the genitals and so is sexually attractive. By association, the product of the anus becomes attractive. Another explanation may start from the fact that to most people feces of all kinds are considered filthy, and cleaning areas where people defecate and so on, is thought by many to be the concern of inferior people. As an extension of this reasoning, those who seek degradation as a sexual favour (*masochism**) may become obsessed with feces. To clean away or to handle or smear the body with human waste therefore provides an opportunity to make a person feel inferior and debased.

Carried to the extreme, some people will actually consume and swallow the feces of a sexually-revered person, a practice called COPROPHAGIA. These deviant practices are frankly dangerous.

Transvestite

(From the Latin *trans*, across, and *vestis*, clothes). This is a compulsion, found in some men (but hardly ever encountered among women), to dress in the clothes of the opposite sex. There are many degrees of CROSS-DRESSING (as transvestism is also called), and it occurs in varying forms among people whose sense of *gender identity** gives rise to problems. An extreme example is the man or woman who lives completely as a person of the opposite sex and would undoubtedly be *transsexual**. The variations are not only difficult to define but are often confusing even to the individuals concerned. The fundamental difference between a transsexual and a transvestite is that the latter, when cross-dressed, still knows he is a man, whereas the former has the distinct feeling of

belonging to the opposite sex. Accordingly, transsexuals usually try to obliterate all traces of their given sex, but transvestites tend not to go to such lengths and may allow some physical aspect of maleness (for example, body hair) to show even when they are fully dressed and made-up as women.

A transvestite's situation is often not static; there can be a momentum towards increasing identification with the opposite sex. Most transvestite men start by deriving a fetishist excitement from contact with female clothes and make-up.

Once they have taken up cross-dressing, they find great pleasure in being able to mix as a 'woman' with other transvestites or with real women. In adopting their pseudo-feminine role, transvestites usually choose a female name which they feel is appropriate to go with their other self—and may call their cross-dressed selves their own sisters.

The most common cases of transvestism are heterosexual men leading otherwise conventional sex lives, often married and with children. Such men find that a short period of wearing women's clothes from time to time relieves sexual tension. Some encounter problems with wives who find this sort of behaviour difficult to accept, though some wives will turn a blind eye for the sake of children. The causes of transvestism are not known, but hormone anomalies which can occur in the early stages of pregnancy, as well as psychological factors due to early upbringing, may be responsible.

The term *drag** is often used carelessly as if it were a synonym for transvestite clothing. Correctly, however, it means theatrical cross-dressing by female impersonators, or the spectacular female garments worn by homosexual men or transsexuals at some social functions.

Pedophilia

(From the Greek words meaning 'love of a boy'.) Sexual desire with children as its object. The children involved can be either male or female. The desire to use children for sexual purposes has a number of possible explanations. To have intercourse or perform other sex acts with infants or juveniles may be felt to have some power of rejuvenation. The deflowering of a virgin has been believed, as a sort of mythology, to help restore an aging man's youth (or even to cure VD), all the more so if the virgin were very young. Indeed, this idea is by no means totally forsaken today. A small child is something both innocent and helpless; its sheer weakness makes it pliable and vulnerable. Therefore, it is all too easy for an adult to force, or subtly trick, a child into taking part in sexual acts. A child will not have the same conception of right and wrong as an adult would and will usually comply with the will of an older person. The seducer clearly feels a sense of power and domination over the child. Adults have the will to decline sex, but children who know little about it seldom have such will.

Freedom from the hazard of one's sex partner getting pregnant has been offered as one reason why some men prefer child sex partners. Another strong explanation for pedophiliac activity is the absence of any fear of comparison. A sexually over-anxious adult may entertain deep doubts about his or her sexual performance, for an experienced partner is able to draw comparisons which may be unfavourable. A child has had little or no experience and the adult thus feels correspondingly secure. Additionally, there is a measure of appeal in novelty and also in the newness and unspoiled quality of a child. There are, therefore, many ways in which a pedophile may regard a child as a potential lover.

Some adults report that they are sexually attracted to children because of their comparative unisexuality—the differences between the sexes before puberty are slight. Both are hairless and have childish, sexless-sounding voices. There are no prominent sex characteristics to threaten an anxious adult. Boys' genitals are insignificant and girls do not have developed breasts. An adult pedophile will often enjoy sexual relations with either a male or female child.

By no means does all pedophilia re-sult from initiation by an adult. Precocious children display a large measure of sexual curiousity. Often they feel little of the sexual shame that can restrain an adult. Thus they can tempt an older person and even flagrantly lead them. This is particularly true of children of both sexes around five to six years old, when sex games of the 'playing doctor' sort start. Also, girls of around 12 to 14, at the so-called 'Lolita' stage, feel the first awakening of sexual change in their bodies and are excited by their newly-found power to attract attention without necessarily being

aware of all the consequences.

Pedophilia often involves actual sexual contact and penetration of children as well as masturbation and general fondling, handling, dressing up and other sex 'games'. Not all pedophilia involves direct sexual contact; in some societies it is sufficient to have child slaves, who may well be sexually trained to play with each other and provide visual entertainment of a sexual nature.

Having sexual relations with children below the legal age of consent constitutes a legal offence and can result in severe penalties. The majority of cases that come before the law are those of adult men committing offences against both sexes. Frequently the child is a member of the offender's immediate family, when *incest** is also involved. Cases of women having relations with children (mostly boys) are less often encountered but are, in fact, more common than is generally realized. Again, such a relationship may be incestuous. A small boy may be invited into a mother's bed, ostensibly for company, comfort or warmth. Masturbation, oral sex or intercourse may then take place.

Children who has been sexually assaulted should never be subjected to intense interrogations or to expressions or adult outrage, or even to excessive physical examination to determine the extent of the assault. This can obviously make children see themselves as injured, polluted, debased or naughty and guilty. Children should be gently discouraged from ever taking rides or any sort of food from strangers, and they should be made to feel secure enough to report sexual attentions from any adult, even from someone fairly well known to them.

20

GROWING UP

The psychology of sex at all stages
of human development.

Psycho-Sexual

The psychology of human sex life is a widely-ranging study, embracing 'normal' development, and also deviations and difficulties, and the relationship between the sexual impulse and other aspects of human expression, such as creativity and aggression.

A central issue in the study of sex is sexual variation. Maleness and femaleness are not unique and mutually exclusive entities in personality, but come in various mixtures in different individuals. Exactly how much of this variation is due to genetic inheritance and how much to social conditioning it is impossible to say.

The most common form of interpersonal sexual expression is the heterosexual relationship, but Kinsey's work established that the *homosexual** relationship is far more common than was at one time supposed. From his large male sample, 37% recorded at least one homosexual experience in their lives and a small proportion (4%) recorded that they were exclusively homosexual. Between the consistently heterosexual and the completely homosexual comes an ill-defined group who enjoy, or have at some time enjoyed, relationships both with their own and the other sex. Some of this group have a clearly-defined sexual preference; others not. According to Kinsey, female homosexuality was much less common than male homosexuality. A small number of individuals are *transsexual**— physically of one sex but feeling, psychologically, that they are the other.

Any individual's precise pattern of sexuality will be unique. Relating to one's own sexuality and to that of others is never entirely easy and may lead to doubts and conflicts. These will tend to be greater in a rigid, inhibited social climate and less in a flexible one.

With children, care must be given at every stage to foster sexual development appropriately, and to ensure that they grow up free from unnecessary blocks, guilt and inhibitions.

Children vary from the start in both gender and temperament. Boys, in general, seem to be more assertive and competitive than girls, who are more sensitive socially, and more interested in caring roles from an early age. Some people regard these differences as culturally conditioned rather than inherited. In practice, the origin of these differences is less important than the fact they exist.

Sexual Development

The sexual development of an individual starts with the young child's initiation into sensual feelings, consciousness of his body, interaction with others, and the sharing of pleasure. Thereafter comes the period of childhood when sexual feelings become comparatively quiescent because the child is deeply engaged in coming to terms with the world at large, and exploring his own potentialities for action and achievement.

A happy and healthy ten-year-old is an extremely competent and integrated young person, aware of his or her sex but not much under the sway of sexual impulse. Then puberty arrives with all its changes and challenges. This can quickly fragment the self-assurance even of the well-adjusted prepubertal child. If the child is not well-adjusted, the impact of puberty can be more unsettling still.

Psychologically, the period between the onset of puberty and the attainment of fulfilled sexual relationships is one of continuous search, growth and adjustment. The individual is faced with the task of discovering not only personal identity as a young adult, but also sexual identity. Each young adult has to learn how to share this more mature personality with others, and how to relate to the other sex through the various stages of friendship and intimacy.

All this can be the source of a great deal of doubt and uncertainty, particularly among those who are acutely aware of not being attractive physically. Many young people worry intensely about whether or not they have what it takes to be desirable and to be successful lovers. Lack of social self-confidence can be especially obstructive at this stage because it inhibits those very relationships through which a secure sense of personal and sexual identity are granted.

If all goes reasonably well during the exploratory period of sexual development, young people gradually gain perspective on themselves, and others, as sexual beings and win through to self-confidence and sensitivity in relating to the other sex. But many young people get caught up in difficulties they cannot handle and need the support and reassurance of good counselling. Ideally, both mother and father should provide this, but often such difficulties arise because of some kind of parental deprivation. Teachers can also help.

Infantile Sexuality

The baby's introduction to the world is highly sensual, since his or her first contacts with life come through the senses—sight, sound, touch, taste. All these are, among other things, components of sexual response. Furthermore, the infant's experiences are very much concentrated on exploring his or her body. This is intensified by the pleasures of feeding, interest in the process of excretion and the fascination of playing with the genitals,

Psychoanalytical theory emphasizes the oral, anal and genital phases of development as crucial to growth and influential in shaping the personality. There are, however, other aspects. From the beginning of life the baby experiences interaction with another person—the mother or mother-substitute. About the same time he begins to be aware of other people too. Relationships with these are also important to his psychosexual growth. Research has shown that animals and birds reared in isolation may grow up socially incompetent. Right from the start, a child is learning to be sensual through the experience of his own body, and learning the pleasure of interacting with others—the essence of sexuality. When Freud broached the issue of infantile sexuality the response was one of shock. But now we realize that it is natural that the origins of adult sexuality should be present in infancy.

CHILDHOOD SEXUALITY is the continuation of infantile sexuality in a less intense form. As the young child becomes mobile and verbal, such a rich and varied world of possibility opens up to him that his body becomes only one of many interesting things and less central to his attention. But, throughout childhood, sexual interest and curiosity continue to be lively. Sex play, either with friends and siblings or alone, is common.

During the infantile and childhood phases of sexual development it is vitally important that a child should be given a good feeling about his body and its functions and should be so treated that no sense of guilt is generated by his sexual curiosity, fantasies and pleasure in sensation. Potty training should be matter-of-fact and cheerful. To make a child feel he is 'dirty' or 'bad' because of his natural functions and interests in various kinds of sex play is to sow the seeds of sexual difficulties later on.

Mother

In spite of trends towards shared parenthood, the mother remains central in the personal and sexual development of children. At the start of life she is the source of food, comfort, love and that subtle sharing of intimacy and feeling that has only recently been receiving close attention. From the mother particularly the young child picks up the assurance of self-value, personal confidence and trust in intimacy that lay the foundations for happy, relaxed, guilt-free sexuality in adulthood. When the natural mother is not available, a loving mother-substitute can play the same role.

The mother's place inevitably gives rise to conflicts within the family. The infant boy may sense that he is the rival of the father for the love and attention of the mother. Young children can be very possessive! Freud called this rivalry the OEDIPUS COMPLEX. Thus, family life generates tensions and jealousies as well as cooperation and affection. The mother is in the centre of it all. The children compete for her attention and love, and the father expects his share, so that successful mothering depends on balancing one claim against another and, as far as possible, meeting the emotional needs of everyone—a highly skilled task.

At the adolescent stage, acute rivalry may develop between mother and daughter. The girl, becoming ever more aware of herself as a young woman, may challenge her mother for the approval and attention of her father. At the same time the mother finds herself sharing the home with a young woman who may be in the full bloom of desirable youth when the mother feels her own attractions to be waning.

Conflict between mother and adolescent boy can also arise, because the young man wants his mother's approval, but resents the fact that she has the power of a parent over him. The boy may then display a disconcerting mixture of affectionate concern and dominant aggression. The resolution of family conflicts has a valuable part to play in the maturation of children.

The natural dependence of children on their mothers may become over-dependence, especially if the mother is too dominating and managing. This can lead to MOTHER-FIXATION—the permanent, excessive dependence of the child on the mother.

Father

A father is a person; he is also the model of masculinity within the home. This remains true even though the sex roles are not as clearly defined as they once were. In the first instance, the boy finds out what it means to be a man by watching his father. This can have long-range influence on a boy's concept of his masculine role. If the father combines strength with warmth and gentleness in his bearing, the boy will grow up seeing manhood in those terms. If, however, the father is afraid of showing feeling, the boy may come to regard tenderness and strength as incompatible, which can cause difficulties when the time comes for him to be a lover.

For the girl too, the father is her initial model of a man. She may begin to experiment with her femininity by flirting with him in little ways at quite an early age. This gives the father great power over his daughter's self-assurance as a young female. Lack of appreciation at any age will undermine her self-confidence and any harsh criticism, particularly of her physical appearance, may do long-lasting damage. The special intimacy that can develop between father and daughter may result in the girl's resenting her mother's presence (ELECTRA COMPLEX). This is not an absolute but an ambivalent attitude: the girl both depends on her mother, loves her *and* resents her sexual and emotional intimacy with the father.

In addition to his role as a model man, the father has an important role as a friendly, encouraging companion who leads children into new experiences.

During adolescence, the father may find himself embroiled with both son and daughter over issues of independence. This can be particularly complicated with the daughter who wants to be admired by him as a young woman but, to her annoyance, is still subject to his authority. Tension can also arise because the father feels that no one is good enough for his daughter. The father may also resent the greater sexual freedom that his children enjoy.

Just as children may become over-identified with their mother, so they may become over-identified with their father. This FATHER FIXATION can obstruct growth towards independence of personality and the development of mature relationships with members of the other sex.

Adolescence

Sexual maturity brings not only physical changes but glandular changes also. The two together generate a strong SEX DRIVE which, sometime during the adolescent years—say 13 to 20— is likely to culminate in complete sexual relations. In early adolescence, however, the main outlet for boys is masturbation, often accompanied by sex fantasies. Studies indicate that masturbation among mature males is virtually 100%. The reported figure for mature females is lower. The usual reason given for this is that girls are subject to less immediate and intense sexual pressure, and seek to be loved as individuals rather than to find opportunities for sexual release. Whatever part masturbation plays, adolescents are spontaneously interested in, and excited by, the thought of complete sexual experience. What proportion attain it during the teenage years is uncertain, but much experimentation takes place. There is also a good deal of anxiety about physical desirability and sexual capacity.

During adolescence, mental and emotional growth are just as marked as physical development. Emotions become more intense and more extensive. The combination of physical drives, surgent feelings and self-doubt accounts for much of the sensitivity and moodiness characteristic of adolescence. The mood swings, in their turn, lead to uncertainty about personal identity at the very time when the young adult is making a strong bid for independence, which itself often leads to conflicts with parents and the feeling of being unloved and misunderstood.

As a part of the struggle for independence, adolescents turn to their peers for friendship and support. This puts their social skills to the test and may lead to happy group life or to a greater or lesser degree of isolation. To be alone and friendless is particularly painful for an adolescent. Adolescents have many other tasks to face such as getting a start in a career and arriving at a set of values by which to live.

In the midst of this turmoil of change and development, to be in love can be an integrating and transforming experience, but brings with it the peril of things going wrong and the resulting devastation of spirit. It is not surprising, then, that psychosexual problems, and problems of relationship are common during the adolescent years.

First Intercourse

First intercourse is a considerable event for both young men and young women. Unfortunately it may be a disappointing one, partly because the glamorization of sex makes expectations unrealistically high; partly because a fully rewarding sexual exchange is the outcome of experience. Furthermore, the circumstances of first intercourse may be far from ideal and the act may be secretive and hurried. Some girls feel let down by their first experience of intercourse, and may wonder why so much fuss is made about it.

Young men are often apprehensive of failure and may have difficulty in maintaining an erection or in controlling ejaculation. 'First night nerves' usually clear up but can be very embarrassing at the time. Even if things are difficult, however, a boy is likely to gain a sense of pride and satisfaction at having had relationships with a girl regardless of the result.

By no means are all first experiences between young men and young women. Kinsey reported visits to prostitutes by boys as young as 14. He found that at least one such visit has been made by 40% of his overall sample before the age of 20. Kinsey's figures show an almost desperate striving of young males to prove their manhood. He reported attempts at intercourse by boys as young as 12. By 15, about 40% of boys had at least tried to have intercourse; a proportion increasing to 70% by 19. The better educated tend to reach the stage of intercourse later. For girls, according to Kinsey, attempts at intercourse are 'less often and later' than for boys. (Kinsey's statistics have probably been outdated today.)

Sometimes a more experienced person may initiate a young man or woman. When this is the result of a kind and loving relationship, the experience for the beginner may be more satisfactory than when two beginners are involved. In some countries, initiation of young men by older women is a socially recognized part of *sex education**.

To make first intercourse happy rather than frustrating, it is important that both young men and women should be prepared for making love. This is an aspect of education more often catered for in primitive societies than in technologically advanced ones.

Virginity

The entrance to the vagina is partly closed in the young girl by a membrane of skin, the *hymen**. Before intercourse, the opening in the hymen is only about large enough for a finger to go through. At first intercourse this opening is stretched to admit the erect penis (DEFLORATION). As well as stretching, the hymen may tear slightly, with the loss of a few drops of blood. If the man is gentle there is no pain at all, or only slight pain. The opening in the hymen may also be enlarged by masturbation, during washing, as a result of vigorous exercise or by a doctor.

In the past, evidence of virginity at marriage—an intact hymen—was highly prized for religious and social reasons. Masculine vanity also came into this; the defloration of a virgin at first intercourse was glamorized as a highly satisfying masculine achievement. Proof of virginity at marriage was sometimes taken to absurd lengths, including scrutinizing the bridal sheets for spots of blood as proof that the bride was *virgo intacta*. Such evidence was proof of the bridegroom's brutality rather than the bride's virginity, as stretching the opening of the hymen does not necessarily lead to tearing it, while enlargement may occur from other causes than sexual relationship.

During the past quarter of a century, and more or less in step with the increased emancipation of women, virginity is less prized by women and less demanded by men. Indeed, the situation has today somewhat reversed so that young men and young women may value a certain amount of experience in their partners.

Enlarging the hymen during first intercourse is not difficult and is achieved by a firm, gentle thrust with the erect penis when the opposition of the membrane checks penetration. There may be a little pain, especially if the woman is tense or anxious. If penetration should prove difficult owing to the hymen being exceptionally thick, or because nervousness reduces the rigidity of the man's penis, the doctor can open the hymen without difficulty or pain to the woman.

'Virginity' in a man is sometimes spoken of, but generally in the sense of his lacking sexual experience. Since even the opening of a female's hymen does not necessarily mean she has already had intercourse, the word has even less meaning when applied to a man.

Learning to Love

Love is the personal element in sex. Girls, in general, are interested in love earlier than boys. This is partly because they mature earlier so that a thirteen-year-old girl may be, in both physique and bearing, a young woman, while her male comtemporaries are still mainly taken up with boyish pursuits. Young hoydens who try to outboy the boys are usually late developers who are over-compensating for a sense of disadvantage by a display of toughness.

The first stage of learning to love is, consequently, rather confused. Soon after puberty, or even before it, girls find themselves seeking to express their incipient, passionate feelings, although there are no suitable partners available, nor are they yet ready to commit themselves in deep personal relationships. This is the stage when their developing feelings are directed to any available objects; among them pop stars, pets, boon companions, admired older friends. 'Crushes' on older people may be directed to members of their own or the other sex. Boys also pass through the hero-worshiping stage, but things are easier for them. When they are ready for pairing relationships, potential partners are available.

Another feature of this generalized need to find an object for love is 'loving-from-afar'. Those who run advice columns in periodicals are used to such *problem letters** as: 'I know a boy who works in a shop near us. He comes to the house sometimes to bring things. I love him very much. How can I get to know him better?' In her fantasies, the girl has endowed the young man with every virtue. Such distant adulation can be the starting point of a long process in which a fantasy of love gradually develops into a loving relationship between real people.

At the same time as both boy and girl are expressing their aspirations in fantasy, they are also making everyday relationships with one another. This is the stage of early pairing-off between girls and boys of about the same age, of going around together but as yet free from deep commitment.

This initial stage leads on to special friendships when young people not only do things together, but talk together a great deal and cuddle and pet together and learn to share one another's feelings. During this period, a boy may have several girl friends, and vice versa. Couples may join up to form a group of friends. Special friendships come and go. As a boy and girl get to know one another better they may find that they are not all that well suited after all. Special friendships may come to an end, often to be replaced quite quickly by another one, even though the break-up, at the time, may seem like the end of the world.

All this experience leads to the gaining of insight about one another and the gradual replacement of fantasy criteria by reality criteria as the basis of selecting partners. Not all, of course, learn from their experiences. Some people make ineffective fantasy choices of love partners all the way through their lives.

As time goes by and each sex becomes more aware of what they value most in the other, longer-lasting relationships are likely to develop. From these, sooner or later, an extra-special friendship may deepen into a new kind of love, a love based not on hopes and imaginings but on a deep feeling of fondness for a particular partner, centred upon what he, or she, actually is. If the friendship continues to grow in strength, instead of fading as time passes, then it may well lead on to engagement and marriage.

Learning to love is a highly personal matter. No individual goes neatly through a precise series of developmental stages. Some jump phases; some get stuck; some lack the self-confidence to start at all. Yet, overall, adolescence provides the experiences that lay the foundation for mature loving. Furthermore, adolescent love can be profound and passionate. It should always be respected and never made light of or ridiculed.

The sincerity of adolescent love is not invalidated by the impression adolescents often give of being hard-baked, even cynical. Most young people are, at first, tentative in their relationships with the other sex, the more so because of the pressures of commercialized sex and the expectation of high performance that it engenders. The brashness and ostentation of adolescents are, for the most part, defences. Tenderness and idealism are just below the surface.

209

Puberty

Puberty is the period when the sex organs become mature. The process takes about two years, and the age of attaining maturity varies. For girls, the normal range is from 10 to 16, with 13 as the commonest age. In Western society over 75 per cent of girls have their first period between 12 and 14. Boys, on average, reach maturity about a year later than girls. The average age for MENARCHE has been decreasing steadily in European countries for more than 100 years. Norwegian records give 17 years and one month as the average for 1840. The chief changes occurring during puberty are:

Physical growth. Puberty is a period of rapid physical growth in both height and weight. During this GROWTH SPURT boys may gain about 5in (12cm) in height in a single year. Skeletal changes include the broadening of the shoulders in boys; the equivalent for girls is broadening of the hips. The girl's limbs and body become more rounded. *Accelerated development of the sex organs.* This is most noticeable in boys. Penis, testicles and scrotum all grow rapidly. The testicles descend deeper into the scrotum. This completes the descent of the testicles, which begins in early life. *Development of secondary sex characteristics.* In both sexes, hair grows under the armpits and around the genital organs and, to some extent, on the limbs and body surface. Among boys facial hair also grows. The girl's breasts usually develop rapidly, although there are great personal variations. Whereas all breasts begin as a mere bud, about 38 per cent end up small, 34 per cent of medium size, and 28 per cent large. Shape also varies. About 20 percent are flat, 60 per cent rounded and 20 per cent conical. The voice deepens for both sexes. During puberty a boy's voice usually drops by as much as an octave. Sometimes a boy's voice changes suddenly or 'breaks'. *First ejaculation (boys) or first menstruation (girls).* If physical maturation and the growth spurt are delayed, adolescents may feel at a disadvantage. This feeling passes as puberty progresses.

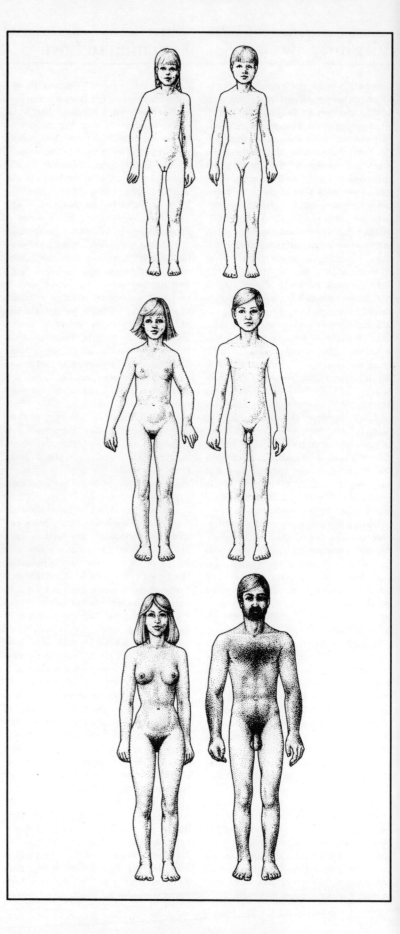

First Menstruation

A girl approaches her first menstruation with a mixture of pride and trepidation. If her mother has prepared her for it and has encouraged her to look forward to it as natural evidence of attaining womanhood, the pride will predominate. If, on the other hand, the parents' attitude has been clouded with inhibition, apprehension and anxiety, this is likely to sow fear, and perhaps shame in the girl's mind. But, in the best of circumstances, the girl is likely to experience a certain amount of shock at her first menstruation because blood *is* frightening, and apparently persistent bleeding more frightening still. This apprehension should clear away after a few periods, when she comes to realize that the bleeding does stop, and that the total amount of blood lost is often quite small.

Nevertheless, the beginning of the reproductive cycle is a considerable physical change which can lead to temporary difficulties. Digestive upsets, with or without nausea and vomiting, may be experienced. Excessive tiredness and listlessness may also occur. Anything thought to be abnormal should be referred to the doctor, whose treatment, or assurance that nothing is wrong, should ease the symptoms and dispel the anxieties. Menstruation of itself is not an illness and should not be treated as such, although a little cosseting, if the girl is nervous and worried, can help her get adjusted.

Well before the onset of the first period, a girl should be fully informed about what will happen physically, and taught the use of sanitary towels or tampons. She should also be prepared for the fact that she may feel tense and irritable, or depressed, for two or three days before her period begins. Until she gets used to having periods, a girl may be embarrassed about other people noticing her condition, or fear that her clothes may get stained without her knowing, or that the odour of menstruation may be obtrusive. Careful hygiene and the mother's reassurance help to overcome these anxieties.

Penis Envy

According to Freud, small girls may resent the fact that boys have penises, and may have unconscious fantasies about having been robbed of this symbol of masculinity. Freud believed that he could trace feelings of inferiority in some of his neurotic women patients to early penis envy. Alternatively, Adler, regarded inferiority feelings as universal but pointed out that women were actually in a socially inferior situation which could provoke them to great efforts to escape from their submissive role. This 'masculine protest' could take either a socially useful or a neurotic form. Presumably, as women gain equality of status, 'penis envy' will disappear.

Obsession

The excessive persistence of an idea or feeling is an obsession. We all experience minor obsessions, as when a tune runs on and on in our heads. Such small quirks of the mind are not to be confused with pathological obsession, a condition in which a single idea may completely dominate the mind. What is called SEXUAL OBSESSION is usually a misnomer. Sex is fascinating, and it is natural that a wide range of stimuli should touch off sexual interest. However, people who never talk about anything else are showing signs of obsession. Such behaviour is often related to feelings of guilt or inadequacy.

Repression

As used in psychiatry, repression refers to the tendency of the mind to push out of consciousness thoughts or feelings that cause pain or embarrassment to the conscious personality. It follows that, in a sexually inhibited society, sexual impulses will often be repressed. There are, however, many other causes for repression. For example, it may be more expedient to repress dislike of a superior than to show it. What is repressed does not disappear. It will find some roundabout mode of expression, sometimes in neurosis. The best answer to repression is to accept our less respectable impulses as normal. Acceptance, not repression, is the basis for control.

Libido

The Freudian term for energy directed to sexual gratification is the Latin word *libido* (meaning 'desire'). Since, in Freudian theory, all creative drive is sexual in origin, libido is also used to describe the dynamic force of the personality. Jung regarded the creative impulses of man as existing in their own right and not only as the secondary effects of sexuality. In Jungian theory, therefore, libido is the sum-total of psychic energy. In its turn, this is related to Adler's concept of man as ceaselessly striving to make his unique mark in life. Libido varies from person to person and with age and state of health.

Sublimation

Sublimation is one of the Freudian 'defence mechanisms' by means of which unacceptable instinctual impulses are seen as becoming transformed into socially approved activities. A classical example of this is the sexually inhibited spinster who devotes herself to animal welfare. The need for the concept arises directly from Freud's insistence that sexual drive or aggression lie behind all human activities. Freud's critics believe that human beings have a considerable autonomous power of decision and regard man as creative from his own potentialities and not merely subject to libidinal and aggressive drives.

Sexual Neuroses

A NEUROSIS is a badly adapted response to life. It is usually associated with repressed motives, thoughts and feelings which are rejected from consciousness because they are unacceptable to the personality. Difficulties with social and sexual relationships are also a feature of neurosis. Neuroses are usually classified according to dominant symptoms, among which are anxiety states, depression and obsessive-compulsive reactions. A simple example of neurotic maladjustment is that of a person who feels compelled to wash every few minutes. A possible interpretation of this would be that the individual is attempting to erase by his symbolic behaviour an acute, unconscious sense of sexual guilt perhaps generated during a prudish upbringing. Such a compulsion is not only a great nuisance, but it will also disturb social and sexual relationships.

A different example of neurotic behaviour is that of an individual who is driven to compensate for an extreme sense of inferiority, established in early years, by striving to make himself, or herself, the constant centre of attention. Such a life style, if taken to excess, is likely to irritate friends, lead to difficulties at work, and inhibit relaxed mutuality which is the foundation for happy sexual relationships. These two cases exemplify what has been a source of argument since the beginning of modern psychiatry.

Freud believed that psychic energy is sexual in origin. Consequently, his system, PSYCHOANALYSIS, placed sexual disorientation at the centre of neurosis. Freud described the human psyche as organized in three functional levels. At the fundamental unconscious level (the ID) are the powerful instinctive drives of our animal natures. These seek immediate gratification. Society, however, cannot exist amid a chaos of uncontrolled impulse. Consequently the EGO developed, to shape, guide and coordinate the basic drives into socially acceptable patterns of behaviour. The struggle between Id and Ego gave rise to values and principles of conduct. These are encountered by children in the matrix of family relationships and are absorbed into the mind as the SUPEREGO. Thus the Ego holds the middle ground between the primitive energies of the Id and the moral force of the Superego. If the Ego is too much threatened by the instinctual drives, or overwhelmed by the demands of a rigid Superego, neurosis may result.

The neurosis itself is, according to Freud, associated with the repression of the conflict into unconsciousness. It is, however, still active, and seeks to express itself in devious ways, such as anxiety. Cure is sought by gradually uncovering the repressed material and helping the individual to understand and accept it.

Freud described the Ego as using various defence mechanisms in its negotiations with primitive impulses and the demands of reality. The effect of these mechanisms is to give the Ego support in maintaining self-esteem. REPRESSION is one of these defences—it rids the conscious mind of the embarrassment of thoughts, desires and feelings that are unacceptable to it. Or the Ego may bolster itself by identifying with someone else. Or it may off-load the sense of shame from its own undesirable impulses by condemning them in others.

Yet another device of the Ego is regression to an earlier stage of life, when things were easier and more pleasant. Little boys, put out by the arrival of a baby, may revert to infant behaviour in an unconscious attempt to recapture lost love and attention. Adults also may take flight from reality by regression.

Freud's method of uncovering the repressed content and elucidating the Ego-defence system was to encourage the patient to verbalize everything that he thought or felt. He also carefully analyzed the patient's *dreams** and fantasies in which he expected to find the unacceptable desires, motives and fears expressing themselves symbolically.

Psychoanalysis deals with the relational aspect of a neurosis by encouraging the patient to work out on the analyst the hostility, dependence, or other emotions, that have obstructed, or are still obstructing, the patient's growth towards maturity.

Alternative explanations of human neurosis appeared in parallel with the development of psychoanalysis, and others have emerged since. Alfred Adler was originally a member of Freud's circle but broke away because he saw neurosis as arising mainly from social relationships, or other influences, which undermine self-esteem, accentuate the normal sense of inferiority, and force the individual to adopt a life style which impairs, or ruins, the individual's capacity to deal with the major tasks of life: friendship, love, and work. C. G. Jung also separated from Freud because he could accept neither Freud's total emphasis on sex, nor his description of the unconscious mental processes. Jung held that the depths of the psyche are rich with potential creativity. He believed that neurosis occurred when the further development of the SELF towards complete integration was blocked in some way.

The variety of theories may seem confusing until one remembers the complexities of the area being explored, and the difficulty of identifying precisely what has the curative effect. Since the classical days of Freud, Adler and Jung, there have been many modifications, expansions, amalgamations and additions to the theory and practice of psychiatry. Some therapists prefer to work in groups rather than with individuals; or individual and group treatment may be combined. The use of tranquilizers, anti-depressants and other drugs has grown enormously in recent years. Another fairly recent addition to the psychiatrist's armoury is behaviour therapy, a technique for reconditioning responses as, for example, in gradually freeing a patient from an irrational fear. Social therapy and *sex therapy** are now independent fields of study and treatment.

Apart from full-scale neuroses, neurotic trends may affect sexual relationships in a variety of ways. Owing to a hangover from past relationships, or experiences, an individual may be too dominant, or too submissive, to build a good relationship with a partner. Or the choice of a partner may be unduly influenced by the unconscious desire to find someone who resembles a parent or other especially loved person. Excessive shyness may inhibit social and sexual relationships. Deep insecurity may make a man vulnerable to sexual failure. Fear of losing her identity may prevent a woman from letting herself respond fully in passionate exchanges of love. Minor difficulties can be worked through—they are part of the normal human situation—major difficulties may be too deep-seated or obstinate to be cleared by experience and may require counselling, psychotherapy or psychiatry.

The study of the relationship between neurosis and SEXUAL DYSFUNCTION brings out strongly the importance of providing children with the love, acceptance, stimulation and encouragement that assure for them a sense of self-value, and lead to a confident relationship with others, and to a liberated, though responsible, attitude to sexual behaviour.

Sex Education

All people have a sex education of one kind or another, if not from parents or school, then more commonly from companions in their own age group. However inaccurate or inadequate the gaining of knowledge about sexual intercourse and 'where babies come from' may be, people learn some basic facts of life in childhood and adolescence.

Ideally, sex education should involve a wide-ranging understanding of all human sexuality. In actual practice many people do not receive the kind of

sex education which ensures that 'human beings may be aided toward responsible use of the sexual faculty and toward assimilation of sex into their individual life patterns as a creative and re-creative force'—the stated purpose of SIECUS, the Sex Information and Education Council of the US.

The consequences of sexual ignorance and lack of good sex education are well known: world-wide venereal disease rates, abortions, illegitimate births, single parent families, shot-gun

weddings (one in five brides are already pregnant on their wedding day, one in three if they are under 20), divorce rates and the hidden distress caused by sexual ignorance in many marriages or in the lives of the sexually unstable. All these demand an awakening of the public in general and educators in particular to the need for teaching people how to enjoy their sexuality responsibly.

So much ignorance and myth remain concerning conception, pregnancy, childbirth, contraception, disease, masturbation, abortion, perversions and aberrations that sex becomes what it should never be, *a problem*. Sexual maturity triggers off difficulties which

amount in many young people to psychological trauma. Private behaviour and public expectation are seen to be two different things. Personal sex drives, ignorance and peer group pressures compete with prejudice, taboos and intolerance.

Young people may be taught about the purpose of the sex act, the sanctity of marriage, the dangers of promiscuity and disease and of the unplanned pregnancy (wrongly labelled 'the unwanted child'). Yet they are fully aware of,

though perhaps mystified by, their own basic sexual urges which have probably led them to masturbation or possibly premature hetero- or homosexual experiences. They suddenly find, in a state of comparative ignorance, that the adult population is concerned with reproductive sex only in so far as it relates to the size of a family. It is otherwise preoccupied with, if not totally committed to, love-sex and fun-sex as regular and necessary functions of adulthood. Love-sex is considered re-creative, while fun-sex is recreational. Double meanings and double standards abound and have to be personally debated by each individual, often without guidance from more mature and experienced persons.

Attempts to adjust to mature sexuality may eventually lead to satisfying and disciplined sexual fulfillment in a warm relationship, but failure to adjust may lead to an over liberal and selfish hedonism, to a guilty and shame ridden denial of sexuality, or to frustration. Intelligent and responsible sex education should lead to the former, and happier, sexuality.

Sex education is not synonymous with teaching the immature and innocent the mechanics of adult coitus (although this forms part of a good sex education) or scaring them about 'the consequences of any sex activity if they are too young. However, sex education is all too commonly thought of as informing children about 'the birds and the bees', of describing copulation and pregnancy in biology classes, of warning about VD, of teaching contraception, demography and population dynamics, and even as an extension of family planning propaganda.

Good sex education in a human context must deal with major problems in society today, many of which are sexually related. Few will deny that there has been a sexual revolution characterized by the sexual emancipation of women, an ever more youthful involvement in sexual activity and a widespread confusion between liberation and liberality, between freedom and licence. There is clearly a need for more education concerning the traditional as well as the emerging role of sex today.

All people should keep in mind the influence of new forces affecting human sexuality when educating their children or when expanding their own sexual consciousness. There is a marked decline in the need for coitus to be primarily concerned with procreation; sexual intercourse for love and pleasure and the release of tension can be associated with spiritual values.

21

MARRIAGE AND SEX

Love solves many things, but rose - tinted glasses do not help much.

Pre-Marital Sex

Until the late fifties or early sixties pre-martial sex, sex before marriage, was an absolute taboo in normal society, in the media anyway, if not in life. It seemed to be an absolute moral precept, based on our Judeo-Christian culture, that every girl should go to the altar a virgin. (Men, of course were different, but they didn't do it with the kind of girl they would marry.)

The ethic of pre-marital purity has developed over the centuries through biological and economic necessity. Virginity was a guarantee of freedom from disease, and that any immediate offspring would be legitimate. Nowadays, a blood test can reveal these factors.

A prime cause of the increase in pre-marital sex must be the decline in religion. Once Christian ethics were not taken for granted young people felt free to make their own moral decisions about basic things like sex before marriage. Once efficient contraceptives had been developed and venereal disease was controllable what harm could there possibly be in such a pleasurable activity? Female emancipation and the acknowledgement of female sexuality must also have played a part. Advocates of women's liberation, such as Germaine Greer and Kate Millet, stressed the active role that women could play in sexual relationships of all kinds.

Statistics are only partially revealing. In 1953 Kinsey reported that about 50% of boys had had full sexual intercourse at least once before marriage but that only 3% of girls had (which may raise some eyebrows: were the 3% girls responsible for the comforts of the 50% of boys, or was there widespread immorality amongst married ladies?). In 1973 R. C. Sorensen surveyed the same age-group and discovered that male sexual knowledge was about the same but that by then about 30% of girls had had sexual fulfilment. In another 1973 study J. Kanter, reporting on over 4000 teenagers, showed that the incidence of pre-marital sex rose from one in seven at 15 years to almost one out of two at 19 years old. In the same year in the United Kingdom, the Opinion Research Centre poll showed that about 55% of the population studied thought that sex before marriage was acceptable if the couple were engaged. We can glean information by looking at the rates for abortions, unmarried mothers and the incidence of venereal disease but these statistics obviously represent only a fraction of what is actually going on. Even Gallup type polls must be suspect because this area of human activity is fraught with psychological sensitivity. People often lie in their responses, answering what they think they should answer.

Although pre-marital sex is widespread there are always biological risks and psychological dangers. A full sexual relationship involves the whole person and few adolescents are psychologically mature enough to cope with such a relationship. There is little doubt that young adolescents—say those under 16—are incapable of a mature union and that sex without love is not much fun really. If they start too young or too promiscuously they may become sexually cynical before their time and never be able to experience a full and pleasant marital relationship. Yet pre-marital sex with a potential spouse surely clarifies at least one aspect of marital harmony (or disharmony). It thus leaves the way clear for the exploration of the more mundane but equally important aspects of the shared life.

For adults, pre-marital sex is now considered normal. Few hotels bother about the marital status of their room-sharing residents. There is little social stigma attached to cohabitation. The media, the barometer of opinion, talk cheerfully about filmstars' 'companions' or 'partners' without dwelling on their marital status or otherwise.

Courtship

Courtship in nature can be defined as the process which takes place between meeting and mating. In the human species we should say it is the process between meeting and marriage, since the end of human courtship is not simply mating but living together.

The phenomenon of courtship has been studied in many species and has many variations and elements. These include sensual attraction through sight, smell, sound and colour, and varied behaviour rituals and responses. Both active and passive roles might be combined during the courtship.

In various species courtship takes different forms. At the appropriate season a male bird will show bright new plumage, change its tune and cavort about in attractive postures. The female bird may start to build a nest and flutter about in the vicinity of attractive males. In canine affairs, the bitch is only sexually available for about a week, twice a year. The approach of her season is announced to the neighbouring dogs by a powerful and presumably attractive odour. They respond by anxious attendance on her doorstep.

This sexual wooing process is influenced and controlled by chemical body messengers, the hormones, and by inbuilt nerve processes, the reflexes. In animals, the courtship phase serves to distinguish those members of the species who are sexually aware and ready and, simultaneously allows the male and female members of the pair to synchronize their mating activity. This helps to ensure a successful conception and the continuation of the species through that pair bond. Aggression is used to determine territorial rights for the potential pairing and to ward off other competitors for—usually—the female partner.

The cultural, religious, ethnic, educational and individual personality features of the human animal when entering the courtship phase make direct comparisons with animals difficult.

The human female is sexually available not for a limited season but at any time for some twenty or thirty years. Human courtship processes are more prolonged, though not really any less ritualized. Aggressive behaviour towards rivals, in the open fashion of animals, is not normally evident, although some human courtship relationships follow a stormy course.

The constructive aim of human courtship appears to be that of 'giving to receive'. This may involve giving presents, money, rings, food or entertainment, or giving less tangible elements like promises, praise, approval and the expression of love. The received portion may be equally material—a home, presents, rings—as well as physical—social contact, sexual contact, companionship—and intangible—love, warmth and affection. The more romantic and non-arranged the courtship pattern, the more the mutual exploitation aspect is played down, and the more altruism and thoughtfulness for the other are emphasized.

In primitive societies, the initial selection of a potential mate went to the tribal leader or group chief; subsequently it passed to the parents in more developed societies. The parents' choice for their child was sometimes influenced by an intermediary—even a professional matchmaker. In close-knit

ethnic groups and orthodox religious societies, the intermediary could generally be relied upon to match up families accurately and effectively. In those societies where matches still tend to be arranged, and in Europe and America until the beginning of this century, the young couple would meet and interact only in the company of a protector or chaperon. The presence of the chaperon was essentially meant to ensure that virginity was preserved. As the couple developed their relationship, they made contact with each other's social network. This included visiting and meeting their families and friends, but in a setting which still precluded 'being alone' together. After a suitable period, agreed by the parents, a formal ceremony of promise in marriage—the BETROTHAL—may have taken place. This was blessed by a family or religious ceremony, and included the ritual exchange of documents, gifts or symbolic jewellery. The betrothal was followed by busy activity between the families, planning the arrangements which culminated in the wedding.

In contemporary Western countries, and increasingly in other societies, the choice of mates for courtship is largely open and determined by the young couple themselves. Various degrees of physical contact can be made, sometimes casually, sometimes purposely, as the couple find out about each other, and approve of each other as physical and emotional partners. Restrictions on their being alone together scarcely exist today. Some courtships can therefore proceed from simple contact, through embracing, kissing and petting, to actual pre-marital sexual intercourse. The description of dating goes from 'casual', to 'going out', to 'going steady', and finally to engagement although formal engagements seem to be going out of fashion.

Meanwhile the same pattern of getting to know each other's social network proceeds. An engagement will probably involve nothing more specific than a party, or it may simply be announced informally or through a newspaper insertion. To confirm their engagement, the couple may exchange gifts or a symbolic item such as an engagement ring for the girl. Today the process may be broken off without social stigma and family outrage as was formerly the case. The ups and downs of human relationships are an accepted part of courtship, and it can be interrupted until reconciliation between the couple, or brought to an end entirely with the return of gifts.

Matrimonial Advertisements

It is an adolescent, romantic dream that a future marriage partner will turn up naturally in one or other area of normal life—at work, in the discotheque, on holiday, at school or college, or through a family connection. But for many, it does not happen so easily. The very shy, the intensely career-minded, may not succeed in meeting a likely partner, and chances diminish as their social peers and workmates themselves marry. Others who have problems meeting potential partners are the widowed, the divorced and the unmarried mother. For them, the solution may be to seek a potential partner by placing an advertisement in personal columns or in 'pen pal' sections of newspapers or magazines.

Apart from the overt self-description of the advertiser, much of his or her real self may be unintentionally revealed by the way the desired partner's physique and personality are described. Another method is to go to a matrimonial agency or 'marriage bureau', which makes the introductions and acts in some degree as a watchdog. Among orthodox Jewish communities, the old-fashioned marriage broker still has a role to play, especially for less affluent families who have traditional ideas about property and matrimony. Asian communities with similar traditions make unembarrassed use of the advertising columns of newspapers in the search for a 'good match'. On the other hand, the recent crop of contact magazines in the USA serves more explicitly sexual purposes. Although phrased like genuine appeals for companionship, the majority of such advertisements has been found, following an investigation by a leading feminist magazine, to be a cover for various forms of commercial sexploitation.

Computer dating should in theory be able to avoid misuse, but reports from users indicate that the systems are not rigorously enough programmed or monitored to provide, as yet, a truly 'clean' and accurate introductions service to their customers.

Trial Marriage

Marriage has no guarantee of being inherently successful, yet many people believe that it can and should work out well, and feel that when they eventually marry it should last for the rest of their lives. They would rather go through a trial period together than go through a divorce. In fact, they take advantage of the present sexually tolerant social climate to attempt to achieve a marriage which will ultimately be as permanent as the uncritically idealized marriage had to be in sexually repressive times.

A trial marriage is more than simple co-habitation. The couple who share the same domestic arrangements and the same bed may describe themselves as 'living together'. Their cynical friends may say they have 'shacked up' together. But their parents or the elders of their society would be happier to describe them as having a 'trial marriage'. It denotes a serious mode of behaviour which is in keeping with modern marriage and divorce.

In the trial period, the couple are to all intents and purposes married. They may keep separate bank accounts and they probably will not take out a joint mortgage, but in all non-financial ways they share everything. Their intention is, if at all possible, to live together for the rest of their lives. The trial marriage period can indicate where their difficulties will lie and whether they can cope with them. One partner may turn out to be compulsively tidy while the other is pathologically untidy. In the courtship period this may not have seemed a serious problem, each admiring the other for not being beset by his or her own problem, but, once married, a difference like that could easily lead to continual and increasing battles. This is the kind of incompatability which can be faced in a trial marriage, but not all problems can be resolved. A couple will not want to have children until they are formally married when the production of a family brings along a whole new set of problems. These will test the couple's characters in ways that even the trial period may not have prepared them for. .

Time will show whether trial marriages reduce the divorce rate. Indeed, they may at least reduce the proportion of marriages which are at present statistically likely to break up within the first four and a half years.

Wedding Customs

There are as many different wedding customs as there are different traditions in the world. Every culture has developed its own ceremonies, but nearly all wedding customs have one thing in common: a symbolic expression of the union of mankind and earth and the general fertility hoped for from the union.

The ceremony is surrounded by symbols of fertility. Whether the place is a church, synagogue or temple, it is usually decorated with flowers. The bride carries flowers and the men sport flowers in their buttonholes. After the wedding, there is always a feast. In some ceremonies the bride and groom share wine, and afterwards cut a cake together.

The symbolic message is that the man is the tiller of the land, the sower of the seed. The woman is the fertile and inactive earth. She is intrinsically his possession. In most ceremonies the man is the active partner and the woman passive. She is packaged in a special virginity-promising gown that she may never wear again. She is brought to the church veiled, by her father who 'gives her away' to the groom. In some Asiatic countries, the veiled bride is sent from her father's home on horseback, while the groom sets out at the same time on his own horse. He 'captures' her and carries her back to his own home. The woman is veiled for complex reasons, she is unknown and a dark quantity, she is passive. Once he has become her husband the groom unveils her. He can release her potential fertility to the eyes of the world. He claims her as his wife by putting a ring on her finger. On the one hand this expresses her bondage; on the other hand it has a phallic symbolism analogous with the act of procreation.

When the couple leave after the wedding ceremony, the onlookers may shower them with rice, sugared almonds or paper confetti. This is a fertility rite which reminds us once again that the husband will sow his seed in the wife. She throws her bouquet to the crowd, offering the hope that one of them, too, will achieve a fertile union.

Pre-nuptial customs vary just as widely, with just the same underlying similarities of meaning. Some very traditional cultures forbid the bride and groom to meet at all before the actual ceremony, while in contemporary American custom they are virtu-ally never out of each other's sight from betrothal to wedding day. Both extremes emphasize in different ways the importance of the period of preparation. The Judaic code advises the bride and groom to fast for a period up to the moment of drinking the wine and receiving the blessing. Some carefully circumscribed opportunities for physical contact, without sex, are allowed to the betrothed couple. Known in some northern European countries as TOBIAS NIGHT or JOSEPH'S NIGHT, they recall the chaste behaviour of those Old Testament worthies. They are euphemisms for sharing a bed without taking one's pants off. Similarly, BUNDLING allows contact while separated by blankets.

Wedding Depression

A prospective bride or bridegroom may begin to feel gloomy, dejected, inactive or even restless as plans for the ceremony progress. It is not unnatural to feel apprehensive about breaking familiar ties, the loss of freedom and the taking on of financial responsibility as the prospect of an entirely new life dawns. Some people feel so depressed that they fail to appear at the appointed time for the wedding. Medical or other professional advice should be sought if a depressed mood or if symptoms such as weight loss, poor appetite or difficulty in sleeping become obvious. In societies where pre-marital sex is absolutely taboo, this state of mind and body can put the newly weds in the worst possible shape for the sensitive beginning of sexual relations.

Honeymoon

The word honeymoon describes a vacation or holiday taken by a newly-married couple following the wedding. Traditionally, a honeymoon away from parents, relatives, friends and familiar surroundings allowed a couple to begin their sexual life in privacy. With increasing pre-marital sex in contemporary Western society, this purpose has declined. (So-called HONEYMOON CYSTITIS often occurs at times remote from the honeymoon period.) 'Honeymoon period' is a figurative expression for the early months of marriage when the partners hold a romantic view of each other as the desired and perfect partner.

Droit de Seigneur

This is a French term which means literally 'the right of the feudal lord'. It is an historical term of sexual innuendo and describes the right of a social superior to DEFLOWER the bride of his inferior. The concept is familiar in Western Europe. In France it is also described with the term JAMBAGE which means downstroke; in Italy the word CAZZAGIO is used which means applying a military rod. Obviously the idea of *droit de seigneur* has been established for centuries as a sexual giggle.

Legally and technically such a right existed from feudal times under the Latin description *jus primae noctis* or the right of the first night. In theory the Lord of the Manor or his equivalent in a local community could demand that a vassal surrender his bride after the wedding ceremony and before consummation. The Lord could exercise his power or right to establish the purity of the bride, to set his blessing on the union and to give them the chance of a 'superior' offspring or merely for the fun of it. In practice it is debatable whether such a right was commonly if at all exercised. Medieval historians suggest that it existed really as a threat to hang over the heads of the unfortunate vassals and as a demonstration of their absolute inferiority to their lord.

The practical result of this right was that the Lord of the Manor had a power which enabled him to levy a sort of marriage tax on his vassals. He would demand money or tithes from them on their marriage, on the understanding that if they didn't pay up then he would exercise his rights.

The ritual defloration of a bride by someone other than her bridegroom exists also in some primitive tribes and is known as the NASAMONIAN CUSTOM because the Greek historian Herodotus first described it among the Nasamonians in the 5th century BC. Various forms of this ritual have taken place at various times and in various cultures perhaps as a way of sharing the defloration of a virgin which had religious taboos associated with it.

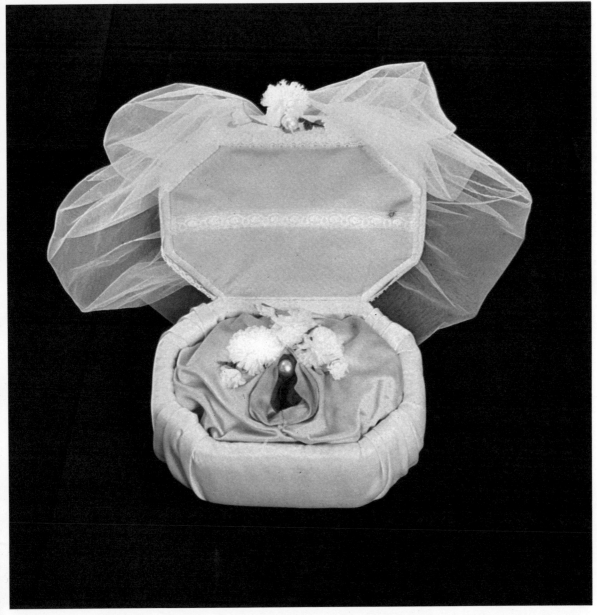

Photo: Paul Levin

Pillow Book

Bedside books, usually containing illustrations of sexual postures, are found in many cultures. In the Far East, the Japanese BRIDAL ROLL was intended to instruct the bashful newly-wed. Japanese erotic prints and paintings are outstandingly explicit and can be studied with advantage by Westerners who are interested in improving their sexual techniques. Pillow books have thus had an educative purpose apart from titillating the reader, for only in the last 100 years has there been any kind of formal education in biology and sexual matters. Until then, sexual techniques were learned by word of mouth or gleaned from bawdy books.

The most famous book of this kind is the Hindu classic, the *Kama Sutra*, written by Vatsyayana in about the 4th century AD and incorporating traditions from much earlier times. It is, in fact, a handbook of civilized manners which treats sexual relations in a quite uninhibited way. There were many Greek and Roman treatises on lovemaking, the best-known probably being Ovid's *Art of Love*. The Renaissance saw the publication of Aretino's sixteen sonnets describing the classic sexual positions, illustrated by his contemporary, the painter Giulio Romano. In the Islamic world, there is the Arabic compilation known as the *Perfumed Garden* of Shaikh Nefzawi.

Any erotic books can be pillow books if they have the right effect on the reader, but the more descriptive they are the more helpful they will be. If such works had been more freely available in the past in Western countries, much of the unhappiness caused by the traditional trial and error process of sexual activity at the beginning of a marriage might have been avoided.

In 1886, the first serious sex manual was published—Dr. Albutt's *The Wife's Handbook*. The first truly modern handbook was Marie Stope's *Married Love*, published in 1918 and, in spite of its seriousness, it was considered scandalous at the time. Men and women today have an extensive range of arousing and informative illustrated books to choose from (*Reader's Guide**).

Matriarchy

A matriarchal society is one in which the mother is the head and ruler of the family group or clan. It is known to have existed in very early times in the Mediterranean and the Near East and is probably associated with the ancient religious cults of mother-goddesses which flourished in that area long after matriarchal societies had been replaced by patriarchal ones. In some ways, matriarchal patterns remain strong even in male-dominated societies, where the mother or grandmother often exerts a powerful influence over basic family affairs and the bringing up of children in a traditional mould. A modern writer, Gordon Rattray Taylor, has detected a pervasive attitude of sexual tolerance and romanticism in those periods of history when society was woman-oriented—possibly a heritage from earlier matriarchal societies. He calls these 'matrist' periods. Jung suggested that matriarchy was a necessary stage in the psychological development of mankind, parallelling the phase of individual development when the mother dominates a young child's world.

Descent through the female line, or the tracing of one's family lineage through the female ancestors, can also be a feature of matriarchy, but the two are not necessarily found together.

Nuclear Family

A nuclear family is firstly a biological group—a male and a female who form a sexual and emotional bond, mate and produce offspring. In the advanced Western industrial societies, it means the closely-knit, basic family group, consisting of a wife/mother, husband/father and immature children, which is set apart from the rest of the community in which it lives and is not in close day-to-day contact with other relatives. This is a comparatively recent by-product of modern technology and its resultant mobility. Since the nuclear family does not usually operate in a wider kinship group, its on-going stability and strength depend on a high degree of personal fulfilment being found within it. It needs continued mutual love as well as social and sexual satisfaction for both husband and wife.

Patriarchy

Absolute authority vested in the male head of a family group or clan is called a patriarchy. Patriarchal societies were the norm for human life until quite recently. Buttressed by the Biblical and clerical traditions of the Church, the 'natural' superiority of the male in all social patterns seemed almost unquestionable. The maleness of God and of the Jewish and Christian priesthoods, the stories of the Old Testament patriarchs, the legends and history of the classical world all pointed to man as the head and leader. The law gave a man wide rights as head of the family and made his wife and her possessions his property, in varying degrees. The attitudes prevailing when the male orientation of society is at its strongest—called a 'patrist' period by Rattray Taylor—are usually restrictive, frowning on gaiety and tending to sexual hypocrisy. Now that the physical strength of a man is no longer important for family survival, and Christian values of male superiority no longer have much force, the traditional discrimination in favour of men is both out of date and unfair. The role of the husband and father is being examined and new patterns of family relations are being tried out.

Extended Family

In a simple form, an extended family exists when 'three generations live under one roof'—a husband, wife, children and grandparents. An extended family features not only a common family or tribal name, but may also share a dwelling, common social activities, common family interests and family ownership of a business or property. A *nuclear family** tends to be part of or subordinate to an extended family when there is a strong dynasty or link between successive generations, or additionally when there is a strong link between brothers, sisters, cousins, aunts, uncles and even adoptive relations and relations-in-law.

Illegitimacy

Any child born to an unmarried mother is described as illegitimate. Developed societies have traditionally taken the view that conception and procreation is only 'legal' when it takes place within a marital unit that has been formally declared lawful in a civil or religious ceremony. This can create later and continuing problems for the child who is born out of wedlock, for he or she may grow up never actually learning who the father is. For some people this creates a deep-seated psychological gap in their development. Sometimes the child becomes aware of the social stigma that surrounds illegitimacy even in the most liberal societies. The term bastard—a quite respectable, formal description of an illegitimate person—may be used in its common and insulting sense against him. In more general language, a bastard object is something inferior, spurious, incompleted, awkward. Naturally a bastard may so come to regard himself in a similar lowly fashion.

In all major developed countries, and most developing countries, a child is registered at birth with the names of his or her parents on some form of birth certificate. When the illegitimate child subsequently is required to present his birth certificate the absence of a paternal name is obvious, and the stigma of illegitimacy is made public. Some countries have adopted a standard 'shorter form' birth certificate which registers birth day, place and name but omits the parents.

Even in tribal and more primitive social groups, where the practice of premarital sexual relationships is not looked at askance, the conception and birth of a child by an unwed mother is considered to be somewhat odious and undesirable. The principle appears to be that society wishes to know that when a child is born there is a paired, responsible unit of husband and wife to ensure its safety, succour and support. Clearly it is realized that fatherless children may in growing up have to be provided for by society to some extent. Developed societies recognize, however, that whatever the official or social proscription on illegitimacy may be, unmarried women will still expose themselves to the risks of pregnancy and unwed motherhood. Therefore, almost all developed countries have caring institutions, originally based on charitable endowments or religious orders, that will look after an illegitimate child in much the same way as they look after an orphan child. Illegitimate babies also provide subjects for adoption by married couples who are unable to conceive themselves and who wish to complete their family.

In Western societies, the illegitimate child and his unmarried mother act as each other's legal heirs. The mother can approach the courts to try and prove who the father of the illegitimate child is, so that she can claim financial support. However, because of the way blood tests are presently administered, it is far easier to prove that a man could *not* have fathered a particular child than to prove definite paternity.

Looked at historically, the fact of being born illegitimate often appears to have had an effect on the drive, ambition and initiative of the individual. Determination to 'wipe out the strain' of the background of being born out of wedlock may account for the rise to fame, sometimes fortune and sometimes to notoriety, of many individuals down through the centuries. The success of the sex bombshell Marilyn Monroe was not only national but global. She shed the tawdry background and colourless, immature personality of Norma Jean Baker, whose mother was a film studio process worker and whose father was 'unknown', to become a star in her own right. Another very successful 'bastard', who is often at pains to draw attention to his beginnings, is the successful if controversial critic, producer and author, Kenneth Tynan. Still in the world of entertainment, a European example of a foundling who rose above the bleakness of her background was Edith Piaf. This tiny woman sang her way from the slums into the hearts of all Frenchmen between the two World Wars, and subsequently into international musical acclaim. And, of course, history is not without famous claimants who were illegitimate. William the Bastard, Duke of Normandy, transformed his title in the history books to William the Conqueror, King of England, as a result of pressing his claims and winning the Battle of Hastings.

Harem

Harems go with the practice of polygamy (or more precisely, *polygyny**). A harem is the part of a polygamist's house where the wives and female servants live. The word itself is Arabic, meaning 'reserved' or 'not to be touched'. Entrance and exit depended solely on the will of its patron. Its inhabitants would never normally be permitted to see another potent male.

Secluded quarters for wives have existed in Jewish, Siamese, Babylonian and Peruvian societies, and in India (*purdah*). In Islam it is a long established institution. The Koran permits a man to have up to four legal wives. This is seen as protecting the marriage against the possibility of the husband resorting to a prostitute for alternative sex. It is also a means of protecting the vulnerable spinster in the Arab communities, by finding her a place among someone's wives. The Islamic tradition recognizes that a man's sexual interests may vary from one year to another, that a woman's response varies from one time to another, and that some men have a greater sexual need than others. The taking of a *concubine**, in addition to the legal wives, is not actively discouraged. Concubines provide a sexual outlet for the custodian owner to enjoy his sexual needs untrammelled by the worries that a wife might care to place before him during his sexual attentions. If he can afford to, a Muslim may enlarge his collection of concubines. Hierarchical problems sometimes arose between the older and newer members of a harem, as well as those who were more popular as sexual companions than others. Over the centuries, Islamic potentates like the Turkish sultans, who were not nomadic, would build themselves suitable palaces with appropriate space for the feminine members of their household who were known collectively as 'the harem'.

The consummate harem was developed by the Turkish sultans. The sultan was allowed seven wives, each of whom he gave her own apartment, gardens and bath. She also had female and castrated male servants. The wives led lives of absolute idleness. Always available to the sultan, their only other preoccupations were gossip and intrigue. They were not known by their names but as *kadin* ('lady') number one, two, and so on. Though the sultan had the right to have pleasure with any of the female slaves (known as *odalisques*), etiquette allowed him to enjoy only those who were chosen for him by his mother or presented to him by state officials. Once the sultan had favoured an odalisque she was relieved of her duties and given her own apartments in the harem. She could never, however, make any demands on the sultan, and it was quite possible that she would only see him once in her life. As only the mother, sister or daughter of the sultan could acquire the regal status and power of sultan, the main concern of the ladies of the harem was the production of the sultan's heir. It did not matter who was the mother, and it could even be an odalisque, if the kadins were not able to forestall it.

Even among nomadic groups in the Middle East, the tendency to multiple marriages is high, and the harem principle may still be in evidence even when an actual residential harem is not possible. Marital contracts are unusual for nomadic men until later on in life, so it may be more difficult to distinguish 'wife' from 'concubine' in a nomadic harem compared with the urban harem.

Partner Swapping

Exchanging married partners for sex is known as 'partner-swapping', 'mate-trading', or less fairly but more often as 'wife-swapping'. It is, in fact, condoned mutual adultery.

Partner-swapping emerged on a wider social scale with the growing affluence of Western society after the Second World War. First described in the USA, it then came to public attention in Britain and other European countries. Post-war swapping may have begun as 'erotic games' at high-spirited parties where inhibitions were loosened by social familiarity and alcohol. Choosing partners occurs in various ways. For example, men throw house keys or car keys into a pile on the floor, and wives choose a partner by selecting a key ring at random. This activity developed on a more regular and sophisticated basis. Two or more married couples might rendezvous at an agreed home or meeting place such as a bar or hotel. After a period of general socializing, the couples would then re-group, not in a casual or chance fashion, but in a pre-arranged selective swap. The rearranged twosomes then retired to somewhere suitable. Couples who swap may know or recognize one another, but a tacit rule is to use first names only.

In the United States, regular swapping became known popularly by the euphemism SWINGING, but is now commonly called swapping. It is not just for fringe or experimental *group sex** devotees, but has become a feature of some otherwise 'respectable' middle class marriages in many communities. Swingers' or swappers' clubs can be formed through personal introductions or carefully worded press advertisements usually in special magazines.

Kinsey's sex studies first suggested that the thirties are the years when women's sexual tensions and needs are likely to be highest. The female partner of the American swapping couple tends to be in her late twenties or early thirties. The male swapper comes from a much wider age range.

Partner exchange activities rarely come to light unless marriage disharmony, mental breakdown or sexually-transmitted infections cause problems. Then swingers may turn to a marriage guidance counsellor, a family doctor or some other medical or social guidance service.

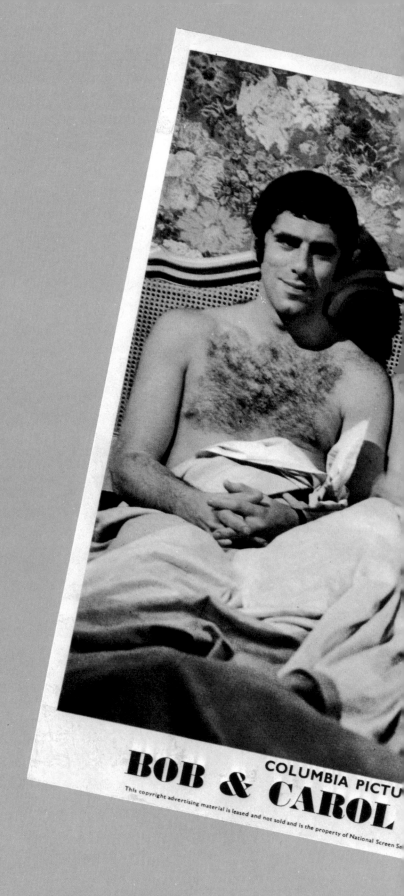

Common Law Wife

A couple who wish to live together and enjoy regular sexual relations are usually encouraged by society to seek a regular monogamous union through a religious or civil marriage ceremony. They are then contracted to one another with specific legal obligations. The couple may, however, decide simply to set up house together and enjoy sexual relations without the legality of a marital contract; and may then stay together indefinitely. The woman may even change her name to that of her male partner 'for convenience'. She becomes known to neighbours and others as 'Mrs'. English, Scottish and American law recognize her after a time (usually seven years) as a Common Law Wife and accord her certain limited rights.

Bigamy

Bigamy (from the Greek for 'two spouses') is different from *polygamy** in that only one of the marriages contracted for is legal. It means that one or the other partner has gone through a form of marriage ceremony while still legally married to someone else. Men tend to indulge in bigamy as an unlawful act more often than women in Western society. There are exceptions to the definition of bigamy which allow for the following situations. When a partner is missing from home or after a major accident, and is either presumed or legally pronounced dead, the surviving spouse may remarry after a certain number of years without being in a bigamous state. The same holds true where the previous marriage was terminated by a legally approved divorce action. Again, if the previous marriage was declared null or invalid for some reason, the partners may remarry without either being open to accusations of bigamy. The problem can arise that—because of religious or civil laws—the country of remarriage does not recognize the earlier divorce in another country as legal. In that case the remarrying spouse might be open to a charge of bigamy.

When divorce was difficult and costly, bigamy offered some husbands an escape from an unsuccessful marriage, though the risks of detection and subsequent imprisonment were particularly high.

Polygamy

The practice of a member of one sex being mated or legally contracted to two or more members of the opposite sex is known as polygamy. The word broadly covers the different kinds of multiple or plural marriages, such as *polyandry** and *polygyny**. In tribal societies and loosely-knit communities in some developing countries, marriages may appear to be polygamous, but are in fact centred on a father or mother figure around whom social and sexual activities revolve. In the societies of developed countries, which historically have a Christian background and practice *monogamy**, polygamy is usually regarded as irreligious and is generally illegal. Problems arising from immigrant families coming from societies (especially Islamic ones) where polygamy is normal, have still to be solved.

Concubine

A concubine is a woman who cohabits (lives and has sex) with a man to whom she is not legally contracted in marriage. In societies which practice *polygyny**, a concubine ranks as a secondary wife, and having a concubine does not preclude a man from having sexual relations with his wife. Unlike the wife, a concubine can be discarded when her sexual attractiveness has worn off. Concubinage has a long history and is mentioned in the Old Testament. Generally speaking, keeping a concubine has been the prerogative of men whose wealth or high social position allowed them this extra luxury.

Polyandry

The version of *polygamy** (plural marriage) in which one woman lives with two or more men in a self-contained setting. The practice appears to be comparatively rare in the world, whereas its opposite, *polygyny** is fairly frequent in both primitive and more developed societies. The sexual frictions and tensions possible within a polyandrous union can be anticipated, as they can be in a polygynous situation. *Partner-swapping** is not a form of polyandry, since the sexual liaisons are usually temporary and remain on a one-to-one basis.

Polygyny

One form of *polygamy** (plural marriage) is polygyny, which literally means that one man is married legally to two or more women. In the Islamic world, celibacy is not considered a state of grace and the Koran permits a man to have up to four wives. (This helped to spare women the vulnerability of being spinsters in a male-dominated world.) Islam apart, mainstream global religions (sects like the Mormons excepted) do not countenance polygyny, though in less developed societies it is not unusual. When the women whom a man marries are sisters, the practice is known as SORORAL POLYGYNY.

Ménage à Trois

Usually, a *ménage à trois*, or 'household of three', consists of a married couple who add a third person to their relationship. The third person may be a lover of either or both of them, and it may be a person of either sex.

Male extra-marital sex for husbands has always been recognized as a possible occurrence away from home and sexual guilt about the relationship could be suitably insulated—the reverse applied to wives until the present century.

Ménage à trois is still a household to be enjoyed by the fringes of society. Something akin to it was however accepted as a formal arrangement in the rich society families of Italy from the 17th to the 19th century. When a wife, for whatever reason, found the attentions of her husband to be inadequate, she would seek out an official lover from among her own social class. The practice was called CICISBEISM and the lover was a *cisisbeo* or *cavaliere servente*. The husband was generally aware of his existence.

Nowadays, a *ménage à trois* is understood to imply the knowledge and consent of all the partners. The wife may still love her husband but need some other outlet for her sexual feelings, or either the husband or the wife may be *bisexual** and want a lover of the same sex, in addition to the spouse.

One form of *ménage à trois* is one in which a husband's unmarried close male friend becomes attracted to the wife. She may or may not be dissatisfied with her husband, but the flattering attentions of the best friend of her husband will make her feel romantic. Finding she is still sexually attractive to men apart from her husband stimulates her. The result may be a *ménage à trois*, in which the husband continues to receive his wife's sexual favours but she also has regular sexual relations with the best friend.

Whatever the cause or the arrangement, the partners can only find mutual happiness and satisfaction in a *ménage à trois* if it is done freely. They will presumably be more liberal in their outlook than the average monogamous couple, and whenever the arrangement fails to work they will feel free to change it without bitter disputes. Its successful maintenance demands a depth of personal understanding which lies outside normal cultural and social conditioning.

Open Marriage

This is a fairly new concept—as a logical development of marriage in the light of modern sexual freedoms. Partners who marry nowadays do so through choice and not through necessity. Society no longer demands a marriage licence before people begin living together. Couples in an open marriage recognize that their behaviour is a matter of mutual consent rather than formal rules. Open marriage implies total mutual trust. A wife, for example, might go out with her friends for an evening, leaving her husband at home, or one of the partners might go on holiday alone. In Victorian times, a lady could never spent the night alone in a house with a man other than her husband. Nowadays it can happen without the immediate assumption of adultery. In an open marriage, a wife seeing her husband with another lady, would approach and introduce herself. No dark suspicion would cloud her thoughts.

But more and more the term open marriage is used to mean full sexual freedom for the partners. This still involves trust, but it also involves condoned extra-marital sex. This may take the form of *partner swapping** where married couples come together for the purpose with the full knowledge of all concerned, or the partners may allow each other complete and private affairs, recognizing that each has sexual and emotional needs that cannot be satisfied by an exclusive relationship.

In this time, when pre-marital sex is normal, contraception fairly efficient, and venereal disease fairly controllable, it may not be a bad thing to bring new ideas into the concept of marriage which, after all, is an institution which can grow and change with the times. Open marriage at its best represents a relationship based on truthfulness and understanding. It does away with sordid furtiveness, but it must be a true mutual understanding, and each of the partners must equally desire it. If one of them is the leader and the other the less willing partner, domestic disruption and distress might result.

Edouard Manet

Monogamy

Having only one marriage partner at any time is called monogamy. Although strictly the word means 'one wife', it describes an exclusive relationship between one man and one woman. Monogamy is enforced in Western civilization by legal and religious authorities, and is accepted as the basis of a stable family unit, which in turn determines the healthy rearing of children and the control of moral standards.

Some people attempt to justify the predominance of monogamy in our society by looking at it in terms of human evolution. Desmond Morris points out that the pair bond relationship in human beings is derived from a courtship process which is generally more prolonged than in other animal species. This strengthens the pair bond and encourages monogamy.

Monogamy does not seem to be an instinctive behavioural pattern in human behaviour, and there have been instances of sophisticated societies where it was not the norm. Greek and Roman myths depict polygamous gods; the Jews practised *polygamy** (David and Solomon had many wives); even in nearly modern America, the Mormons approved of polygamy for members of their church. The dominance of monogamy may perhaps be ascribed to cultural conditioning rather than to basic human nature. Fairy stories invariably culminate in monogamous unions. Mythical lovers go in couples (Romeo and Juliet, Hero and Leander, Jack and Jill, etc) and we associate a third person in a relationship with threat and disaster.

We find no difficulty in accepting the notion that a parent can equally love several children and we expect children to accept this shared status without undue sibling rivalry. Yet we do not easily assimilate the idea that a man or a woman can simultaneously love more than one mate. Society does accept the concept of SERIAL MONOGAMY, that is to say, a sequence of one-to-one relationships, one after another. Most people have had several consecutive relationships before they settle into orthodox marriage. With the easing of the divorce laws, more and more people divorce and remarry. Society accepts that it is possible to love more than one mate; it is only taboo to love them simultaneously.

The choice of partner in a monogamous relationship may be made either from within the individual's own social, cultural or ethnic group, or from outside personally familiar groups. The former is called *endogamy* and the latter *exogamy*. When marriages were invariably arranged by the leader of the tribe, the feudal lord, or the parents, then the monogamous marriage was invariably an example of endogamy. In contemporary developed societies, the social and territorial mobility of young people combines with personal freedom in choosing a marriage partner. This makes a modern monogamous marriage almost as likely to be in the form of exogamy as of endogamy. This is a comparatively recent development.

Equality

In primitive and undeveloped societies, there was no question of equality of legal or any other kind of rights for husband and wife. In fact, the wife was invariably regarded as being 'owned' by the husband in the manner of an object or chattel. Her fixed role was that of worker, child breeder and caretaker of the family's daily needs. She had no property of her own and was entirely dependent on her husband.

In contemporary developed societies, the idea that both husband and wife should be sexually and legally equal in terms of rights and opportunities is a fundamental part of the on-going sexual revolution. There have been profound changes in women's sexual roles, in their identity and even in their personalities as a result of the demand for equality with males. This is bound to be more far reaching in the future, and will have an influence on the character of the marriage relationship. As the roles of men and women undergo changes, with increasing equality for women, legal rights, better pay for work and recognition of their achievements, traditional patterns of submission and dominance, of breadwinner and homemaker and of sexual aggression and reception will result in both man and woman undertaking marriage as an equal, mutually responsible team which shares all the work and rewards of the marital and family relationship.

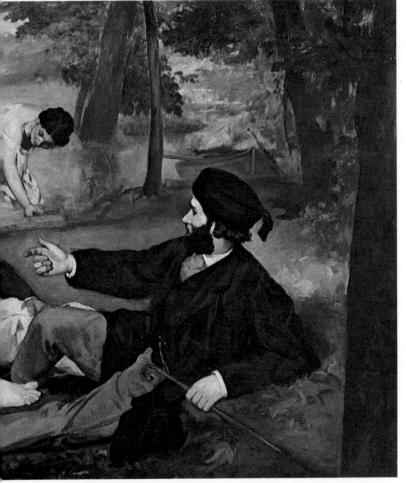

Childlessness

Childlessness may be voluntary by the use of *contraception** or *abortion**. Involuntary childlessness is also called *sterility**, INFERTILITY or sometimes BARRENNESS. Involutionary childlessness results from a failure of function in the husband in about one-third of couples, a failure in the wife in about one-third and a combination of minor factors to be found in both partners in the remaining third. About 15 per cent of all marriages are infertile.

In the male there may be psychological reasons making intercourse difficult or impossible, or breaks in the control of the sexual function by accidental injury such as a fractured spine. Intercourse for men requires conscious active behaviour under control of the will, just as drinking a glass of water does. This controlled behaviour is later followed by ejaculation which, once a certain stage of excitement has been reached, is no longer under the conscious will and is therefore called a reflex.

To be fertile, a man has to be able to have an erection of his penis, maintain the erection and ejaculate healthy sperm inside his female partner.

Female fertility depends on the ability of the woman's ovaries to produce at least one egg suitable for fertilization in most months of the year, and on healthy internal genital organs.

Sometimes there are several combined factors contributing to childlessness. For example, a fertile husband may not have intercourse with his wife on the correct days when an egg can be expected to be available for fertilization. These factors usually cause childlessness when the fertility of one or the other (or both) partners is weak. Without help from a doctor who can calculate accurately, with the aid of the woman's temperature records and other tests, intercourse may always occur on days unlikely to produce a baby. Furthermore, the degree of acidity in the vagina or cervix (the neck of the womb) may prevent the sperms passing through on their way to the egg. Sometimes the position the couple adopt for intercourse may militate against successful fertilization. Sometimes ejaculation occurs too low down in the vagina, so that most of the seminal fluid is lost. These faults are easily corrected with expert advice. About 60 per cent of all childless couples can be helped by experts to have children.

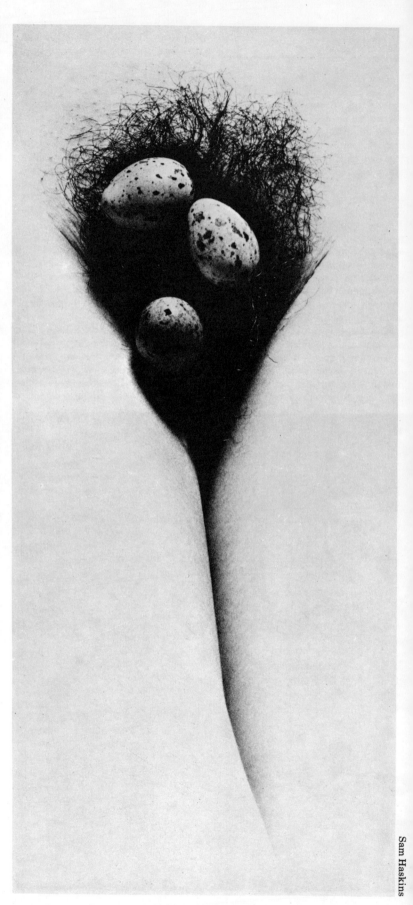

Sam Haskins

234

Artificial Insemination

Sowing seeds is called insemination. The normal way for human beings to reproduce is for a man to sow his seed or introduce his semen into a woman by intercourse. The fusion of the nucleus in the head of one of his seeds or sperm with the nucleus in her egg constitutes fertilization. Though normal intercourse is the standard way for reproduction to occur, it is not always successful. There may be a need to resort to artificial insemination in order to achieve fertilization of a female egg.

Artificial insemination may be performed using the husband's semen (AIH, or Artificial Insemination by the Husband). This need may arise when a husband has some psychological inability to have intercourse successfully. A typical case would be where the husband ejaculates prematurely before entering his wife's vagina, but where it is known by testing with the microscope that his semen can produce pregnancy. Most cases of *premature ejaculation** can now be cured, but it may take time and the couple may be in a hurry to start a pregnancy. Another typical cause may be where the man produces a small quantity of fertile semen but not enough to bathe the cervix sufficiently to ensure penetration by live healthy spermatozoa. Occasionally when the vagina is very capacious, as when the woman has already had many children, the semen may not be retained but flows out. There are some women who just cannot relax adequately to permit normal intercourse. Such women may accept a small syringe introduced into the vagina so that the semen can be placed on or near the cervix where it should be to start the whole process of having a baby in the normal way.

If, however, donor's semen is used, the procedure is known as Artificial Insemination by Donor (AID). This is necessary when the difficulty in having a baby arises from absence of spermatozoa in the husband's semen or he has such a low sperm count that it is unlikely that he will ever fertilize his wife.

A few doctors use mixed specimens of the husband's and a donor's semen for artificial insemination so that nobody can be 100 per cent certain that it is the donor and not the husband that has fertilized the wife.

When artificial insemination from a donor is carried out this is usually done in a doctor's office under conditions of the greatest possible confidentiality. A donor is selected with as close a physical resemblance to the husband as possible, so that when the child is born no one will suspect that it has not been fathered by the husband. Usually only the doctor performing the procedure and one nurse or trusted secretary knows the details. It is rare indeed for the mother-to-be to be told who donated the semen with which she has been fertilized. Doctors feel it would be unethical for her to know, because once having the child she may be so grateful, that she might wish to meet the donor and perhaps acquire a closer relationship. For this reason all doctors carrying out artificial insemination using donor's sperm keep secret from the recipients the identity of the donor.

During artificial insemination the sperm is drawn out of the container in which it has been collected, and a small amount placed with a special syringe on the outside surface of the cervix and perhaps a droplet just inside the cervix. The semen is not placed inside the womb, because spermatozoa have to pass through the cervix under their own power in order to become capable of fertilizing eggs. Furthermore, fluid placed inside the womb is quite often rejected, especially if it is placed there forcibly under pressure. The timing of artificial insemination from the husband or from a donor has, of course, to coincide with the date on which the patient is expected to be ovulating. Any other time will be useless.

When the husband's semen is used for artificial insemination, the same technique as for a donor may be used, but the same need for the procedure to be carried out in the doctor's office is not present as a couple can learn relatively easily how to perform artificial insemination at home. Also husbands may find it difficult to masturbate at a definite hour of the day in the rather clinical atmosphere of a doctor's office, so this arrangement works well. Artificial insemination at home can be carried out by the couple at their own convenience using a specially invented cap that fits over the cervix and which has a plastic tube passing through its centre. The cap is made of plastic and is fairly rigid, and so long as the right size is chosen a woman can be taught by her doctor fairly quickly how to apply it over her own cervix. The tubing hangs down into the vagina and out through the lips of the vulva. A small screw tap slides over the tubing. An ordinary syringe can be fitted on to the end of the tubing. The husband ejaculates into a plastic container and the seminal fluid is then drawn up into the syringe. The syringe is applied to the end of the tubing and the tap is opened and the seminal fluid injected through the tubing into the cap which has been fitted on to the cervix. The tap is then closed. The cervix adaptor, as it is called, is left in position for about eight hours. By this means one can be sure that the cervix is bathed in the husband's seminal fluid for all of this time and the chances of insemination are greatly increased, particularly when the husband produces only small quantities of semen or the vagina is lax or there are bars to normal intercourse.

According to the laws of most countries, every child born in wedlock is presumed to be a natural child of the husband. It is obvious that a child born as the result of insemination with a donor's semen is really a natural child of the donor and not of the husband. This is true in spite of the fact that the donor has never had intercourse with the mother of the child. The child must inherit features from the donor in the same way as it would from a natural father. In view of this, the greatest care must be taken in making a decision for or against artificial insemination from a donor. It is not surprising, therefore, that those doctors who carry out the procedure have become quite expert in counselling couples as to the likely reactions to pregnancy and as to the legal position of the child. There is no doubt at all that artificial insemination from a donor is a perfectly legal procedure. If it is carried out with the consent of the husband, it can not be considered as adultery in the eyes of the law and it can not be a reason for the husband seeking a divorce in the future.

In a large majority of cases the child is accepted by husband and wife equally as their own child and the manner in which the child was conceived is nearly always forgotten. In many ways the procedure is preferable to adoption, partly because the child is the natural child of one of the parents and partly because today there is a shortage of babies put up for adoption.

There is one small snag common to both adoption and artificial insemination from a donor, and that is the tendency for some parents to blame the true father of the child for any faults in behaviour found in the child.

Adoption

The adoption of a child is a choice on the part of the new parents and the change of relationship means that a child becomes for all legal purposes the child of its adopting rather than its natural parents. The adopting couple assumes all the normal responsibilities and rewards of being father and mother for the chosen adopted child.

In theory, adoption is simple. A mother who may be married, but often is not, gives birth to a child she cannot keep. More or less reluctantly she gives it for adoption by a couple who often, but not necessarily, cannot have a child themselves for medical reasons. The mother usually does not know to whom the child has gone and the adopting parents usually do not know the identity of the natural mother.

In practice the reactions of the adopted child are as important as those of the adopting parents, and the ability to predict the future success of a particular adoption requires skills that have until now not always been recognized. Social and welfare workers have long been involved in the specialized work of arranging adoptions, which for choice should nearly always be through a recognized adoption agency, although so-called 'third party' adoptions can still be arranged. Such recognized agencies comprise both voluntary or charitable societies and many local government agencies who handle adoptions. They receive applications from prospective parents and information from social workers working in maternity hospitals and in homes for children who have had to be put 'into care', and who thus get to know of babies who will be offered for adoption. Some adoption agencies specialize in trying to improve adoption opportunities for children with special needs—those with physical or mental handicaps, disturbed children and children over six years of age.

Prospective parents are urged to examine their reasons for adopting most carefully. One unsatisfactory reason is to help bolster an unstable or unhappy marriage. It is very important that *both* partners want to adopt—no one should agree to adoption or simply go along with it just to please their spouse. Another poor reason is to patronizingly give a home to a child in need. The new relationship must be such that mutual love can develop between the child and the new parents.

Due to more liberal abortion laws and attitudes towards illegitimacy—many unmarried women now choose to have children and 60 per cent of all unmarried mothers keep their babies. It is presently very difficult to find babies for adoption. There are, however, older children in need of care such as multiracial children who have been placed 'in care' and who would benefit by adoption by mature parents. There are, of course, added problems in adopting a child who is no longer an infant. Children who may have spent several years in an institution as part of a larger group may find it very difficult to adjust to the emotional climate of a small family group.

Non-Consumation

A marriage is consummated when the husband's penis enters into the wife's vagina. By law, even partial penetration of the vagina constitutes consummation of the marriage. If the wife is a virgin, the hymen must be torn or stretched sufficiently for at least part of the penis to pass through it. For full intercourse to take place, virtually the whole length of the penis has to be introduced into the vagina.

Even today, evidence of consummation in many societies is derived from finding blood on the underwear or sheets after the first act of intercourse. This is not a sensible test for previous virginity. It is only a crude indication of whether the hymen has been torn at intercourse. Today, few courts would accept failure to find blood as evidence of non-virginity on the part of the wife. This is because many virginal women wear internal tampons which stretch the hymen.

Failure of consummation is almost always a failure by both husband and wife. It is seldom that either partner is entirely responsible, although the man must of course be anatomically able to function and the wife anatomically able to relax sufficiently to allow him to function.

A man must be able to have a durable erection of his penis, and maintain that erection for long enough to penetrate his wife in order for the marriage to be consummated. Rarely is there a structural, anatomical fault in the penis serious enough to prevent erection, but an erection may easily be lost if the husband is frightened of hurting his wife or if he becomes so rapidly excited that he has an ejaculation before penetrating. Failure to achieve an erection is nearly always psychological in origin.

When the wife is primarily responsible, as is in the condition known as *vaginismus**, the commonest reason for non-consummation of marriage, the causes stem often from fears that she will be hurt, damaged or split. Lack of experience, clumsiness and, above all, repeated failure, with the inevitable subsequent 'self-watching' all contribute to make things worse.

The situation is not helped if the couple have no true privacy. Some of the worst cases of failure of consummation occur in those marriages where the couple have been given a bedroom next to that occupied by other members of the family (often the bride's parents). This adds to their shyness with one another and the embarrassment that the sounds they make in intercourse may be heard in the next room.

The problem, incidentally, is far more common than most people imagine. A proportion of all married patients who attend infertility clinics have failed to have children because of nonconsumation of the marriage.

Masters and Johnson devote 15 pages in *Human Sexual Inadequacy* to vaginismus to show with very good diagrams how tightening of the muscles at the entrance to the vagina can make intercourse impossible. They emphasize that the teaching of the anatomy of the organs, and especially of the musculature, is one of the first essentials in their treatment. They also show that the sexual history taken from the wife is very important indeed because it is not only virgins who suffer from virginismus. Women who have previously had intercourse normally and then suffered the results of an awful episode such as rape or even gang rape may subsequently be unable to consummate. They emphasize, too, that in many cases the man is unable to maintain his erection and they show in their book ways in which he can be helped to do this.

It is emphasized by Masters and Johnson and by most other sex therapists that a very strict upbringing is one of the causes of failure to be able to achieve pleasure in intercourse.

Time and time again sexologists report that the doctor's role is to give the patient 'permission' to enjoy sex, 'permission' which was felt to have been refused by the attitude of the parents when educating their children.

All are now agreed that for the successful treatment of non-consummation the doctor's help must be sought and he in turn must have the co-operation of the husband as well as the wife. In almost all cases the first step is to take a general medical history very carefully from each partner. This medical history involves enquiry as to menstrual function, age of sexual development of the breasts and other secondary sex characteristics, and details of previous illnesses which may be relevant. Then a full physical examination is carried out to confirm that non-sexual physical development is normal and this is followed by a careful and very gentle examination of the genital organs to ascertain their state of normality or otherwise. No experienced doctor will hurt a patient by forcing a vaginal examination on her.

The sexual history-taking also involves quite lengthy enquiry into the past sexual attitudes of the couple. Once both partners have been given an opportunity to talk out their feelings about sex, marriage and religious attitudes to intercourse, as well as the education received at home, training to overcome the spasm which is almost always the cause of the non-consummation of the marriage can be started.

Different doctors use different techniques. Masters and Johnson from the outset obtain the collaboration of the husband and demonstrate to him how the muscles at the entry to the vagina are in spasm. With this demonstration the wife, too, learns the cause of the husband's failure to be able to penetrate. Other experts such as doctors de Senarclens and Pasini in Geneva who have made a special study of this subject, teach the woman to examine herself first and encourage her to become acquainted with her body and to stretch her vagina. Often they show her with the aid of a mirror what she is doing to herself. Most people agree that once the woman is able to stretch her vagina either with her own fingers or with a glass dilator, the next step is for her to allow her husband to do the same, for this gives him self-confidence, without having to prove himself.

Everybody, according to de Senarclens and Pasini, should first be at ease with himself or herself in order to obtain good relationships with others. This is why, unlike Masters and Johnson, they concentrate first on teaching the woman how to explore herself.

Most doctors believe that once a woman has overcome the spasm at the entry to her vagina, it is helpful if the first attempts at intercourse are carried out with the wife in the superior position. She squats over her husband and lowers herself gently on to his erect penis. If necessary the penis is lubricated with an ointment such as K-Y jelly.

A few psychiatrists feel that psychological treatment is indicated before the physical treatment is attempted. Certainly in some cases psychotherapy may be essential in order for full appreciation and handling of problems that are interfering with the enjoyment of sex. One of the worst fears in nonconsummation cases is that the woman may feel that she is either not a true woman or not worthy to be woman. It may require quite a lot of skill by a psychiatrist to improve such patients' estimation of themselves.

Surrogate Therapy

The word surrogate simply means substitute. However, since *Masters and Johnson**, the American sex researchers, used the word to describe the SUBSTITUTE SEX PARTNERS they used in treating male patients with sexual problems, it is in this special context that the word is now most often used.

The fact that substitute, replacement or surrogate sex partners in *sex therapy** programmes are helpful in treating certain problems should be self-evident—but it is not. There is an enormous and often quite irrational resistance to the use of surrogates in the treatment of sex problems. Probably the most frequent objection is that unless sex takes place within the context of a loving relationship it becomes devalued and is worthless. Of course, if one believes this to be so without exception, then one is unlikely to have much faith in surrogate therapy. Those who oppose the use of surrogates on these grounds are expressing a personal point of view and one which does not necessarily accord with the facts of human sexuality. Moreover, such opinions are normally only held by those who do not have serious sexual problems themselves, at least of the type which are curable. However, many thousands of patients and potential patients feel intuitively that surrogate sex therapy is their only hope. Why should they feel this way?

Take, for example, a young man in his mid-twenties who, having attempted intercourse on a number of occasions, discovers that he is impotent, that he is unable to achieve a sufficiently hard erection to penetrate the female vagina. *Counselling**, psychoanalysis or psychotherapy (talk therapy) are unable to help this patient. No doubt the patient can obtain a proud erection when he masturbates alone but that is of little consequence if he cannot perform when he is with his chosen sex partner.

Surrogate sex therapy involves practical intervention where a patient has the active and sympathetic cooperation of a partner to help overcome fear of sexual failure. The cure lies in learning how to become both relaxed and aroused in a sexual situation. Clearly one cannot just talk a patient into that frame of mind. Very often a doctor will tell a male patient to go away and get himself a girlfriend and then instruct them to come back together later. How-

ever, it is obvious to the patient, if not to anyone else, that he is caught in a vicious circle. He needs a partner to help him gain confidence and sufficient self-esteem to escape from his fear of failure. But he cannot risk finding a partner because of his fear that he might fail—and so he opts out in order to avoid the humiliation of failing and making a fool of himself. Indeed, he may opt out of forming relationships altogether for several years, even for a lifetime, for want of a sympathetic partner. By offering him something besides a prescription for a tranquilliser or giving him a pep talk, by providing a substitute, sympathetic sex partner, at least half, if not more, of the patients with a fear of sexual failure can become satisfactory and satisfied lovers.

There is no magic in the sex surrogate method. In the first place, the patient is aware that his surrogate partner knows about 'the problem', and so he does not have to go through the agony of deciding whether or not to tell her. Because *he* knows that *she* knows, half the battle is won and a load of anxiety is immediately lifted from his mind. Secondly, in surrogate sex therapy the patient and surrogate do not jump into bed at the first meeting. Normally patient and partner meet socially on two or three occasions or even for longer, if necessary, until they feel relaxed with each other. And then stage by stage, usually at weekly intervals, they will talk about the relevant sex problem and progress through the early stages of sex play, the surrogate determining how fast they should proceed from the response of her partner, ensuring above all that each meeting ends on a point of success. For example, she would not begin to undress him completely until he was sufficiently relaxed to be able to enjoy such activity without feeling anxious about what comes next. Nor would she normally attempt to stimulate his penis directly until he became sexually aroused as a result of her stimulating him elsewhere on his body. Naturally, penetration and intercourse would not begin until the stage was reached where he was able to get good erections and hold them for some time.

A female sexual problem which may occasionally require the help of a male surrogate is known as *vaginismus**. This is a condition where the vagina fails to dilate sufficiently to allow the penis to enter. Usually this can be treated by the woman herself either by learning *muscle consciousness**, by using her fingers or special dilators of

graded sizes which will help her to relax the vaginal muscles. At a later stage her partner will then be able to begin, in stages, to insert his penis. However, if a woman hasn't got a regular partner, or has opted out as a result of a history of failures, or has a partner who has become impotent as can happen to husbands or boyfriends of women with vaginismus, then the help of a surrogate male is often the only way she can gain enough confidence to dispel her anxieties about her inability to participate in intercourse.

The use of surrogates for patients who are married or have steady relationships perhaps needs some further justification. The fact is that many married couples simply cannot help each other when sexual problems affect their relationship. Indeed they ask for the cooperation of a surrogate to help either one or the other or both with their problems. On reflection this is not surprising because many sex disorders, particularly *premature ejaculation** in the male and so-called *frigidity** in the female, where she fails to become turned on sexually, are problems which very often arise *because* of the relationship. By directing attention to an individual's specific problems instead of concentrating on the personal relationships, one can significantly increase the chances of successfully helping the person in question. A happy, sexually confident individual is much more likely to be able to relate to a marital partner or other person and to transfer satisfaction from the initial success with a surrogate to a marital partner or other future partners.

One of the most important reasons why surrogate sex therapy is successful is that it necessarily bypasses the 'burden of a loving relationship' which so often can be sexually counter-productive. Without such a burden, fears of humiliation, rejection or loss of face are reduced. Moreover, the newness of the patient-surrogate relationship will be more arousing sexually and the freshness and novelty implicit in these short-term therapeutic relationships can restore confidence and a sense of sexual well being to a patient that would be otherwise unobtainable. There is, of course, no guarantee that such improvement can be automatically transferred to a martial relationship, although subsequently it very often is. Often each partner begins to grow and understand themselves and their needs and with that added insight can then make more mature judgments.

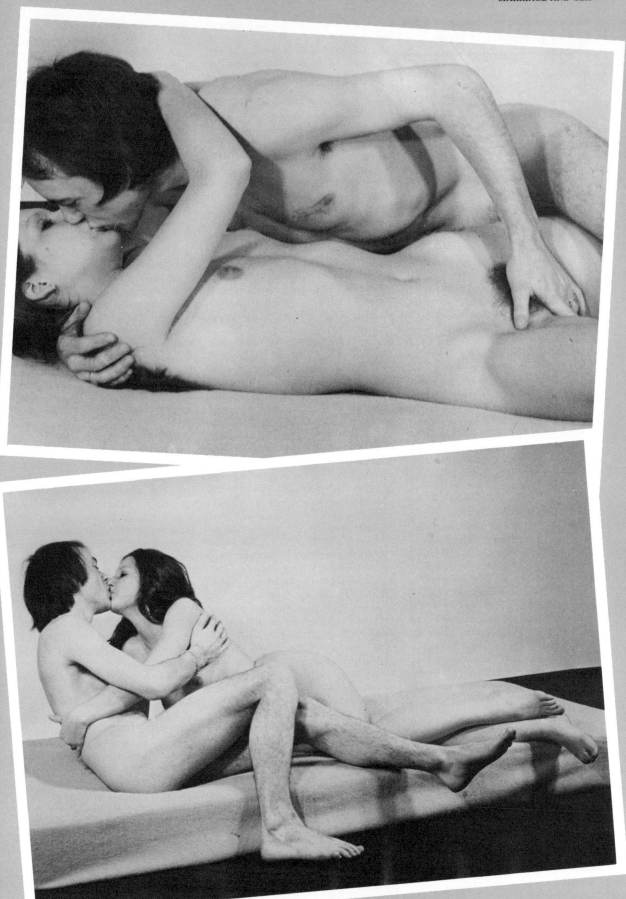

Extra-Marital Sex

Different civilizations and different cultures look at extra-marital sex in totally different ways. In Judeo-Christian cultures the Biblical commandment stated, 'Neither shalt thou commit adultery' and people who did so were ostracized from society or severely punished. On the other hand, adultery by men was often overlooked by society as long as it was carried on without general public knowledge, hence the popularity of the secret AFFAIR.

A culturally interesting form of extra-martial sex occurred among black women from the West Indies, even when living away from their homeland. They tended to have quite large families of children by different men before finally settling down with one partner in marriage toward the end of their active reproductive lives. The historical background for this behaviour lies in the *extended family** developed in the West Indies when slavery existed. Slave owners there and in other cultures, including the American South, treated their female slaves as breeders of high-class slave stock, and encouraged mating with different males in order to 'improve the stock'. The older women, grandmothers and aunts, looked after the children when the mother went out to work in the fields or the slave-owner's house. There was much warmth in these large family relationships and the men, even if not permanently linked in marriage with their sexual partners, did have homes to turn to. Marriage was recognized for companionship toward the end of life and once married, the husband and wife stayed reasonably constant to each other. This social pattern of extra-marital sex persists even today, but there are more disadvantages than advantages. The extended family system is not usually in operation in the last quarter of our century and all that remains is the unfaithfulness, the lack of security and the necessity of baby-minders to take over the care of the children while mothers go out to work.

Today in most of the Western world, adultery or extra-marital sex is viewed somewhat more lightly than a few years back. Until the recent past, a single act of adultery was considered adequate grounds for divorce, but this is no longer so. Even in the 1960s a husband would blatantly take a strange woman to a hotel and stay the night there in order to provide his wife with the evidence of his unfaithfulness as shown by the hotel bill or being caught by a private detective *inflagrante delicto* (in the act of committing an offence, in this case adultery). Today such an act of adultery would not constitute sufficient grounds for divorce, which has become much easier to obtain anyway. Divorce by mutual consent after obvious breakdown of the marriage is slowly becoming commonplace—a much more logical and intelligent view than a single adulterous act.

Adultery seems to be on the increase. *Partner swapping** and 'swinging', where groups of couples come together for parties which lead to sexual intercourse with one another's spouses, are becoming more commonplace too. These activities do nothing to improve marriage. On the contrary, they usually harm it for a degree of marital fidelity is still the normal and acceptable behaviour.

In middle-aged men, adultery quite often starts as an affair with a younger woman. Sometimes this occurs if something at work arises to lessen self-confidence, such as someone else being promoted over the head of the older man. He then seeks to reassure himself that he is still as 'good a man' as he ever was by what is considered the ultimate test of virility—the seducing of a younger woman. Some younger women are flattered by the attention of an older man, and so an affair starts. Older women, too, may succumb to the flattery of seduction by younger men, but these affairs often die out fairly quickly. The reasons for anybody starting such an affair are quite often not clear cut. Many 'just happen' and the couple find themselves in a situation from which it is difficult to extract themselves. Even today many girls find themselves pregnant by men they thought they were engaged to, but who finally turn out to be already married or about to marry someone else.

There are, of course, more permanent, moderately stable extra-marital relationships. The secretary with her married boss is a common example. His wife may or may not know about the relationship. Sometimes there is a fine degree of mutual connivance. Wives, of course, may have relationships with other men while their husbands are at work or away from home on business. Sometimes it is argued that these relationships help a marriage—initially they may take some built-up tensions away or they may provide relief from boredom with the marital partner.

One of the reasons that *prostitution** tends to flourish is because some men need constant reassurance of being able to perform sexually whenever they want to without any risk of being refused—by their wives or more permanent partners. Prostitutes, by the nature of their function, do not refuse a man.

In all adulterous relationships, it is claimed someone almost inevitably suffers. If a man goes with a prostitute he can pick up a sexually-transmitted disease and then transfer it to his wife. The unmarried mistress of an older man may suffer, if only because in the end she may well be deprived of the chance of having a completely fulfilled life—the times of seeing her lover may well be restricted, any necessary secrecy in the relationship may grow tiresome and she may miss the chance of having a marriage and family of her own if she wants this. When a wife realizes she has been deceived she suffers, because few people enjoy feeling that they have been fooled or cheated or that their husband is shared with another woman. A wife's pride may be even more hurt if her husband's relationship with a mistress is an open one—this adds insult to injury. It is sometimes the only way a man can force his wife into getting a divorce, especially if she is dead set against getting one whether he feels their marriage is a failure or not. If a man in turn suffers, it is often from the strain of keeping up two separate relationships which, as he ages, becomes more and more tedious to maintain. Adultery can be financially draining on a man, and it can be emotionally exhausting to 'lead a double life'.

If a wife takes a lover and is found out, the husband is almost inevitably hurt, at least his pride is hurt. For most married couples, the marriage partner is not only a partner but a most precious possession; and adultery is seen often as nothing but robbery. It may not be a very attractive fact that most couples regard the marital partner as an object and specially a *sex object** to be possessed, but it is an emotional fact, and people can be driven to extremes of jealousy when confronted with a partner's extra-marital sexual life.

In an age where 'sex appeal' is considered to be wholly admirable, a man or woman who can attract other partners inside or outside of marriage may temporarily achieve some form of admiration because of his or her prowess. But in the end, extra-marital sexual relationships often turn out to be less fulfilling and less pleasurable than they seemed likely to when the affair or affairs started. There is an excitement in a new extra-marital sexual relationship which often fascinates those taking part in it. This excitement comes about partly from a feeling of success at sexual conquest and partly from the stimulus of meeting a new challenge and knowing a new person in an intimate way, emotionally and sexually.

The emotional involvement, however, with the new partner may often make it very difficult to break off the relationship once it becomes boring. An impossible situation sometimes arises when either the wife or mistress says, 'You have to choose between us'. The choice is often difficult, especially if the man is sensitive and really in the end wishes to hurt no one. However, once any affair is started this is pure male wishful thinking—and his desire not to hurt anyone often leads to everyone getting more and more hurt.

The main trouble with most extra-marital sex is that almost inevitably someone is hurt–for jealousy, remorse and very often feelings of guilt remove and dull the pleasure of the adventure. For every adultery that turns out to be a worthwhile and rewarding experience in the fullness of time, there are many more that end in disappointment, disillusion and mutal disgust. Although free-thinking tends to include free-love, even modern men and women seem unable in most cases to cope with its inherent problems, although notable exceptions clearly exist.

Tomi Ungerer

Divorce

Divorce is the legal dissolution of a marriage. Since one in four of the marriages contracted each year is likely to end in divorce, it must now be considered as a normal facet of human life.

There are two types of divorce: those where children are involved and those where there are none. The former is vastly more complicated than the latter. The actual divorce may be the final act in a long process of increasing bitterness and disillusion which has extended over many years, during which the couple have lived together in an empty shell of a marriage, struggling to find ways of improving the relationship and unwilling to take the final step. The possible 'other' man or woman in many cases is not as significant in the break-up of the marriage as

it might appear, although frequently he or she might be used as a scapegoat for the hostile feelings of the deserted spouse, as well as providing one or other partner with the impetus to leave an already crumbling marriage.

Negotiations over access and custody, when young children are involved, are notoriously prone to bitterness and hostility. Children are frequently used as pawns in battles between the parents. Although the courts may resolve such struggles at a legal level, their solutions cannot work satisfactorily without the couple's mutual cooperation. *Counselling** may be needed to achieve this. The manner in which a marriage is dissolved and the degree to which each partner is aware of his personal responsibility for its breakdown, is of enormous importance to any children of the marriage. If possible, their loyalties must not be harmfully split and both parents must help them to come to terms with the situation.

The feelings experienced by many people after divorce are often similar to those accompanying a bereavement—feelings of loss and disorientation, as well as of bitterness and anger. Such feelings may take months or even years to resolve. The status of newly divorced people can also be confusing to themselves and to those around them. Their presence can be a source of unease to other couples who may view them as a threat to their own marital security. An individual who is no longer part of a safe couple may be unwelcome to anyone who suspects that their own marriage is shaky. Divorced women with young children are particularly vulnerable and they may feel themselves 'trapped'. They find that, despite the great social changes in the post war years, they still face great difficulties—financial, social, and sexual—in adjusting to their new status.

Tomi Ungerer

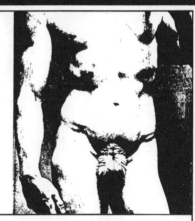

22

SOCIETY AND SEX

Public angles on private life.

Women's Liberation

The women's liberation movement really began in the latter half of the 19th century and in both the USA and Britain was closely associated with the struggle for female suffrage. This was achieved in the USA in 1919 and in Britain in 1928, thanks largely to the efforts of such feminists as Elizabeth Cady Stanton, Susan B. Anthony and Emmeline Pankhurst, who were additionally concerned with fundamental rights like equal pay, co-education and college education for girls, women's rights over children and to property and wages. From such beginnings the struggle broadened to include birth control and equality in professional life. In the 1960s, a new dimension appeared: sexual equality. With the publication of Germaine Greer's *The Female Eunuch* and Kate Millet's *Sexual Politics* the new wave of women's liberation began. The Women's Liberation movement challenged the notion that men have a superior role in life. Its purpose in doing this was not to undermine the male ego but to rescue the female ego. This was, and is, a necessary operation. The women's movement tries to change stereotyped ideas about what women are capable of doing and how they should behave to fulfil their potential as individual people with individual talents and with particular sexual needs.

The movement has opponents: people of both sexes who fear that liberation means neglected child-rearing and unstable marriages (or even no marriages at all); and men who do not want to compete with women for money, jobs or power. Many of these opponents do not realize (or do not believe) that the movement cuts two ways; if women are free to choose their own roles, be it as mother and housewife or breadwinner (or a combination of both), so are men. Men who are tired of shouldering the responsibility, earning the money, never seeing the children, acting aggressive, and generally inviting ulcers and/or heart attacks, will benefit from a spreading of each sex's traditional load. This important and practical aspect of the women's rights movement has led to the opening of job opportunities for *both* sexes, because of the breakdown of stereotypes and traditional roles. There are now, for example, more male telephone operators and secretaries; more female truckers, mechanics and fire-fighters.

Age of Consent

Ordinary legal maturity now comes at the age of 18 for both sexes. Below this age, a person is referred to as a MINOR, and the years of growing up are a person's *minority*. In sexual matters, however, a minor is one below the age of consent. Until she is 16, a girl may not legally consent to intercourse, and a male (whether adult or minor) having intercourse with an under-age girl is guilty of child violation, which can be regarded as rape. (In Britain, intercourse between consenting male adults has been legal since 1967, but for this the age of consent is 21.) However, a male minor may legally have sexual relations with any female over 16. With the average age of puberty in girls falling to around 13 today, they are becoming mature long before childbearing is acceptable. Consequently, it is not surprising that pregnancies in girls below 16 have risen.

Sexual activity with and between children is an emotive subject. A long tradition makes us pretend that children do not have or feel, sexual attraction. Yet a boy just after puberty has the strongest sexuality of his entire lifetime. If two children have sexual intercourse, the law will generally not be involved, and before puberty such experiences are best treated as part of childhood play. Although sexual advances by an adult rarely injure a child physically, psychological damage may result, perhaps much later in life. Far more upsetting to a child can be the police inquiries and legal proceedings.

Incest

In almost all societies, sexual intercourse has been forbidden between close blood relatives (brothers and sisters, parents and their children) and in some it may be condemned among all the several hundred members of a clan. Breaking this prohibition is termed incest. Understanding of genetic inheritance is very recent, but almost all societies must have long since found out by painful experience that human inbreeding tends to disaster. In rare cases, ancient traditions approved—Lot's daughters had to start two new families without husbands to make them pregnant, and the pharaohs of Egypt were required to intermarry for religious reasons—but these breaches of the general rule were not extended to the people at large.

The scientific reason for endorsing the ban on intercourse between blood relations is the danger that a baby may be born suffering from a serious inherited disease. Many such diseases affect only the person who inherits the trait or gene from both parents. These are recessive diseases and cystic fibrosis is an example. Some genes for such recessive disorders occur in all families, so the chance that two will come together is higher if blood relatives mate.

If, on the other hand, a gene is potent enough to affect the individual, although he receives it only from one parent, it is called a dominant gene. Natural selection quickly weeds out from the population the dominant genes that cause grave disease, but this does not apply to recessive genes which can hide in healthy people for generations. A majority of the serious inherited diseases are therefore recessive, and the mating of close blood relatives is then much more likely to produce seriously diseased offspring than to create children who are to be in some way better than average.

It might be expected that babies born to two intelligent parents would be brighter than either one of them. It does not seem to work that way. The children will tend to be not as much above average as the parents are. Certain characteristics are inherited, not by a single gene-pair from father and mother —several pairs are involved. This seems to be true for the inherited part of intelligence. If family ambitions are high, disappointment is frequent.

How much incest actually occurs within families cannot be known, but it seems to be found more often in socially disadvantaged groups or among people of below-average intelligence. If proven, it is a serious criminal offence, but even if not discovered publicly, incest must carry a grave threat to the happiness of a family. It probably plays a large role in male and female subconscious desires, and at this level, incestuous feelings between children and parents form a significant element in Freud's theory of the working of the Oedipus complex.

Indecency

Really this means what you want it to mean. It implies that our sense of propriety or acceptability is offended. Defecating in the street is offensive or indecent and we forbid it. But nowadays the word indecency is used mainly for sexual matters, causing great confusion.

The commonest of the indecent offences before the courts is *indecent exposure**, sometimes called 'flashing'. This is a man's wilful exposure of his sex organs to passing females. The distress some of the girls or women feel is largely a result of our suppressive and secretive traditions. Any kind of sexual approach to a partner who is unwilling or is below the age of consent can be called 'indecent assault'.

'Gross indecency' is anal intercourse or sodomy. The law prescribes heavy sentences for this act even between married couples. However, it will not now prosecute consenting adult homosexual men for it provided the act takes place in private.

Shows or published photographs that are sexually stimulating may be judged indecent. Publishers of girlie and pornographic magazines need constant legal advice on such matters to avoid prosecution which is essentially erratic, irrational and believed by many to be ridiculous.

Feticide

Feticide, or abortion as it is commonly called, is the premature ending of a pregnancy, by natural or artificial causes, before a baby has been fully formed. A baby is theoretically able to live independently at about 28 weeks after conception. Probably 20 per cent of all pregnancies end spontaneously by abortion. This is often nature's way of getting rid of faulty embryos. The word MISCARRIAGE is widely used when there is a natural failure of a pregnancy.

About eight weeks after conception, the developing embryo begins to look a bit like a baby. It is then called a 'fetus'. The word FETICIDE means the wilful termination of a pregnancy during this period. Some physical illness is caused in about four per cent of all abortions and there is also a risk of about five per cent that subsequent pregnancies will be unsuccessful. The dangers are smallest when the operation is performed early before the twelfth week, and by experuenced doctors. Then it carries a risk of only two per hundred thousand.

Abortion is now a fairly safe and, indeed, routine aspect of medical prac-

tice, but it is nonetheless never pleasant. Added to which, evidence is growing that frequent abortion may lead to subsequent problems of fertility. Providing abortion facilities as a nation-wide service (as in Britain since the 1967 Abortion Act) is also costly, and it puts many gynecologists and nursing staff in a dilemma if they have religious scruples. For all these reasons, it should never be regarded as a first line of defence against pregnancy. It should be seen as a reserve to be used only when serious attempts at family planning by more routine contraceptive methods have failed, particularly for married women whose families are already as large as they can manage.

Internationally, terminating pregnancy so as to prevent the birth of a child is a matter of enormous public concern. In the modern period, it has been treated by law as a serious crime, the reason being that the baby forming in the womb was considered to be already a human being. It is therefore surprising to discover that abortion was not prohibited until fairly recently. In Britain, termination before quickening was legal until 1803. In America it was Connecticut that was the first state to outlaw it in 1921. Even then the proscription applied only to abortion after quickening.

In 1929, it was enacted in Britain that abortion could be undertaken in good faith to preserve the mother's life. In 1938, a British gynecologist was tried for aborting the pregnancy in a girl of fourteen who had been raped. The trial judge established more lenient principles which allow consideration of the woman's health to influence the decision. In the 1967 Abortion Act, the effect of further childbirth on the health of the mother or on existing children, and her environment, could also be considered.

Vociferous pressure groups campaign against legalized abortion. They claim that the fetus should be protected by the sanctity of human life. In weighing this argument, it is useful to get some idea how the people who use it have approached the questions of the death penalty and pacifism. Abortion, unlike execution and war, relieves rather than causes human anguish and degradation. Humane people will also consider the risk of serious unhappiness for a child born to a mother who does not welcome it.

The moral and legal aspects of abortion have yet to be really solved. (See also the medical article *abortion** under BIRTH CONTROL.)

Phallic

Anything that is associated with or looks like a penis (Latin for 'tail') or phallus (from *phallos*, Greek for 'sweller') is described as phallic. Because the penis is of such importance for the regeneration of life, symbols for it play a conspicuous part in magic and religion. It might seem that widespread display of phallic objects indicated a sense of male dominance in society. In fact, they are found far more commonly in connection with old fertility cults, in which women play a significant and more or less equal part as priestesses, vestals, oracles or witches (with important female deities standing for the complementary life-bearing female principle), than they do in male-dominated or patrist societies, which tend to a certain stern prudishness on these matters in public.

As Freud realized in his studies of dreams, any vertical object can be a phallic symbol, and one can end up by reading too much meaning into the motives of the builders of church steeples or skyscrapers. More immediate in their erotic associations are objects that can be put into the mouth and suggest fellatio—bananas, fat cigars, chocolate bars, lipstick, asparagus, lollipops, and the like. The shape and explosive power of a handgun has strong phallic symbolism, especially when worn close to the genitals or fired from the hip. A rock guitar is almost always played at an angle from the thigh, as if it were a giant, artificial penis.

Wearing penis substitutes openly—such as the primitive penis sheath or the European cod piece—denotes a society that accepts sex without any sense of guilt.

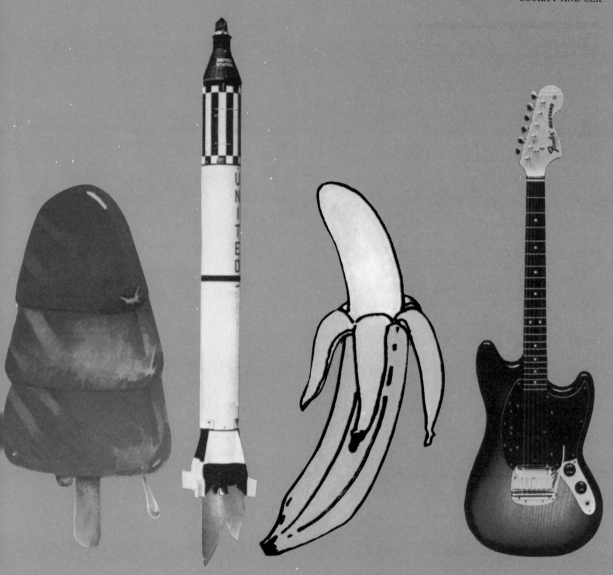

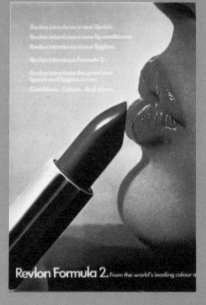

Revlon Formula 2. From the world's leading colour a

Phallic

At the dawn of civilization, humans imagined a male heaven fertilizing a female earth or vice versa. In many different ways, the processes of nature (rain, seasonal floods, plant growth, etc) seemed to them to parallel sex, conception and birth. Nature spirits were assumed to be revelling in sex all around them, setting the right example for nature. Much of primitive fertility magic consists of rituals meant to imitate the infinitely more powerful actions of the spirits. In Hinduism, the stone or metal model of a penis or *lingam,* representing the life-giving power of Shiva, is a central cult object, found in many homes. The lingam is usually set in a socket that represents the vulva or *yoni,* of the female principle. Ancient Egyptian religion recognized an earth-god Geb (who was shown in coitus with the sky-goddess), an orgiastic god Bes, not unlike Bacchus, and a fertility god Min, in whose guise, complete with a huge erection, the reigning pharaoh would often be depicted. The ancient Greeks pictured the fertility gods Hermes and Priapos, and the mythical male woodland creatures known as satyrs and *silenoi,* as all having conspicuous erections. Described as ITHYPHALIC, these images were touched on the genitals for good luck and hung with garlands on holidays. The high spot of the Greek festival of Dionysus, the *phallophoria,* was carrying the gigantic model of an erect penis in procession. On the whole, ithyphallic deities seemed to have rather jolly natures.

Among less advanced prehistoric cultures, standing stones had a phallic meaning along with various other practical or symbolic uses. In modern primitive cultures, such stones or wooden posts are often carved explicitly in the shape of a penis. The semi-sacred reputation of the oak tree may be partly due to the phallic form of acorns, which are shaped like a glans emerging from the foreskin.

(Top, left) *phallic post outside a Mongol monastery, deterring female demons.* (Top, right) *oro-genital joke in a Roman drinking-bowl.* (Centre) *female devotee carrying the great phallus in the Dionysia festival.* (Right) *earth and sky as ithyphallic Egyptian gods.*

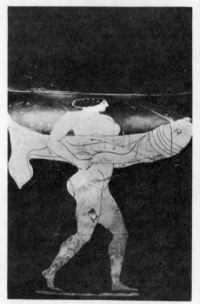
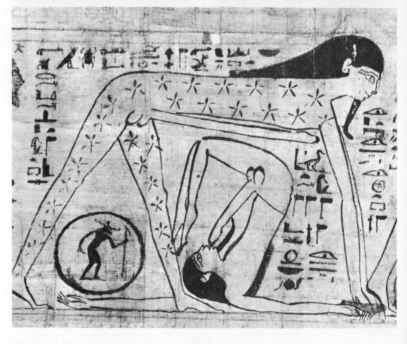

Vulvic

Closely linked with phallic symbolism is its female counterpart, vulvic symbolism (from *vulva**, the general term for a woman's external sex organs). On cult figures made of bone, clay or stone, the 'divine triangle' of the mother-goddess was prominently marked with lines and filled with dots to represent the pubic hair, or the vulva itself was shown as a vertical incision. These figurines seem to be universal at particular stages of human development: in Europe they date from the old Stone Age, in the Near East from about 4,000 BC, in the Aegean from about 3,000 BC, in Japan up to the 4th centure AD, and in most primitive cultures today they are still current. The most widely worshipped goddess in the ancient Near East, known as Ishtar (Babylon) or Astarte (Syria), was depicted like this. No wonder the Old Testament denounces the goddess of fertility and love as the 'abomination of Ashtaroth'.

The central cult object in most forms of Hinduism is the *lingam* (the male principle of Shiva, shown as a symbolic penis) set in a socket to represent the YONI, the female principle, shown as a vulva. In the many forms of Hinduism, the female genitals are depicted as powerful images. Sometimes, as in the erotic sculptures on the temple at Konarak, they are seen on the statues of the heavenly consorts (*apsarases*); sometimes they are a formalized design like an ikon; sometimes, as in Tantric practices, they are shown as a source of supernatural energy, symbolized by a snake emerging from the vagina. In Hindu paintings and statues of the ecstatic union of a god and his *shakti* or female counterpart in coitus, the depiction of the act is vivid, physical and give emphasis to the female role.

(Top, left) *vulva-worship on a Tantric icon.* (Top, right) *gold pendant of Astarte, 1600 BC.* (Left) *creative energy (the snake) emerging from the vulva of a female yogi.*

Vulvic

Vulvic

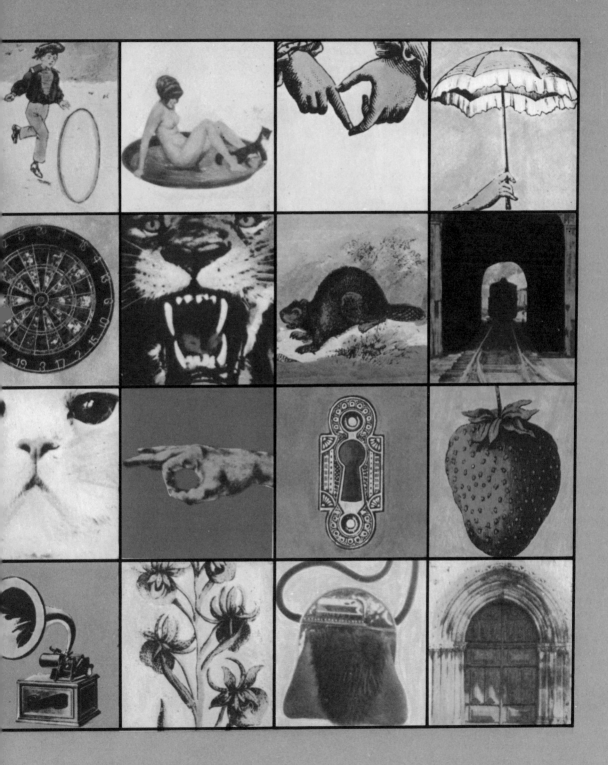

Circumcision

A fold of skin, with a membrane lining it, covers the sensitive glans, or head of the penis. This is the foreskin or *prepuce**, and after puberty, it usually becomes slack enough to be rolled back easily. During erection, this happens spontaneously. Cutting away the foreskin, known as male circumcision, with the result that the glans of the penis is permanently exposed, is carried out for one or both of two reasons—one medical, the other cultural.

The medical reason is hygienic, for the simple removal of the piece of skin and membrane reduces opportunities for infection due to uncleanliness and accretion of *smegma** underneath the base of the foreskin, round the corona of the glans. Medical circumcision is now carried out generally on infants (especially in the USA), but until recently it was uncommon except in cases of adults suffering from *phimosis**.

The cultural reasons are deeply rooted in traditions and religions. In Judaism and Islam, circumcision has the sanction of religious law. The custom is found among the ancient Egyptians and in pre-Columbian America, as well as in present day Africa, Southeast Asia, Australia and Oceania. Sometimes circumcision is part of an initiation rite of adolescent youths into manhood, when the pain of the operation forms a severe test of their courage. Elsewhere, there is a remote connection between betrothal ceremonies and circumcision of the bridegroom. Interestingly, the Hebrew word for 'circumcizer', *mohel*, is thought to have an archaic meaning that refers to 'father-in-law'. A slit in the foreskin suffices for circumcision among some peoples, while some Australian aborigines cut into the passage of the urethra (SUBINCISION) and leave it open from the scrotum to the opening (meatus) in the glans.

Mutilation of the external sex organs is also performed on girls in some cultures, involving cutting off the clitoris (FEMALE CIRCUMCISION) or, more rarely, the labia minora (NYMPHECTOMY), and even the brutal ripping of the vulva (PHARAONIC MUTILATION). The intention is to reduce the sexual responsiveness of women thus making them safer wives. Although it does not have much direct effect on their responsiveness, the operation is proof of the degraded position of women in such societies. *Infibulation**, a milder version of the

same idea, consists of clasping or stitching the labia together. To the end of the late 19th century, this practice was common in European brothels to create the semblance of virginity in young prostitutes. Pharaonic mutilation creates a scar which wholly prevents vaginal entry, and further cruel incisions are necessary for marriage and again to permit childbirth.

Instruments employed for male and female circumcision vary from the human fingernail or prehistoric flint knife to exclusively shaped steel blades. The male operation often involves the use of a pierced disc or board through which the foreskin can be drawn and cut off without danger of the glans on the other side. The amount of bleeding is normally small. There is recent evidence that the incidence of cancer of the cervix is lower among wives of orthodox Jewish husbands than in the rest of the population, which suggests that a health advantage accompanies cultural circumcision in Western countries.

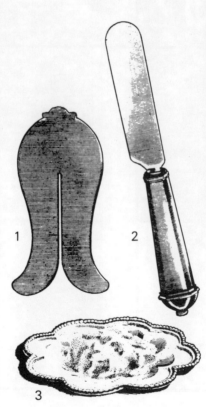

Circumcision in the Portuguese synagogue in the 18th century (right). *The ladies are non-Jewish spectators. The* mohel *is equipped with* bartzel (1), *knife* (2) *and basin of sand* (3).

Religion and Sexual Behaviour

Religions are systems of ideas which guide vast groups of people in their personal lives—down to minute details of cleanliness, in many cases. Sex, as a major factor in life, has occupied a place in the moral teaching of all religions, sometimes in an antagonistic and sometimes in a receptive manner.

At the roots of all the world's religions we can recognize *fertility cults** and the awe felt by primitive humans for the forces of nature. Important rules controlling people's behaviour were worked out and imposed on them, as it was felt that the regenerative powers of nature—and especially the fecundity of crops and livestock—could be influenced by human actions. The primary duty of religious systems ever since, though tempered and enriched by the growth of philosophic ideas and moral speculations, has been to lay down unshakeable laws for its followers to obey. Edicts by the deity are the cornerstone of the Jewish, Christian and Muslim faiths, and they all bring human sex life within their scope.

The systems which display the least conflict with the natural world are the ones which are the least obsessed with sex as a moral issue: in Hinduism and Taoism (both reaching back very far towards prehistory), sexuality is actually structured into the religious life; in Buddhism (the most extremely spiritual of world religions) it is brushed aside as just one of the many forms of 'illusion' that enslave the spirit in the material world; in Jewish ethical teaching, the concern is more with regulating sex within a family setting than with dogmatically condemning it as an enemy of the spiritual life; in Christianity, sex acquired a phobic association with sin and has always presented theologians with the fine problem of differentiating between love and sex, *agape* and *eros, caritas* and *amor.* Sects like the dualistic Cathars and the Shakers went to the length of banning even procreation among their followers.

Humanity has always been taught that its sex-life has a meaning in a divine scheme of things. Thus the predominance of a faith with an antisexual bias is favourable to the development of sexual inhibitions and phobias among the people of that time or place. We see this, for example, in 16th and

17th century Europe and New England, (especially wherever the Puritan ethic had a hold on the authorities) in the cruel epidemic of witch-hunting. Salem's monstrous persecution of 1692 was parallelled in Catholic Europe by the events among the hysterical nuns at Loudun in 1634 and their aftermath on the scaffold. Christianity has had a long tradition of sexual repressiveness, but although St. Paul's writings seem to have set the church early on that course, it has been realized by recent scholarship that antisexual ideas were already current in the later period of classical culture. The Greeks had sought refuge from the destructiveness of erotic passions in philosophy and refined pederasty, while the Romans were half-heartedly hoping to recapture the bygone austerity of republican times. In the end, the early church fathers hammered out a doctrine of sex which eradicated freedom and joy from physical love—perhaps the only major religious teachers to do so successfully. Chastity became so precious that it was the mark of the Latin priesthood, and some women attained sanctity by refusing their husbands' advances. Celibate monks and nuns seemed to be closer to heaven than ordinary mankind.

Many influences combined to prevent medieval Christendom from developing thus into an asexual paradise —not least among them, the human nature of priests and popes themselves —but the imprint of centuries of sexual guilt is stamped heavily on modern Europeans. It is only some seventy years—one generation—since enlightenment about sex and understanding of humanity's sexual nature made its appearance in the writings of Freud and Havelock Ellis. The preceding Victorian era had reinforced the deep traditional guilts ever wider areas of a fast multiplying population. That period and that outlook are still not so far away from us as we usually suppose.

Most restrictive European and American attitudes towards sex draw their strength from inherited Christian precepts, even though the people who hold them may not think of themselves as religious. The law of many countries still enshrines, on the subjects of marriage, divorce, abortion and homosexuality, moral values which derive from a Christian past. Individuals today often find themselves in conflict with the law and the state over actions which they, and society generally, regard as proper and acceptable. This is one of the ways in which religion still affects a non-religious society.

The strength of prohibitions can be greater than freedom of choice. The self-punishing streak in human nature easily responds to a call for sacrifice—especially in physical mortification. Renunciation of the world and its temptations has been the mark of many noble natures, yet it requires only a little distortion, a bit too much zeal, for these values to lose their basis in love and become a dogmatic hatred of all the joyful eroticism of life. It is significant

that extreme political ideologies tend to call on the same anti-permissive, self-denying traits in their dedicated followers as used to be demanded from Christians by their preachers.

The secularization of human thought now permits a modern person to make moral decisions without consulting a religious guide. It also puts all religions, cults and moral systems on an equal footing, so that they can be compared on their merits. A Westerner

may now consider that we have come a long way from the primitive farmer who perhaps whips a phallic field-marker in the belief that it will make the grain sprout for certain. The dignity and sublimity of the religious framework we have inherited (but already left behind) appears to have been a higher stage in human progress. Then we should look at other civilizations and consider the violent sexual ecstasy of the divine figures in tantric Bud-

dhism—making their coitus resemble a storm of cosmic energy—or the almost infinite variations of human sexual intercourse that writhe around the Hindu shrines of Konarak and Khajuraho, and ask ourselves whether we have missed out something in our ideas of what is holy and good. As pious men have pointed out before, a zeal for purification can be an excuse for persecution, and purity itself can be a disguise for dryness of spirit.

Religious Eroticism

Many sincere people find it hard to accept that there could be an erotic content in much Christian iconography, and would regard the idea as being offensive to their religious sensibilities. They might regard the display of sexual feeling as a sign of 'paganism', yet some of the most powerful statements of Christian spirituality use unmistakably erotic images, especially the 'pietist' hymns and certain mystical writings. St. Teresa of Avila gives the most direct example of this in her *Life* (1565), where she describes her mystical union with Christ in terms that could be used to describe an orgasm: 'the pain was so great that I screamed aloud; but simultaneously I felt such infinite sweetness that I wished the pain to last eternally. It was not bodily, but psychical pain, although it affected to a certain extent also the body. It was sweetest caressing of the soul by God.'

The vivid sculpture portraying this episode (in Sta. Maria della Vittoria, Rome, 1645–52) is considered to be Bernini's masterpiece. The swooning ecstasy of the saint in marble is parallelled by ancient Greek portrayals of ecstatic female devotees of Dionysus, called the Maenads or Bacchae, who became 'possessed' by their god. The same orgasmic response can be seen: heads thrown back, eyes unfocussed, mouths open in a moan. Eroticism strongly tinged with sadism frequently appears in pictures of the sufferings of Christian martyrs and of the torments of the damned, particularly those guilty of carnal sins.

Pray
for
Rosemary's
Baby

Paramount Pictures Presents

Mia Farrow
In a William Castle Production
Rosemary's Baby

also starring
John Cassavetes
co-starring
Ruth Gordon
Sidney Blackmer
Maurice Evans
and Ralph Bellamy

Incubus. Succubus

In European demonology, incubus (Latin for 'nightmare', from a verb meaning 'to lie upon') and succubus (medieval Latin, from *succuba*, a prostitute) were the names for evil spirits which were supposed to have intercourse with people in their sleep. These delusions of sexual activity with ghosts or spectres are known as SPECTROPHILIA. While confessions of intercourse with such creatures were commonly extracted under torture in witchcraft inquiries, many other people genuinely had delusions of sex with demons. Spectrophilia tended to be reported in celibate communities of monks or nuns. Such delusions are the emotional fantasies of people suffering from extreme sexual repression, and probably from feelings of guilt about masturbation as well. In some cases, the belief could be played on to explain away an illegitimate pregnancy. Comparable legends are found in many cultures, especially in Japan.

Self-Mutilation

People are led to mutilate their own bodies by various kinds of mental pressure. Even psychosomatic illness can be seen as self-mutilation, whether subconscious or (as with the malingerer who can create an ulcer) deliberate. Visible mutilations are sometimes used for sexual display (*Cosmetic Deformity**), and self-*flagellation**, especially as a public penance, is a known form of religious excess. In its most acute manifestation, the deep psychological link between sex and religious practice can be seen in the recorded instances of self-castration. The priests of Attis (consort of the goddess Cybele) performed a ritual self-emasculation and buried their genitals. The idea that a mediator with the gods would be better for being a sexless individual (a *transsexual** or a *eunuch**) is found not only in the ancient Near East, but also in the ambiguously sexed medicine-men of Asia and North America. Voluntary sacrificial gelding, took place in ancient Egypt and, as an ascetic practice, among some dervish sects. The most famous Christian example is Origen, the 3rd-century Alexandrian church father. Members of a Russian sect, the Skoptzy, revived castration in the 18th century.

Fertility Cult

From earliest times people needed desperately to ensure the fertility of the earth. They believed that the sexual union of human beings would magically increase nature's bounty. Fertility rituals and orgies were organized, as in the worship of Dionysus. The spring ceremony of raising the maypole was accompanied in medieval times by sexual promiscuity. Phallic symbols appear on field workers or on religious shrines. Women were made to labour in the fields, partly because they were themselves the fertile sex. To stimulate their fertility they were sometimes

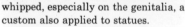

whipped, especially on the genitalia, a custom also applied to statues.

Primitive people tried by magic and sacrifice to guarantee the regular course of nature's seasonal changes of death and rebirth. Some tribes ritually killed their kings to replace them by strong young men. In the worship of Cybele, her devotees cut off their genitalia, which were ritually buried.

Temple prostitution developed in the service of fertility gods, and was itself a kind of religious fertility ritual. When fees were paid, at least part went as a sacrifice to the treasury of the temple. Another idea was that the bleeding caused by defloration was dangerous and taboo, similar to the 'barren' blood of menstruation. Strangers, or such magically protected men as priests, were therefore called upon for the service of taking the bride's virginity before the husband did.

(Far left) *A bowl painted with a rain-making dance of Hopi Indian men wearing artificial phalluses* (Opposite page, below) *Two Celtic carvings of a woman displaying her vulva, called Shelagh-na-gig figures, surviving on English parish churches*

(Left) *A humorous Greek view of the fertility images called herms, with their prominent carved stone phalluses* (Below) *Garlanding the genitals on a herm was one way in which the Greeks paid their respects to the powers of growth in nature*

Taboo

Originally this Polynesian word referred to some action that must not be performed, otherwise the whole community would be punished by the supernatural powers. Now it is used to mean something we avoid for fear of offending public opinion.

Frazer, in *The Golden Bough,* gives many instances of taboo in the literal meaning. The Ainus of Sakhalin forbid a pregnant woman to twist ropes, as this would save her baby from twisting in the womb. Menstruating Aborigine women in Australia were utterly forbidden to touch anything used by men.

The long and hypocritical tradition that people should be virgin at the time of marriage made it taboo for bridegrooms to admit sexual competence. A pretended clumsiness must have distressed many brides.

COUVADE may be a curious instance of taboo. This is a custom by which a husband pretends to be pregnant instead of his wife. The 'expectant' father takes to his bed and receives the good wishes of friends. His wife, poor woman, tries to pretend she is not affected. This rigmarole was probably a superstitious attempt to draw evil influences away from the wife and baby.

Body contact can promptly arouse sexual excitement, as most people know, and this probably led to the remarkable taboo Anglo-American society placed upon touching between strangers. Carried over into much of ordinary life, the no-touching taboo has a lot to answer for in the growth of sexual inhibitions.

Even doctors can hardly use taboo words when talking of sex or excretion to their patients. On the other hand, the mechanical repetition of a taboo word like 'fucking' betrays a feeling that the word possesses a kind of 'big medicine', which endows the speaker with the power of outrageous daring.

Taboos may sometimes provide a useful conservatism, adapting the speed of change in society to a tolerable level. Margaret Mead reported that some children developed neurotic traits when parents suddenly abandoned the old taboo against nakedness. The children were startled by the difference between their own bodies and their parents! Because they had not lived in a society where nakedness was widely accepted, they did not see other childish or adolescent bodies going through the stages of growing up.

Eunuchs & Castrati

Men's external reproductive organs are sometimes removed by CASTRATION or EMASCULATION either to make the victims useful in specific ways or as a form of humiliating punishment. They are then known as EUNUCHS, from a Greek word meaning 'keeper of the bedchamber', recalling the principal service to which castrated males have been put.

Sterility is inevitable if both testes are removed, but other effects are variable, depending in part on the cause of the emasculation and whether it was performed before or after puberty. Desire and potency may be lost, but this is not inevitable, and many such men retain libido and ejaculation. For servicemen suffering castration by war wounds, the support of a loving sex partner has sometimes permitted the recovery of some sexual function. Some are also helped by administration of the male sex hormone testosterone. A boy castrated before puberty will fail to develop the primary and secondary sexual characteristics of a normal male that would otherwise be stimulated by hormones produced by the testes. He retains his small penis and high voice and the softer tissues and rounder body outline of a child or woman. The usual purposes for which eunuchs were made were partly domestic and partly sexual. Their chief use was as servants or slaves who could safely be made responsible for the women of a household. Their girlish attributes made them, in addition, desirable sexual objects to their owners. In some circumstances, a eunuch could also perform without risk as a sexual partner in the harem. In despotic or oriental societies, eunuchs often became trusted functionaries and achieved high social position, even exercising political power in the state.

Castration as a punishment or in vengeance has sometimes followed a sexual liaison, the best-known case in history being that of Peter Abelard, the controversial philosopher who taught at Paris in the early 12th century.

The vocal qualities of men whose voices remained unbroken as a result of being castrated before puberty ('strange, sexless, superhuman, uncanny' in one description) have long been recognized. The CASTRATI male sopranos of Italian opera were famous in the 17th and 18th centuries, a few lingering on into the 19th century (the last of them died in 1922).

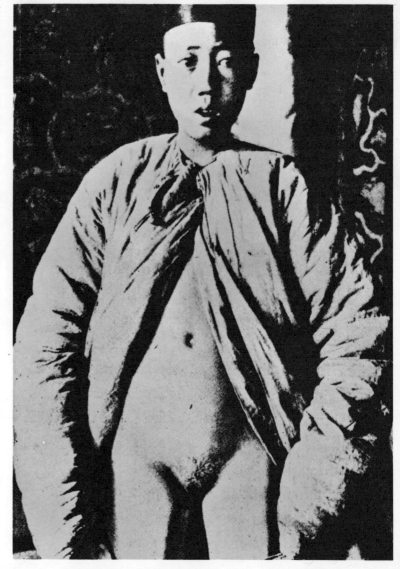

I made love to 10,000 women

TOP thriller writer Georges Simenon has made the astonishing claim: "I've made love to 10,000 women."

By MIRROR REPORTER

Simenon—wealthy creator of the French detective Maigret—says that his life of womanising began when he was thirteen. He is now seventy-four.

The man who sold 350 million books during his writing career insists that the 10,000 figure is accurate for his bed-time career. He told a Swiss newspaper:

● I needed women physically and I also had a need for communication.

Whenever I see a beautiful woman my first thought is, 'How is the expression on her face during orgasm?' I chased after that all my life—to know which one is the true woman, the one who is all dressed up and wears diamonds, or the one who cries out at a certain moment without knowing it.

That is the key to a woman. I contend that you know a woman only after you have slept with her. I wanted to know women—I wanted to learn the truth.

I do not know those 10,000 women any longer. I have forgotten them all. But I am beginning to know ● the true woman.

Belgian-born Simenon, a one-time reporter, has two broken marriages behind him. In a book of memoirs he once told how he used to get people drunk at his home.

"I forced cocktails on my guests to produce more quickly the release that would

SIMENON: Truth-seeker

permit me to see them naked," he said.

Simenon's life style has been in dramatic contrast to the family-man image of the detective who made his fortune—pipe-smoking Maigret.

The final Maigret book came out four years ago when Simenon decided to retire and take things easy.

Reason: He was having dizzy spells.

Hogarth ridicules an operatic castrato's ungainly physique (top, left). *A Chinese victim of the 'clean sweep', with a tube to permit urination* (left).

Casanova caricatured from the life (top) *and his modern competitor* (above).

Erotomaniac

Since sexologists tell us there is no such thing as 'too much sex', the idea of erotomania may seem meaningless to the modern reader. But when we consider the idea more closely, it turns out that the 'sex maniac' is always after something other than lots of sex. In fact, the most innocent kind of sex maniac is the man or woman who wants very little sex with lots of people. Darker types are the compulsive Peeping Tom or *voyeur**, the flasher, the rapist and even the murderer—men who like their audiences, partners and victims to be involuntary. (The female of the species, known as nymphomaniacs, seem to be free of these particular compulsions.)

The carefree seducer and the wife-murderer are images that have had a powerful appeal in most cultures at most times and doubtless represent many unconscious—or at least unspoken—wishes or fantasies. The Bluebeard myth—the husband who murders a succession of wives—is common to European, African and Eastern folktales, but most Western versions (they now include Bartok's opera *Bluebeard's Castle* and Chaplin's film *Monsieur Verdoux*) stem from Perrault's *Tales of Mother Goose* (1697).

The Don Juan story is in a lighter vein. Tirso de Molina, author of the first widely known play on the theme (1630), is said to have been inspired by a notorious Spanish seducer who ended his days as a devout abbot. The figure became a popular one in theatricals and puppet shows all over Europe. The rehearsals of the first production of *Don Giovanni* in Prague in 1787 were assisted by a living 'Don Juan', the aging Casanova (1725–1798). Lord Byron, author of the great 19th-century poetical version of *Don Juan*, comes close to capturing the zestful, anarchic and unrepentant spirit displayed by Casanova, who titillated Europe with his erotic adventures.

Whatever secret feelings these myths betray—perhaps a latent hatred and fear of the opposite sex—society must ultimately contain them within the social framework, and most Bluebeard and Don Juan tales focus on the failure and/or punishment of the hero (in both Molière's play and Mozart's opera he is dragged off to hell). Yet the fascination of these figures lies in what they get away with: a glorious freedom from the constraints of monogamy.

Rape

Legally, the crime of rape is committed when a man has sexual intercourse, with a woman, without her consent, by force and/or fear of significant bodily harm. In British law, to have sexual intercourse with a woman without her consent, by fraud, also constitutes rape. Rape must be by penis in the vagina, and evidence of penetration only (without ejaculation) is enough to bring a charge of rape. This applies in Britain and the USA, although tests of corroboration and consent vary. An alleged rapist who uses the common defence of consent is basically saying that the woman voluntarily agreed, is now lying, and has some malicious purpose in bringing the charge. Only four percent of rape allegations are considered by the police to be false when the complaint is made—no higher than false allegations for any other crime.

Wives cannot be raped by their husbands in the eyes of the law, and there is pressure on both sides of the Atlantic to change this. Boys under a certain age may be too young to have 'criminal intent' and this will affect the degree of punishment. Any sexual intercourse with a minor, or a mentally defective woman, is illegal and gives rise to the charge of 'statutory rape' or 'unlawful sexual intercourse'. The use of drugs to render a victim unconscious or impersonation of a husband also constitutes rape. On the other hand, forced anal and oral penetration, the use of bottles, fingers, broom handles, knives and guns, and spitting, urinating or defecating on the victim, humiliation and forced imprisonment are not covered by the law of rape in Britain, but are in some US states.

The commonest place where rape occurs is in a woman's own home. After this, in decreasing frequency, in cars, hospitals, parks and drinking places. About half the number of rapists are already known to their victims, and may be from her family.

A raped woman will react in many different ways, and whatever reaction it is, is it right for her. She is expected to become hysterical and uncontrolled, but roughly half will appear calm, controlled and subdued, which may only mean that they will have greater difficulty in getting people to believe them. A woman in hysterics is likely to be told to pull herself together, and for her the difficulty may be in giving a coherent account.

Any rape can possibly result in pregnancy and sex-related disease. Sympathetic and immediate medical attention and the availability of pregnancy prevention are what is needed. Raped women, especially when they meet with anger and hostility from those closest to them, need a great deal of emotional support as well as legal and medical information. Rape crisis centres have been set up on a self-help basis to provide this support. Rape counselling, which lets a woman explore her feelings in safety, soon after the rape, can help to prevent serious problems of a psychosexual, psychological and emotional kind from developing.

By far the most damaging experience for a raped woman is not to be believed and to be treated as a 'victim', rather than a person who needs to regain control of her life through her own efforts.

Reporting rape to the police is never easy, but if a woman wants to, then there are certain actions she must take. She should tell someone of the attack as soon as possible, so that they can bear witness to her emotional state and early complaint. She must try to remember the sequence of events, important details, and whether there may have been witnesses. On no account must she wash, take a bath, or change her appearance. In doing so, she may destroy valuable forensic evidence. She should avoid taking drugs or alcohol, and report to the police quickly. She should take a change of clothes with her, since those she is wearing may be taken for evidence. The raped woman can expect to spend several hours with the police being interrogated, being examined internally and externally, making a statement, identifying the rapist if caught, or looking through mug shots. Police treatment varies and it is always best to take someone along for support. The woman may be in for a heavy time.

Not all allegations of rape lead to convictions. In Britain, about 50% of all reported rapes reach trial, and only 60% of these resulted in convictions. Rape is notoriously under-reported and even assuming reporting to be as high as 25%, this would mean that 90% of rapists get off.

Several months later, the case will be tried by jury. For many women this is the worst part of the ordeal. In Britain and some states of the USA, women cannot be questioned on their past sexual history (apart from previous relationship with the defendant) except at the judge's discretion. The raped woman and the accused have the right to anonymity in Britain and some US states. Prosecution styles vary, but the defence's attacks on the woman's character are hardly even rebutted. She will find her whole life, morality and credibility on trial. It is his word against hers, and the whole weight of the anti-female myth ('she provoked it') will be stacked against her. The accused's previous record will not be made known to the jury and, since sexual experience tends to enhance rather than malign a man's character, there is no defence mileage to be gained from this type of questioning. Where there is no evidence of bodily damage, he stands a good chance of getting off, even though he may have used a knife to threaten the woman.

Perhaps the severest blow for a woman is when 'twelve good men and true' acquit the accused. She knows that not only has she been raped she has also been found guilty by implication of being a promiscuous, malicious liar. Acquitted rapists are reassured that society, from prejudice or by default, condones their behaviour. Recent British studies show that 14% of men acquitted of rape are later convicted for sexual offences.

There are numerous reforms, current and proposed, which go some way to satisfying both the feminist and civil liberties lobbies. Some states have changed rape to a form of sexual criminal assault which takes into account the degrees of damage done to the woman when sentencing.

Reform does not stop rape, and damaging male myths need to be countered. Seventy percent of rapists plan their attacks and ninety percent of these are gang rapes. Less than four percent of convicted rapists are found to be in need of psychiatric help, and many make the same score on aggression and attitude-to-women tests as 'normal' men.

In a society were man is seen as initiator and woman as consentor, as predator and prey, wolf and chick, aggressive and passive, rape is the extreme logical end of the spectrum of male-female sexual relationships. But rape brutally opposes a woman's right to sexual self-determination. It is not just a violent form of sex, rather it is a physical assault, using the penis as a weapon, and causing degradation, pain and humiliation.

23

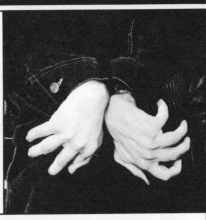

DISABILITY AND SEX

Physical obstacles that handicapped lovers can learn to overcome.

Disability

Disabled people are *people* first and foremost, with all the sexual urges and needs of people everywhere. Yet the disabled or deformed person, regardless of other physical attractiveness or personal charm, is too often written off as a non-sexual being by society. Indeed, many handicapped people, adopting the outlook of those around them, hold this negative view of themselves, although their sexual capability may be equal to other people's.

Certainly, sexual problems can often arise for the handicapped: research has shown that most disabled people meet with them at some time or another. But the first obstacle which they must overcome is that of prejudice. Once past this obstacle, their problems can usually be solved, or at least reduced. 'Sex in a wheelchair' is by no means an impossibility.

The front part of the brain and the central nervous system (the brain itself and the cord of nerves which runs from it down through the spine) control the physical changes which take place immediately before and during sexual activity (erection in the man, enlargement of the clitoris and vagina in the woman, etc.) 'Messages' are carried from the base of the spine through the nerve fibres that run to the sexual organs. Thus, interruption of the spinal cord—if it is damaged (as with paraplegics) or if it does not develop properly (as in spina bifida)—will prevent the messages getting through. Depending upon the completeness and position of the nerve-break, function and/or feeling in the sexual organs (among other parts) may be lost, reduced or interfered with. A similar complete or partial effect may result from damage to the nerves leading from the spinal cord to the sexual parts.

Other problems, less directly connected with sexual function, can arise. Paralysis may have little effect on the sexual organs, but can make certain sexual positions or movement impossible. Discomfort or pain can reduce these or bar them altogether. Rheumatism and arthritis are examples in this connection. Unintentional contractions of muscles causing jerking or rigid limbs (as in cerebral palsy or muscular dystrophy) may raise obstacles to sexual intercourse. Real problems of physical danger may arise where *severe* breathlessness or palpita-

tions accompany sexual excitement, where bones are brittle or (more rarely) when epileptic convulsions are triggered by intercourse.

Handicaps in hearing or sight may carry special problems. For the deaf, communication with most people is difficult and there is not even an official sign language for sexual concepts at present. Blind people often depend on others for social contact and not being able to read the facial expression of others is itself a sexual handicap. Moreover, young deaf and blind people are specially hampered in sex education, which is still in its infancy for these groups. Physical problems may be aggravated by mental or emotional ones, or the latter may arise independently.

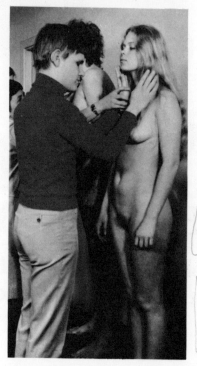

The poor view of themselves held by some disabled people—and it can sometimes be extreme—may get in the way of sexual relationships.

Since sexual ignorance and inhibitions are still fairly wide spread, many disabled people are prevented from finding their own solutions to the problems they may meet. Until recently, only a minority was able to obtain advice or counsel about them. Until the last few years, little attention was paid to the sexual aspects of disability, or to the solutions which exist in sexual problems which may arise for the handicapped. Happily, there is now increasing interest and action on their behalf.

It is seldom that postural difficulty or bodily deformity totally prevents sex in one position or another. Intercourse is possible while lying, sitting, standing or kneeling, with the man in front of or behind the woman, above or below her. Techniques also exist of which some disabled people are unaware. Methods of intercourse when the penis is not fully rigid and means for extra stimulation of both the penis and clitoris are important examples. Such knowledge could be significant for many disabled people and can now be obtained from organizations concerned with the problem.

Artificial aids—either extemporized (such as use of a pillow or cushion to adjust bodily position or restrain a recalcitrant limb) or manufactured aids available— can be immensely useful. Aids vary from small devices for maintaining or hardening erection to an artificial penis or vagina.

Where intercourse *is* impossible, the caressing of the genitals of one partner by the other, or both together, can be almost equally pleasurable. This can be done either with hands or orally. There are many techniques for this kind of lovemaking which are easily learned and put into practice (*oral sex**).

Many people whose disability has caused a total loss of feeling in the main sexual area find that their sensitivity in other parts of body—even those not usually recognized as sexual areas (*erogenous zones**)—increases. Caressing or stroking of these parts can give intense pleasure. Even people who are virtually incapable of movement and have little or no feeling in their body report far more than usual sexual pleasure and satisfaction simply from being held close to their partner.

The time may not be far ahead when disabled people automatically receive information or advice on the sexual elements of their disorders in the course of treatment and rehabilitation. This does not alter the fact that there are many thousands of the handicapped who have never received such advice. For these, organizations have been set up to deal with the problems involved.

But the first obstacle remains, and it can be reduced only by radical change in the social outlook on disability. Disabled people are capable of love, sex and sexual or marital partnership. Sometimes, they need assistance—but such assistance is worthwhile if it leads to a full and satisfying sexual life for two people.

Victor Hancox

THE *Intimate Room*

701 7TH AVE.

701 SEVENTH AVE.

Frankfurters

FRESH FRUIT

DR NK

Venga
Hacia
Abajo
Estamos
Abiertos
7 Dias
Semenal

10
COMPLETE

Solamente
$10

BEAUTIFUL
GIRLS

$10
COMPLETE
NO OTHER CHARGES

24

SEXPLOITATION

Trade-boosting titillation techniques that put sex into everything.

Pornography

(From the Greek, *porne*, prostitute and *graphein*, to write). Strictly this means 'writing about prostitutes'. We use it to refer to material which is meant to produce strong sexual arousal. It may be written as some sort of story, generally with illustrations. It may be photographs, drawings, a film or a recording. Unfortunately, because of the long tradition of sexual repression, the word has come to imply something contemptible or even criminal. Human needs have created a large market for such products. This is particularly true for very repressive societies and periods.

A whole range of pornographic publications exist, ranging from the slightest sexual allusions to the most frank expression of intense erotic excitement, activity or fantasy. Much is available on open display which, in the present climate of opinion, is unlikely to be prosecuted successfully. This is SOFT PORNOGRAPHY. 'Girlie' magazines generally provide excellent examples. Popular newspapers use sexy pictures and articles to titillate their readers. This was known in journalism as 'cheesecake' or 'tit pictures'.

So-called HARD PORNOGRAPHY (or hard-core porn) is so candid that prosecution is always a great risk. Some security is gained by selling it discreetly. This is an administrative protection rather than a legal one. It reduces the chance that the material will fall into the hands of children, which appears important to the authorities. A great deal lies between these two categories. Any clear-cut distinctions are really misleading. The contents of magazines and books selling freely overlap considerably with the wares to be purchased in 'adults only' book shops.

Pornography deals with the whole range of sexual responses. For the ordinary heterosexual person there are albums of nudes. These may be simple bosom and bottom shots (or 'tit and bum').

In the further stages of frankness 'beaver' and 'split beaver' shots show the hairy vulva, reminiscent of that furry animal. Publications of this type are sold generally in plastic wrappings so that the contents are available only after purchase. Books illustrating sexual penetration, even of the vagina, are generally reserved for controlled sale.

Sexual responses range, of course, far beyond the acknowledged sequence from attraction to kissing and embracing to intercourse. A whole variety of stimuli can lead to a variety of responses. Many people are wholly or partly homosexual and youths are specifically attractive to some homosexuals. The thought of cruelty can be exciting to a minority and some articles of clothing may be very important to those addicted to fetish responses. Similarly *rubber** and *leather fetishes** exist.

The mechanisms in the human brain causing sexual responses are closely associated with those dealing with violence. Sadism and masochism are common, though usually as mild and certainly not universal traits in our characters. Magazines with such names as

Spankers cater for this tendency. *Flagellation** is widely represented in pornography because it can be so exciting erotically.

Sexual penetration, so tenderly described as the 'merging' of the partners, may be vaginal, or it may be in the mouth or in the anus. Some pornography will portray and revel in all these many types of sexual experience. For some people the playful dominance and submission which is part of intercourse expresses itself in bondage or humiliation. All are natural to some people—amusing and harmless if the partners care for each other.

To a considerable extent the buyers are men, sadly discontented with the type or quantity of sex life has to offer them. These are often called unkindly 'the dirty macintosh brigade'.

A scatter of men undoubtedly buy pornography to provide an extra filip in their marriage. Though women do respond, pronography sales are almost entirely made to men.

The difficulty we have in being honest and charitable about the realities of sex is the main reason for our difficulty in dealing properly with pornography. To a large extent, one's erotic reactions are contrary to one's aesthetic sense, and even more they tend to deflate one's self-importance. Unless a particular item of pornography matches the customer's personality and mood it may be very displeasing. Some people may be upset by sexual provocation because the frustration it produces irritates them. Others have been so brought up that they cannot joyfully accept their own impulses. Such people are especially likely to be aggressive and interfering *prudes**, as anxious therefore to punish others as to protect themselves from anxiety.

Pornography is condemned on the ground that it may lead to harmful consequences. During the last ten years or so considerable research has failed to give evidence of such harm. There is some evidence that persons who are disturbed sexually have had less than average experience of pornography, especially in childhood. The rapist seems to use pornography as a safety valve to reduce his unacceptable impulses. If we condemn the fantasy literature of sadistic sex we should also condemn our children's books of history and entertainment. Goldstein and Kant (who contributed to the 1970 Presidential Commission on Obscenity) found that a strong response to pornography is associated with qualities that are encouraged by education. They report that adults using pornography seem to have a compulsion to compensate for sexual disappointment. G. L. Simons emphasises that censorship has largely prevented the development of a commendable literature of eroticism. Novels and plays help us in other parts of human understanding; similarly we need good pornography to help us to adjust properly to ourselves and to each other in this most sensitive and vulnerable part of human relationships. This is particularly true for sadomasochism.

The law as it stands leads to confusion and shame. Jurymen require unusual honesty and courage to take the side of people accused of obscene publication. Pornography, like sex, is for private use.

Books & Magazines

While books of erotica (*Reader's Guide**) have been produced and circulated almost since writing was invented, it is a recent development for magazines to be published with a 100 per cent sexual content, apart from medical manuals. This is in part because it is easier to stock and sell a 'naughty' book discreetly than it is to handle and display pornographic magazines. Fetishistic magazines—usually of a very poor quality—specially catering for a readership interested in flagellation, etc., have been around for a hundred years or more, but it is the so-called sexual revolution that has made possible the arrival of the all-round sex magazine.

Where 'Playboy' (picking up the trail from the pre-war 'Esquire') discussed sexual topics openly and coolly in combination with other features on general topics, the 1960s arrivals like 'Forum' had a single-minded dedication to the subject of sex. This must have been what the public was waiting for. The boom took off with titles like 'Penthouse', 'Playgirl', 'Viva' and many others, to be followed by 'Screw', a send-up of sex magazines which outrageously broke all previous existing taboos in printed matter.

Advertising

The advertising industry's purpose is not only to inform the public about new and available goods and services, but also to persuade the public to buy, regardless of need. Human sexual responsiveness, both conscious and unconscious, is used for these purposes. Two main theories about human sexuality which were proposed by *Freud** are used over and over again in advertisements—the idea that if the LIBIDO or sexual energy is prevented from finding a direct outlet, then it finds an alternative means of expression; and that the alternative channel is some kind of creative expression called SUBLIMATION. So, buying a powerful car may be a 'creative' way of expressing aggressive masculinity.

Advertising uses LIBIDO and SUBLIMATION in combination with traditional male and female role-playing (*sexism**) to persuade people to buy—anything from a lawn mower to the latest body deodoriser. Advertisements exploit human ideas about sex and sex roles by insinuating in words and pictures that if you buy something you don't really need it will help you to achieve a desired *psychosexual identity**.

The use of human sexuality in advertising can be amusing and harmless, but it can also be extremely harmful. Advertising has given a generation of women a 'complex' about supposed vaginal *odour**; it has promoted an image of smoking and of drinking alcohol as social activities which enhance sex appeal and make one feel at ease in sexual situations. The use of sexual themes plays upon readers, or viewers, self-confidence in dealing with the opposite sex. While adults may be more immune to advertising, adolescents, searching for a grown-up sexual identity, are conditioned by advertisements to believe in the glamourization of sex. This misleadingly engenders both 'high performance' sex expectations as well as the idea that sexuality equals romance—which can lead to severe disappointment in real life and a feeling that 'something must be wrong with me'. Sexploitation in advertisements seeks to tell the public that the problems of human sexuality are easily solved by the purchase of manufactured goods.

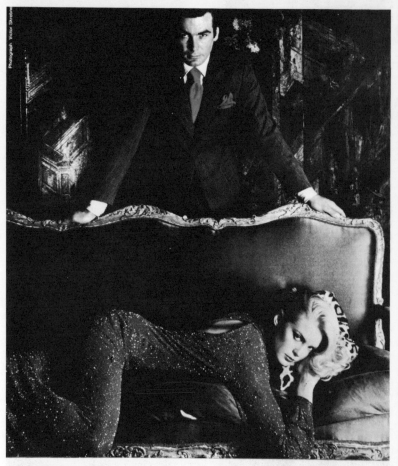

Cloth for Men..... BY DORMEUIL

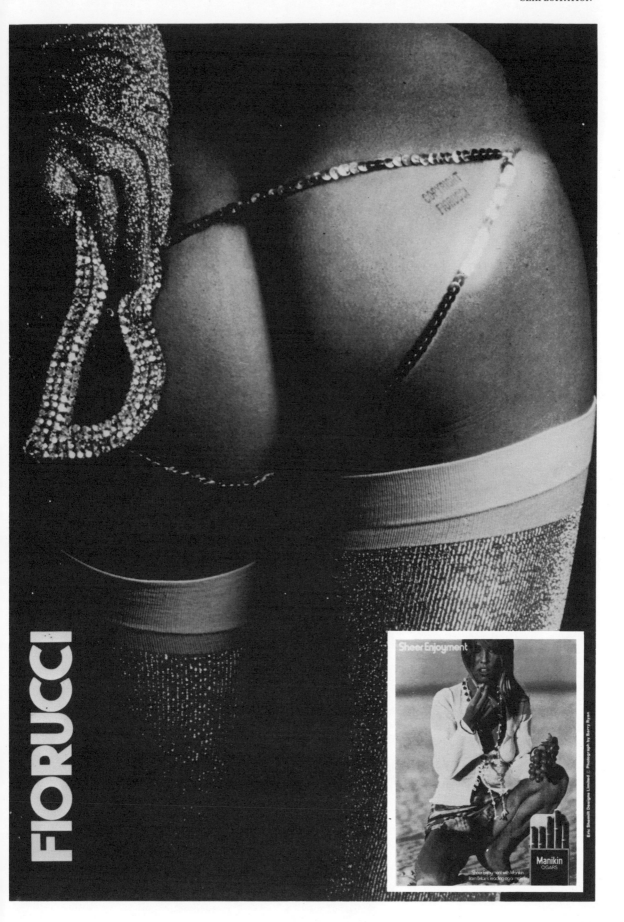

FIORUCCI

Skin Flicks

A skin-flick (that is to say, a film show-ing nakedness) or blue movie is the cin-ema's equivalent of the erotic picture book, but with the added advantage of movement. There are two main outlets for this kind of product: packaged one-reelers for private projection, and the X-rated showing at commercial sex theatres. One other minor use, but a valuable one, is as a prelude to arousal during *sex therapy**.

The pornographic content being all-important, blue movie makers usually take little trouble over plot-line, char-acterisation or technique. They may even, in some cases, serve their viewers very short on really erotic scenes, since prospective customers cannot run through the cassettes before purchase, or demand their money back from the box office if dissatisfied. However, cut-throat competition combined with a more lenient interpretation of the law

in many countries can be expected to put a premium on increased quality in new productions. Unless they just fol-low a trend towards sadism and exces-sive shock, blue movie makers may come to see their chances of survival and success in a technically better product than they have got away with until now. The arrival of the 'art movie' in soft porn—for example the 'Em-manuelle' series—may be a pointer in this direction. Perhaps the institution of an Oscar for the best hard porn movie of the year might give the producers an incentive to quit conning their public.

Most of the production is concen-trated in a few small companies, which market their reels internationally un-der various names—often in order to circumvent postal censorship prob-lems. Some of the directors may also be involved in straight work for television commercials, while others are dedi-cated to underground activities, both pornographic and avant-garde. Profits are reputedly high, and often evade taxation, but stability in the business is low.

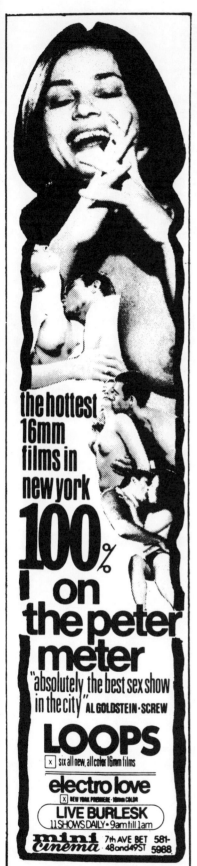

Sex Shows

The basic stimulus to sexual excitement is the provocative display of the human body. This can vary from simple titillation to candid protrayal of intercourse or of erotic fantasies. Extreme frankness probably occurs only at private parties. The danger of prosecution greatly restricts the entertainment available for purchase.

Can-can dancing from France, with frilly knickers and bottom shows, high kicks to show thighs and panties of the music hall dancing troupes, belly dancers of the Mediterranean countries delight millions of men. Night clubs and restaurants may use waitresses whose clothing emphasises and partly reveals their sexual attributes. Bunny-girl uniforms, see-through cat suits—all find a place in the sex show. Undress is of course not essential to sexiness. The contortions of male pop singers with their microphones often mimic the movements of coitus.

Striptease dancers progressively remove their clothes as the act proceeds. Then they ogle the audience with naked body. Simple stage tricks may suggest intercourse. Lesbian love-making is portrayed, but seldom homosexual male activity or heterosexual intercourse. The legal dangers have placed striptease as an activity on the fringe of the underworld. This makes them scarce, expensive and occasionally dishonest.

Many men react to such shows with growing warmth, amused light-heartedness, a sense of beauty and gladness more marked than eroticism.

25

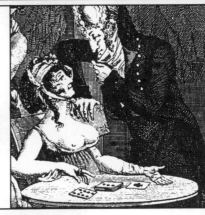

PROSTITUTION

The workers whose job it is to provide pleasure-for a price.

Prostitution

Sex has been for sale throughout the ages and, despite the fact that more and more people are marrying, persists. The human sex drive is fundamentally promiscuous. Marriage and family life, with all the attendant advantages, modify and reduce the sex drive somewhat, but do not abolish it. Whatever one's moral view, it is almost certainly true that the majority of males is interested in sexual variety, and for a number of reasons may pursue this outside marriage. Prostitutes cater to all tastes, ranging from straight intercourse to non-coital, sado-masochistic rituals, or role-playing games. The customer gets what he pays for, without emotional hang-ups or commitment. Prostitution is thus a consequence of male erotic desire and not the instigator of it. Advocates also argue that in a primarily monogamous culture, prostitution may be expected to reduce illegitimacy, abortions, adultery and divorce, rape and attacks on children. Whether or not this is the case has not yet been proved.

The so-called 'pro' or 'professional' makes her living by being ON THE GAME. She may be relatively high class, dealing with just a few regulars, usually by appointment, or be a common streetwalker plying her trade to all comers. New tougher legislation in recent years has cracked down hard on street girls. Of course, prostitution did not disappear, it was simply pushed underground, and the era of the call girls, masseuses, models, escorts and other euphemistic titles was born.

The non-professional prostitute is often employed and/or married. She offers sex as a means of augmenting her income, although occasionally, her behaviour may be at least in part, a means of combating boredom. These acts of amateur prostitution may be fairly regular, or a single experience to meet an immediate financial need. It has been observed that the amateurs seem to be increasing their numbers at the expense of the professionals. The number of all girls 'on the game' and the relative proportion of 'amateur' to 'professional' reflect both male demand and the level of official repression.

The motives for anyone becoming a prostitute may be diverse and confused, but the following can often be found:
1 Rewards are far higher than those in most female occupations. A high-class call girl working for herself in a big city can comfortably earn as much as a senior business executive does in a week.
2 The better class of prostitute may meet interesting, intelligent and even prominent men. Her life is, therefore, likely to be more exciting and glamorous than that of the average girl going out to work.

3 Surprisingly, some male clients become emotionally attached to prostitutes and there is the ultimate prospect of getting married to such a man.
4 Addiction to drugs, supporting a family, or meeting some other major financial obligation.
5 Satisfaction of various drives like self-punishment, punishment of others, hostility towards males, etc.
6 A few girls are so highly sexed they actually enjoy most of their contacts.

For them, prostitution is the best way to combine business with pleasure.

7 There are some girls so inadequate, lazy or dull that they drift into prostitution as the only way they can earn a living.

Nothing has been established about the characteristics of the men who use prostitutes, and it would seem that they come from all walks of life and represent all levels of intelligence. Certain men, however, may have special reasons, of which the most typical are:

1 They require a variety of sexual activity unavailable from any other source.

2 They are too shy, physically handicapped or too old to find a sexual partner any other way.

3 They may be seeking satisfaction of a deviated sex urge, such as sado-masochism, fetishism, etc.

Over the years, the attitude of the law makers towards prostitution has been capricious and even hypocritical. Nowhere is this more the case than in the USA, where for all practical purposes, prostitution is illegal. The numerous brothels which operate illicitly in most big cities are often forced to buy immunity from law enforcement agencies, politicians or gangsters. Traditionally, the last, especially the Mafia, has organized and profited from prostitution. In Britain prostitution as such is not illegal, but soliciting for the purpose is, and so is living on immoral earnings, or procuring, or taking part in the management of a brothel, or knowingly committing premises to be used either as a brothel or for the purposes of habitual prostitution. Most other European countries have outlawed brothels and the girls, driven underground, may suffer harassment of varying degrees from their 'exploiters', be they the police or the pimps.

The attitude of the Christian church towards prostitution has been confused and arbitrary, although it has never actually condoned it. In the middle ages, the church condemned prostitution as 'original sin': sex was meant only for procreation; pleasure, even in the marriage bed, was denounced. Laws at the time were savagely punitive, and prostitutes could even be put to death.

Venereal diseases became widespread in Europe after 1492 and an epidemic of syphilis was rightly attributed to the brothels. Following this scourge, medical examinations and registration gradually became commonplace, and in some countries prostitutes were segregated into 'red light' districts.

Demi-Monde

(From the French, *demi* meaning 'half' and *monde*, 'society') This is an old-fashioned term for the 'half world' in which glamorous women of doubtful morals and no social standing lived. Such women were known as *demi-mondaines* and included actresses, music hall and vaudeville performers, courtesans and other good-time girls

Aubrey Beardsley

who frequented cafés and theatres at a time when 'nice' women did not dine out in public or go to the theatre. The term was popular in the 'gay nineties' and until the first World War when aristocrats and other men of breeding and social standing thought it exciting to frequent places of entertainment with women of loose reputation. These women living in a half or twilight world of petty criminals often became common prostitutes when they had lost their youth and looks.

Gigolo

(The masculine form of the French term *gigole*, a dance hall woman.) A professional male companion or escort for females who is paid for his company, for sexual favours or for his role as a confidant. A gigolo is usually heterosexual but occasionally bisexual or even homosexual. Characteristically, a gigolo is young and physically attractive and tends to ply his trade in fashionable circles of society in big cities and resort areas. A gigolo may be employed on a semistable basis by a middle-aged or elderly woman of means and accompany his patron while she travels. Gigolo was originally another name for a pimp or even a paid dancing partner.

Call Girl

A higher class of discriminating prostitute who supplies sex to comparatively few males, usually on the basis of an appointment made by telephone call, is known as a call girl. They do not solicit clients on the street or in bars, but deal with businessmen, politicians and society figures who can afford higher fees and who pass on the girls' names to friends and associates.

Call girls often live alone in tastefully furnished apartments suitable for entertaining their clients. Some work in expensive hotels, or night clubs, providing their 'entertainment' in a client's own bedroom or suite. Call girls may work for a madam or a pimp or rely on a contact woman with whom they split their earnings.

All types of sexual activities may be catered for. A call girl may be taken out for an evening on the town before servicing her escort's needs. In addition to her professional fee, she may expect and be given presents. Call girls sometimes accompany their clients on holidays or business trips, and they may be kept as mistresses for several months until one or the other party tires of the arrangement.

Jane Fonda in 'Klute'

Hetaera

These were the higher class of prostitute or courtesan in ancient Greece. Rather like the Japanese *geisha**, hetaerae were skilled in the art of conversation—and especially of argument, a talent prized by Athenians. Their sexual skills are illustrated in a number of vase paintings, but entertainment by music and dancing was usually left to a class of performer called *auletrides* or 'flute-players'.

Heterae paid taxes to the state according to their commercial success, and were far from being despised like the common prostitutes or *pornia* (from which the word 'pornography' is derived). In fact, they were envied for their freedom and accomplishments, especially by married women whose lives were a tedious round of domestic duties within their own households. The base from which a hetaera operated could be a recognized brothel or equally a temple like that to Aphrodite Pandemos, which was identified with extra-marital sex. Prostitutes whose trade was closely connected with temple service were a different class. They were known as 'sacred servants' or *hierodules*.

Geisha

A geisha is a traditional Japanese entertainer and hostess who has been trained in all the social graces and arts to provide complete entertainment for men. For a fee she acts as companion for an evening's sophisticated pleasure, and is skilled at conversation, singing, dancing, playing musical instruments, performing a traditional tea ritual, serving food and often in sexual activities, although not always. A common question of Westerners is: 'Is a geisha a prostitute?' In the sense that they are paid for their services and that these may include sex, the answer is yes; but the profession of geisha is highly respected in Japan. It has a long and honourable history and many geishas have risen high in the social hierarchy.

Child Prostitution

The reason that children go into prostitution is more often the need for money after running away from home than any precocious or abnormal sexuality. Increasing numbers of children below the *age of consent** leave home as part of a rebellion against parental or social values and end up penniless in a big city.

However, not all child prostitutes are runaways—some operate from a home base unknown to their parents. A small number, especially in disadvantaged families, may be compelled by unscrupulous parents, or by a procurer, to submit to adult clients with the taste for sexual experience with children (*pedophilia**). The most common sexual services provided by either boys or girls are masturbation and fellatio. Actual intercourse is less frequent but may be part of the repertoire of more physically mature children.

Some younger children whose sexual experiences belie their years spend their earnings on chocolates, comics, soft drinks or movie tickets, while harder and more worldly-wise juvenile prostitutes have been known to blackmail their clients, for the law takes a serious view of sexual interference with children.

Pimp

The role of a pimp (also known as a PONCE OR PIMP) is to manage a female or male prostitute and live off the earnings, which is a criminal offence. Pimps often supply emotional support, as well as physical protection from perverted or sadistic clients. Pimps may run the household, taking care of everyday chores, like paying bills. They may also, but not always, act for clients as procurers of prostitutes.

A pimp may get part of his sexual gratification from his 'charge' (some pimps are married to their prostitutes), which does not prevent many pimps from being physically violent towards them. This can be a way of scaring an unwilling woman into continuing with a profession that (unlike the pimp's) is in itself not illegal, or to ensure that she hands over her hard-earned money. Despite being ill-treated in this way, few prostitutes make official complaints to the police against pimps—partly out of fear of reprisals and partly because law enforcers are not over-sympathetic to anyone 'on the game'.

Few pimps limit their criminal activities to the exploitation of prostitutes. Because of their contacts with

the underworld and intimate knowledge of the illicit sex scene, they are frequently involved in pedalling drugs or pornography, in obtaining illegal abortions, and may even blackmail their prostitutes' clients. Pimps with a reputation as police informers are often despised by other criminals and law enforcers alike. If convicted of 'living off immoral earnings' and imprisoned, they may be badly treated at the hands of fellow inmates.

Recently, pimps trafficking in teenage male prostitutes have become increasingly prevalent. The young boys who go into prostitution are often runaways. A pimp will introduce such a boy to the drug scene and, once he is hooked, the pimp can ensure that he stays 'on the game' to get money for drugs.

Brothel

Colloquially, a brothel refers to any premises in which sex services may be bought, whether there are one or twenty prostitutes working there. In law, a brothel is defined as: premises in which two or more women offer their bodies for lewd hire, so a prostitute or a call girl cannot be prosecuted for keeping a brothel if they are working on their own.

The word brothel comes from an Old English word which simply meant a worthless man or woman. Brothels have a long history and come in all shapes and sizes. In Europe and North America most brothels (or bawdy houses) have now been outlawed. However, there has been a corresponding rise in massage clinics, ESCORT SERVICES and *call girl** rings.

The origin of organized brothels is strangely entangled with ideas of temple-service to the gods of fertility in ancient times. In India, the *deva-dasi* operated from temples, as did the *hierodules* in ancient Greece (*religious and sexual behaviour**). By Roman times, the religious connection had grown much weaker, and with the coming of Christianity it disappeared altogether. In the Middle Ages, the public bath-houses usually functioned as brothels—hence Shakespeare's name for a bawdy-house was 'the stews'.

Brothels were traditionally managed by a brothel-keeper called a MADAM; she was often an older prostitute with a good head for business, and looked after all aspects of the girls' welfare. This included regular health inspections, for a house which got a reputation for diseased girls would not stay in business very long. As well as negotiating the best possible terms, a madam would also act as a sort of public relations officer ensuring as far as possible that all parties got a square deal. The importance of the brothel and its madam in prostitution, at least in Western Europe, declined as the law became more moralistic and prohibitive. Despite this, brothels are not totally extinct—they are found in many Western countries in so-called red light districts, where the prostitutes' traditional sign, a lighted lamp with a red shade, indicates 'business as usual'.

A modern version of the brothel-keeper of yesteryear is the CONTACT WOMAN who instead of running a house runs a 'string of fillies' or call girls by means of the telephone.

Massage Parlour

A massage parlour or clinic can rarely be found to offer body massage and nothing more. In many cases, it is a euphemism for a *brothel** or at least a place where various non-coital sexual favours may be bought, or an initial introduction effected in which the 'masseuse' and client contract to rendezvous later for agreed sexual services. Massage parlours generally advertise sauna, massage and 'assisted' showers. Most proprietors, who are only too familiar with the law, vehemently deny they are in the business of procuring or prostitution, or that they are acting as pimps. These establishments, however, have proliferated simply because the services offered are so ambiguous, and thus may appear to be perfectly legal.

When a masseuse is in conversation with her would-be client she uses a form of verbal shorthand to assess his level of interest and sexual requirements. She may ask innocently, 'Do you have an all-over, Sir?' (meaning masturbation) and if he answers affirmatively she will casually mention that such a service is additional—in other words, it costs more than the advertised fee for massage. In other cases, if the 'vibrations' are right, she will dispense with the pretence and simply detail her sexual repertoire or ask the client outright what he wants.

Most massage parlours, in fact, offer massage and masturbation—known as relief massage—although more elaborate forms of stimulation, soft pornography and even coitus may be available on the premises, if requested. Naturally, these extras inflate the price, which in any case tends to be high. Some parlours offer high colonic irrigation or *enemas** and various types of vibrator experience. Massage is such an ambiguous description that it lends itself to cynical exploitation of clients seeking sex activity. Many operatives con their clients into parting with high fees for little more than a 'slap and tickle'. When a hoped-for sexual service fails to materialize, the place becomes known as a 'clip joint'.

The introduction of the Finnish SAUNA now provides a similar cover for sexual services, so that what is in its land of origin a normal and purely social facility has suffered early corruption when transplanted to other countries, although it might have become a welcome health pursuit.

26

MARITAL NOVELTIES (Gift Boxed)
Nothing ever has been made to equal these items. More than conversation pieces.
A MINI VIBRATOR FITS BEHIND EACH FACE.

JILL SLEEVE
16A- $19.95

JILL TONGUE
16B- $19.95

JACK SLEEVE
16C- $19.95

JACK TONGUE
16D- $19.95

1970'S MAN
16E- $20.95 w/hair

LIFE LIKE VAGINA
16F-w-Hair - $19.95
16G-no/Hair- $17.95

IN THE SEX STORE

Merchandise that spices humdrum sex- so why not, if it helps?

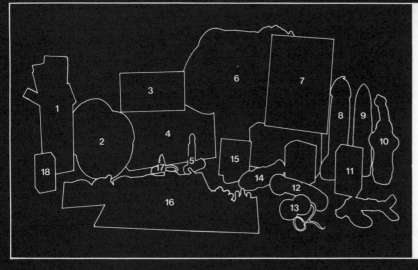

1. 'Sex Packet'
2. Sailor's Sweetheart
3. Penile Splints
4. Harness Dildo
5. Pocket Tingler
6. Underwear
7. Finger Tinglers
8. Phallic Candle
9. Black Vibrator
10. Rintintin Vibrator
11. Arab Strap
12. Double Delight
13. Vaginal Balls
14. Extension Sheath
15. Love Ring
16. Special Condoms
17. Rejuvenating Tablets
18. Clitoral Stimulator

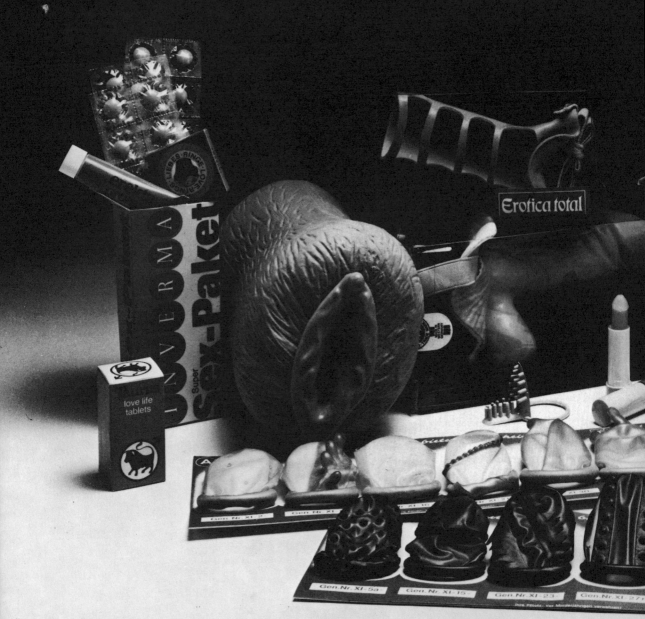

CHINESISCHER
Lustfinger
"LAMELLO FING"

Der «Lamello Fing» erweckt die Kunst des Vorspiels zu neuem Leben!
Dieser Fingerring aus reinem Latex macht die Frau bereit für die Liebe.
Seine weichen Noppen reizen sanft aber intensiv die Klitoris und den
vorderen Scheideneingang der Frau. So kann in Erregungsanstieg be-
schleunigt werden, und es ist Ihr möglich, gemeinsam mit Ihrem Partner
den Orgasmus zu erleben.

1.
Der «Lamello Fing» paßt auf jeden Finger und läßt sich leicht an- und ablegen.

2.
Der «Lamello Fing» ist diskret und wirksam. Gönnen Sie sich und Ihrer Partnerin nächsten Liebesabend mit dem «Chinesischen Lustfinger»!

3.
Der «Lamello Fing» ist aus hygienischem, reinem, weichem Latex.

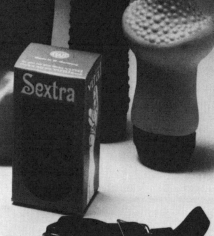

MATA
KAMBING

Gen.Nr. XL-30a

JuT

Sextra

DOH
BERWICK
LONDON
Tel 01-43

Underwear

The erotic function of underclothes might seem too flimsy a subject (like the garments themselves) to merit discusion, but it is a matter that has interestingly contradictory connotations. In the first place, erotic underwear works one way for men and another for women. It is generally confirmed by women that while men can be excited by the sight (real or imagined) of female undies, even when these are not being worn by anybody, women are not excited by actually wearing them, but rather by the response they create in their male sex partners. It is on these grounds that most women dress sexily, even where it cannot normally be seen. *Vice versa*, men who wear 'athletic' briefs usually enjoy a minor but constant stimulation as a result of the cupping support which these give to the male genitals, while women's erotic interest is mainly stimulated by just this heightened response in men.

Dildo

An object that can be used as a substitute penis for intercourse or masturbation is called a dildo, or many other names. Manufactured ones resembling a real male penis (sometimes complete with testicles) are on sale in many shapes, sizes, materials and colours. Various embellishments can make the shaft of the dildo a lot more interesting in size and texture than many specimens of the real thing. There are hollow types that can be filled with warm water, oil or milk and squeezed to 'ejaculate'. Some are fitted with electrical vibrating devices (*vibrator**). Elastic waist belts with straps are sometimes attached to dildos so that a female can play a male role in homosexual intercourse. Nothing should be used which has to be forced into the vagina or rectum, and all dildos should be kept scrupulously clean.

Clitoral Stimulator

This is a ring, usually made of latex rubber, which fits around the base of an erect penis. Attached to the ring is some kind of stimulating surface—it may be a pad or air cushion with a stippled surface, or bare soft rubber projections,

looking like a coarse nailbrush. A stimulator (or LOVE RING) is placed so that it is squeezed between the area at the base of the penis and the clitoris, thus increasing a woman's sexual arousal. It also exaggerates the friction of male pubic hair against the woman's corresponding area.

Many kinds of fancifully shaped rubber devices, called FRENCH TICKLERS, can be placed over or around the penis or made as part of special condoms. They are intended to stimulate the vagina during intercourse, but, as Masters and Johnson discovered, the upper two-thirds of the vagina is almost insensitive to any touch.

Penile Splint

A penile splint is a cylinder of soft rubber with one or two thin curved plastic plates embedded in it. Its purpose is to keep a soft or impotent penis sufficiently rigid for penetration. When in position, the plates in the splint hold the penis out from the body. With careful handling and *lubrication**, the penis can be inserted into the vagina even without having an erection. The glans or sensitive tip of the penis is not covered and gaps in the sides of the splint also permit intimate contact. It is a useful male sex aid. There is medical evidence that assistance like this can reduce anxiety and eventually encourage a return to a natural state of erection (*impotence**).

Pills, Creams, Sprays

All products sold as exciters, improvers or prolongers of sexual performance are a confidence trick (*aphrodisiac**). Vitamin pills can help but only as part of a general improvement in health (*fitness**). Tranquiliser pills can assist in sex problems by relaxing the mind and body, but only doctors should recommend or prescribe these. Anesthetic creams and sprays can reduce sensation in the genital area and have some slight effect on *premature ejaculation**, but a doctor's advice should be sought before use. Creams which are supposed to increase sexual potency are useless and may contain irritating substances. Mild irritants (such as a pinch of cayenne pepper in butter) offer slight help but can also burn and blister the sensitive genitals.

27

CLINIC

Checking up for signs of things that may go wrong.

Gynecology

Gynecology is one of the most recent specialities in medicine. Although minor gynecological operations had long been performed, gynecology was really an American invention. It was developed as a special skill by a handful of backwoods obstetricians, delivering babies in Virginia, Kentucky, Vermont and Pennsylvania in the early 19th century. Most of them had received their training as 'man-midwives' in Scotland at Edinburgh University and hospitals. At that time, the practice of gynecology was, for most doctors, confined to examining the vagina by means of a primitive SPECULUM, prototypes of which had been around for centuries. A speculum is an expanding hollow instrument that opens the vagina, allows air to enter it (normally the vagina is closed, with no space between its walls) and thus allows the doctor to see inside. He can also visually inspect the neck of the womb (*cervix**). This makes it possible to diagnose a little more accurately various vaginal discharges, diseases in the cervix and get an idea of the common *womb prolapses** and displacements that trouble many patients.

Today, a routine gynecological examination includes an examination of the lower abdomen (*palpation*), and of the external sex organs, including the clitoris, the vulva and the perineum. Then the physician examines the interior of the vagina with his fingers, and can also feel and examine the womb (*uterus*), and if possible the *Fallopian tubes** and *ovaries**. Often at this time his other hand will be pressing gently on the woman's lower abdomen. In this way, the various organs within the pelvis can be carefully examined. Finally, the doctor will pass a speculum into the vagina and make a visual examination of that and the cervix. Sometimes he will also take a smear test from the cervix or the vagina and also from around the opening of the *urethra** (urine tube).

This simple routine examination produces a wealth of information, and in most cases no further investigations are necessary to clinch a diagnosis. Most cases of vaginal discharge can be diagnosed in this way. The very copious *trichomonia** (a smelly, greenish discharge) can be differentiated from the itchy, cheesy, *candidiasis** (thrush) discharge that sticks to the vaginal walls and may bleed when removed. In doubt,

swabs can be sent for laboratory examination. If *gonorrhea** is suspected, a special swab is taken from around the urethra and will often allow an accurate diagnosis to be made.

Inspection of the inside of the vagina can disclose signs of syphilis, abnormalities of the cervix, prolapses, hormone deficiency and various abnormal positions of the uterus which cause the cervix to 'point' in an unusual direction. By means of the two-handed (bimanual) examination, the size and positioning of the internal gynecological structures can allow a diagnosis of ovarian cyst, fibroid or other enlargements of the uterus and certain abnormalities of the Fallopian tubes to be

made. Examination of the external sex organs will also find evidence of prolapse, swelling of Bartholin's glands, varicose veins, tumors and various diseases of the sexual skin.

Sometimes it is necessary to proceed to other tests to reach an accurate diagnosis. The doctor may want to know the condition of the inside lining of the womb, in which case he will dilate (open up) the CERVICAL CANAL, the central opening of the neck of the womb, and either suck out a specimen through a flexible tube called a CANNULA, or scrape off some of the womb's internal lining with a spoon-like instrument called a CURETTE. In the latter case, this little operation of 'dilation and curettage' (D & C) is done under an

anesthetic. Similar operations are carried out to terminate a pregnancy (therapeutic *abortion**).

At times it is necessary to see inside a patient's pelvis to make an accurate diagnosis. In the past, the only way a gynecologist could do this was to make an incision (cut) into the lower abdomen and have a look round (a LAPAROTOMY operation). Gradually, however, instruments were devised that contained optical systems to allow an internal view without the necessity of making large cuts in the skin. This led, first of all, to an instrument that was pushed through the vaginal wall (a CULDOSCOPE), giving a limited view of the pelvic organs. More recently the LAPAROSCOPE was developed. This instrument is pushed through a small incision near to the patient's navel. At the same time, C_2O gas is introduced into the abdomen to produce a ballooning effect. Very good visualization is then possible through the laparoscope, through which minor operations can be also performed. This technique has revolutionized gynecological diagnosis since the mid-1960s.

1. Speculum 2. inserted into vagina and opened 3. Cervix 4. Bladder 5. Womb 6. Rectum 7. Anus 8. Spatula 9. scrapes surface cells from cervix 10. Opening into womb

Dilation and Curettage (D&C):
11. Vagina 12. Dilator inserted into cervix 13. Dilators in increasing sizes 14. Curette 15. scraping the womb lining

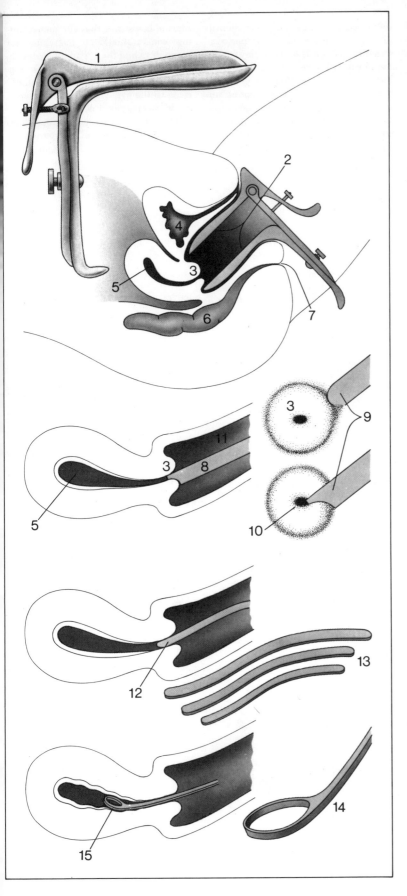

Hygiene

William Smellie, an eminent Scottish obstetrician, wrote a book on female anatomy in the middle of the 18th century. It did not endear him to his doctor colleagues, who called it 'the most bawdy indecent and shameful book the press has ever brought into the world', but it was the start of sex hygiene as we understand it. In a general medical sense, hygiene got going in Germany with a Bavarian doctor called Max von Pettenkofer (1818–1901). His advances in controlling cholera and typhoid by devising good house and city drainage and proper ventilation systems, and by popularizing healthier clothing, set a new standard for the world.

Hygiene means health, from Hygeia, the Greek goddess of health. A hygienic or healthy approach towards sex is still far from being universal. Women are still at a disadvantage, it seems, due partly to a degree of female 'modesty' that persists despite emancipation. The existence of successful advice columns in magazines the world over, phone-ins and self-help organizations demonstrates the need for more knowledge on sex hygiene—knowledge that does not seem to be readily available from the medical profession. The rules of sex hygiene for women are simple. Always see a doctor if an unusual lump, change of shape, bleeding or discharge develops. Do not ignore any change in your menstrual pattern unless your doctor has examined you. Finally, undergo smear tests every three years at least.

About 16,000 women in Britain and 50,000 in the USA develop breast cancer each year. Modesty encourages late diagnosis, so the overall survival rate is less than 35 percent. Only about 20 percent of all womb cancers are diagnosed early enough to be cured, whereas if really early diagnosis occurs, a cure rate of 80 percent seems likely. Most womb cancers occur on the cervix, and regular smear tests and early investigation of gynecological problems would prevent most of them from becoming incurable.

One famous expert in gynecology from Columbia University is on record as saying that if everyone—patient, diagnostician and therapist—were to act in a perfect manner, cancer of the cervix would disappear as a problem.

The hygiene of sex-related diseases and vaginal discharges are discussed in the section on *health**.

Menstrual Cycle

Woman is the only creature that has evolved a menstrual cycle. 'Menstrual' and 'menses' come from Latin words for 'monthly' and clearly our forefathers connected menstruation with the waxing and waning of the moon. Even

today, women talk about their 'monthlies' as an alternative to 'periods'. Other terms like 'the curse', 'my friend' or 'unwell' all have interesting psychological overtones. Often in primitive communities there is a concept of 'uncleanness' associated with menstruation and there are religious interdictions with regard to the menstrual cycle that are widely observed today.

Mosaic law states that the menstruating woman should be 'put apart' for seven days and that 'whosoever toucheth her shall be unclean'. Hebrew communities built bath-houses, usually close to the synagogue, where women could wash away this uncleanness.

Even in modern times medical folklore, often regrettably supported by doctors, added to the 'unclean' myth

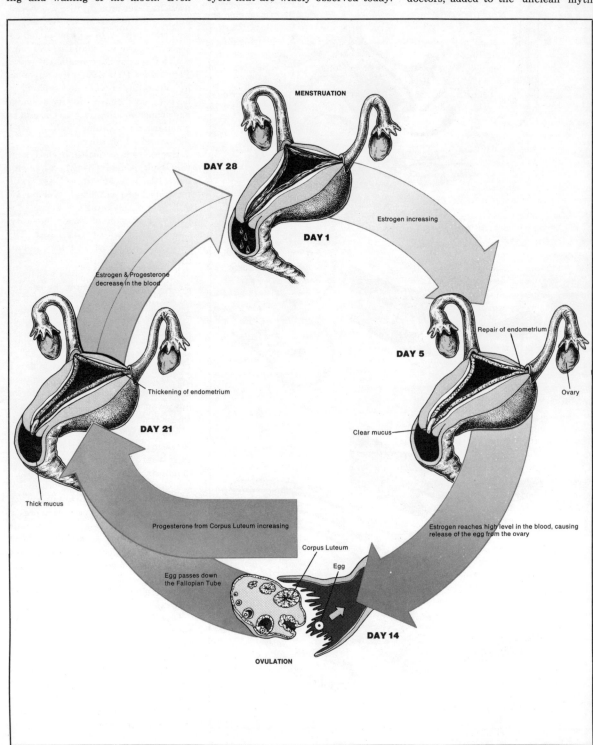

of menstruation. Even in the 19th century, the eminent *British Medical Journal* declared that hams were spoiled when handled by menstruating women, and in this century two American gynecologists supported the idea that flowers wilted excessively fast if touched by one, and they proceeded to describe what they called a 'menotoxin', thought to bring about this amazing effect. Not too long ago, mothers advised girls not to bathe or wash their hair if they had a period and, of course, sexual intercourse with a menstruating woman (always taboo in Jewish law) was widely and erroneously thought to bring to the male many venereal diseases. Not washing oneself at this time only induces the somewhat antisocial menstrual odour. Yet many women who rightly wash, shower or bath daily, including periods, feel bound to use a vaginal deodorizer as well in the interests of sex *hygiene**, so sure are they of a state of 'uncleanness' at this natural time.

The menses appear during the body changes known as puberty (from the Latin word for 'maturity') and this is known as the MENARCHE. After the pelvis starts to widen in girls (7-11) the breasts begin to develop (9-10). Then hair starts to grow over the pubis. The skin on the external sex glands and sometimes around the eye, mouth and nipples, tends to darken and then menstruation soon appears. Later, underarm (axillary) hair develops. The first period arrives usually between the age of 10 and 16 (average 13.0 years in Britain, 12.5 years in North America). In more underdeveloped countries, a later menarche occurs (India: 13.5 years). In Britain this has dropped from 17 to 13 years in the last 100 years and still appears to be dropping at the rate of about four months every 10 years.

Before a girl first menstruates, she often has a white vaginal discharge. She undergoes profound psychological changes in most cases and changes from a self-conscious or tomboyish creature into a more mature woman. The sexual urge is often homosexual at this time, a phase to be replaced sooner or later by heterosexual influences. After the first period has passed, everybody anxiously awaits the next. It may be some time in arriving, for the regularity of a girl's periods usually takes about 30 cycles to establish itself.

Although the menses are related to the calendar, they do not ever appear on an exactly regular basis. One analysis of 17,000 menstrual cycles in 1,265 women showed the average cycle to be 28.4 days long. That is to say, a period followed its predecessor by 28 days and 6 hours. It also showed that the average woman must expect one-third of all her cycles to depart by more than two days from her normal cycle. Variations from two to seven weeks in the time between cycles occur commonly in all age groups. The length of the actual period varies, too. In a series of 800 menstrual cycles in 76 healthy women, the average period lasted 4.6 days. The normal range is from three to six days during each cycle. About one to five ounces of blood are lost during each period.

DYSMENORRHEA (*painful periods*): Girls have painless periods until after about 20 cycles, when ovulation occurs in regular association with the menstrual cycle. This occurs about 14 days before the appearance of each menstrual period. Once ovulation happens, the adolescent girl becomes a fertile woman. (Very occasionally ovulation occurs before the periods show themselves. The absence of period pains cannot be relied upon as a practical contraceptive.) Thus, painful periods, if they are to be a problem, commonly arise between the age of 15 and 18.

At one time gynecologists believed dysmenorrhea was caused by 'an unsatisfied sexual appetite', while a more modern view is that it occurs in 'highly sensitive, apprehensive, self-centred girls who are sexually rather immature'. Neither view is tenable. Apart from a few girls whose painful periods are due to some abnormality (and because of this, all dysmenorrhea sufferers should be examined by a doctor), the basic cause is unknown. A healthy life with plenty of regular exercise and no restrictions on activities during menstruation seems to lessen both the incidence of painful periods and the severity of the condition. A few cases need more than simple pain killers, and modern treatment, including oral contraceptives that inhibit ovulation, is very effective.

AMENORRHEA (*stopped or missed periods*): Doctors talk of 'physiological' amenorrhea (pregnancy, the menopause, after childbirth, the amenorrhea of the young menstruant) and 'pathological' amenorrhea. The commonest causes of the latter are anxiety and stress, malnutrition, obesity, chronic intoxication (lead poisoning, addictions), the pill and certain illnesses (tuberculosis, anemia, cancer). Amenorrhea always needs to be investigated by a doctor. Periods should not be 'brought on' by hormones, as these will not be real menses, but hormone-induced bleeds which solve no problems and create new dilemmas.

MENORRHAGIA (*heavy periods, hyper menorrhea*): This means regular periods in which the woman looses more blood than usual. These can be short but heavy menorrhagia or long periods with a lighter daily loss. Menorrhagia is common at the beginning and end of a woman's menstrual life. The causes are various and include physiological causes (see above), fibroids, polyps, blood diseases, upsets in hormone levels, and the so-called idiopathic, or unknown causes. An older term for menorrhagia was an issue of blood or a *flux*.

METRORRHAGIA (*metrostasis*): Is a term used to describe periods or bleeding from the womb which is irregular (not cyclical). It can be continuous or intermittent. It occurs in abnormal pregnancy states (*abortion**, *ectopic pregnancy**) or as a result of a 'surface bleed' in the reproductive tract. In the interests of health, it needs prompt investigation by a gynecologist.

POLYMENORRHEA (*epimenorrhea*): This is regular (cyclical) bleeding which is normal in amount, but which occurs too frequently (perhaps a period of four days occurring every 20 days). Usually in such cases the womb is normal, but there is a disturbance of the complicated relationship that exists between the *pituitary** gland and the ovaries. Treatment can be with hormones.

EPIMENORRHAGIA (*polymenorrhagia*): This implies regular (cyclical) bleeding which is both too frequent and in excess of normal amounts, for example a period pattern of eight days loss every 21 days. Usually it means that both the ovaries and the womb are disturbed in function. Often the internal sex organs become temporarily overfilled with fluids. It is also seen in anxiety states and in pelvic inflammation.

PREMENSTRUAL TENSION: About 20–30 percent of all women experience premenstrual tension (or blues). Usually, they are said to be ultra-feminine and have well developed breasts and nipples, but this does not always apply. The three characteristics of pre-menstrual tension may be summarized as a triad of irritability, depression and lethargy. If it is making life difficult for a woman, medical treatment with hormones, tranquilizers, etc., is successful.

Pregnancy Tests

A large amount of the chorionic gonadotrophic hormone starts circulating in the blood and urine of a recently pregnant woman. The first reliable pregnancy test, called the Ascheim-Zondek test (first described in 1927) involved injecting immature female mice with the urine to be tested and examining their ovaries for egg-ripening changes 100 hours later. This was widely superseded by the Hogben test, which used to make the xenopus toad lay an egg and give a quicker result. Modern tests do not use animals but chemicals, and can be 'read' with accuracy within seconds. Few tests can exclude pregnancy with a high degree of accuracy until 10 days after a woman's period has been missed. X-rays can show the body of a developing fetus within 9-12 weeks of pregnancy. An experienced doctor can diagnose pregnancy by means of an internal examination at about 8–12 weeks.

Early pregnancy is characterized by one or more of the following symptoms: 1. stopping of periods (amenorrhea); 2. morning sickness, unexplained nausea or appetite changes; 3. pain and tenderness in the breasts; 4. an increase in the frequency of passing urine. There are also other early signs of pregnancy. From the sixth to the eighth week of the pregnancy, the surface veins on the breasts appear more obvious, the nipple and its surrounding areola darkens and small enlarged lumps (Montgomery's tubercles) appear. The doctor will also note that the vagina inside looks blue rather than pink, and when it is examined with a speculum, enlarged arteries are visible, pulsating high up in the vagina. Also, the cervix may feel softer than usual. Soon the womb begins to feel softer too. It may also be felt to contract and is larger than would be expected in the non-pregnant state. Between the eighth and twelfth week, it is possible to demonstrate *Hegar's sign:* the doctor places his left hand firmly on the patient's lower abdomen while examining her internally with the right hand: if she is pregnant, the doctor can by gentle pressure feel the fingers of both hands virtually meeting, because the enlarged womb has already started to rise up out of the pelvis into the abdomen.

Later in pregnancy, the breasts enlarge and may show stretch marks on them. The areola becomes enlarged and a little fluid (called colostrum) can be expressed from the nipple. At the same time, the baby (fetus), which started as a ZYGOTE (the cell resulting from fertilization of the two cells of sexual reproduction, the sperm and the egg), is now enlarging the womb greatly and is felt as a hard abdominal mass which contracts from time to time. Later it will be felt to move, its heart beats can be heard and a single dark line, the *linea nigra,* will appear, running down the centre of the abdomen, together with stretch marks both there and perhaps on the thighs.

At an early stage in pregnancy it is necessary for a woman to be examined by a doctor. As well as a gynecological and general examination, various blood tests will be carried out. These will avoid many pregnancy hazards and give advanced warning of others, and will at least include a blood group and anemia testing, a test against syphilis and tests for 'Rh' (Rhesus) grouping.

RHESUS FACTOR testing is most necessary. It gets its name from the little Rhesus monkeys used in the experimental work that produced important new knowledge in the management of pregnancy and the health of the newborn baby. By far the larger number of people are Rhesus-*positive,* but there is a racial variation—White Europeans and Americans are 85 per cent positive, Negros are 90 per cent positive and Mongoloid races are 100 per cent positive. If a woman is Rhesus-*negative,* a problem exists if she had previously been sensitized to the more common Rhesus-positive blood, which can happen if she has carried a Rhesus-positive baby in her womb, or has had an injection or transfusion with Rhesus-positive blood. If, once sensitized, she again falls pregnant with a Rhesus-positive baby, antibodies caused by her own prior sensitization can pass through the placenta and enter the developing fetus and cause damage to its blood cells. (This does not happen when a Rh-negative woman is pregnant for the first time.)

In the past, the so-called Rh-incompatability disease often caused severely jaundiced and anemic babies to be born. Their blood sometimes had to be exchanged by transfusion at birth, and many babies died. Now, in hospitals, all Rhesus-negative mothers are given an injection of Rhesus antibody (obtained from male volunteers) at the end of labour or abortion. This 'mops up' any possible sensitizing material and prevents antibodies that can be dangerous in a subsequent pregnancy.

Fallopian Tube

Gabriele Fallopio, a 16th-century anatomist, discovered and described, among other things, the ovaries and the paired tubes *(oviducts)* that transport eggs from the ovary down towards the womb. If intercourse takes place at the favourable time (between the eighth and the eighteenth day of a 28-day cycle), then an egg (ovum) will probably be in the middle third of the 4in (10cm) long tube of a fertile woman, the only place where fertilization can take place. The fertilized egg then will immediately start to develop as it floats downwards towards the womb, where it implants itself into the lining of the womb and starts to grow into a baby.

The Fallopian tube has several parts. At its farthest end from the womb it lies very close to the ovary, and is shaped rather like the 'bell' of a trumpet. The rim is covered with little tentacle-like structures that wind themselves around the ovary and pick up the newly-produced egg from its surface. The wide end of the tube gradually tapers down to a very narrow portion *(isthmus),* where the chances of sperm meeting egg are high. Finally, the 'near end' of the Fallopian tube dives through the wall of the womb and opens into its internal cavity. The cells lining the inside of the wider half of the Fallopian tubes have tiny hairlike cilia on their surface. These waft the egg gently down towards the middle of the tube to meet the upward-swimming sperm cells.

Nature does not often make mistakes, but when she does even small ones can be devastating. If an egg cell is fertilized and for some reason instead of passing down into the womb it chooses to develop in the Fallopian tube, or much more rarely floats back into the abdomen, trouble occurs. Such an out-of-place pregnancy is called an *ectopic pregnancy*.*

The Fallopian tubes can also become infected, in which case the condition is called SALPINGITIS. (*Gonorrhea** may cause salpingitis.) Most troubles in the Fallopian tubes can be diagnosed by a vaginal and abdominal examination. The LAPAROSCOPE is used to help diagnose difficult cases.

Ectopic Pregnancy

Ectopic means 'out of place' and refers to what happens if a fertilized egg does not go on down the *Fallopian tube** to the womb in the normal way. Usually there is some mechanism to hold the fertilized egg in the tube for just three days, after which it continues its downward journey, which probably takes a matter of hours only. The dividing egg still floats around the womb for two more days before it clings to the wall somewhere and burrows into the lining. This whole mechanism is complex and not yet completely understood. Like all complex mechanisms it can go wrong.

In about one in 300 pregnancies, the egg is halted in its journey down and stays in the tube for the full five days after which is burrows to obtain nourishment to survive. Not finding itself in the womb, it burrows into the wall of the tube—quite the wrong place for any dividing live egg to be,

because it has a thin wall with a thin muscle and a lining unsuitable to the developing egg. All the same, the egg will quite often survive, go on dividing and even form a tiny fetus. The future health of the mother and *very* rarely, of the child, too, depends on what happens next. Just once in a blue moon, there is almost miraculously a large enough blood supply for the nourishment of the embryo, and it can grow as well outside the womb as if it had been implanted in the wall. More often, however, the fetus just dies and nobody knows that this has happened or that anything is wrong, except that the tube may be blocked and the reason for this may never be discovered.

The most frequent sequence of events is as follows. The growing, burrowing egg finds its way into a small blood vessel, and some bleeding occurs around the place. This bleeding gives rise to pain low down in the abdomen, which may not be very severe. A little blood is lost from the vagina and a little blood comes out of the end of the tube

into the peritoneal cavity and causes more pain. There may be frequent bleeding episodes, each time accompanied by pain, and these may be repeated several times over in the course of the following six weeks or more.

If a large blood vessel is eroded there is an emergency. Much bleeding takes place, the patient feels faint and often does faint. She looks pale and she lies down. When this happens, the blood in the peritoneal cavity flow up underneath her diaphragm and she feels pain referred into one shoulder or both of them. This dramatic but everyday occurrence is known as a ruptured ectopic pregnancy, and every gynecologist has operated on many of them.

The presence of an IUD contraceptive seems to make ectopic pregnancy much more likely to occur. All women who miss a period while using a IUD need very careful medical supervision and an early pregnancy test.

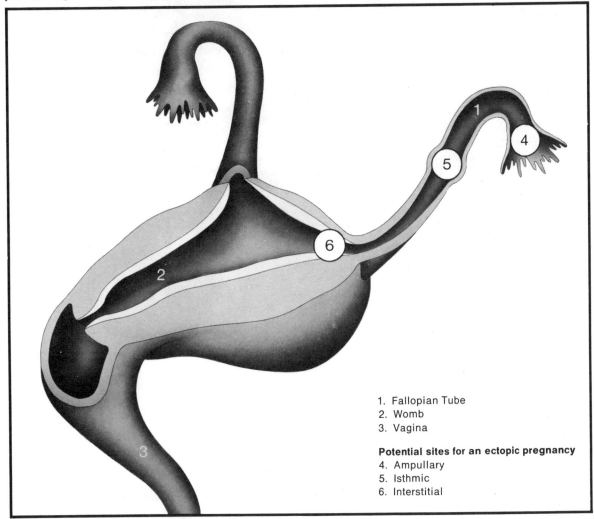

1. Fallopian Tube
2. Womb
3. Vagina

Potential sites for an ectopic pregnancy
4. Ampullary
5. Isthmic
6. Interstitial

Glands

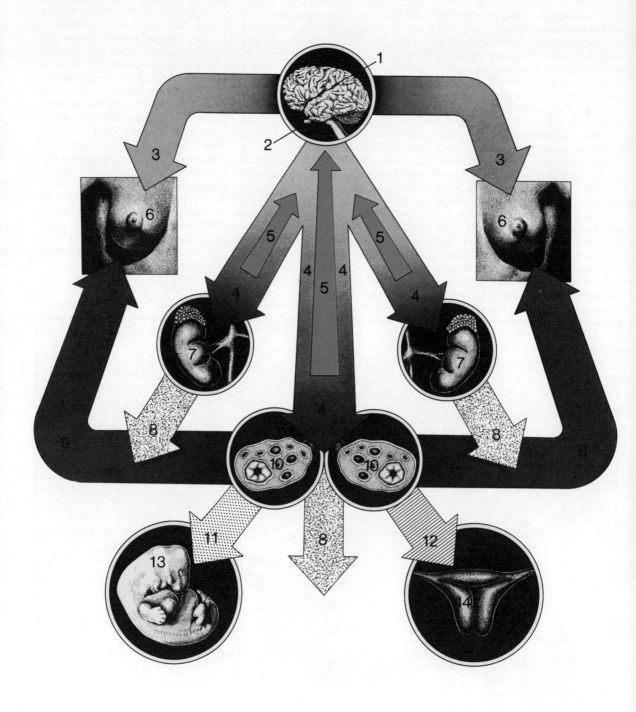

1. The brain
2. Hypothalamus and Pituitary glands
3. Lactation hormones
4. Gonadotrophic hormones
5. Hormone feed-back to brain
6. Lactating breast
7. Kidney with Adrenal gland
8. Male hormones
9. Ovarian hormone
10. Ovary
11. Progesterone
12. Estrogen
13. Fetus
14. Secondary sex organs

The *ovaries** are the primary sex glands in the female. Hormones from the *pituitary** gland control the process of egg-cell expulsion (*menstrual cycle**). The ovary also produces hormones on its own account and in this it resembles the *testes**. Estrogens and progesterones are the main hormones produced by ovaries, but woman also produces at least three male sex hormones as well. The main function of the hormone *estrogen* is the stimulation of the *secondary sex organs*, vulva, vagina, Fallopian tubes, womb and breasts. Progestogens are mainly involved in the maintenance of a pregnancy should one occur and, together with estrogen, also affect various parts of the secondary sex organs.

The PITUITARY is a tiny, hazel-nut-sized gland situated below the centre of the brain in both sexes. It is a sort of master computer that programmes every gland in the body and monitors and controls its various 'slave-station' glands, especially the ovaries. It produces hormones that 'tell' the ovary when to develop and shed eggs and also when to produce progesterones. The latter are also produced in big production sites in the *placenta* in the pregnant woman. The pituitary also produces a multipurpose hormone called *prolactin,* one of the functions of which is to stimulate the breasts to produce milk. The *hypothalamus* is a part of the pituitary complex.

The ADRENAL glands are situated over each kidney in both sexes. They share a complex function which includes sexual differentiation. They produce variable amounts of many of the sex hormones. If they become overactive, they can produce large amounts of male sex hormone in both sexes, as a result of which women change in appearance quite strikingly to resemble men. Their clitoris enlarges, their faces become hairy, and muscles develop in size. These women also lose their heterosexual impulses. Most of these changes can be reversed by modern medical treatment.

The THYROID is a single gland situated in the neck. Its main function is the control of the body's metabolic rate. Only if it goes wrong does it produce secondary sexual effects. An enlarged thyroid gland, giving an attractive fullness to the neck, occurs in many adolescent girls to such an extent that this is sometimes referred to as a secondary sex characteristic.

The *prostate** in the male, apart from its directly sexual function, produces prostaglandin.

Cryptorchism

Cryptorchism, (or cryptorchidism, meaning literally 'hidden testes'), is commonly referred to as undescended testes, but not all *hidden* testes are really cases of UNDESCENDED TESTES. To protect the testes from injury, they can be forced back inside the pelvis (where they originated in the fetus) by a powerful reflex of the Cremaster muscle. The Cremaster (or Cremasteric) reflex can be shown in action if the inner side of the thigh is lightly stroked. The muscle itself is hidden from view inside the body, and moves the testes upwards by its connection with the covering of the scrotum and the spermatic tube. A typical effect is seen by any male who takes a plunge into icy water. Real undescended testes fail to migrate down into the scrotum as they should by the time a child is born. Though cryptorchism of a reflex nature does not develop until a baby is a few days old, it is possible to recognize undescended testes at birth.

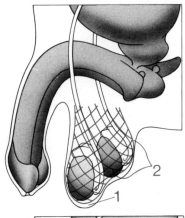

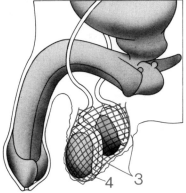

1. Scrotal sac
2. Relaxed Cremaster muscle net
3. Retracted Cremaster muscle net
4. Testes drawn upward

Orgasmic Dysfunction

Orgasm is an involuntary thing, like a sneeze, and cannot be willed. Most people find out how to get to orgasm either by experience with a partner, or by masturbation, and if anybody doubts if they have had an orgasm, one can be sure they have not. A satisfactory definition of orgasm has not yet been produced, but the modern sexology pioneered by *Masters and Johnson** has coined many new phrases to help us understand it. One such phrase is orgasmic dysfunction. When scientists put 'dys' in front of a word they mean 'bad'; thus orgasmic dysfunction means bad functioning of orgasms, in the same way as dysmenorrhea means bad functioning of menstruation. However, in that case, *painful* menstruation is really the common-sense use of the word, and in rather the same way, when we talk about orgasmic dysfunction we do not really mean bad orgasm, instead we mean *difficulty* with orgasm. It can occur in the male in various ways. In some cases, a man can have his orgasm so quickly that he cannot wait to penetrate the vagina at all, or he ejaculates so quickly during intercourse that his partner has no chance to reach a high level of sexual excitement. This is called the orgasmic dysfunction of *premature ejaculation**.

A common female orgasmic dysfunction is caused by another 'dys' problem —dyspareunia—literally meaning badly mated, but in actual fact describing the condition of painful intercourse. If a woman experiences painful sex, she certainly will not have an orgasm. Sometimes a woman reacts to painful sex by developing the condition known as *vaginismus**. (For quaint historical reasons, the name of the condition has generally retained its German form when mentioned in English.) A woman suffering from vaginismus tightly closes her vagina by contracting all the muscles of her perineum and those of her thighs as well. The physical causes of vaginismus include a host of gynecological conditions, and the doctor at his clinic should be able to diagnose them. A vaginal discharge (*leucorrhea**) may make a woman sore inside and therefore make penetration by the man painful. Skin conditions can sometimes make the sexual skin tender, itchy or painful. Psychological upsets can also cause vaginismus. (See also *Frigidity**.)

Cyst

A cyst is a growth that has a very fine, tough wall and is full of liquid. It can develop from several sex organs. Ovarian cysts are rarely diagnosed until they reach the size of a pigeon's egg, unless a LAPAROSCOPE is used. Sometimes they stay small, but they can grow enormously. Some of the earliest gynecology involved operations to remove ovarian cysts that were so large that they prevented their owners from walking about. Nowadays ovarian cysts are easily removed by the operation of ovarian cystectomy. A few ovarian cysts undergo malignant changes and so early removal becomes essential.

Cysts of BARTHOLIN'S GLANDS in the vulval region occur commonly. Once infected, they make walking, standing, sitting and intercourse very uncomfortable. The gland produces normally a colorless secretion that keeps the lips of the vulva moist. When inflamed, a swelling occurs at the base of one of the labia minora and a minor operation is necessary.

FIBROIDS (*Fibromyoma, myoma*) are common gynecological tumors and are made almost entirely of muscle of the womb. Usually a 'fibroid' is really a mass of little ones—as many as 200, but commonly from 5–30. They are seldom completely round and are more likely to have an irregular shape. They are slow to grow but can get to be quite large. They occur in 10 percent of women over 40 and cause symptoms generally between the age of 35–45. The commonest symptom produced is MENORHAGIA. The usual treatment is by removal of the womb (*hysterectomy**) if symptoms become worrying. However, more doctors are now performing MYOMECTOMY, an operation which leaves the womb whole while removing enlarged fibroids.

Cancer of the main part of the womb usually occurs between the age of 50–60, although it can develop in young women. It is most common in women who have not been pregnant. Usually, the only symptom is irregular bleeding and a not very heavy vaginal discharge. Pain of an unusual character is noted in 15 percent of all patients with this cancer. It appears in the stomach or in both sides of the pelvis and lasts for only one or two hours each day. Diagnosis of this type of cancer is by a D & C* operation in most cases.

Cancer of the cervix can be diagnosed before it develops into a true malignancy. A routine SMEAR TEST is taken, in which cells from the cervix are rubbed off onto a wooden spatula (a bit like an ice cream stick) and are then examined on a glass slide under a microscope. Cancer of the womb is a very dangerous disease. About 10% of all women who die of cancer, die of womb cancer, and in 6.5% of these cases the cancer is on the cervix. Sometimes the first sign of a cancer of the womb is a red spot on the cervix called a CERVICAL EROSION. But in almost all cases of erosion, the smear test excludes cancer. When cancer is suspected from a smear test, a minor operation (*cone biopsy*) removes some of the cervix for special sectioning. Often no further treatment is required, but if a growth is found, hysterectomy is performed.

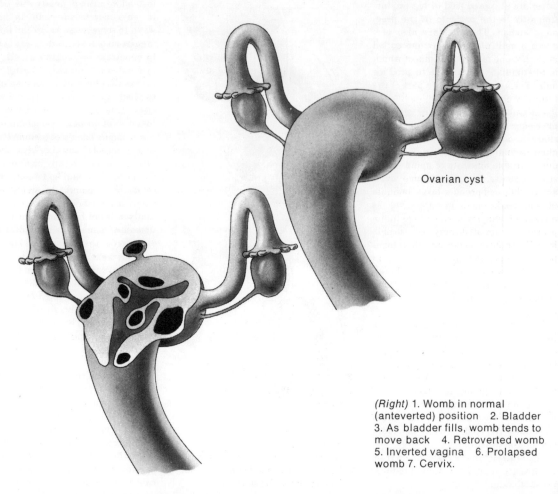

Ovarian cyst

(*Right*) 1. Womb in normal (anteverted) position   2. Bladder 3. As bladder fills, womb tends to move back   4. Retroverted womb 5. Inverted vagina   6. Prolapsed womb 7. Cervix.

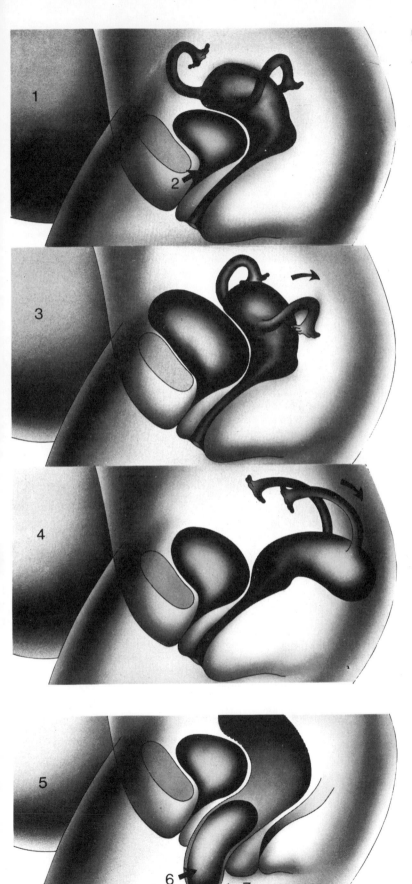

Womb Prolapse

The ancient Greeks believed that the womb (*hustera* in Greek) moved about inside the body. When women behaved strangely, they thought it was because they were having trouble with their wombs moving about and upsetting them. Thus we get the word 'hysteria'— a disease predominently occurring in women. We now know this idea is ridiculous, for the womb does not change places or cause hysteria. It does, however, undergo a variety of changes in position within the pelvis.

Usually, the womb rests on top of the bladder and is therefore lying roughly at an angle of 90° to the vagina. In other words, it is pointing forwards, towards the front of the body and we say it is ANTEVERTED. A doctor, or a woman herself, feeling the inside of her vagina, will then be able to feel her cervix, or neck of the womb, pointing out from the forward part of her vagina. Sometimes, however, the womb lies with the main part of its body pointing backwards. In this case we say the womb is RETROVERTED, and the cervix is then usually felt right at the top of the vagina or slightly more pointing out from the back wall of the vagina. As well as the whole womb lying in a different position, it can bend—often where the neck of the womb joins the main body of the womb. About 15 per cent of all wombs are retroverted. In the large majority of cases this causes no problems, although sometimes it can be responsible for *dyspareunia**.

The other way in which a womb may move out of its usual position is by prolapsing. It can even end up right outside the body—doctors call this *procidentia*, from the Latin for 'to fall'. There are various reasons for *prolapse** of the womb. Sometimes a woman is born with rather poor or weak supports to the womb. Sometimes the supports of the womb are disturbed by childbirth. A woman can start a prolapse by gaining weight, lifting very heavy weights, or straining repeatedly to open her bowels. At times, a small tumour in the womb makes itself known first of all as a prolapse. A sensation of swelling or fullness of the vagina, or that something is 'coming down inside' announces a prolapse and urinary symptoms—difficulty in passing the motions, backache, discharge or MENORRHAGIA— occur. A doctor can easily diagnose and treat prolapse.

Menopause

The menopause (stopping of periods) is the period in a woman's life, lasting from one to five years, during which various changes take place in her sex organs as a result of changes in hormone production by the ovaries. These changes are sexual and physical. The sexual ones can be summarized as follows:

1 The sexual response of women over fifty is slower. It takes about one to five minutes of sexual foreplay for the vagina to lubricate sufficiently to allow comfortable penetration to occur.

2 The vagina does not expand as much during sexual intercourse as it does in younger women. This added tightness during the climacteric often makes for very satisfactory sexual sensation in the male.

3 The labia (lips) of the vagina are less liable to show the colour changes that occur in younger women during sexual foreplay, and they no longer flatten out and become raised as they do in the young female when she is sexually excited.

4 There is a lesser degree of separation of the labia during sexual excitement.

5 The hood over the clitoris tends to shrink as a woman ages. This tends to expose the clitoris more easily to sexual stimulation.

6 The fat under the mons veneris (pubis) tends to disappear and the pubic hair becomes thinner.

There are changes in the workings of sexual intercourse during the CLIMACTERIC, too. The duration of the orgasm is reduced. The vaginal contractions that characterize orgasm remain, but their number is reduced by about half, as are the womb contractions that occur in orgasm. Most surveys show that women masturbate more frequently in the climacteric and this carries on until they reach the age of about sixty, then this urge for sexual stimulation gradually decreases.

The average age when periods cease varies widely throughout the world. In the USA, fifty is the generally accepted age, and in Britain the average is about forty-seven. In the islands north of Scotland, however, it moves up to fifty-five. In most civilized countries, the menopause comes later now than it did —approximately four years later than in the last century. The age at which it occurs does not depend on what a girl's age was when the periods started.

Strangely, the monopause and climacteric are peculiar to humans, for in animals egg release, and therefore fertility, continues into old age.

There are more old wives' tales about the menopause than any other aspect of human sexuality. It is not related to how many children a woman has had, what sort of periods she has experienced (heavy or slight), how many times she has had intercourse, or whether she lives in a hot or cold environment. The only factors that seem to influence it are social, economic and family circumstances.

The commonest way of knowing that the menopause has arrived is for the periods to decrease gradually in the amount and in the frequency of the menstrual loss of blood over a period of several months or even years. Sometimes, however, the periods just stop and that's that. Excessive and prolonged bleeding is never a sign of a normal menopause, and any bleeding that occurs after the menopause makes a visit to the doctor a *must*.

The breasts will sometimes change at the menopause, but quite often they do not. This is because most of the breast tissue is fat, and it is only the small glandular part of the breast that tends to disappear. If women gain weight at the menopause and through the whole of the climacteric, it is due to nothing but overeating.

The most difficult part of this CHANGE OF LIFE for women is the psychological side of things. Largely, this is due to a conditioning process, the result of years and years of a thoroughly unscientific attitude to life that equates the *change* with a change for the worse. In fact, many women find it is a change for the better. A study that involved 4,000 women doctors disclosed that in 90 per cent of them the menopause and the climacteric did not interfere with their way of life. About 5–10 per cent of women experience emotional problems including depression, headaches, insomnia, hot flushes (not flashes), heart thumping (palpitation) or excessive dryness of the vagina during the climacteric. Medical treatment will always help. One form is hormone replacement, in which synthetic or natural hormones are given to replace those no longer being produced by the ovaries to any large extent at the menopause. This is very effective in the management of a 'bad' menopause, but does sometimes provide its own problems, affecting a person's hormone balance generally. Further medical advice should be sought if this happens.

Fertility, Sterility

The Latin word *fertilis*, from which we derive our present-day concept of fertility, literally meant 'fruitful'. Today, fertility has an almost exclusively procreative sense (e.g., eggs, seeds, men or women are fertile or infertile), although we do still use the word in its older and wider sense (e.g., 'a fertile imagination').

The basic facts of human fertility were learned largely as a result of the development of simple microscopes about 300 years ago. The human egg cell (ovum) is very much like the egg cells of all animal species. Even under the microscope, the eggs of mice and women are difficult, if not impossible, to distinguish. But an egg cell is unlike other cells in two prime ways: it is much larger (the human egg can just be seen by the naked eye), and it has in it only half the full number of chromosomes for a cell (23 instead of 46). This clearly leaves the egg cell incomplete and it is incapable of a separate existence for more than a few days. If, however, it is fertilized by a sperm cell (a minute structure compared to the egg—1/1000 of an inch (.025mm) in diameter at its head end with a 12/1000 inch (0.305mm) long tail), which also has 23 chromosomes, it will start to grow and eventually form a fetus.

Thus, we see the dual nature of fertility. The child is the result of a union of two fertile people. There are many occasions where the fertility of the union can be interrupted, leading to sterility. Yet sterility is seldom considered a dual concept, and one partner or the other tends to be blamed for the defect. In many ways this is unfair. A low-powered fertility may come about as a result of the sum of the fertility of both partners. It is more sensible to think of *relative infertility* in place of the old concept of one-sided *sterility*.

Of course, sterility can be specific to one partner. A man with no testes or a woman with no ovaries is unarguably sterile, but a woman with, for instance, an abnormality of her Fallopian tubes may be *relatively* infertile. Whether the union is a fertile one or not will depend on the relative fertility of her mate. If he is highly fertile, the union may still result in a child, but if he has low fertility, the chances could be lower.

The common causes of infertility or sterility are as follows:

In the male:

1 failure to produce sperm in sufficient numbers and with the capacity to fertilize.

2 obstruction of the epididymis, vas or ejaculatory ducts.

3 failure to deposit sperm in the vagina.

In the female:

1 failure to produce eggs frequently or to produce eggs capable of being fertilized.

2 pelvic adhesions interferring with the passage of the egg.

3 partial or complete obstruction of both Fallopian tubes.

4 hostility to the newly fertilized egg or the sperm in the womb, cervix or vagina.

5 specific hostility to the sperm by sperm 'antibodies'.

6 age (female fertility falls sharply after 35, and sterility is total at 52).

7 certain pelvic tumours and endometriosis.

8 coital errors.

Statistically, the prime cause of infertility is found much more often in the woman than the man. Some 40 per cent of all male partners are found to be *subfertile* when a union appears infertile. But only one man in a hundred who enters into a union with a desire to produce progeny proves to be sterile.

Investigation of the infertile union is usually delayed for two years after regular sexual intercourse (without contraceptives) starts to take place. This is because out of every hundred couples who desire a child, 65 will have started a pregnancy within six months, 80 per cent in a year and 90 per cent in two years. This means 10 per cent of all couples remain childless without medical aid after two years of regular unprotected coitus. Complete and skilled medical investigation of the infertile union will bring success in about half of these cases. A drop-out rate of about one in three occurs, and if more couples completed the course, it is likely that the failure rate could be lower.

Fertility investigations of a purely clinical nature usually start with the woman. If she appears to be normal gynecologically after a simple examination, it is usual to examine two or three samples of the man's sperm. Only if there appears to be nothing abnormal after this examination is it justifiable to go on to further, more sophisticated female tests.

Hysterectomy

Hysterectomy (womb removal) is one of the most misunderstood operations. It is also probably the operation that is most likely to be carried out for no good reason. Countries vary widely in the percentage of women who have it carried out. The highest rate for hysterectomy is the United States, and among highly developed countries the lowest hysterectomy rate occurs in Britain's National Health Service.

Hysterectomy is what might be called a popular operation with gynecologists because it is relatively easy to perform, warrants a high fee and theoretically should remove all a woman's gynecological problems, as the most common form of the operation only leaves the patient with her vagina. Some patients view hysterectomy as a salvation if gynecological problems have been a constant worry. Afterwards, however, even if they have passed the age of child-bearing, there is often the sense of 'mourning' experienced in the loss of fertility and of an organ that, although unseen, is a badge of femininity.

Broadly speaking, there are two types of hysterectomy—total *(Fig 1)* and subtotal *(Fig 2)*. In the subtotal operation, the cervix is not removed with the body of the womb. There are also two ways of doing hysterectomy operations: through an incision (cut) in the abdomen or through the vagina (vaginal hysterectomy). The choice of operation depends on many things. Sometimes it is not feasible for purely mechanical reasons (i.e., there is not enough room to remove a very large womb through the vagina).

Whether or not the ovaries are removed during a hysterectomy operation depends on many things, particularly on whether or not they appear healthy. Surgeons often remove them in menopausal women who have a hysterectomy for the sake of completeness. One wise gynecologist has said, 'Two ovaries are better than one, one is better than none, save them when you can, remove them when you must'.

The commonest cause for hysterectomy operations being carried out are *fibroids** which are causing severe gynecological symptoms. Sometimes it it feasible just to remove the fibroids (a MYOMECTOMY) and leave the rest of the womb, the Fallopian tubes and the ovaries behind. Often this is, however, technically impossible. A 'good' hysterectomy carried out by a 'good' surgeon for a 'good' reason leaves a woman in better health than she would have been without surgery and has no effect on her sex life.

Phimosis

Phimosis is a shrinking up of the opening of the foreskin in the uncircumcised male. A true phimosis is comparatively rare, but a secondary form is extremely common. In some babies, the foreskin and the head of the penis are not always perfectly separated at birth, and trying to retract the foreskin then leads to a tearing of this little structure. As the body repairs injury, it lays down fibrous tissue which shrinks as it matures, and this what tends to produce a secondary phimosis. Sometimes phimosis occurs in the elderly, and secretions trapped behind the foreskin can produce *balanitis**. A true and permanent phimoisis makes *circumcision** necessary, as otherwise sexual intercourse becomes unsatisfactory and painful.

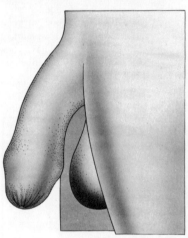

Balanitis

This term describes a condition in which the glans (the bulbous head of the penis) becomes inflamed. It most commonly occurs in uncircumcised men. It is often caused by a retained secretion (*smegma**) underneath the foreskin, so frequent washing and soaking in a warm bath usually settles the condition in a few days. If *phimosis** occurs as well, then *circumcision** should carried out. There are, however, other causes of balanitis, including herpes infection, syphilis, gonorrhea and various tropical diseases involving the male sex organ. A simple form of balanitis is sometimes seen in male babies in conjunction with nappy rash. As this responds to adequate treatment, the condition clears quickly.

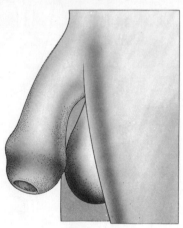

Epididymitis

This is a general inflammation of the *epididymis**, the small structure mainly composed of tubes which lies at the back and above the testicles. If they are inflamed as well, the term used is EPIDIDYMOORCHITIS. Symptoms are rather like those of 'flu'—a generally unwell feeling and an aching sensation around the testicles. In INFECTIVE EPIDIDYMITIS, gonorrhea, syphilis or, more rarely, tuberculosis may be present. Sometimes, mumps can affect the testes and turn into epididymitis called MUMPS ORCHITIS. NON-INFECTIVE EPIDIDYMITIS often follows the strain of lifting something heavy while the bladder is full. This forces urine back down into the tube (vas) connecting the epididymis to the urethra and sets up a 'sterile' inflammation.

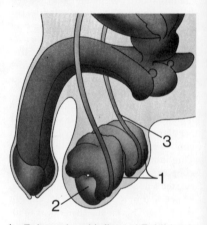

1. Enlarged and inflamed Epididymis
2. Testis
3. Vas Deferens

Hydrocele

Hydrocele (literally, a water tumor) is a condition in which a watery fluid collects around the testes and the *epididymus**. It tends to increase inside and inflate the scrotal sac, producing a condition sometimes referred to as 'big balls'. Light from a low-wattage lamp held close to the scrotum will cause a hydrocele to glow, showing its shape and size. The commonest type of hydrocele occurs in elderly men, for no known reason. Rarely, a hydrocele develops as a result of an injury to the testes, or secondarily to a tumour or disease. Sometimes it will occur in babies. Although small hydroceles need no treatment and can be left as they are (provided that they are accurately diagnosed as such by a doctor), large ones can be released by 'tapping' (perforation with a large-bore needle under local anesthetic) or by operation.

Urethritis

This is inflammation of the urethra, the tube that leads from the inside of the bladder to the exterior. In the male it passes through the prostate gland and is usually about 8 to 9in long, and in the female it is only about 1½in in length. The urethra can become inflamed in the same way as any other tissue as a result of invasion by bacteria, viruses or chemicals, by rough usage (trauma) or due to things being introduced into it. The female urethra seems more vulnerable in this way than the male urethra, and because of its comparative shortness the inflammation is more liable to spread and involve the bladder, causing *cystitis**.

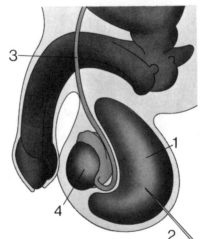

1. Hydrocele behind testis
2. Needle for tapping
3. Vas Deferens
4. Testis

Priapism

Priapism is named after Priapos, the Greek god of gardens and fruit bearing, who was always shown with an enlarged and deformed penis. In the medical sense, it is a rare condition in which a prolonged erection occurs that is not associated with, or relieved by, sexual desire and intercourse. Priapism is always a surgical emergency, because unless the condition is relieved within 24 hours, the penis becomes very painful and *impotence** commonly follows as a complication. The operation consists of draining the organ of blood and stopping any further blood being pumped in. Strangely priapism is relatively common in men who are on dialysis (kidney machine) because of renal failure. It has nothing to do with SATYRIASIS (from satyrs, the woodland creatures in Greek mythology, who were usually shown with erect penises) which is a psychiatric condition of excessive sexual desire in the male.

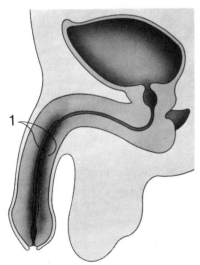

1. Inflamed region

Male Menopause

When a better knowledge of the physiology of *aging** is with us, the question whether or not a male climacteric of menopause occurs may be answered. What is certain, however, is that once intercourse is interrupted, or feared, in the older man, secondary impotence commonly occurs. With loss of potency many men feel older than their years and claim they are 'past it' or 'too old to change'. A very few men actually develop female menopausal symptoms, hot flushes and the like, in the same way as some men develop pregnancy symptoms when their wives are pregnant.

The changes that take place in the sexuality of the older male are well documented. At 50-plus, as compared to 50-minus, the following changes often occur:

1 Erection is delayed. Most older men do not become tumescent until several minutes of sexual stimulation have occurred, but once the man reaches the plateau phase, a stable erection is maintained

2 Testicular elevation and engorgement are less obvious and pre-ejaculation emission does not occur

3 The plateau stage of coitus lasts longer and can indeed be prolonged voluntarily for a considerable time

4 Ejaculation tends to take place in a single stage

5 The volume of semen ejaculated at each coital experience decreases with age. After 24 hours of continence, it is about 0.10–.20 fl oz (3-5 ml) in young men and .07–.10 fl oz (2-3 ml) in older men

6 Even more noticeable is a reduction in the force of semen expulsion—from 1-2 feet (30-60 cm) down to 3-12 inches (8-30 cm)

7 The refractory period after orgasm is extended. This is probably the greatest change, and the period is altered from minutes to hours

8 Detumescence is very rapid, and in old men the penis often collapses immediately after orgasm.

It appears that, provided the aging man's partner enjoys her sexuality and can relate well to her older lover, then there is no deterioration in the quality of the male orgasm. If, however, there is an unsatisfactory or 'turn off' partner, the older man will often experience a better orgasm by masturbation than by coitus. Male fertility persists often into very old age, and in this sense there is no real male climacteric.

Tomi Ungerer

Prostatitis

The prostate gland lies at the base of the bladder in the male. The prostatic urethra goes through it to allow urine to be passed. Prostatitis is a vague disease of an uncertain nature. It is said to be common in people with sedentary occupations and in those having a great deal of sex. It is also said to be brought on by exposure to cold, too much alcohol, a lowered resistance, urinary infection, anemia and debility, as well as a secondary effect from chronic prostatic obstruction. When medical conditions are connected with such a wide variety of possibilities, it usually means that the condition is ill-understood. Some authorities are ex-tremely sceptical about the condition of chronic prostatitis. The aching pain in the perineum, the frequency of water passing and the pain on passing water suggests that anxiety and worry, per-haps sexual anxiety especially, are more involved than anything else. Surgeons who believe that prostatitis really exists, describe the gland as being swol-len, tender and hot when it is examined by a finger placed in a victim's rectum. Prostatitis of the chronic type is often treated by prostatic massage by the rectal route and this is said to be fol-lowed by the passage of urine that is cloudy and from which various germs can be grown. Doubtless much 'pros-tatitis' is really due to enlargement of the prostate gland and subsequent 'prostatism'.

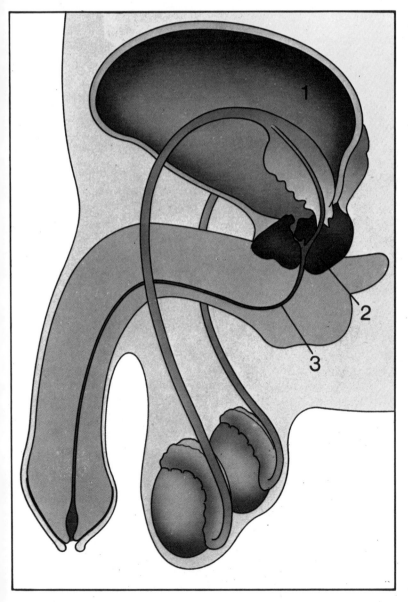

Rejuvenation

This possibility, especially with refer-ence to sexual performance, has fasci-nated mankind since the beginning of history. The earliest remedies involved magic and sorcery, and powerful re-juvenating procedures are mentioned in ancient scriptural works of Asia like the *Veda*. An extract of the fifteen-leaved soma plant was recommended by the famous Indian physician, Su-shruta. Other plants, especially ery-ngo (sea holly), rocket fenugreek, the buttercustard (durian tree fruit), and saw palmetto musk seeds, have had quite serious rejuvenating claims made for them by enthusiastic sponsors, but have never been tested in a modern therapeutic way. Animal and insect substances have also been used, especi-ally the cantharides beetle (Spanish fly), which was popular in Europe from the 16th century onwards. Many of these preparations really act as *aphrod-isiacs** rather than as restorers of youthful health.

Another popular phase in the history of rejuvenation was GLAND TRANS-PLANTS as practised by 'Dr' J. R. Brinkley of Kansas in the 1920s (using goats' testes) and by Serge Varanoff in Europe in the 1930s (using monkeys' testes). Both were really echoing the work of a famous gland-rejuvenation researcher of the previous century, Charles Edouard Brown-Séquard (1817–94). One of the most interesting facets of rejuvenation theory is based on the work of the Austrian physiologist, Eugen Steinach (1861–1944), who found he could rejuvenate sexually inactive rats by what was, to all intents and purposes, a vasectomy operation. Stein-ach's operation became tremendously popular and was carried out on a world-wide basis until the 1940s, but never underwent a well-designed clinical trial. The wealthiest and most popular modern rejuvenationist was undoubt-edly Paul Niehans who ran the famous clinic at Montreux in Switzerland, and rejuvenated kings, politicians, film stars and at least one pope, by the process of cellular therapy (the injec-tion of embryonic sheep's cells) well into the 1960s. Biologists doubt that such cell therapy is anything more than an elaborate con.

1. Bladder distended with retained urine
2. Enlarged Prostate gland
3. Urethra

Acne

This an infuriatingly common disease of both sexes which is closely linked with the developing of sexual function. For some ill-understood reason, the sudden upsurge of sex hormones during adolescence and early adult life causes the character of the grease in the glands in the skin (sebum) to change. Instead of acting as a useful lubricant, it becomes very thick and viscous. This causes blackheads, whiteheads or comedos to form. It seems likely, too, that a germ called *propionibacterium acnes,* often found in the depths of the grease glands, also plays a part in the accumulation of sebum in these glands, and induces them to rupture into the skin. Then the various fatty substances (horny cells, lipids and fatty acids) cause small toxic abscesses to develop in the skin of the face, shoulders and back.

Knowledge of the dual nature of acne (hormones plus acne germs) has lead to several very effective treatments. Certain antibiotics (drugs called tetracylines and erythromycin) tend if taken by mouth to accumulate in the grease-secreting glands. This does not occur with penicillin or the 'sulpha' drugs, and quite small (subtherapeutic) doses of such drugs can control acne on a long-term basis, until the condition commonly subsides of its own. Usually, this is at the passing of the teenage years, but occasionally untreated acne tends to persist into adult life. Another substance called benzoyl peroxide seems to have the same antibacterial effect, but acts faster, and has the advantage of being applied locally in five per cent to 10 per cent solution.

Another treatment called retinoic acid seems to work by breaking down cell adhesions within blackheads, so that cells cannot become impacted and thus form large blackheads and thus encourage acne spots to develop. Old-fashioned remedies (sulphur, phenol, resorcinol) relied on this principle but they could not penetrate the skin as easily as does retinoic acid.

Acne has nothing to do with dirtiness, 'bad living', masturbation, constipation or eating improper food. A combination of the remedies known to be most effective usually clears the condition quickly and so removes a barrier that tends to spoil the young lives of many people with the feeling of isolation and shame that acne often brings. Due to its own intrinsic disturbance of hormone levels, the commonly used 'combined pill' often cures acne in young women.

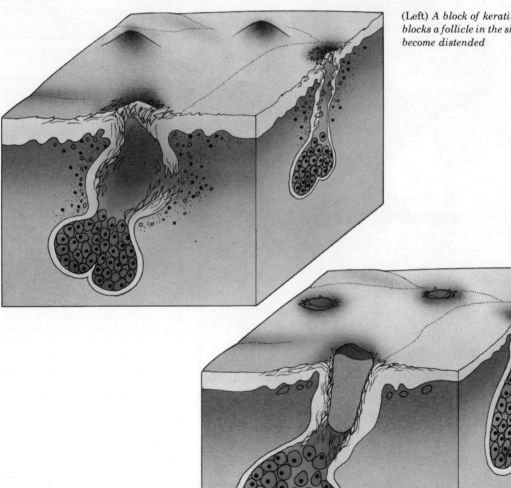

(Left) *A block of keratin (or blackhead) blocks a follicle in the skin, causing it to become distended*

(Right) *The contents of the follicle rupture into the skin, and a small abcess or pustule is formed*

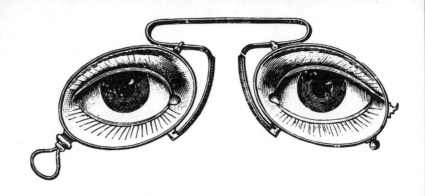

READER'S GUIDE

The best of the world's erotica - plus
classified further reading lists.

Erotica

The Song of Solomon
Aristophanes, The Lysistrata
Musa Puerilis *in the Greek Anthology*
Apuleius, The Golden Ass
Ovid, The Art of Love (*Ars Amatoria*)
Lucian, Dialogues
Boccaccio, The Decameron (1353)
Pietro Aretino, Postures, *also known as
the* Sonnets (*Sonetti Lussuriosi, c.* 1527)
Pietro Aretino, Discussions
(*Ragionamenti, c.* 1536)
Michel Millot, L'Escole des Femmes
(1655)
Brantôme, Lives of Gallant Ladies (*Les
Femmes Galantes*, 1666)
Rochester, The Farce of Sodom (*c.* 1680)
John Cleland, Fanny Hill (1749)
Casanova, Memoirs (*complete edition*,
1960)
Choderlos de Laclos, Les Liaisons
Dangereuses (1782)
de Sade, The 120 Days of Sodom (1785)
Robert Burns, The Merry Muses of
Caledonia (*c.* 1786)
de Sade, Justine (1791)
de Sade, Juliette (1797)
Restif de la Bretonne, Anti-Justine (1798)
André de Nerciat, Le Diable au Corps
(1803)
'*Alcide de M—*', (*Alfred de Musset*)
Gamiani (*c.* 1840)
de Lautréamont, Les Chants de
Maldoror (1867)
anon., Aus den Memoiren einer Sängerin
(1868, 1875)
anon., The Romance of Lust (1873–6)
Mark Twain, 1601 (1876)
anon., The Pearl, A Journal of Facetiae
and Voluptuous Reading (1879;
reprinted 1968)
Sacher-Masoch, Venus in Furs (*Venus
im Pelz*, 1886)
The Whippingham Papers (1888)
'*Walter*', My Secret Life (*c.* 1890)
Paul Verlaine, Femmes (1890)
Paul Verlaine, Hombres (1891)
anon., Teleny, Or the Reverse of the
Medal (1893)
Aubrey Beardsley, The Story of Venus
and Tannhäuser (1895)
Aleister Crowley, White Stains (1898)
Baron Corvo, Letters from Venice
Apollinaire, Memoirs of a Young
Rakehell
James Joyce, Ulysses (1922)
Frank Harris, My Life and Loves (1922)
anon. (*attributed to Jean Cocteau*)
Le Livre Blanc
Georges Bataille, The Story of the Eye
(*Histoire de l'Oeil*, 1928)
D. H. Lawrence, Lady Chatterley's Lover
(1928)
Henry Miller, Tropic of Cancer (1934)
Henry Miller, Tropic of Capricorn (1939)
Stanley Kauffmann, The Philanderer
(1953)
Pauline Réage, The Story of O. (*Histoire
d'O.*, 1954)
Vladimir Nabokov, Lolita (1955)
Terry Southern & Mason Hoffenburg,
Candy (1958)
William Burroughs, The Naked Lunch
(1959)
William Burroughs, The Ticket that
Exploded (1962)
Hubert Selby jr., Last Exit to Brooklyn
(1964)
Gore Vidal, Myra Breckinridge (1968)
Philip Roth, Portnoy's Complaint (1969)
Tomi Ungerer, Fornikon

Further Reading

GENERAL

Everything You Ever Wanted To Know
About Sex But Were Afraid To Ask *by
Dr. David Reuben*
The Modernization of Sex *by Paul
Robinson*
Sex in Human Loving *by Eric Berne*
The Art and Science of Love *by Albert
Ellis*
The Folklore of Sex *by Albert Ellis*
Living is Loving *by Inge & Sten Hegeler*
An ABZ of Love *by Inge & Sten Hegeler*
Catalog of Sexual Consciousness *ed. by
Saul Braun*
Total Sexuality *by John Warren Wells*
Sexual Behavior in the Human Male *by
Dr. Alfred Kinsey*
Sexual Behavior in the Human Female *by
Dr. Alfred Kinsey*
Human Sexual Response *by Dr. William
H. Masters and Virginia E. Johnson*
The Encyclopedia of Sexual Behavior *ed.
by Albert Ellis & Albert Abarbanel*
Fundamentals of Human Sexuality *by
Herant A. Katchadourian & Donald
T. Lunde*
Human Sexual Expression *by Benjamin
A. Kogan*
Human Sexuality *by James L. McCary*
The Sex Handbook *by Handman &
Brennan*
For a Better Sex Life (*SIECUS Study
Guide*)
My Secret Garden, Women's Sexual
Fantasies *by Nancy Friday*
Primal Sensuality *by Paula Newhorn*
Sex and the Nature of Things *by N. J.
Berrill*
Sexual Myths and Fallacies *by James L.
McCary*
Sexuality and Man (*SIECUS Study
Guide*)

(Art)

The Erotic Arts *by Peter Webb*
Studies in Erotic Art *ed. by Bowie &
Christenson*
Eroticism *by Georges Bataille*
Eroticism in Western Art *by Edward
Lucie-Smith*
Erotic Art of the West *by Robert Melville*
Erotic Art of the East *by Philip Rawson*
Primitive Erotic Art *ed. by Philip
Rawson*
The Pin-up, A Modest History *by Mark
Gabor*
The Nude *by Kenneth Clark*
Woman as Sex-object, Studies in Erotic
Art *ed. by Thomas B. Hess & Linda
Nochlin*

4. GENDER

Man Woman, Boy Girl *by John Money &
Anke A. Ehrhardt*
The Transsexual Phenomenon *by Dr.
Harry Benjamin*
The Bisexual Odyssey *by John Paul
Hudson*
Sex and Gender: On the Development of
Masculinity and Femininity *by
Robert J. Stroller*
Sex, Gender and Society *by Ann Oakley*
The Male Machine *by Marc Feigen
Fasteau*
Males and Females *by Corinne Hutt*
The Other Women *by Barry Kay*
Sex Differentiation and Development *ed.
by Colin R. Austin*
Transvestites and Transsexuals: A
Mixed View *by Deborah H. Feinbloom*

1. The LIBERATORS

What Freud Really Said *by David
Stafford-Clark*
Selected Writings *by Wilhelm Reich*
Psychopathia Sexualis *by Dr. Richard
von Krafft-Ebing*
The Sex Researchers *by Edward M.
Brecher*
Studies in the Psychology of Sex *by H.
Havelock Ellis*
Three Essays on the Theory of Sexuality
by Sigmund Freud (ed. James Strachey)
The Sexual Radicals *by Paul A.
Robinson*

2. A SEXUAL GALLERY; 11. PERSON TO PERSON

Games People Play *by Eric Berne*
The Presentation of Self in Everyday Life
by Erving Goffman
The Book of Daniel *by E. L. Doctorow*
People in Love *by Claire Rayner*
Sex and Love *by James Hemming &
Zena Maxwell*
The Book of Love *by David Delvin*

5. SEXUAL DISPLAY

Free Beaches, A Phenomenon of the
California Coast *by Leon Elder*
Nudism Today (*International Naturist
Federation, CH-2075 Thielle,
Switzerland*)
Nudist Society *by William E. Hartman
and others*
Dress and Undress *by Paul Tabori*

6. AROUSAL; 8. ORAL SEX; 9. POSITIONS; 10. ORGASM

An Analysis of 'Human Sexual Response'
ed. by Ruth & Edward Brecher

The Key to Feminine Response in Marriage by Ronald M. Deutsch
The Nature and Evolution of Female Sexuality by Mary Jane Sherfey
The Hite Report by Shere Hite
The Sensuous Woman by 'J'
The Sensuous Man by 'J'
The Joy of Sex by Alex Comfort
More Joy by Alex Comfort
Secrets of Sexual Success by James Archer
The Intimate Kiss by G. Legman
Total Sex by Dr. Herbert A. Otto & Roberta Otto
The Enjoyment of Love in Marriage by LeMon Clark
Understanding the Female Orgasm by Seymour Fisher
The Female Orgasm: Psychology, Physiology, Fantasy by Seymour Fisher
Male Sexual Performance by Sam Julty
The Myth of the Vaginal Orgasm by Ann Koedt
Sex Manners for Advanced Lovers by Robert Chartham
Sex Manners for Men by Robert Chartham
Total Orgasm by Jack Lee Rosenberg
Touching: The Human Significance of the Skin by Ashley Montagu

7. WORRY BLOCKS
Understanding 'Human Sexual Inadequacy' by Fred Belliveau & Lin Richter
Masters and Johnson Explained by Nat Lehrman
Intimate Strangers, Surrogate Sexual Partners by Barbara Roberts
Inside the Sex Clinic by Peter & Barbara Wyden
The New Sex Therapy by Dr. Helen Singer Kaplan
The Illustrated Manual of Sex Therapy by Dr. Helen Singer Kaplan
Sex Without Guilt by Albert Ellis
The Power to Love by Edwin W. Hirsch
Sex in Later Life by Ivor Felstein
Sex and the Over-fifties by Robert Chartham
Sexual Life After Sixty by Isadore Ruben
A Good Age by Alex Comfort

13. WORDS & GRAFFITI
Playboy's Book of Forbidden Words ed. by Robert A. Wilson
The Penthouse Sexindex by Lynn Barber
The Queens' Vernacular, A Gay Lexicon by Bruce Rodgers
(Censorship)
The Illustrated Presidential Report of the Commission on Obscenity and Pornography ed. by Earle Kemp
Not In The Public Interest by David Williams
The End of Obscenity by Charles Rembar
Sex and Society by Martin Seymour-Smith
The Obscenity Laws, A Report by the Working Party set up by . . . The Arts Council of Great Britain (1969)
Mrs. Grundy, Studies in Sexual Prudery by Peter Fryer
The Case Against Pornography ed. by David Holbrook
The Longford Report Against Censorship (National Council for Civil Liberties)

14. BIRTH CONTROL
Sex with Health (Consumers Association)
Contraceptive Technology by Dr. Robert A. Hatcher
Pill on Trial by Paul Vaughan
Vasectomy: The Male Sterilization Operation by Paul J. Gillette
What Every Woman Needs To Know About Abortion by Helene S. Arnstein

15. HEALTH
Microbes and Morals, The Strange Story of Venereal Disease by Theodore Rosebury

16. SEX FOR ONE
Liberating Masturbation, A Meditation on Self Love by Betty Dodson
The Anxiety Makers by Alex Comfort

17. DUO-PLUS
Beginner's Guide to Group Sex by Caroline Gordon
The Groupsex Tapes by Herbert F. Margolis & Paul M. Rubenstein
A History of Orgies by Burgo Patrridge

18. SAME-SEX PARTNERS
Gay Spirit, A Guide to Becoming a Sensuous Homosexual by David Loovis
Lesbian Images by Jane Rule
The Gay Mystique by Peter Fisher
Lesbian Woman by Del Martin & Phyllis Lyon
The Second Sex by Simone de Beauvoir

19. PARAPHILIAS
Sexual Deviation by Anthony Storr
S-M, The Last Taboo by Gerald & Caroline Green
The Complete S&M Questionnaire (D&H Studios)
The Complete Golden Shower Guide (D&H Studios)
The Complete Enema Guide (D&H Studios)
Masochism in Sex and Society by Dr. Theodor Reik
Psychology of Sex Offenders by Albert Ellis
Sexual Deviance and Sexual Deviants ed. by Goode & Troiden
Must We Burn De Sade? by Simone de Beauvoir

20. GROWING UP
Knowing About Sex (3 volumes, each for a different age-group) by James Hemming & Zena Maxwell
A Young Person's Guide to Life and Love by Dr. Benjamin Spock
Boys and Sex by Wardell B. Pomeroy
Girls and Sex by Wardell B. Pomeroy
Facts about Sex for Today's Youth by Sol Gordon
Sex and the Adolescent by Maxine Davis
Sexual Behaviour of Young People by Michael Schofield
Show Me! A Picture Book of Sex for Parents and Children by Will McBride & Helga Fleischauer-Hardt

21. MARRIAGE AND SEX
The Intimate Enemy by George R. Bach & Peter Wyden
Love Today, A New Exploration ed. by Herbert A. Otto
The Future of Marriage by Jessie Bernard
Sexual Adventure in Marriage by Jerome & Julia Rainer
Pairing by George R. Bach & Ronald M. Deutsch
Beyond Monogamy ed. by James R. Smith & Lynn G. Smith
Open Marriage by Nena & George O'Neill
The Complete Handbook For a Sexually Open Marriage by John & Mimi Lobell
The Joys of Open Marriage by Peter & Suzanne Heck
The Affair, Unfaithful Wives and Husbands Reveal Their Secret Lives by Morton Hunt
The History of Human Marriage by Edward A. Westermarck
Renovating Marriage: Towards New Sexual Life Styles ed. by Roger W. Libby & Robert Whitehurst
Jewish Marriage ed. by Peter Elman

22. SOCIETY AND SEX
Eros Denied by Wayland Young
Love in Action by Fernando Henriques
Legal Abortion, The English Experience by A. Hordern
Aspects of Love by Susan Lilar
Male and Female by Margaret Mead
Model Penal Code (2 vols) The American Law Institute

Sexual Behavior and the Law ed. by Ralph Slovenko
The Cradle of Erotica by Allen Edwards
The Jewel in the Lotus, A Historical Survey of the Sexual Culture of the East by Allen Edwards & R. E. L. Masters
(Women's Liberation)
The Female Eunuch by Germaine Greer
The Feminine Mystique by Betty Friedan
The Descent of Woman by Elaine Morgan
Woman's Consciousness, Man's World by Sheila Rowbotham
Our Bodies, Ourselves ed. by The Boston Women's Health Book Collective
Getting Clear, Body Work for Women by Anne Kent Rush
Sexual Politics by Kate Millet
Woman in Sexist Society: Studies in Power and Powerlessness ed. by Vivian Gornick & Barbara K. Moran
(Rape)
Patterns in Forcible Rape by Menachem Amir
Against Our Will, Men, Women and Rape by Susan Brownmiller
A Record of Rape and its Results by Joan Jones
Against Rape by Medea & Thompson
Rape as Social Control by Janice Reynolds
The Politics of Rape by Diana Russell
(Eunuchs & Castrati)
The Keeper of the Bed by Charles Humana
Peter Abelard by Helen Waddell
Recollections of T. G. Jackson by B. H. Jackson
The Castrati in Opera by Angus Heriot
(Religion and Sexual Behaviour; Phallic; Vulvic; Fertility Cult)
The Golden Bough (abridged ed.) by J. G. Frazer
Sex in History by Gordon Rattray Taylor
Sexual Relations in Christian Thought by Derrick S. Bailey
Sex Laws and Customs in Judaism by L. M. Epstein
Sex and Sex Worship by O. A. Wall
Phallic Worship by G. R. Scott

23. DISABILITY AND SEX
Entitled to Love by Wendy Greengross
Not Made of Stone by K. Heslinga
Sexual Options for Paraplegics and Quadraplegics by Mooney, Cole & Chilgren
Life Together by I. Noordqvist
Sex and the Physically Handicapped by W. F. R. Stewart
Human Sexuality in Health and Illness by N. F. Woods
Sex and the Spinal Cord Injured by Eisenberg & Rustad

24. SEXPLOITATION
The Undergrowth of Literature by Gillian Freeman
Pornography Without Prejudice by G. L. Simons
Pornography and Social Deviance by M. J. Goldstein & H. S. Kant
The Other Victorians, A Study of Sexuality and Pornography in Mid-19th-century England by Steven Marcus

25. PROSTITUTION
Prostitution and Morality, A Definitive Report by Harry Benjamin & R. E. Masters
Prostitution and Society by Fernando Henriques
The Call Girl, A Social and Psychoanalytic Study by Harold Greenwald
History of Prostitution by Paul Lacroix

27. CLINIC
Hormones and the Body by Stuart A. Mason

Index

Blackheads, 306
Blackmail, 186, 282
Bladder, 37, 39, 40, 65, 72, 110, 148, 154, 155, 290, 299, 302, 303, 305
'Blame game', 84
Bleeding, 132, 150, 211, 260, 290, 293, 295, 300
  irregular, 298
  menstrual-like, 142
Blessing (wedding), 220
Blind-folding, 183, 187, 190
Blindness, 148, 150, 159, 266
Blisters, 149, 152, 153
Blood, 77, 108, 110, 112, 150, 154, 155, 183, 184, 209, 211, 237, 261, 293, 294, 295, 303
  menstrual, 137, 260, 300
  Rhesus-negative, 294
  Rhesus-positive, 294
  stream, 148, 150, 154
  See Thrombosis.
Blood pressure,
  high, 68, 72, 87, 88, 132
Blood test(s), 146, 149, 150, 153, 216, 226, 294
Blow job, a, 95
Bluebeard myth, 263
Blue movie, 274
Blues, 293
Bodies, dead, 197
Body, 78, 80, 94, 100, 106, 107, 108, 110, 112, 132, 148, 150, 152, 153, 158, 159, 161, 180, 182, 183, 187, 190, 192, 194, 197, 202, 203, 210, 237, 238, 266, 276, 288, 297, 302
Body contact, 69, 152, 261
Body language, 74
Body maps, 33-40, 62
  man, 37-40
  woman, 34-37
Body piercing, 60, 190
Body sensitivity, 92
Body sprays, 80
Body therapy, 19
Bondage, 14, 60, 74, 183, 187, 190, 194, 220, 271
  erotic, 26, 27, 52, 188, 190-191
Boobs, 51
Books and magazines, 192, 270, 271
Boot(s), 183, 190, 192, 194, 195
Boredom, 62, 95, 106, 240, 278
Born out of wedlock, 226
Bosom, 104, 270
Bottom(s), 172, 270, 276
Bowels, 154, 299
Bowsers. See Pubic wigs.
Boxing, 183
Boyfriend(s), 146, 147, 238
Bra burners, 29
Brain, 15, 46, 64, 68, 70, 72, 108, 110, 112, 116, 150, 266, 296, 297
Branding, 183
Brank, 190
Breast(s), 24, 32, 42, 46, 47, 53, 58, 62, 66, 68, 78, 100, 101, 122, 126, 130, 132, 152, 160, 172, 194, 200, 210, 237, 293, 294, 296, 297, 300
  slang words for, 126
Breast cancer. See Cancer(s).
Breath(ing), 107, 108, 112, 187, 190
'Bridal roll'. See Pillow book.
Bridal sheets, 209
Bride(s), 209, 220, 221, 222, 261
Bridegroom(s), 209, 220, 221, 222, 254, 261
Bridle of a horse, 190
British Pregnancy Advisory Service, 124
Broadframe, 43
Brothel(s), 17, 186, 192, 254, 279, 281, 284
Brothers, 225, 230, 246
Buboes, 149, 153
Buckles, 190
Buddhism, 256, 257
Buggery, 169, 171
Bundling, 220
Bunny girl, 276
Butch, 76
Butch female homosexual, 42, 169, 174
Butch male homosexual, 43, 172
Butter, 77, 288
Buttercustard (Durian) fruit, 305
Buttocks, 53, 58, 100, 126, 149, 152, 154, 155, 172
  slang words for, 126

Calendar method, 130, 138-9
Call girl(s), 26, 278, 280, 284
Camel's milk, 77
Camp, 171
Cancer(s), 122, 291, 293
  breast, 291
  cervix, 153, 254, 298
  womb, 291, 298
  See Smear tests.
Candida Albicans, 154
Candidiasis, 154, 166
Candidosis, 154
Cannula, 290
Cantharidin, 65
Cantharides beetle. See Spanish fly.
Cap. See Diaphragm.
Carbohydrates, 72
Caress(ing), 84, 94, 100, 108, 197, 266
Caritas, 256
Carunculae, 35
Casanova, Giovanni Giacomo, 24, 134, 263
Cassolette, 96
Castrati, 89, 262
Castration, 89, 144, 259, 262
  anxiety, 89
Castration complex. See Castration anxiety.
Cathars (sect), 256
Cauterization, 153
Cavaliere servente, 232
Cazzagio, 221
Celibate, 231, 257, 259
Cellular therapy, 305
Censorship, 128, 271, 274
Cerebal palsy, 266
Cervical canal, 35, 141, 148, 290
Cervical cap (diaphragm), 136
Cervical erosion, 298
Cervical mucus. See Mucus.
Cervical smear test. See Smear test.
Cervix, 24, 34, 35, 36, 37, 110, 112, 130, 135, 137, 143, 148, 234, 235, 290, 291, 294, 299, 301
Cervix adaptor, 235
C-film, 135
Chains, 116, 187
Chain sex, 164
Chancre, 150, 153
Chancroid, 146, 153
Change of life, 34, 139, 300
  See also Menopause.
Chaperon, 217
Chaste, 24, 220
Chastity, 32, 257
Cheeks, 78, 161
Cheesecake, 112, 170
Cherry. 77
Chest, 76
Chick, 264
Chicken queen, 171
Child-bearing, 246, 301
Childbirth. See Birth.
Childhood, 202, 203, 214
Childlessness, 234
Child molester, 169
Child prostitution, 282
Child violation, 246
Children, 88, 158
Chlamydia, 149, 151
Cholera, 291
Christianity, 256, 257, 284
Christian Church, 32, 188, 225, 279
Chromosomes, 35, 42, 43, 46, 300
Chukchee, 169
Cicisbeism, 232
Cinnamon, 77
Circulation, the, 107
Circumcision, 40, 58, 122, 254, 302
  female, 254
Cirrhosis, 69
Citizens for Decency through Law, 128
Civil liberties lobbies, 264
Civil rights movement, 176
Clams, bearded, 77
Clap, the. See Gonorrhea.
Classicism, 80

Cleanliness, 256
Client(s), 280
Climacteric, 300, 304
  See also Menopause.
Climax, 60, 80, 82, 84, 88, 108, 110, 190
  See also Orgasm.
Clinic, 289-306
Clip joint, 284
Cliques, male, 116
  homosexual, 171
Clitoral orgasm(s), 20
  See also Orgasm.
Clitorial stimulator, 288
Clitoris, 20, 34, 36, 37, 47, 58, 62, 63, 66, 67, 68, 78, 94, 96, 100, 107, 108, 126, 158, 161, 254, 266, 288, 290, 297
  enlarged, 42
  hood of, 60, 66, 100, 300
  prepuce of, 40
  slang words for, 126
  tip (glans), 34, 62
Clomipramine, 68
Closet case, 171
Closet queen, 171
Closets, 171
Clothing, 52, 192, 197, 270, 276
  see-through, 276
Clyster treatment, 197
Cocaine, 68
Cock-leash, 190
Cock-ring, 52
Cock-tease, 31
Codpiece, 53, 192, 248
Co-education, 244
Co-habitation, 216, 220, 230
Coil, morning-after, 140, 142
  See also IUD.
Coil (Saf-T coil), 140, 141
Coital variations. See Kama Sutra; Positions.
Coitus, 29, 35, 37, 40, 77, 106, 214, 250, 251, 257, 276, 284, 301, 304
  See also Intercourse.
Coitus incompletus, 141
Coitus interruptus, 130, 141, 159
Coitus reservatus, 141
Coitus saxonicus, 141
Collective Subconscious, 23
College education for girls, 244
Colonic irrigation. See Water Games.
Colostrum, 294
Colt, Rip, 172
Columns, advice, 122, 209
Combination Pill, 132, 142
Comedos, 306
'Coming', 89, 108
'Coming out', 171, 174
Commission on Obscenity and Pornography
  Presidential Report of the, (US), 128
Companionship, 108, 218
Compatibility, 114
Competition, 107, 110
Compulsions, 263
Conception, 70, 130, 132, 214, 216, 226, 246, 250
Concubine, 226, 227, 230
Conditioned reflexes. See Reflexes.
Condom(s), 106, 130, 134, 135, 136, 137, 142, 146, 149, 288
Condylomata, 153
  accuminata, 153
  lata, 150, 153
Cone biopsy, 298
Congress, 104
Consciousness-raising sessions, 174
Consenting adults, 16, 120, 246
Constipation, 306
Consummation, 220, 237
Contact, physical, 118
Contact lenses, 132
Contact magazines, 218
Contact services, 118
Contact woman, 280
Contraception, 18, 24, 130, 132, 134, 136, 137, 138, 140, 141, 142, 144, 214, 232, 234
  'morning-after', 140, 142
  Table of Choices, 130
  See Birth control
Contraceptive(s); 24, 122, 126, 130, 132, 135, 136, 137, 140, 146, 216, 247, 293, 301
  foam(s), 135
  information, 85
  slang words for, 126

See Narcotics.
Herpes, genital, 153, 302
Herpes simplex, 153
Hetaera, 281
Heterosexual(s), 19, 22, 76, 169, 170, 172, 174, 190, 202, 214, 270, 280, 293
Hidden testes. *See* Cryptorchism.
Hierodules, 281, 284
Hinduism, 250, 251, 256
Hippocrates, 15
Hips, 100, 210
   broad, 43
Hirschfeld, Magnus, 13, 17, 169
Hitting, 104
Hogben test, 294
Holding hands, 62, 74, 182
Homo-erotic art, 172-173
Homoerotophobia. *See* Homophobia.
Homophile, 169, 171, 176
Homophobia, 180
Homosexual, 16, 17, 19, 20, 22, 28, 146, 150, 170, 171, 172, 180, 182, 190, 202, 214, 246, 271, 280, 293
   activity, 276
   behaviour, 169, 170, 180
   desires, 19
   dress codes, 52
   female, slang words for, 127
   male, slang words for, 127
   See also Same Sex Partners.
Homosexuality, 13, 16, 17, 76, 118, 120, 124, 169, 176, 180, 257
   female, 174-175, 202
   male, 170-171, 174, 180, 202
   See also Same-Sex Partners.
Honey, 77
Honeymoon, 24, 155, 220
Honeymoon period, 220
Hood (prepuce), of clitoris. *See* Clitoris.
Hooker, 278
Hops, 64
Hormonal changes, 106
Hormone replacement therapy (HRT), 20, 300
Hormones, 64, 70, 77, 142, 216, 262, 293, 297, 300, 306
   male, 37, 43, 296
   steroid, 70
   synthetic female, 132
Hostility, 87
Hot flushes, 300, 304
HRT. *See* Hormone replacement therapy.
Human development, 15, 19
   anal phase, 203
   genital phase, 203
   oral phase, 203
   See Growing Up.
Human psychology, 19
Human Sexuality Program, The, 92
Human Sexual Inadequacy, 20, 237
Human Sexual Response, 20
Humiliation, 182, 187, 238, 271
Husband(s), 147, 148, 224, 225, 226, 232, 233, 235, 240, 246
   impersonation of, 264
Hustera, 299
Hustler, 74
Hyde, 180
Hydroasiatica, 65
Hydrocele, 303
Hygieia (Greek goddess of health), 291
Hygiene, 72, 94, 96, 291, 293
Hymen, 35, 37, 209, 237
Hypermenorrhoea. *See* Menorrhagia.
Hypnosis, 15, 17
Hypocrisy, 20, 24, 225
Hypothalamus, 296, 297
Hysterectomy, 47, 144, 298, 301
Hysteria, 15, 17, 80, 298

Ice cream, 77
Id, 15, 213
Identity, gender. *See* Gender identity.
Ignorance, 86, 146

sexual, 20, 122, 158, 214, 266
Illegitimacy, 16, 226, 235, 259, 278
Immaturity, 117
Impotence, 17, 20, 65, 68, 69, 82, 84, 85, 86-87, 88, 89, 92, 141, 144, 166, 288, 303
Impotent, 82, 87, 88, 127, 166, 192, 238
   slang words for, 127
Impregnate, 29
Inadequacy, 89, 212
Inbreeding, 246
Incest, 200, 246
Incompatibility, physical, 114
Incontinence, 106
Incubus, 259
Indecent exposure, 192, 246
Indecency, 12, 128, 246, 291
Indrani, 104
Infantile sexuality, 203. *See also* Sexuality, childhood.
Infatuation, 117
Inferiority, 117, 212, 213
Inferiority complex, 16, 82
Infertile, 43, 70, 130, 234, 300, 301
Infertility clinics, 237
Infibulation, 60, 254
Inflagrante delicto, 240
Inhibitions, 16, 24, 69, 82, 84, 85, 88, 106, 114, 118, 120, 126, 164, 166, 211, 228, 256, 261, 266
Initiation rite, 254
Inner lips. *See* Labia minora.
Innocence, 200
Insecurity, 117, 213
Insemination, 234, 235
Insomnia, 300
Intercourse, 19, 26, 27, 46, 60, 63, 84, 86, 89, 95, 100, 101, 106, 110, 112, 134, 137, 138, 139, 140, 156, 164, 192, 200, 209, 216, 234, 235, 237, 238, 240, 246, 257, 259, 266, 271, 276, 282, 293, 297, 298, 302, 303, 304
   first, 207, 237
   incomplete, 141
   serial, 164
   sexual, 24, 34, 62, 69, 72, 74, 80, 89, 107, 135, 142, 146, 152, 155, 214, 264, 300, 301
   See also Anal intercourse.
Intermarry, 246
The Interpretation of Dreams, 15, 16
Intersex, 42-43
Intimacy, 24, 202, 204, 205
Intra-uterine device. *See* IUD.
Introitus, 35, 110
Intromission, 110
Introverted, 118
Ipsation, 17
Irritation, 85
Irrumatio, 95
Isolation, 203, 206, 306
Isthmus, 294
'Itch', the, 152
   Norwegian, 152
Ithyphallic, 250
IUD (Intra-uterine device), 130, 140, 295

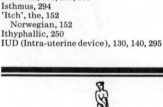

Jackboot, 195
Jambage, 221
Japan, 251, 259
Jazz. *See* Music.
Jealousy(ies), 89, 117, 166, 204, 240, 241
Jellies, 106
Jelly, spermicidal. *See* Spermicide.
Jockstrap, 52
Johnson, Virginia, E., 20
Joints, 72
   arthritic, 100. *See also* Arthritis.
Joseph's night, 220
Juliette, 14
Jung, Carl Gustav, 16, 19, 23, 112, 212, 213, 224
Jus primae noctis, 221
Justine, 14

Kadin, 226, 227
Kama Sutra, 60, 100, 104, 222
Karmen cannula method (abortion), 142
'Keep fit' exercises, 72
Kegel, Alfred, Dr., 106
Kegel exercises. *See* Exercises.
Keratin, 306
Kidney(s), 37, 65, 296, 297
Kinsey, Alfred Charles, 19, 20, 112, 159, 169, 170, 171, 174, 176, 180, 202, 207, 216, 228
Kiss(es), 31, 63, 66, 69, 78, 94, 96, 114
   body, 96
Kissing, 62, 66, 78, 94, 95, 96, 104, 169, 217, 271
   See French kiss.
Kitsuse, 180
Klinefelter's syndrome, 43
Knaus's method. *See* Rhythm method.
Knees, 96, 100, 106, 161
Knickers, 276
Konarak, temple at, 251, 257
Koran, the, 226, 231
Krafft-Ebing, Richard, Freiherr (Baron) von, 13, 14, 15, 16, 17, 184
K-Y jelly, 106, 237

Labia, 60, 62, 94, 300
   majora, 34, 36, 37, 46, 100, 110
   minora, 20, 35, 36, 37, 40, 110, 298
Labour (in childbirth), 294
Lactation, 68
   hormones, 296
Laparoscope, 37, 290, 294, 298
Laparoscopy, 144
Laparotomy, 290
Larynx, 37, 95
'L-clinic', 24
L-dopa, 68
Learning to Love, 209
Leather, 187, 190, 194
Leather club, 52, 76
Leather scene, 52
Legs, 58, 62, 100, 101, 104, 132
Le minimum, 56
Lesbian, 20, 174, 276
Leucorrhea, 297
Lewd, 164
Liberation,
   female, 29
   of love life, 120
   sexual, 12, 17, 29
Liberators,
   sexual, **12-20**
Libertine, 24
Libido, 15, 16, 47, 68, 182, 212, 262, 272
Licentious, 164
Licks, 63, 66, 96
Licking, 78, 94, 95, 96
Life force, 19
Life rhythms. *See* Biological rhythms.
Life-style, 213
Limbs, 101, 210
   amputated, 195
   artificial, 195
   delicate, 100
Linea nigra, 294
Lingam, 104, 250, 251
Lip(s), 60, 66, 69, 74, 78, 94
   See also Labia majora and minora; Vulva, lips of.
Lipstick, 192, 248
Liquorice, 64
Literature,
   sexual, 17
Littré's glands, 148

vulval, 96, 272
See also Smell.
Oedipus complex, 16, 89, 204
Oestrogen(s). *See* Estrogen.
Oestrus. *See* Estrus.
Old age, 88, 169, 300
Old Testament, 220, 225, 230, 250
Old wives' tales, 88, 159, 300
Onanism, 159
The 120 Days of Sodom, 14
On heat. *See* Estrus.
Onions, 77
'On the game', 278, 282
Opposite sex, the, 62, 80, 118, 192, 230, 272
'Opposites attract', 180
Opthalmia neonatorium, 148
Oracles, 248
Oral contact. *See* Kiss; Kissing; Sucking.
Oral contraception. *See* Contraception.
Oral sex, 63, 74, 78, **93-98**, 108, 148, 153, 164, 182, 96, 197, 200
Organs, sexual. *See* Sex organs.
Orgasm(s), 13, 19, 20, 51, 62, 66, 68, 82, 84, 88, 94, 95, 96, 101, **106-112**, 114, 158, 159, 161, 162, 170, 182, 186, 190, 195, 197, 258, 297, 300, 304
  clitoral, 108
  female, 20, 72, 100, 106, 108-109, 110
  female failure to reach, 86
  inability to reach, 88, 114
  male, 40, 100, 234
  multiple, 20, 24, 107
  second, 107
  simultaneous, 98, 112
  vaginal, 108
Orgasmic dysfunction, 84, 85, 297
Orgasmic peak, 107
Orgasmic response, 37, 66, 112, 122
Orgy(ies), 14, 15, 27, 127, 164, 171, 260
  slang words for, 127
Orgone energy, 19
Orientation, sexual, 17, 169, 176, 180, 202
Orifice(s), 82, 94
'Original sin', 279
Os, 36
Os pubis, 39
Ovarian cyst, 290
Ovarian cystectomy, 298
Ovarian hormone, 296
Ovaries, 35, 37, 101, 130, 135, 148, 290, 293, 294, 296, 297, 300, 301
Oviducts, 294
Ovulation, 130, 132, 138, 139, 293
Ovum. *See* Egg.
Oxford Rub, 169, 171
Oysters, 77

Pain, infliction of, 184, 188
Pair-bond, 216
Palmetto, musk seeds, 305
Palpitation(s), 266, 290, 300
Panites, 194
Pap test, 00
Parachlorophenylanine (PCPA), 68
Paralysis, 15
Paraphilia(s), 12, **181-200**
Parasympathetic autonomic nervous system. *See* Nervous system.
Parent(s), 202, 204, 206, 213, 220, 226, 233, 236, 246
Parkinson's disease, 68
Partner-swapping, 24, 147, 164, 228, 230, 232, 240
Passion, 77, 78, 80, 114
Passive role, 74
Pathology, sexual, 17
Patriarchy, 225
Pavlov, Ivan Petrovich, 17
Pederasty, 257
Pediculosis capitas corporis. *See* Pubic lice.
Pediculosis pubis. *See* Pubic lice.
Pedophile(s), 31, 200
Pedophilia, 200, 282

Peeping Tom, 192, 263
Pelvic abscesses, 148
Pelvic-floor exercises. *See* Exercises.
Pelvic floor muscles, 106
Pelvic inflammation, 293
Pelvic muscles. *See* Muscles.
Pelvis, 46, 72, 100, 290, 293, 294, 297, 298, 299
Penetration, 29, 31, 40, 84, 89, 95, 100, 101, 106 135, 160, 200, 209, 235, 237, 238, 264, 270, 271, 288, 297, 300
Penicillin, 149, 150, 151, 306
Penicillinase, 149
Penile piercing, 60
Penile splint, 288
Penilingus, 95
Penis, 20, 34, 37, 40, 43, 46, 47, 52, 58, 62, 63, 68, 74, 78, 86, 89, 94, 95, 100, 101, 106, 107, 110, 122, 127, 134, 135, 141, 148, 149, 150, 153, 154, 161, 164, 182, 187, 195, 210, 234, 237, 238, 248, 250, 251, 254, 259, 264, 288, 296, 303, 304
  artificial, 248, 261, 262, 266
  envy, 212
  erect, 88, 160, 209
  glans (tip of), 37, 39, 40, 60, 95, 110, 134, 149, 302
  head of, 60, 78
  prepuce, 39
  shaft of the, 95, 110, 134
  slang words for, 127
Penis-enhancers, 60
Penis sheaths, 53, 248
Penthouse, 271
Pepper, 77
  cayenne, 288
Peptic ulcer, 68
The Perfumed Garden, 77, 222
Peritoneal cavity. *See* Abdomen.
Peritonitis, 148
Perineum, 37, 39, 40, 60, 66, 95, 290, 297, 305
Periods (menstrual), 122, 292-293, 300
Peripheral neuropathy, 69
'Permissive' society, 128, 146
Permissiveness, 120, 146
Personal columns, 218
Perversion(s), 12, 182, 192, 214
Perverted, 89, 180, 195, 282
Person-to-person, 107, **113-120**
Pessary(ies), 130, 135, 137, 142, 154
Petroleum jelly, 106
Petting, 62, 169, 209, 217
Phallic, 77, 248-249, 250
  symbolism, 248, 249, 251, 260
Phallophoria, 250
Phallus, 47, 248, 261
Pharaonic mutilation, 254
Phenol, 306
Pheromones, 80
Phimosis, 154, 254, 302
Phobia(s), 15, 256
Phthirus publis, 155
Physical fitness. *See* Fitness.
Physical sexual therapy. *See* Sex therapy; Surrogate therapy.
Physique(s), 172
Pierced ears. *See* Body piercing.
Piercers, 60
Pill (contraceptive), the, 69, 106, 130, 132-133, 137, 146, 149, 154, 293
  combined, 132, 142
  for men, 130
  morning-after, 142, 149
  progesterone-only, 132
  'stick-on', 130
Pillow book, 222
Pills, creams, sprays (aphrodisiacs), 288
Pimp(s), 279, 280, 282, 284
Pin-ups, 172
Ping-pong infection, 147, 154
Pipe. *See* Urethra.
Pituitary gland, 293, 294, 297
Placenta, 294, 297
Planned parenthood. *See* Birth Control; Contraception.
Plastic surgery, 58
Plateau phase, 20, 107, 108, 304
Playboy, 271
Playgirl, 271
'Playing doctor', 200
Play therapy, 92
Pleasure, 17, 78, 98, 100, 106, 107, 202, 203, 237, 279
Plural marriage. *See* Polyandry; Polygamy; Polygyny.

Poker-back, 151
Pokes, 51
Point of no return, 110
Pollen, 64, 77
Polyandry, 230
Polyester. *See* Terylene.
Polymenorrhagia. *See* Epimenorrhagia.
Polymenorrhoea (too frequent periods), 293
Polygamy, 226, 230, 233
Polygyny, 226, 230, 231
  sororal, 231
Polyps, 293
Ponce, 282
Pop (music). *See* Music.
Pop stars, 209
Pornai, 281
Pornographic bookshops, 14
Pornographic films, 197, 274
Pornographic magazines/books, 28, 190, 192, 270
Pornography, 128, 270, 271, 281, 282
  hard, 270
  soft, 270, 274, 284
Position(s), 96, **99-104**, 108, 222, 234, 266
  face-to-face, 100, 182
  Kama Sutra, 104
  male on top, 100, 182
  'missionary', 100
  rear entry, 100, 101, 182
  standing, 96, 101
  slang words for, 127
  woman on top, 100
Possessive(ness), 117, 204
Postillionage, 101
Potency, 195, 262
Potensan Forte, 68
'Prairie Oysters', 65
Preferences, sexual, 15, 182, 192
Pregnancy, 85, 89, 106, 122, 124, 132, 140, 142, 158, 214, 226, 235, 237, 246, 264, 290, 293, 294, 295, 297, 301, 304
  accidental, 130, 132
  early, 34, 294
  ectopic, 148, 294, 295
  unwanted, 18, 24, 69, 130, 132, 134, 137, 141, 142, 144, 154, 214
Pregnancy tests, 142, 294, 295
Pregnant, 122, 127, 154, 200, 240, 246, 261, 298, 304
  slang words for, 127
Prejudices, 88
Premature ejaculation, 17, 20, 68, 89, 158, 235, 238, 288, 297
Pre-marital sex, 216, 217, 220, 226, 232
Pre-menstrual tension, 70, 293
Prepubertal child, 202
Prepuce, 36, 40
Presidential Commission on Obscenity, 271
Priapism, 65, 303
Priapos, Greek god of gardens, 250, 303
Priestesses, 248
Prick-tease, 31
Prince Albert. *See* Dressing ring
Princeton Rub, 169, 171
'Pro'. *See* Prostitute.
Problem letters, **121-124**
Problems, sexual, 23, 69, 82, 85, 87, 89, 92, 112, 122, 158, 164, 206, 214, 238, 264, 266
Procidentia, 299
Procreation, 77, 138, 220, 214, 226, 256, 279
Prolapse(s), 290
  vaginal, 88
See also Womb.
'Professional'. *See* Prostitute.
Progestasert, 140
Progestin. *See* Progestogen(s).
Progestogens, 130, 140, 297
Progesterone, 132, 296
Progonasyl, 149
Prolactin, 297
Promiscuous, 24, 146, 148, 153, 214, 260, 264, 278
  slang words for, 127
Propantheline, 68
Propionibacterium acnes, 306
Prostaglandin, 142, 297
Prostate (gland), 39, 40, 88, 101, 148, 151, 154, 297, 303
  enlarged, 305
Prostatic Utricle, 39, 40
Prostatism, 305
Prostatitis, 305
  chronic, 305

Truffles, 77
Trust, 114
Tubal ligation, 144
Tuberculosis, 154, 293, 302
Tubules (of testes), 40
Tumescent, 304
Tumour(s), 150, 290, 298, 299, 301, 303
   water. *See* Hydrocele.
Turned-off, 82
Turned on, 62-63, 65, 120, 164, 238
   See also Arousal.
Turner's syndrome, 43
Typhoid, 291
Tyson's glands, 148

Ulcers, 149, 150, 153, 244, 259
Ulcusmolle, 153
'Umbilicated papules', 149
Uncircumcised, 302
Under age partners, 171
Underwear, 76, 196, 237, 288
Undescended testes. *See* Cryptorchsim.
Unfaithfullness, 146, 240
Unguent, 104
Unisex, 46, 200
Unmarried mother. *See* Mother.
U.S. (USA), 64, 128, 130, 142, 146, 148, 150,
   169, 176, 180, 218, 228, 244, 254, 259, 264, 276,
   293, 300, 301
Unsafe days, 138
Unwanted pregnancy(ies). *See* Pregnancy.
Upbringing and conditioning,
   female, 42
   male, 43
Urethra, 37, 39, 47, 110, 148, 151, 154, 254, 290,
   302, 305
   prostatic, 40
Urethral syndrome. *See* Cystitis.
Urethritis, 303
Urinating, 106, 146, 148, 151, 155, 197, 264
Urine, 37, 65, 70, 72, 154, 197, 294,
   302 , 305
   elimination of, 88
'Urnings', 169
Urolagnia, 74, 127, 197
   slang words for, 127
Uterus. *See* Womb.

Vacuum aspiration, 142, 143
Vagina, 20, 34, 35, 36, 37, 46, 47, 62, 63, 68, 78,
   86, 89, 94, 96, 100, 101, 106, 107, 108, 110,
   112, 127, 130, 134, 135, 137, 140-144, 148-150,
   153, 154, 156, 159, 161, 195, 197, 209, 234, 235,
   237, 238, 251, 264, 270, 288, 290, 294, 295, 297
   299, 300, 301
   artificial, 160
   slang words for, 127
Vaginal balls, 106, 159, 162
Vaginal discharge(s), 132, 148, 154, 155, 156,
   290, 291, 293, 298
Vaginal douche. *See* Douche.
Vaginal lips. *See* Labia; Vulva, lips of.
Vaginal muscles, 94, 101, 110
'Vaginal odours', 80
Vaginal orgasm, 20
Vaginal walls, 63, 106, 110, 290
Vaginitis, 154, 166
   tricomonal, 154
   vulvo, 154
Vaginismus, 237, 238, 297
Vamp, 31
Variations. *See* Paraphilias.

Varicose veins, 290
Vas (tube), 301, 302
Vas deferens, 37, 39, 40, 144, 302, 303
Vasectomy, 134, 144
   rejuvenation of rats, 305
Vaseline, 106, 134, 137
Vatsyayana, 222
Vault cap. *See* Dumas cap.
Venereal diseases. *See* Sex-related diseases.
VD Clinics, 146, 154
Venery'. *See* Love-making.
Venus, 146
Vestals, 248
Vestibule, 37
Vibrator, 37, 101, 161, 284
Vinegar, 149
Violence, 116
Virgin, 77, 154, 200, 209, 216, 221, 237
   slang words for, 127
Virginity, 35, 209, 216, 217, 220, 237, 254, 260
Virginity, to lose one's,
   slang words for, 127
Virgo intacta. *See* Virginity.
Virility, 26, 51, 77, 240
Virtue, 24, 32, 209
Vision, 80, 100
Vitamin(s), 69, 72, 288
Vitamin E, 65, 77
Voice(s),
   boys', 89, 262
   deep, 68, 210
Voice changes, 210
Voluptuary, 24
Voluptuousness, 51
Vomiting, 142, 182, 211
Voyeur, 96, 122, 164, 192, 196, 263
   slang words for, 127
Voyeurism, 56, 192
Vulva, 34, 37, 66, 96, 149, 150, 154, 155, 195,
   235, 250, 251, 254, 261, 270, 290, 297, 298
   see also Labia.
   lips of the, 94, 96, 108, 110, 161, 162, 190
   slang words for, 127
Vulvic, 251

Wank, 51
Warts, 150
   ano-genital, 153
   genital, 153
   vulval, 153
Water games, 197
Water retention, 68
Wedding, 217, 220
Wedding depression, 220
Wednesday Circle, 16
Weight, 70, 101, 132, 136, 220
Wet dreams, 89
Wheat germ, 77
Whipping, 14, 187, 188
Whippingham Papers, 188
Whiteheads, 306
Wife, 147, 148, 186, 224, 226, 230, 231, 232, 233,
   240, 241, 254
   common law, 230
Wife-swapping. *See* Partner swapping.
Wig(s), 160
Wine, 69
Wish-fulfilment, 16
Witchcraft, 197
Witch-hunting, 256
Witches, 248
Withdrawal, 141, 159
Wolf, 264
Woman. *See* Body maps.
Womb cancer. *See* Cancer(s).
Womb, 24, 35, 36, 37, 130, 132, 135, 136, 138,
   140, 141, 142, 143, 144, 148, 235, 246, 261, 290,
   293, 294, 295, 297, 300, 301
   anteverted, 299
   neck of. *See* Cervix.
   prolapse of the, 106, 140, 299
   removal of the, 88, 289, 301
   retroverted, 299

Women's clothes, wearing, 43
Women's liberation, 29, 216, 244
   movement, 174, 244
Women's rights group, 144
Words and Graffitti, 125-128
Worry blocks, **81-92**
Wrists, 152, 161, 187, 190

Yaws, 151
Yeast infection. *See* Moniliasis
Yohimbine, 65
Yoni, 104, 250, 251
Young adults, 88
Y-typical congenital malformation, 43

Zoophilia, 196
Zygoté, 294

Acknowledgements

To Peter Webb, Senior Lecturer in the History of Art, Middlesex Polytechnic, and author of *The Erotic Arts* (1974), who greatly assisted the creation of this book with his advice and the use of his own collection of books and photographs, the publishers wish to express their special thanks.

To the following, who have also given valuable help, advice and information, the publishers are grateful:
Dr. C. N. Armstrong; R. M. Coleman (Gold Star Publications Ltd.); The Family Planning Association; Christopher Gotch, RIBA; Malcolm Hoare; Barry Kay; Ministry of Agriculture, Fisheries & Food, Pest Infestation Control Laboratory, Slough, Bucks; Alan Oversby; Philip S. Rawson (Gulbenkian Museum of Oriental Art, University of Durham); Michael Rubinstein.

Drawings by Tomi Ungerer, © Diogenes Verlag AG, Zürich, 1974, and Jonathan Cape Ltd.

The publishers would also like to thank all the studios, artists, photographers and companies who could not be traced before this book went for publication.

Endpapers, photo Jeff Dunas, © Viva International Ltd.; 14 (both) Mary Evans Picture Library; 15 Mansell Coll.; 16 Mansell Coll.; Mary Evans Picture Library; 17 Bildarchiv Preussischer Kulturbesitz, Berlin; Popperfoto; Mikhail Nesterov, Mansell Coll.; 18 International Planned Parenthood Federation; photo E. O. Hoppé, 1932, Mansell Coll.; 19 the Wilhelm Reich Infant Trust Fund; Popperfoto; 20 Popperfoto; 21 Kobal Coll., 'Yellow Lily'; 23 Chris Jones; 25 Peter Till ('Knave', Vol. 8/3); 28 (Marilyn Monro) Popperfoto; (Jayne Marie Mansfield) Syndication International; (Raquel Welch) Rex Features; (Mae West) Kobal Coll.; 29 (Dean) Kobal Coll; (Bogart) 'High Sierra'; (Brando) Ronald Grant; 30 Kobal Coll.; 31 Kobal Coll.; Ronald Grant; 32 Liutholt von Seven, Codex Manesse, early 14th Cent., Heidelberg Univ.; Love Story Picture Library No. 1429. © IPC Magazines Ltd.; 33 'Light on Dark Corners' by Jefferis & Nichols, 1894; 37, 39 QED; 40A *tl*. Popperfoto; *b*. Camera Press; 1977; *tr*. Popperfoto; 40B Rex Features; 41 The Chevalier d'Eon, Mary Evans Picture Library; 42-3 research & visualization by Karen Gunnell, graphics by Howard Dyke; 47 © United Artists; 48 The Times, 29.10.76; 56 *t*. Rex Features; *cl*. Fotogram/Topham; *cr*, *b*. Camera Press; 60 *t*. Fotogram/Topham; *b*. Camera Press; *r*. Shoeshine Studio; 61 photo Robert McFarlane, © Marshall Cavendish; 62-3 © Marshall Cavendish; 64 *tl*. photo © TCP. Ltd.; 65 *tr*. British Museum (Natural History); 66-7 photo Robin Clifford, © Marshall Cavendish; 71 photo Viva International Ltd., graphics QED; 74-5 Mike Reid; 79 graphics by Terry Pastor; 80 Tina

Turner, © London Features International Ltd.; 82 Ernest Thesiger in 'The Bride of Frankenstein'; 88 Ch'ing dynasty ginger-jar, coll. of the Rt. Hon. Malcolm Macdonald; 89 unpublished illustration for *Lysistrata;* 90-1 photo © TCP. Ltd. 1977; 92 photo John Garrett © Marshall Cavendish; 94 'Black & White Head', liquitex on canvas, 1966; 95 *Inside Linda Lovelace*, © Pinnacle Books Inc. & Heinrich Hanau Publications Ltd., 1974; 97 'Red & Black Pillows', liquitex on canvas, 1966 (coll. of John & Kimiko Powers); 98 Wood-block by Kunisada, from *Oyagari no Koe*, Boston Museum of Fine Arts; 100-1 Orissan posture book, early 19th cent., © P. S. Rawson; 102 cup by the Triptolemos painter, Tarquinia Museum; 105 Camera Press; photo Robin Clifford, © Marshall Cavendish; 107 Photo J. Garrett, © Marshall Cavendish; 108 QED; 109 photo Jean Rougeron; 111 photo Malcolm Hoare; 112 QED; 113 photo G. P. Raba, © ZEFA; 115 © Marshall Cavendish; 116 'Aunt Louisa's National Album' *c*. 1870 from *Punch & Judy: A History* by George Speaight; 117 Michele Mortimer; 120 'Copenhagen Candids' by Bogren, Camera Press; 126 *tl*. Reg Boorer; *bl*. Roger Perry; 128 *tl, tr*. Roger Perry; *c, bl, br*. John Topham Picture Library; 129 Topham; 131 © Health Education Council, London; 133-7 photo © TCP. Ltd; 138-9 diagrams by Shoeshine Studio; photo © TCP. Ltd.; 141 Shoeshine Studio; 142-3 Len Whiteman/Gordon Cramp Studios; 144 Len Whiteman/Gordon Cramp Studios; 147 Shoeshine Studio & Ken Taylor; 149, 151 Nigel Marks; 152, 155 Scanning Electron micrographs, Pest Infestation Control Laboratory; dorso-lateral view of *Sarcoptes Scabiei*, x336; dorsal view of *Phthirus pubis* x56; 153 Nigel Marks; 155 graphics by Shoeshine Studio; 156 Nigel Marks; Twyfords Ltd. Stoke-on-Trent; 158 'Nude Masturbation Drawing (Brunette)', 1968-74, pencil & liquitex on rag paper, 11″ x 14″, courtesy Sidney Janis Gall., N. Y.; 159 Paul Sample; 160 photo © TCP. Ltd.; 162 photo © TCP. Ltd.; 164 Musée du Louvre, Paris; 167 Jean Cocteau; 168 detail from etching 'In Despair' from *Fourteen Poems* by C. P. Cavafy, 1966 (Petersburg Press Ltd., London); 170-1 *tl*. Mansell Coll.; *tc*. drawing by F. E. Régamey; *tr*. Library of Congress, Feinberg Coll.; photo John Seymour, © Marshall Cavendish; 172-3 photo Konrad for 'Man's Image'; 'Quaintance' from *Homo-Erotic Art* by Barrington; Colt © The Colt Studio 1974; 177 *tl*. photo John Heim, San Francisco; 178 *t*. © ZEFA/A. Liesecke; *b*. Camera Press; 179 Camera Press; 180 Roger Perry; 186 Louis Malteste; 187 leather fashion by Atomage of London; 188 *t*. Mansell Coll.; 189 National Film Archive, Stills Library, London; 192 photo Eric Schwab Fotogram/Topham; 193 model & photo by Shirtsleeve Studio; 194 *l*. © Allen Jones; 196 *b*. Roger Perry; 200 detail from 'The Secret Garden', courtesy of the Piccadilly Gallery and Waddington & Tooth's Galleries, London; 203 Mihály Zichy, 1875; 206 Viva SA/Cristoph Kahn; 207 *t*. Camera Press; 210 Nigel Marks; 211 Phedon-Salou; 212 'Le Viol', Arts Council of Great Britain; 215 'A York Dialogue between Ned and Harry',

Topham; 217 montage © TCP. Ltd. 1977: photos I. C. Rapoport (Camera Press) & Viva International Ltd., retouching by Sally Slight; 221 Wedding Box by Carol Frank from *Hardcore Crafts*, © Tree Communications Inc. 1976 (publ. Ballantine Books); 222-3 *t. b.* Trustees of the British Museum, London; 224-5 retouching by Sally Slight; 228-9 Ronald Grant; 230-1 Union Pacific; 232-3 'Le Déjeuner Sur l'Herbe', Musée du Louvre, Paris, Photographie Giraudon; 236 Mia Farrow, Popperfoto; 243 Mansell Collection; 245 Camera Press; inset: John Topham; 248-9 design, Reg Boorer, © TCP. Ltd., 1977; 250 *tl*. John Topham Ltd.; *cr*. Stiftung Staatlicher Kulturbesitz, Berlin; *b*. Trustees of the British Museum; 251 *tr*. Trustees of the British Museum; *tl, b*. Ajit Mookerjee Collection, photo Jeff Teasdale; 252-3 design, Ellen Moorcroft. © TCP. Ltd. 1977; 254 Mansell Collection; 255 details from 'La Circoncision des Juifs Portugais', Mansell Coll.; 256 'The Long Engagement' (1859) by Arthur Hughes by permission of Birmingham Museums & Art Gallery; 257 Cerne Abbas giant, Dorset, England, Aerofilms Ltd.; 258 *t*. photo Alinari; *br*. detail of amphora by the Kleophrades painter, Staatliche Antikensammlungen, Munich; *bl*. Topham; 259 *b*. woodcut from *Compendium Maleficarum* by F. M. Guazzo (Milan, 1608); 260 *tl*. *The Erotic Arts* by Peter Webb, page 49, n 285; *l, b*. National Monuments Record; 261 Attic amphora from Nola, Musée Municipal de Laon, photo Lauros/Giraudon; 262 (both) Trustees of the British Museum; 263 presumed caricature, from *Giacomo Casanova und sein Lebensroman* by Gustav Gugitz, 1921; 265 Stafleu's Wetenschappelijke Uitg., Leiden; 266 experimental sex education for blind teenagers in Sweden, by courtesy of Dr. Maj-Briht Bergström-Walan, Svenska Sexualforskningsinstitutet, Stockholm; 267 photo David Ellis; 268-9 Photo Mark Antmann Fotogram/Topham; 270 *b*. Roger Perry; 272 'Boxer' © Virgin Records Ltd. 1975; photo Victor Skrebneski © Dormeuil Ltd.; 273 Eric Schemilt Designs Ltd., photo © Barry Ryan, © Fiorucci Spa.; J. R. Freeman & Son Ltd.; 274 *l*. Michael Putland/LFI; *t., b*. Robert Edwards; 275 *tr*. Michael Putland/LFI; *b*. Fotogram/Topham; 276 *t*. Michael Putland/LFI; *b*. Roger Perry; 277 detail from engraving by T. C. Naudet, Mansell Coll.; 278 Fotogram/Topham; 278-9 Camera Press; 280 *r*. Kobal Coll.; 281 *t*. detail from an oinochoë by the Shuvalov painter, Stiftung Staatlicher Kulturbesitz. Berlin; *b*. Popperfoto; 282 Ronald Grant; Toulouse-Lautrec; 283 Kobal Collection; 284 Aubrey Dewar; 286-7 photo © TCP. Ltd. 1977; 291 Len Whiteman/Gordon Cramp Studios; 292 Karen Gunnell, graphics by Shoeshine Studio; 295 Len Whiteman/Gordon Cramp Studios; 296 research & visualisation by Karen Gunnell, graphics by Shoeshine Studios; 297 Nigel Marks; 298 Len Whiteman/Gordon Cramp Studios; 299 Len Whiteman/Gordon Cramp Studios; 301, 302-3, 305, 306 graphics by Nigel Marks.